American Furniture

AMERICAN FURNITURE 1998

Edited by Luke Beckerdite

Published by the CHIPSTONE FOUNDATION

Distributed by University Press of New England

Hanover and London

CHIPSTONE FOUNDATION BOARD OF DIRECTORS
Luke Beckerdite   *Executive Director*
Dudley Godfrey, Jr.
Charles Hummel
Brock Jobe
W. David Knox, II.   *President*
Jere D. McGaffey
John S. McGregor
Philip L. Stone
Allen M. Taylor   *Chairman*

EDITOR
Luke Beckerdite

BOOK AND EXHIBITION REVIEW EDITOR
Gerald W. R. Ward

EDITORIAL ADVISORY BOARD
Luke Beckerdite, *Executive Director, Chipstone Foundation*
John Bivins, Jr., *Conservator and Decorative Arts Consultant*
Edward S. Cooke, Jr., *Associate Professor, Department of the History of Art, Yale University*
Wallace Gusler, *Master of the Shop–Gunsmith, Colonial Williamsburg Foundation*
Morrison H. Heckscher, *Curator of American Decorative Arts, Metropolitan Museum of Art*
Brock Jobe, *Deputy Director of Collections, Conservation, and Interpretation, H. F. du Pont Winterthur Museum*
Robert F. Trent, *Conservator and Decorative Arts Consultant*
Gerald W. R. Ward, *Associate Curator, American Decorative Arts & Sculpture, Museum of Fine Arts, Boston*
Gregory R. Weidman, *Researcher and Decorative Arts Consultant*
Philip D. Zimmerman, *Museum and Decorative Arts Consultant*

Cover Illustration: Detail of a firescreen attributed to Nathan Lombard, southern Worcester County (possibly Sutton), Massachusetts, 1800–1805. (Private collection.)

Design: Wynne Patterson, Pittsfield, Vermont
Photography: Gavin Ashworth, New York, New York

Published by the Chipstone Foundation, 7820 North Club Circle, Milwaukee, WI 53217
Distributed by University Press of New England, Hanover, NH 03755
© 1998 by the Chipstone Foundation
All rights reserved
Printed in the United States of America   5 4 3 2 1
ISSN 1069–4188
ISBN 0–87451–892–X

Contents

Editorial Statement *Luke Beckerdite*	VII
Preface *Allen M. Taylor*	IX
Introduction *Luke Beckerdite*	XI
The Making and Marketing of Boston Seating Furniture in the Late Baroque Style *Joan Barzilay Freund and Leigh Keno*	1
Germanic Craftsmen and Furniture Design in Philadelphia, 1820–1850 *Charles L. Venable*	41
Labeled Randolph Chairs Rediscovered *Philip D. Zimmerman*	81
The Christian M. Nestell Drawing Book: A Focus on the Ornamental Painter and His Craft in Early Nineteenth-Century America *Nancy Goyne Evans*	99
Sophistication in Rural Massachusetts: The Inlaid Cherry Furniture of Nathan Lombard *Brock Jobe and Clark Pearce*	164
A Seventeenth-Century Carpenter's Conceit: The Waldo Family Joined Great Chair *Peter Follansbee*	197
Notes about New "Tinkham" Chairs *Robert F. Trent and Karin Goldstein*	215

Book Reviews 239

The Furniture of George Hunzinger: Invention and Innovation in Nineteenth-Century America, Barry R. Harwood; review by Milo M. Naeve

Honoré Lannuier, Cabinetmaker from Paris: The Life and Work of a French Ébéniste in Federal New York, Peter M. Kenny, Frances F. Bretter, and Ulrich Leben; review by Wendy A. Cooper

New England Furniture at Winterthur: Queen Anne and Chippendale Periods, Nancy Richards and Nancy Goyne Evans, with Wendy A. Cooper and Michael S. Podmaniczky; review by Wallace B. Gusler

The Shaker World: Art, Life, Belief, John T. Kirk; review by Scott T. Swank

Upholsterers and Interior Furnishing in England, 1530–1840, Geoffrey Beard; review by Jeffrey H. Munger

Southern Furniture, 1680–1830: The Colonial Williamsburg Collection, Ronald L. Hurst and Jonathan Prown; review by Robert A. Leath

Recent Writing on American Furniture: A Bibliography 273
Gerald W. R. Ward

Index 285

Editorial Statement

American Furniture is an interdisciplinary journal dedicated to advancing knowledge of furniture made or used in the Americas from the seventeenth century to the present. Authors are encouraged to submit articles on any aspect of furniture history, essays on conservation and historic technology, reproductions or transcripts of documents, such as account books and inventories, annotated photographs of new furniture discoveries, and book and exhibition reviews. References for compiling an annual bibliography also are welcome.

Manuscripts must be typed, double-spaced, illustrated with black-and-white prints or transparencies, and prepared in accordance with the *Chicago Manual of Style*. Computer disk copy is requested but not required. The Chipstone Foundation will offer significant honoraria for manuscripts accepted for publication and reimburse authors for all photography approved in writing by the editor.

Luke Beckerdite

Preface

The Chipstone Foundation was organized in 1965 by Stanley Stone and Polly Mariner Stone of Fox Point, Wisconsin. Representing the culmination of their shared experiences in collecting American furniture, American historical prints, and early English pottery, the foundation was created with the dual purpose of preserving and interpreting their collection and stimulating research and education in the decorative arts.

The Stones began collecting American decorative arts in 1946, and by 1964 it became apparent to them that provisions should be made to deal with their collection. With the counsel of their friend Charles Montgomery, the Stones decided that their collection should be published and exhibited.

Following Stanley Stone's death in 1987, the foundation was activated by an initial endowment provided by Mrs. Stone. This generous donation allowed the foundation to institute its research and grant programs, begin work on three collection catalogues, and launch an important new journal, *American Furniture*.

Allen M. Taylor

Introduction

Luke Beckerdite

When we established *American Furniture* in 1993, one of our main concerns was whether we could secure enough articles to sustain the publication on an annual basis. Six volumes and fifty-nine articles later, it appears as though our reservations were unwarranted. New discoveries are always on the horizon, and scholars have continued to build upon and revise existing research.

In this volume, Joan Barzilay Freund and Leigh Keno's article, "The Making and Marketing of Boston Seating Furniture in the Late Baroque Style," links their and Alan Miller's earlier research on Boston Georgian seating with findings by Neil D. Kamil, Roger Gonzales, and Daniel Putnam Brown on Boston and New York leather chairs. During the last four years, the history of Boston's colonial chairmaking industry largely has been rewritten in *American Furniture*.[1]

Nancy Goyne Evans's articles on vernacular seating furniture have appeared in three previous volumes. Here she analyzes and reproduces nearly all of the images in the Christian Nestell Drawing Book. As Evans's work reveals, we have only begun to explore and publish the many account books, day books, drawing books, and other important documents that survive in public and private collections.[2]

No scholar has done more to further our understanding of seventeenth-century American furniture than Robert F. Trent. In this volume, he and Karin Goldstein reexamine Plymouth County chairs in the "Tinkham" tradition. Building on research by Benno M. Forman and Robert Blair St. George, Trent and Goldstein identify Dutch and Boston influences in the tradition and suggest that Tinkham chairs are the products of several shops rather than the work of a single individual.[3]

The rediscovery and exposition of seventeenth-century woodworking technology has been a major focus of research by Trent, Peter Follansbee, and John D. Alexander. Follansbee's research on the unique Waldo family armchair, which he discusses in his article, involved both archival work and bench work. Information he gleaned from reproducing the chair supports Trent's earlier attribution of the piece to John Elderkin and sheds light on the divergence and intersection of the carpenters' and joiners' trades in seventeenth-century New England.[4]

Like the Waldo armchair, the desk-and-bookcase illustrated at the beginning of the article by Brock Jobe and Clark Pearce has long been recognized as a monumental achievement in New England furnituremaking; however, its origin and authorship have remained elusive. Building on earlier research by Charles Montgomery and William Short, Jobe and Pearce have identified forty objects from the same shop and attributed them to Massachusetts cabinetmaker Nathan Lombard. Their work also points to related groups of objects and stylistic influences that remain to be discovered.[5]

The Randolph labeled chairs discussed in Philip Zimmerman's article show how attributions and opinions change as new information comes to light. Once considered benchmark pieces of Philadelphia rococo furniture, the chairs were removed from view at the Museum of Fine Arts, Boston, after their authenticity was questioned in 1972. Zimmerman's analysis reveals that the chairs are period examples with modern modifications and suggests how objective and subjective perceptions can influence our conclusions about material culture.[6]

Much has been written about the influence of immigrant Germanic artisans on eighteenth-century Pennsylvania furniture, but little is known about the impact of nineteenth-century Germanic tradesmen. Charles Venable's article, "Germanic Craftsmen and Furniture Design in Philadelphia, 1820–1850," examines the Continental and American contexts in which these artisans flourished and shows how the structural and stylistic details they introduced "played a vital role in transforming furniture design."

Interest in American furniture continues to grow at a steady pace. The 1999 volume, which will be a special issue devoted to Rhode Island furniture and its influence in other regions, is already filled, and a number of articles are committed for the year 2000. For information on the 1999 volume and past issues of *American Furniture,* please contact the Customer Service Department at University Press of New England, 23 South Main Street, Hanover, New Hampshire, 03755.

---

1. Leigh Keno, Joan Barzilay Freund, and Alan Miller, "The Very Pink of the Mode: Boston Georgian Chairs, Their Export, and Their Influence," in *American Furniture,* edited by Luke Beckerdite (Hanover, N.H.: University Press of New England for the Chipstone Foundation, 1996), pp. 267–307; Neil D. Kamil, "Hidden in Plain Sight: Disappearance and Material Life in Colonial New York," in *American Furniture,* edited by Luke Beckerdite and Bill Hosley (Hanover, N.H.: University Press of New England for the Chipstone Foundation, 1995) pp. 191–251; Roger Gonzales and Daniel Putnam Brown, Jr., "Boston and New York Leather Chairs: A Reappraisal," in Beckerdite, ed., *American Furniture 1996,* pp. 175–95.

2. Nancy Goyne Evans, "Design Transmission in Vernacular Seating Furniture: The Influence of Philadelphia and Baltimore Styles on Chairmaking from the Chesapeake Bay to the 'West'," in *American Furniture,* edited by Luke Beckerdite (Hanover, N.H.: University Press of New England for the Chipstone Foundation, 1993), pp. 75–117; Nancy Goyne Evans, "Identifying and Understanding Repairs and Structural Problems in Windsor Furniture," in *American Furniture,* edited by Luke Beckerdite (Hanover, N.H.: University Press of New England for the Chipstone Foundation, 1994), pp. 2–29; Nancy Goyne Evans, "Frog Backs and Turkey Backs: The Nomenclature of Vernacular Seating Furniture, 1740–1850," in Beckerdite, ed., *American Furniture 1996,* pp. 17–57; Nancy Goyne Evans, *American Windsor Chairs* (New York: Hudson Hills Press in association with the Winterthur Museum, 1996).

3. Benno Forman, *American Seating Furniture, 1630–1730* (New York: W. W. Norton for the Winterthur Museum, 1988), passim. Robert Blair St. George, "A Plymouth Area Chairmaking Tradition of the Late Seventeenth Century," *Middleborough Antiquarian* 19, no. 2 (December 1978): 3–12; Robert Blair St. George, *The Wrought Covenant: Source Material for the Study of Craftsmen and Community in Southeastern New England, 1620–1700* (Brockton, Mass.: Brockton Art Center, 1979), pp. 50–51, figs., 46–49.

4. See Peter Follansbee and John D. Alexander, "Seventeenth-Century Joinery from Braintree, Massachusetts: The Savell Shop Tradition," in *American Furniture,* edited by Luke

Beckerdite (Hanover, N.H.: University Press of New England for the Chipstone Foundation, 1996), pp. 81–105. Robert F. Trent, "The Waldo Chair: A Monument of Early Connecticut Joinery," in *Connecticut Historical Society Bulletin* 48, no. 4 (Fall 1983): 174–88.

5. Charles F. Montgomery, *American Furniture, The Federal Period in the Henry Francis du Pont Winterthur Museum* (New York: Viking Press, 1966), no. 177, p. 221.

6. Edwin J. Hipkiss, *Eighteenth-Century American Arts: The M. and M. Karolik Collection* (Cambridge, Mass.: Harvard University Press for the Museum of Fine Arts, Boston, 1941), no. 89, pp. 152–53; and Albert Sack, *Fine Points of Furniture: Early American* (New York: Crown Publishers, 1950), p. 37. John Kirk, *American Chairs: Queen Anne and Chippendale* (New York: Alfred A. Knopf, 1972), pp. 172–74.

American Furniture

Joan Barzilay Freund and Leigh Keno

The Making and Marketing of Boston Seating Furniture in the Late Baroque Style

I have seen your sumptuous Buildings, your gallent Furniture, your Costly Clothing, . . . the profuseness of your Tables, and . . . a great deal of other Extravegance, I have been always afraid what the consequence of these things would be. . . . As to Silver and Gold we never had much of it in the Country . . . and of all Men, you in Boston, especially the merchants should be silent as to the matter for you shipped it off, and yet now complain of the want of it. . . . Your Advice as to setting up and encouraging Manufactures we very humbly approve of; and you may depend upon it; we in the Country shall . . . raise our own Provisions and wear clothing of our own making as far as possible and live out of Debt.

▼ IN THE 1995 VOLUME of *American Furniture*, historian Neil Kamil showed how Boston merchants and artisans produced and exported vast quantities of leather chairs and other manufactured goods to compensate for the lack of a profitable staple crop. Boston's mercantile strategy was to assume the role of a British metropolis, and its success hinged on making style a commodity. In a 1707 letter to his New York agent Benjamin Faneuil (b. La Rochelle, France, 1658, d. New York, 1719), Boston upholsterer Thomas Fitch (1668/69–1736) wrote, "leather couches are as much out of wear here as steeple crowned hats. Cane couches or others we make like them . . . are cheaper, more fashionable, easy and useful." Boston's shipping industry and broad client networks enabled the city's merchant upholsterers to dominate the market for seating furniture in New England and New York. By 1700, appraisers throughout the colonies referred commonly to leather chairs as either "Boston," "New England," or "Boston made."[1]

During the first half of the eighteenth century, Boston chairmakers continually developed faster and more efficient ways to construct seating furniture. The use of patterns, structural shortcuts, and piecework purchased from turners, carvers, and other specialists gave the city's merchants, upholsterers, and entrepreneurs a financial edge over their competitors in other ports. Early in his career, Fitch's apprentice Samuel Grant (1705–1784, fl. 1728) purchased chair frames from John Leach, James Johnson, and Edmund Perkins (1683–1781), the latter of whom bought parts from Samuel Mattocks, Jr. and Sr. These frames were upholstered either in Grant's shop or by contractors such as Thomas Baxter. Grant's trade network, which probably developed from the one established by his master, subsequently expanded to include chairmakers Thomas Dillaway, Samuel Ridgway, Clement Vincent, Henry and William Perkins (Edmund's sons); joiner Daniel Ballard; and carvers Benjamin Luckie and John Welch (1711–1789).[2]

Figure 1 Side chair, Boston, 1710–1720. Maple and oak. H. 47½", W. 18", D. 14½". (Private collection; photo, Gavin Ashworth.)

Figure 2 Side chair, Boston, ca. 1725. Maple and oak; original leather upholstery. H. 43¾", W. 18½", D. 15". (Private collection; photo, Gavin Ashworth.)

Grant also capitalized on the commercial contacts established by Fitch during the first quarter of the eighteenth century. In our recent article written with furniture historian Alan Miller, "The Very Pink of the Mode: Boston Georgian Chairs, Their Export and Their Influence," we traced Grant's shipments to New York and Newport and demonstrated that a large group of seating furniture formerly attributed to those cities was, in fact, made in Boston between 1730 and 1755. Earlier scholars who were unaware of the vast network of family and commercial connections emanating from Boston had erred in assuming that a chair with a New York or Newport provenance was made there. Traditional notions about Boston seating furniture in the late baroque, or "Queen Anne," style are similarly flawed. This essay examines the evolution and distribution of Boston chairs made from the early to mid-1720s, when late baroque stylistic features began to emerge there, to the mid-1750s, when the city's export trade began to wane.[3]

Antecedents of Boston Seating Furniture in the Late Baroque Style

Between 1700 and 1725, the mainstay of Boston's furniture industry was the turned and joined leather chair (fig. 1), a "provincial adaptation of the fashionable London cane chair." Fitch's letterbooks and ledgers record numerous shipments of leather chairs to New York, Rhode Island, and other ports in New England. In 1706, he wrote Faneuil, "I would have sent yo some chairs but could scarcely comply with those I had promised to go by these sloops." The leather chairs exported by Fitch and his competitors were gen-

Figure 3 Side chair, Boston, 1710–1720. Maple. H. 45 1/4", W. 17 1/2", D. 14 3/4". (Private collection; photo, Gavin Ashworth.)

erally described as being "plain top'd" or "carv'd top." On July 11, 1709, Fitch noted that he had sold "many of that sort to Yorkers . . . I make six plain to one carv'd; and can't make the plain so fast as they are bespoke."[4]

Although turned and joined leather chairs remained popular throughout the 1720s, Fitch began making examples with crooked backs and molded stiles by 1722/23 (fig. 2). These new designs were probably inspired by imported and locally made cane chairs and upholstered chairs. On October 6, 1725, Fitch wrote his London factor, Silas Hooper:

> Cary. Litherhed bot for Mr. H[enr]y Deering Some frames, the fore feet of the same fashion [at 13s as] those Charg'd [me] at 21[s of which] 14 have but 37 holes and part of them not Walnutt but only culler'd over, so that the maker ought . . . to make you a further considerable allowance [the chairs] being so much over Charg'd.

Determining precisely when crooked backs and molded stiles first appeared on Boston chairs is complicated by the absence of documented examples and by the fact that Fitch's ledger entries do not begin until 1719 and his correspondence from the winter of 1717 to the spring of 1724 is missing. As furniture historian Benno Forman has suggested, a small group of Boston cane chairs with straight backs, molded stiles, and either turned legs or sawn cabriole legs may predate their leather counterparts by about five years. If so, the late baroque style probably emerged in Boston by the early-to-mid-1720s rather than circa 1730 as previously thought.[5]

The side chairs illustrated in figures 3 and 4 are part of a group of at least thirty related examples, several of which have the capital letter "F" punched

Figure 4   Side chair, Boston, ca. 1725. Maple. H. 43", W. 19", D. 15". (Private collection; photo, Gavin Ashworth.)

Figure 5   Side chair, Britain, ca. 1725. Beech. H. 44 1/2", W. 17 3/4", D. 15 1/8". (Private collection; photo, Gavin Ashworth.)

on their rear stiles or seat rails. Structural and stylistic variations among the chairs in this group indicate that their components were made by several different turners and carvers. In 1724, Samuel Mattocks, Sr. and Jr., sued chairmaker Edmund Perkins for debt, which suggests that they had furnished him with turned components or other piecework. The Mattocks, in turn, commissioned John Lincoln for carving. Such interdependence makes it difficult to determine if the chairs in this group were assembled in one shop that offered a number of stylistic variations or in several shops. The columnar side stretchers on several of these examples (see fig. 3) are similar to those on a small group of Boston easy chairs that appear to date between 1710 and 1720 (see fig. 13). The chair shown in figure 3 probably falls near the end of that range. It is very similar to one that originally belonged to Reverend Daniel Perkins (b. 1697), who graduated from Harvard College in 1717. In 1721, he married Ann Foster of Charlestown and became the minister of Bridgewater.[6]

Two side chairs from the aforementioned group (see fig. 4) have sawn and beaded cabriole legs, a late baroque detail presumably introduced by British imports (see fig. 5) or by immigrant tradesmen such as John Jackson. London furniture makers such as Thomas Phill and Thomas and Richard Roberts began making chairs with sawn cabriole legs about 1715. Samuel Grant's ledgers contain the earliest documentary reference to cabriole legs in Boston. On November 31, 1730, he charged Nathaniel Green £2.12 for "1 couch frame horsebone foot." In eighteenth-century shop parlance, the term "foot" often referred to leg. The chairmakers in Grant's network

Figure 6 Side chair, Boston, ca. 1725. Maple. H. 45", W. 19", D. 15½". (Courtesy, Winterthur Museum.)

undoubtedly made frames with cabriole legs before 1730. On October 14, 1729, he sold New York merchant and ship captain Arnout Schermerhorn "1 Chair of red Chainy" and "1 d⁰ New fashion round seat." The earliest Boston chairs with "round" or compass seats probably had turned cabriole legs and pad feet, although the latter features are not described in Grant's accounts until January 13, 1731/32, when he billed Messrs. Clark and Kilby £12 for "6 Leathr Chairs . . . horbone round foot & cush Seats." Considering the fact that turned cabriole legs and pad feet are stylistically later than sawn cabriole legs, it is logical to assume that the chair illustrated in figure 4 dates from the early to mid-1720s. Some of the "new fashion'd chairs" sold

Figure 7 Backstool, Boston, ca. 1725. Maple. H. 43 1/8", W. 19 13/16", D. 16". (Private collection; photo, Gavin Ashworth.)

by Fitch during this period probably had sawn cabriole legs as well as "crook'd" backs with leather upholstery.[7]

Transitional Seating Forms with Late Baroque Details
Boston seating furniture in the late baroque style can be divided into three categories: transitional forms made during the 1720s, avante-garde forms made between 1725 and 1740, and standardized forms made from the early 1730s to the mid-1760s. On the transitional examples (see figs. 4, 6), "new fashioned" details such as cabriole legs occur in conjunction with midbaroque, or "William and Mary," features such as straight molded stiles and carved Spanish feet. In *American Seating Furniture, 1630–1730*, Benno Forman noted that the side chair shown in figure 6 was "basically a stiff-back cane chair of the Boston school—molded stiles, great heels, Spanish front

Figure 8 Side chair, Boston, ca. 1725. Maple. H. 43 3/16", W. 18 1/4", D. 14 3/4". (Private collection; photo, Gavin Ashworth.)

Figure 9 Armchair, Boston, 1715–1725. Maple. H. 46", W. 23", D. 16 1/2". (Courtesy, Winterthur Museum.)

feet, stretchers, double ogee apron (now integrated into the seat rail)—with overtones of the crest rail and rectilinear seat of the leather chair, onto which have been grafted elements of the 'newest fashion,' carved horsebone legs, . . . banister splat, and cushion seat." Although Forman was correct in his assessment of these disparate details, the chair probably dates about 1725 rather than circa 1730 as he thought.[8]

A backstool and a side chair from the same shop are among the most fully developed transitional forms (figs. 7, 8). Both have over-the-rail upholstery, sawn and beaded cabriole legs, side stretchers with elongated rear balusters and compressed front ones, and center stretchers of essentially the same pat-

Figure 10   Side chair, London, 1715–1725. Beech; japanned green and gold on a red ground. H. 45½", W. 21½". (Courtesy, Victoria and Albert Museum.)

Figure 11   Easy chair, Boston, 1690–1710. Maple with pine; original foundation upholstery. H. 42". (Photo, Winterthur Museum.)

Figure 12   Side chair, Boston, 1690–1700. Maple and oak. H. 35½", W. 18½", D. 18½". (Private collection; photo, Gavin Ashworth.)

tern—extremely attenuated balusters and deep scotias flanking a sharp torus molding—like those on many Boston cane chairs and leather chairs from the 1710s and early 1720s (see fig. 9). The scrolled crest rail on the backstool is similar to those on Boston easy chairs made during the first quarter of the eighteenth century (see fig. 13), whereas the crest rail, molded stiles, and stay rail on the side chair are related to those on a large group of Boston leather chairs (see figs. 2, 9). The simple, crooked banister, or "India back," of the side chair is an extremely sophisticated detail that may have been derived from imported London chairs (see fig. 10). On May 31, 1718, London upholsterer George Remey sold "24 fine wallnuttree chairs wth turned feet, India Backs & India feet."[9]

A small group of Boston easy chairs supports the date range assigned to the aforementioned backstool and side chair. Easy chairs do not appear in Boston inventories prior to 1712, but they were undoubtedly made there

Figure 13 Easy chair, Boston, 1700–1710. Maple with oak. H. 50 3/4", W. 27", D. 21". (Courtesy, Winterthur Museum). The feet are worn and have lost their laminated facings.

Figure 14 Easy chair, Boston, ca. 1725. Maple. H. 48½", W. 27⅜", D. 21". (Courtesy, Winterthur Museum.)

earlier in the century. A remarkable example formerly in the collection of Roger Bacon has a small, squarish seat and straight arms with vertical supports (fig. 11), details that occur on London easy chairs made during the late seventeenth and early eighteenth centuries. Based on these features, Forman dated the Bacon example to 1695–1705. The stretchers connecting the front legs, the side stretchers, and the rear legs support his conclusions. Their distinctive turning sequences are repeated on a late seventeenth-century Boston "Cromwellian chair" (fig. 12) and on what Roger Gonzales and Daniel Putnam Brown, Jr., have termed "first generation" leather chairs. Their research strongly suggests that "first generation" leather chairs passed out of fashion in Boston about 1710.[10]

The easy chair illustrated in figure 13 is one of four with center stretchers similar to those on the Bacon chair. Like many Boston cane chairs, it has symmetrical, columnar side stretchers, an ogee-shaped front rail, and carved

Spanish feet. Several easy chairs related to this example survive. Most have chamfered heels, double-scrolled arms, slightly flared cheeks, and relatively low-arched crests. The "new fashioned" chair shown in figure 14 has a rear stretcher similar to the front one on a Boston low chair made between 1710 and 1720. This stretcher design also appears on a "crook'd back" side chair with virtually identical cabriole legs and Spanish feet (fig. 6) and on numerous leather chairs made during the first quarter of the eighteenth century (see figs. 2, 9). Similarly, the side stretchers on the easy chair are closely related to those on the backstool and side chair shown in figures 7 and 8. Collectively, these chairs suggest that Boston artisans developed a relatively standardized design for easy chair frames by 1715 and that they began incorporating late baroque details by the early to mid-1720s.[11]

The Avante-Garde in Boston Seating Furniture

In 1735, John Oldmixon (1673–1742) noted that "a gentleman from London would almost think himself at home in Boston when he observes . . . their houses, their furniture, their tables [and] their dress." Given Boston's extensive trade with Britain and the city's preeminent position as "the first city of New England, and of all North America," the notion that it took the late baroque style over a decade to travel from London to Boston is implausible. Relying too heavily on the ledgers, account books, and correspondence of Fitch and Grant, scholars have overlooked the fact that furniture makers in much smaller colonial towns and cities began producing late baroque forms during the 1720s. Because Grant purchased most of his frames from other artisans, it is unlikely that he was the first to embrace the "new fashion." Grant, moreover, may have sold chairs with "round seat[s]" and "horsebone feet" years before he began using those terms to describe seating made primarily for the middle market and for export. Boston chairmakers invariably introduced new details in objects made for the local elite. Once accepted, those details became standardized and incorporated into forms that could be mass produced and marketed to a broader clientele.[12]

During the mid- to late 1720s, Boston chairmakers abandoned sawn cabriole legs in favor of more stylish "horsebone round feet." Two armchairs and a closely related side chair (figs. 15–17) suggest how this process took place. Both armchairs have carved yolk crest rails, molded stiles and stay rails, vasiform splats, and bold scrolled arms with turned, baluster-shaped supports. Although they are approximately the same date and possibly from the same shop, one has sawn cabriole legs whereas the other has "horsebone round feet" and applied bosses rather than knee blocks—a feature occasionally found on British seating from the mid- to late 1720s. The side chair shown in figure 17 also had bosses (the current ones are replacements), but its curvilinear back, rounded stiles, and a delicate vasiform splat distinguish it from the two armchairs. Several technological shifts occurred with the introduction of these late baroque details. During the early 1720s, for example, Boston chairmakers began using spokeshaves to simulate turned elements, as the rear stiles and cylindrical passages on the back legs of the side chair reveal.[13]

Figure 15 Armchair, Boston, 1725–1730. Birch and cherry. H. 40¾", W. 22⅞", D. 17⅛". (Courtesy, Winterthur Museum; bequest of Dr. and Mrs. Newberry Reynolds.)

Figure 16 Armchair, Boston, 1725–1735. Maple. H. 43 1/4", W. 20 11/16", D. 17". (Courtesy, Winterthur Museum.)

Figure 17 Side chair, Boston, ca. 1730. Walnut. H. 41", W. 19 3/16", D. 15 3/4". (Private collection; photo, Gavin Ashworth.) The crest rail may be a replacement.

Immigrant artisans and imported furniture were undoubtedly the source for many details found on Boston seating in the late baroque style. Boston cabinetmaker William Price (1684–1771) reportedly made "recurring visits" to England and employed at least one London journeyman. In 1726, he advertised "All Sorts of Looking-Glasses of the Newest Fashion & Japan Work, viz. Chests of Drawers, Corner Cupboards, Large and Small Tea Tables &c. done after the best manner by one late from London." Thomas Fitch imported British chairs and textiles and corresponded with London upholsterers. On several occasions he instructed John East to send the "newest fashion'd" valence and headcloth patterns. Customhouse clear-

Figure 18 Elbow chair, Boston, 1725–1735. Mahogany with maple. H. 34 3/4", W. 23", D. 19". (Courtesy, Winterthur Museum.)

Figure 19 *Abraham Redwood, II*, attributed to Samuel King, Newport, 1773–1780. Oil on canvas. 42 1/2" × 33 1/2". (Collection of the Redwood Library and Atheneum, Newport.)

ances published in the *Boston News-Letter* and *Boston Gazette* document the arrival of 122 ships from London between 1725 and 1729. This intercourse led one petitioner to complain, "the abundance of European goods sent over . . . exposes the inhabitants to appear in extravagant garbs who would gladly avoid the same, were they to receive money in lieu of their labor, manufactures and trade."[14]

Two elbow chairs (see fig. 18) with a history of ownership by Newport merchant Abraham Redwood II (1709–1788) have hooped arms and upholstered, lobed backs that are based on British seating from the 1720s and stretcher turnings that relate to those on Boston cane chairs (see fig. 4). Despite these early antecedents, furniture historians have dated the Redwood chairs as late as 1745–1765. Some scholars assumed that the chair depicted in Samuel King's portrait of Redwood was one of the "two roundabouts" that the merchant purchased through his Boston agent Stephen Greenleaf in 1749 (fig. 19). If the roundabouts had hooped arms, then the

Figure 20 Armchair, Boston, ca. 1725–1730. Walnut with maple. H. 43½", W. 23", D. 18⅜". (Courtesy, Winterthur Museum.) The center stretcher is replaced.

Figure 21 Side chair, Boston, ca. 1725–1730. Walnut with maple. H. 40¼", W. 20", D. 16". (Courtesy, Winterthur Museum.)

reasoning was that the elbow chairs were contemporary with them. As Nancy Goyne Evans has shown, however, hooped arms are incompatible with the structure of roundabout chairs, so the chair depicted in the portrait may actually be one of the elbow examples. Redwood's absence from Newport during a stay in Antigua between 1737 and 1741 has also been cited as evidence that the chair dates no earlier than the mid-1740s; however, it is far more likely that Redwood either inherited the elbow chairs from his father, Abraham (who settled in Newport in 1712), or purchased them about 1730. Although one scholar has suggested that the chairs' mahogany primary wood supports the notion that Redwood purchased them after returning from the Carribean, Boston joiners and turners made a substantial quantity of mahogany furniture during the second quarter of the eighteenth century.[15]

Figure 22 Side chair, London, ca. 1720. Walnut with lightwood inlay. Dimensions not recorded. Illustrated in Nicholas Grindley, *The Bended-Back Chair* (London: Barling, 1990), no. 17.

Figure 23 Detail of the knee carving on the armchair illustrated in fig. 20.

Figure 24 Detail of the knee carving on the side chair illustrated in fig. 21.

The Boston armchair and side chair shown in figures 20 and 21 are based on English prototypes (see fig. 22) influenced by Ming Dynasty seating. Both have India backs, hooped stiles, chamfered rear legs and heels, and cabriole front legs with turned pad feet and flat stretchers. Chairs with hooped stiles and veneered splats with marquetry (usually cyphers, arabesques, or floral designs) were popular in London from about 1715–1725. The backs of the Boston examples are black walnut veneered on soft maple, the core wood preferred by that city's chairmakers. Their center panels are book-matched and outlined by triple-line stringing and crossbanding, but differences in the figure of the veneer suggest that the chairs are from different sets. They are, however, from the same shop. The armchair almost certainly had a center stretcher and seat rail brackets like those of the side chair. Not only is the carving on the chairs by the same hand (figs. 23, 24), but the leaves on the knees are related to those on the two original finials and appliqué of an early Boston desk-and-bookcase in the Palladian taste (figs. 25, 26). The carving on the desk-and-bookcase is similar to work attributed to John Welch (fl. 1732–1780), one of the most prolific carvers in eighteenth-century Boston, but it appears to be a generation earlier. Welch probably apprenticed with Boston carver George Robinson (1680–1737), whose granddaughter he married in 1735.[16]

The armchair (fig. 20) reputedly belonged to John (b. 1758) and Sarah (May) Holland (b. 1772) of Boston; however, their birth dates indicate that they were not the original owners. Another armchair (in the Henry Ford Museum) that appears to be from the same set has an oral tradition of ownership by a "Captain Johnson who lived in Salem . . . and moored his . . .

Figure 25 Desk-and-bookcase, Boston, ca. 1730–1735. Mahogany with oak and white pine. H. 94", W. 41 1/4", D. 24". (Courtesy, Art Institute of Chicago, major acquisitions Centennial Fund.) The feet and one finial are replaced.

Figure 26 Detail of the carved appliqué on the desk-and-bookcase illustrated in fig. 25.

ship in Boston harbor." Despite these Boston area associations, scholars have traditionally attributed both armchairs and the side chair to Newport. Much of the confusion regarding other Boston chairs in the late baroque style stems from similar misattributions.[17]

The side chair illustrated in figure 27 may be from the same shop as the other examples with hooped stiles and India backs, but its sinuous cabriole legs, deeply carved C scrolls, and relatively flat pad feet are similar to those on a large group of easy chairs, backstools, and side chairs made in Boston during the late 1720s and 1730s. The earliest chairs in the group (see figs. 28, 29) have side stretchers with bold baluster turnings like those on transitional seating forms from the early to mid-1720s (see figs. 7, 8, 14). The easy chair illustrated in figure 28 also has a medial stretcher similar to those on many Boston leather chairs (see fig. 9) and tight, double-scrolled arms like the examples shown in figures 13 and 14. These features suggest that the easy chair dates to about 1730, when "new fashion'd round seat[s]" and "horse-bone round feet" first entered the mainstream of Boston chair production.[18]

A closely related side chair (fig. 29) supports the date assigned to the easy chair and other seating furniture in the group. Not only does the side chair

Figure 27 Side chair, Boston, ca. 1725–1730. Mahogany with maple. H. 41", W. 21¹/₄". (Collection at Hunter House, Preservation Society of Newport County; photo, John W. Corbett.)

share features with the example with applied bosses (see fig. 17) but its crest rail and "banister" are variants of one depicted in John Smibert's 1732 portrait of Mary (Fitch) Oliver (1706–1732) and her son Andrew, Jr. (b. 1731) (fig. 30). Mary was the daughter of upholsterer Thomas Fitch. References to her husband, Andrew, and Smibert appear in Fitch's accounts, although not for the purchase of chairs. Smibert completed the Oliver portrait in June 1732, nearly seven months after Samuel Grant began using the term "banister" to describe chair splats. On December 17, 1731, Grant sold export merchants Jacob and John Wendell "10 Leath Chairs @ 26/6 . . . £13.5," and "2 Elbow d°: Banist Backes 48/ . . . £4.16." A more accurate description of the chair in Mary Oliver's portrait can be found in Grant's April 29, 1732, invoice to

Figure 28 Easy chair, Boston, ca. 1730. Maple. H. 48", W. 33³/₄", D. 29". (Courtesy, Museum of Fine Arts, Houston, Bayou Bend Collection; gift of Miss Ima Hogg.)

"Jnº Breck Cooper at north End" for "8 Leathr Chairs horsebone feet & Banist backs . . . £10.12." The tradesmen in Grant's network undoubtedly made chairs with banisters before 1732, however. The side chair shown in figure 29 does not have a history, but an example from the same shop descended in a Boston family.[19]

Samuel Grant began selling backstools, or "low chairs," with cabriole legs by 1731/32. In February of that year, he billed Clark & Kilby for "1 Crimson Chainy Easie Ch: . . . £9.18" and "1 Low chair horse bone foot cush^n Seat . . . £2.17." Although considerably more expensive than side chairs, backstools became popular in Boston during the late 1720s. John Smibert's study for *The Bermuda Group*, commissioned in the summer of 1728, shows John Wainwright seated on a backstool with cabriole front and rear legs (fig. 31). Sir Robert Walpole's accounts for furnishings at Houghton show how quickly London fashions made their way to Boston. In 1728, he ordered "12 fine wallnuttree Chair frames stuff'd back and seats, . . . a wallnuttree set-

Figure 29 Side chair, Boston, ca. 1730. Mahogany; beech slipseat frame. H. 44", W. 19", D. 21". (Courtesy, Museum of Fine Arts, Houston, Bayou Bend Collection; gift of Miss Ima Hogg.)

Figure 30 John Smibert, *Mary Fitch Oliver and Andrew Oliver, Jr.*, Boston, 1732. Oil on canvas. 50 1/2" × 40 1/2". (Private collection; photo, Frick Art Reference Library.)

Figure 31 John Smibert, detail of a study for *The Bermuda Group*, ca. 1729. Oil on canvas. 69 1/2" × 93". (Courtesy, National Gallery of Ireland.)

tee frame," and two large "walnuttree Couch frame[s]" from London joiner Thomas Roberts. These "fine wallnuttree Chair frames" (fig. 32) are only slightly more ornate than the backstool depicted in Smibert's painting and three contemporary Boston examples (see fig. 33).[20]

As Grant's and Walpole's accounts reveal, backstools often accompanied other upholstered forms. Although possibly made a decade apart, the Boston backstool and easy chair illustrated in figures 33 and 34 give the impression of being en suite. Both have compass seats, cabriole legs with C scrolls and pad feet, turned rear stretchers, and flat side stretchers with cove-molded edges. Samuel Grant first mentioned flat stretchers in a February 3, 1741/42, bill to Benjamin Dolbear for "2 Chairs false Seats Flat Strechers . . . £6," but Boston chairmakers undoubtedly made them much earlier. The

Figure 32 Backstool from the shop of Thomas Roberts, London, 1728. Walnut. H. 41", W. 23½", D. 25". (Courtesy, Christie's.)

Figure 33 Backstool, Boston, ca. 1730. Walnut with maple and beech. H. 40", W. 21", D. 25". (Chipstone Foundation; photo, Gavin Ashworth.) The backstool originally had silk upholstery.

medial stretcher on the easy chair is replaced, but it probably resembled the carved one on the backstool (see fig. 33) or was cove-molded like those on the side chair and easy chair shown in figures 36 and 38. Similar stretchers occur on many English and Irish chairs of the period. The construction of the backstool and easy chair also suggest that they are from the same shop. Both have flat seat rails with lap-joints at the front corners. Each joint is pierced by a quarter-round tenon cut from the upper leg stock and reinforced with wooden pins (pegs) (fig. 35). This structural detail also occurs on more conventional Boston seating forms such as the easy chair shown in figure 50.[21]

During the mid-1730s, wealthy Bostonians began responding to new stylistic impulses emanating from London. A renowned set of side chairs commissioned by merchant Charles Apthorp about 1735 (see fig. 36) has broad, baluster-shaped splats with vibrant walnut veneers, angular "crook'd" stiles, cabriole front legs with claw-and-ball feet, tapered rear legs with small, squarish feet, and shell-carved crests and knees—features associated with

Figure 34 Easy chair, Boston, 1730–1740. Walnut with maple. H. 49". (Courtesy G. W. Samaha Antiques, Milan, Ohio; photo Jeffery Dykes.)

Figure 35 Detail of the seat rail and front leg joint of the backstool shown in fig. 33. (Photo, Gavin Ashworth.)

urban British chairs made during the reign of George II (see fig. 37). The Apthorp chairs and a closely related easy chair (fig. 38) may be from the same shop as the backstool and easy chair shown in figures 33 and 34. All of these chairs have classic Boston "arrow-shaped" rear stretchers and cove-molded flat stretchers. The front legs of the easy chair shown in figure 38 are attached with large dovetails that are exposed on the front and wedged rather than with quarter-round tenons, but such variations were relatively common in large shops that employed journeyman laborers and commissioned piecework from other tradesmen.

The carving on the Apthorp chairs and easy chair is attributed to John Welch. All of these examples have embryonic claw-and-ball feet that are similar to those on London seating from the early 1730s (figs. 36–38). In laying out the feet, Welch positioned the ball off center, toward the front corner of his stock, rather than centering the ball to fully utilize the dimensions of his material. By the early 1740s, he began using the more conventional, centered approach.[22]

Figure 36 Side chair, Boston, ca. 1735. Walnut and walnut veneer with maple and white pine. H. 38⅝", W. 20¾", D. 18½". (Courtesy, Metropolitan Museum of Art, gift of Mr. and Mrs. Benjamin Ginsburg; photo, Gavin Ashworth.)

Figure 37 Side chair, London, 1725–1735. Walnut and walnut veneer. (Courtesy, Sotheby's.)

Samuel Grant had business dealings with Apthorp as early as 1736, when the upholsterer credited the merchant's account with "2 doz. chairs" valued at £36, "2 Elbow ditto" valued at £10.16, a "Couch Frame & Squab" valued at £7.7.9, and "Canvas & packing" valued at £1.5. The references to canvas and packing suggest that the seating was for export. Between 1738 and 1748, Apthorp received over 300 chairs from Grant.[23]

By the end of the 1730s, chairs like Apthorp's were the avante-garde in Boston seating furniture; however, the city's chairmakers continued to produce examples with rounded stiles, slender vasiform splats, and pad feet well into the third quarter of the eighteenth century. Much of this later seating was standardized in the sense of being produced quickly (and often rather

Figure 38 Easy chair, Boston, ca. 1735–1740. Walnut and maple. H. 44", W. 31", D. 22". (Courtesy, Winterthur Museum.)

coarsely) and in large quantities. The level of production is suggested by Grant's payments to Edmund Perkins during the 1740s: £695.5.2 for unspecified work in 1742, £694.12.7 for "chair frames etc." in 1745/46, and £790.18.6 for "chair frames etc." in 1746/47. The use of piecework increased production and gave patrons a wide range of features from which to pick and choose. During the seventeenth and early eighteenth centuries, turners, joiners, and carvers provided a variety of components for chairmakers. This practice persisted and expanded later in the eighteenth century as other specialists became involved in the production process. When fire swept through Boston in 1760, chairmaker John Perkins lost "220 wallnot Feet for Chairs," whereas his competitor, Joseph Putnam, lost " 350 wallnot feet." Mass production did not eliminate variety, however, for many standardized late baroque forms made from the late 1730s to past midcentury display creative combinations of British and Anglo-Boston details.[24]

Standardized Seating for Local Consumption and Export

In his study of the shoemaking business in colonial and federal America, economic historian John R. Commons asserted that new markets determined craftsmen's "forms of organization." The three levels of production that he identified have precise parallels in Boston's chairmaking industry: custom-made or "bespoke" work for an immediate local market; standardized work, which required increased output and was geared to a broader retail market; and "order" work, which focused on standardized products made in vast quantity and sold at wholesale prices to outside markets. As the accounts of Fitch and Grant suggest, most of the seating furniture made in Boston during the first half of the eighteenth century conformed to Commons's last two levels of production.[25]

Figure 39 Side chair, Boston, 1735–1755. Walnut. H. 38 7/8", W. 19 3/4", D. 16 1/4". (Courtesy, Winterthur Museum.)

Figure 40 Side chair, Boston, 1735–1755. Walnut with maple. H. 39 5/8", W. 21 3/4", D. 21 1/4". (Courtesy, Winterthur Museum; gift of Mr. & Mrs. George M. Kaufman, Martin E. Wunsch, and anonymous donor.)

Standardized side chairs similar to those shown in figures 39 and 40 were produced in Boston from about 1730 until past midcentury. Materials, structural options, and decorative details determined the price. The least expensive chairs, many of which represented "order work" made for outside markets, were made of maple and painted or stained to resemble a more expensive wood such as mahogany. These chairs typically had trapezoidal frames, loose seats, chamfered rear legs and heels, turned cabriole legs with pad feet, turned stretchers, flat stiles, vasiform splats, and yolk-shaped crests. Imported woods, rounded stiles, compass seats, carving, and over-the-rail upholstery increased the price, usually in proportion to material and labor costs. Grant's accounts during the early 1730s suggest that the average price of a basic walnut chair like the one illustrated in figure 39 was approximately 26s. On September 8, 1732, Grant charged Jonathan Fayerweather for "6 Leath Chairs ban. back 26/6 . . . £7.19," "6 Maple Chairs cush^n Seats of green chᵃ 37/ . . . £11.2," and "8 Black Walnutt chairs cushⁿs of Leath. . . £12." A comparable chair with a compass seat and over-the-rail upholstery probably cost a few shillings more (see fig. 40).[26]

A side chair that reportedly belonged to William Ellery, Jr. (1727–1820), of Newport (fig. 41) and another that descended in the Moses Brown family of Providence (fig. 42) are more expensive variants of standardized Boston trapezoidal and compass seat forms. Ellery's chair may have been a bequest from his parents, William (1701–1764) and Elizabeth (Almy) (d. 1783). Like many Newport merchants, William, Sr., conducted a good deal of business in Boston. On November 23, 1745, his sloop *Phoenix* left Boston for Mary-

Figure 41 Side chair, Boston, 1730–1740. Walnut. H. 41¾", W. 20½", D. 20". Illustrated in Anderson Galleries, *Colonial Furniture, the Superb Collection of Mr. Francis Hill Bigelow of Cambridge, Massachusetts*, New York, January 17, 1924, lot. 142.

Figure 42 Side chair, Boston, 1740–1750. Walnut; maple slip seat. H. 40½", W. 21¾". (Courtesy, Moses Brown School.)

land with a cargo that included "1 Desk & 2 Tables" and "2 doz. chairs." Although the rounded stiles and ogee-shaped front rail of the Ellery chair distinguish it from the most basic of the standardized side chair forms, it would have been substantially less expensive than the example illustrated in figure 42. Chairs with carved shells, curved rails, and slip seats were probably more costly than comparable forms with over-the-rail upholstery, assuming that the same textiles were used. The Brown chair probably dates from the early to mid-1740s, as does the claw-and-ball foot example shown in figure 43. By that time, Boston merchant-upholsterers like Grant were exporting standardized versions of Georgian seating along with late baroque forms. As the Ellery chair and shipping records reveal, Newporters purchased large quantites of Boston seating for both personal use and resale.[27]

Standardized seating clearly included more than just plain "order work." The relatively coarse construction of the side chair illustrated in figure 44

Figure 43 Side chair, Boston, 1740–1755. Mahogany; maple slip seat. H. 38 1/2", W. 22", D. 21 1/4". (Chipstone Foundation; photo, Gavin Ashworth.)

marks it as a standardized form: The front rail was hastily sawn and undercut, and the flats on either side of the center drop are not parallel; saw kerfs from the shaping process are visible on the face of the front rail, inside edges of the stretchers, and around the scroll volutes on the front legs; prominent spokeshave marks remain on the rear legs; and the leg-stretcher joints are poorly finished. Despite these features, the chair is a very fashionable example of Boston seating. Its crest rail, crooked stiles, broad vasiform splat, and lambrequin-carved knees are quite similar to those on side chairs attributed to London joiner Giles Grendy (1693–1780). In addition to working for prominent Britons such as Richard Hoare and Sir Jacob de Bouverie, Grendy produced large quantities of furniture for export. A magnificent bombé bureau with cabinet that belonged to Boston merchant

Figure 44 Side chair, Boston, 1735–1750. Walnut. H. 40 3/4", W. 20 5/8", D. 17 3/4". (Private collection; photo, Gavin Ashworth.)

Figure 45 Side chair, Boston, 1735–1745. Walnut. H. 40 3/4". (Courtesy, Wayne Pratt Antiques.)

Charles Apthorp may be from his shop. Apthorp probably purchased the cabinet between 1735 and 1745, which would make it roughly contemporary with the Boston chair (fig. 44). Chairs exported by Grendy or one of his contemporaries may have influenced the basic design of the Boston example.[28]

A pair of side chairs that descended in the Bromfield family of Boston (see fig. 45) and a set from the Huse family of Greenland, New Hampshire (see fig. 46), display other options that were available in standardized formats. The Bromfield chairs share details with the preceding example—compass seats, carved rear feet, front legs with lambrequins and C scrolls—but they have different backs, stretchers with rounded outer edges, and carved slipper feet. The crests of the Bromfield chairs look back to the hooped

Figure 46   Side chair, Boston, 1735–1745. Walnut; maple slipseat frame. H. 40⁷/₈", W. 21¹/₁₆", D. 17¹/₈". (Courtesy, Museum of Fine Arts, Boston; gift of Miss Dorothy Buhler.)

forms that were popular in Boston during the late 1720s and early 1730s (see figs. 20, 21, 27). Multigenerational shop traditions, such as those established by members of the Perkins family, probably account for the longevity of certain styles and patterns as much as the conservatism of some of their patrons. Rounded stiles, yolk shaped crests, and slender vasiform splats were fashionable from the late 1720s to about 1750. John Singleton Copley's portrait of Bostonian John Barrett (fig. 47) painted in 1758 shows a chair with lambrequin knees and carved C scrolls similar to the ones on the Huse chairs and the Boston examples shown in figures 44 and 48.[29]

Most of the easy chairs produced in Boston during the second and third decades of the eighteenth century were standardized forms. Between 1739 and 1747 alone, Grant sold at least fifty-four easy chairs. Many were purchased by ship captains or sold with packing materials indicating that they had been earmarked as venture cargo. On August 15, 1759, Grant billed Boston shopkeeper John Scollay £4.18.6 for "a Green [worsted] Easie Char & packing" (fig. 49). The following day, Scollay sold the chair to Jonathan

Figure 47 John Singleton Copley, *John Barrett*, 1758. Oil on canvas. 50" × 40". (Courtesy, Nelson-Atkins Museum of Art, Kansas City, Missouri; gift of the Enid and Crosby Kemper Foundation.)

Figure 48 Side chair, Boston, 1740–1750. Walnut. H. 40¼", W. 20¾", D. 24". (Private collection; photo, Gavin Ashworth.)

Sayward of York, Maine, for the same price, which suggests that Scollay was acting as an agent for Grant. Grant's ledger entries indicate that Clement Vincent and George Bright furnished most of his easy chair frames in 1759. Vincent typically received about 14s. per frame while Bright received approximately 16s.[30]

Sayward's easy chair is typical of most Boston examples made from about 1730 through the 1770s. It has rear stiles that extend to form the legs (maple stained to match the walnut front legs and stretchers), slightly flared cheeks, vertical arm scrolls, turned stretchers, and cabriole front legs that are dovetailed to the seat rail. The Boston easy chair shown in figure 50 is similar, but its front legs have quarter-round through-tenons and its double-scrolled arms recall those on earlier forms (see figs. 13, 14, 28). Different shops clearly developed different production methods; however, standardization, the use of piecework components, and specialized labor were the determining factors in the evolution of the Boston easy chair.

Although a variety of design options such as leg form, stretcher shape, and ornamental carving were available in Boston easy chairs, the upholstery was invariably the most expensive component. On December 8, 1729, Grant billed Nathaniel Green for:

1 Easie chair fraim	2.0.0
6 1/2 Yd. chainy @ 6.8	2.13.4
1 Yd 1/8 print 4	0.4.6
18 Yd. silk bindg. 12	0.16.6
Tax 5 girtweb Thred & line 3	0.8.0
4 lb. curld hair 10 4 lb. feathers. 14	1.8.0
1 1/2 Yd Ticken 9.4 crocus & Ozna: 12	1.1.4
makg: a Easie chair	1.15.0
Total	10.6.8

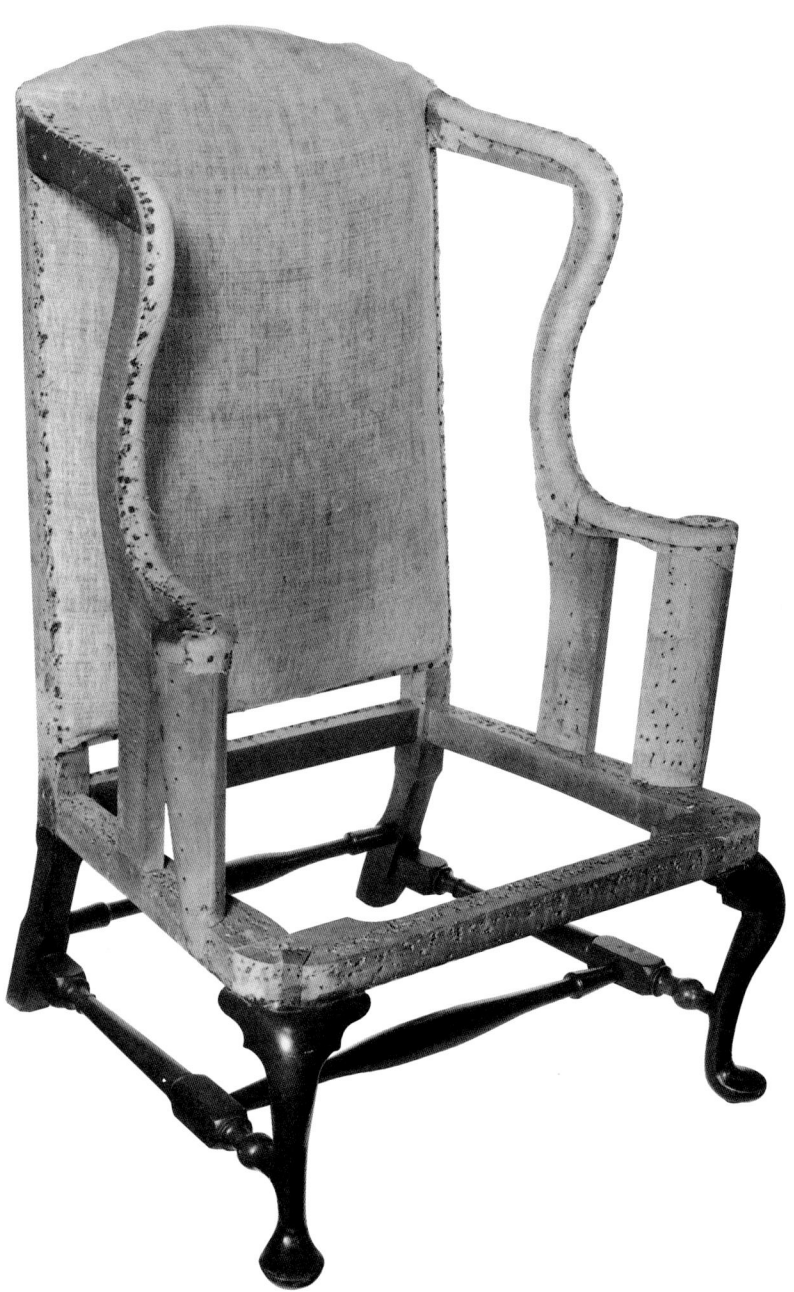

Figure 49 Easy chair by Clement Vincent or George Bright with upholstery by Samuel Grant, Boston, 1759. Walnut and maple with maple and white pine. H. 46 1/8", W. 33 7/8", D. 21 3/4". (Courtesy, Society for the Preservation of New England Antiquities; photo, Richard Cheek.) The front feet are replaced.

Figure 50 Easy chair, Boston, 1735–1755. Walnut with maple. H. 48", W. 32". (Courtesy, Leigh Keno American Antiques.)

Next to couches and settees, easy chairs were the most costly seating forms. As Grant's bill reveals, the upholsterer's materials and labor generally accounted for at least two thirds of the cost of an easy chair. Most of the easy chairs mentioned in Grant's accounts between 1728 and 1732 were covered in cheney, a coarse-grained or ribbed worsted. Harateen, another relatively coarse worsted, became increasingly popular after 1738, although it had been used in Boston since the mid-1720s. On March 26, 1726, Thomas Fitch wrote Madame Anna Hooglant of New York:

> I concluded it would be difficult to get Such a Calliminco as you propos'd to cover the Easie Chair, and haveing a very Strong thick Harratine which is vastly more fashionable and handsome than Calliminco I have sent you an Ease Chair Cover'd wth sd Harrateen wch I hope will Sute you.

Fitch and Grant understood the importance of satisfying their clients' desires for the latest London fashions *and* accommodating regional tastes.

Figure 51 Easy chair, Boston, ca. 1758. Walnut and maple with maple. H. 46 3/8", W. 32 3/8", D. 25 7/8". (Courtesy, Metropolitan Museum of Art; gift of Mrs. J. Insley Blair.)

In December 1731, Fitch instructed London upholsterer John East to send "a pattern or figure of [a] Fashionable Vallance & the figure of a headboard & headcloth. . . . he may send some with a little more work, our people too generally choosing them somewhat showy."[31]

Whether for bedsteads or easy chairs, fashionable textiles gave Boston consumers the opportunity to distinguish their furniture from that of their peers. Grant's records reveal that his clients occasionally replaced or updated upholstery. On October 26, 1756, he billed John Scollay for "new cov^d easie chair & 2 window squabs." Several Boston easy chairs retain their original upholstery, but few are as elaborate as the one shown in figure 51. The front of this chair is covered with Irish-stitch needlework, and the back panel is embroidered with a rural landscape. The crest rail is inscribed "Gardner Junr/ Newport May/ 1758/ W." Such inscriptions usually identify either the owner or upholsterer. The one on this chair may refer to Caleb Gardner, who died in Newport in 1761. His son, Caleb, was born in 1750 and did upholstery work for Abraham Redwood in 1774. Although the Gardner chair has been attributed to Newport, its stretcher turnings, integral rear stiles and legs, and basic frame design have parallels in the Sayward

Figure 52   Side chair, Boston, 1735–1745. Walnut. Dimensions unrecorded. Illustrated in Anderson Art Galleries, *Philip Flayderman Collection*, January 4, 1930, lot 492.

Figure 53   Easy chair, Boston, 1735–1745. Walnut. Dimensions unrecorded. Illustrated in Anderson Art Galleries, *Philip Flayderman Collection*, January 4, 1930, lot 493.

chair and many other examples with Boston-area histories. Evidence suggests that both the frame and landscape panel of the Gardner chair were shipped from Boston to Newport. Textile historian Amelia Peck has attributed the panel to an anonymous Boston needlework school, based on its composition and stitching.[32]

Distribution and Misattribution

Given the Rhode Island provenances of many Boston chairs, it is understandable that scholars attributed some of them to Newport tradesmen. Much of the confusion can be traced to a set of six side chairs and an easy chair that descended in the Eddy family of Warren, Rhode Island (figs. 52, 53). These objects have been erroneously associated with Job Townsend (1699–1765) ever since they appeared in the Philip Flayderman sale at Anderson Galleries in 1930. Although the sale catalogue failed to provide documentation for the attribution, when the chairs sold again in 1932 they were described as part of a group of furniture "made by Job Townsend for the Eddy family of Rhode Island in 1743. One of these pieces, which bears Townsend's label, still remains in the possession of this family." The fact that the Eddy family may have owned a piece labeled by Townsend does not mean that the chairs came from the same source. Judging from Townsend's surviving account books, which span the years 1751–1757, the principal output of his shop was case furniture and tables. No chairs are listed during that period.[33]

The hooped crests, flat stretchers, and carved C scrolls on the Eddy chairs clearly establish their Boston origin. Based on their relationship to the earlier "India back" arm chairs and side chairs shown in figures 20, 21, and 27 and later standardized examples with flat stretchers (see fig. 44), the Eddy chairs appear to date from the 1740s. A ship captain named Jeremiah Eddy transported a large number of Boston chairs to Rhode Island during that decade, so it is conceivable that these chairs or other Boston examples descended in a branch of his family. Harbor clearances listed in the *Boston News-Letter* indicate that Eddy sailed to Newport at least twenty times between January 3, 1739, and December 27, 1744. Eddy was a native of Swansea, Massachusetts, which bordered Warren, Rhode Island (incorporated on January 27, 1746/47).[34]

Since the 1930s, furniture historians have used the design vocabulary of the Eddy suite to attribute numerous Boston chairs to Job Townsend and other Newport tradesmen. Similar misattributions can be traced to a set of chairs that descended in the Moses Brown family of Providence (see fig. 42). A 1927 *Bulletin of the Rhode Island School of Design* noted that the set could be the "Leather Chairs" that Brown purchased from John Goddard in 1763. The Brown chairs clearly date from the 1740s or 1750s, however. Like a set of chairs once owned by Charles Barrett, Sr., of Concord, Massachusetts (and later New Ipswich, New Hampshire), the rounded stiles and shell-carved crests of the Brown chairs take their design cue from earlier British models. Because the Townsends, Goddards, and other Rhode Island cabinetmakers used carved shells on much of their case furniture, scholars cited the shells on the crests of the Brown chairs as evidence of Rhode Island manufacture. Not only does the carving on the Brown chairs speak to a strong Boston tradition, but the shells on Newport seating from the 1760s on were derived from Boston chairs imported into Rhode Island during the second and third quarters of the eighteenth century. A Boston desk-and-bookcase with a probable history of ownership by William Cabot of Salem has a lobate shell on its scrollboard that is almost identical to the shells on the Brown set.[35]

Rhode Islanders purchased seating furniture in Boston because it was the dominant center of upholstery and chairmaking in the colonial Northeast. Between 1729 and 1739, the output of Samuel Grant's enterprise alone amounted to 2,006 chairs, 138 stools, 49 couches, and 44 easy chairs. Between 1725 and 1730, at least 278 vessels sailed from Boston to Rhode Island.

Figure 54 Robert Feke (1706/1707–1752), *John Banister*, 1748. Oil on canvas. 50⁹/₁₆" × 40⁹/₁₆". (Courtesy, Toledo Museum of Art.)

Thomas Fitch, whose primary trade was European textiles, had over thirty-two clients in Rhode Island. Boston's command over chairmaking and upholstery is underscored by the sheer numbers of its industry. Between 1730 and 1750, eighty-eight cabinetmakers and joiners, twenty-two chairmakers, fourteen upholsterers, six carvers, five turners, six japanners, one glazier, and one chair caner worked in Boston—far more than in any other colonial city. During the same period, thirty-seven cabinetmakers and joiners and three carvers worked in Newport, but records identify only one chairmaker and no upholsterers.[36]

Rhode Island ship captains and merchants were among the principal importers of Boston seating furniture. One of the most ambitious Newport merchants of the 1730s and 1740s was John Banister (fig. 54). In a 1739 letter to John Thomlinson of London, Banister noted that Newporters desired "to make themselves Independent of the Bay Government to whom they have a mortal aversion." Banister's frustration stemmed from his own dependence upon Boston suppliers such as upholsterers William Downe and Samuel Grant, from whom he purchased "12 Lea: Chairs " for £19.4 and "18 Lea Chairs" for 32s. respectively, in 1739. Banister's account books reveal that he purchased 144 chairs in Boston between 1741 and 1743.[37]

The chairs Banister purchased represent a variety of Boston export styles. On March 31, 1743, he "bought by Mr. Hugh Vans in Boston & Shipped on board the Sloop Ann, Joseph Dean Master for Newport" two dozen chairs, including "6 Leather chairs @ 34 . . . 10.4," "6 Lea back Red @ 34 . . . 10.4," "6 ditto Black @ 38 . . . 11.8," and "6 ditto Horsefoot @ 38 . . . 11.8." Two weeks earlier he had received a cargo via "Capt. Eady" of "30 Chairs Leather Backs & Bottoms @ 38/" totaling £57 and "6 ditto Leather Bottoms @ 35/6" totaling £10.13. "Eady" was likely the aforementioned Jeremiah Eddy, whose name appears frequently in Banister's accounts of that year. Banister also purchased work from John Welch. An invoice of July 1, 1743, indicates that Banister received "a Lyon Head . . . from Welch" valued at £35.2, which was presumably a ship's figurehead.[38]

By the mid-1740s, Rhode Island was entering into an era of improved productivity and prosperity. Local industries were growing, and the colony's merchants and entrepreneurs were beginning to establish regular and direct trade routes with London, Bristol, and other European ports. Before midcentury, Newport did not have the artisan base to support a chairmaking industry, but after 1755, local tradesmen like the Townsends and Goddards began making and exporting seating furniture. Jeanne Sloane estimated that fifty-six cabinetmakers were active in Newport between 1745 and 1774, compared with sixty-four in Boston—a city with a much larger population. Additional measure of Newport's improved industry can be taken from southern port-of-entry records. Between April 6, 1756, and December 24, 1775, at least 128 ships arrived in Annapolis from Boston and at least 67 arrived from Newport. Despite Boston's numerical dominance, the Newport cargoes had a higher percentage of case furniture, tables, and chairs. Newport vessels carried an average of nine pieces per vessel, whereas Boston ships carried an average of three. During this period, 25 case pieces, 20 tables, and 380 chairs arrived in Annapolis from Newport.[39]

In 1738, Banister traveled to London to begin developing trade alliances that would challenge Boston's dominance in intercoastal shipping. His invoice book of 1739 describes one of his first London cargoes, which included "4 Pier glasses in neat wallnuttree Frames . . . £7.12," "4 Ditto Carv'd edge & Shell . . . £7.12," "3 Ditto . . . wth out gold . . . £3.18," "a Walnuttree Card Table . . . £2.5," "a Bewroe table wth a Desk . . . 2.10," "8 Walnuttree Chairs w. Seats Covered with black Span: Leather . . . £9.12," and "1 Elbow Chair . . . Ditto . . . £1.11.6." Signaling things to come, Banister wrote his London suppliers Thomas and James Hayward on May 28, 1739:

> my hurry obliges me to Proceed upon the Head of Business, which at present Looks with an Incouraging prospect the people of this Colony being resolved to Brake of their Dependence for Boston therefore have Generously purchased the Greatest part of my cargoe already.[40]

ACKNOWLEDGMENTS For assistance with this article, we thank Gavin Ashworth, Luke Beckerdite, Merrilee Posner, Allan Breed, Michael K. Brown, Amy Coes, Wendy A. Cooper, Jane Furr Davis, Linda Epich, Frank Fuller, Elisabeth D. Garrett, Constance and Dudley Godfrey, Roger Gonzales, Nicholas Grindley, Anne Rogers Haley, Clifford and Ralph Harvard, Morrison H. Heckscher, Brock Jobe, Marybeth Keene, Leslie Keno, Alan Miller, Ruth Oliver Morley, Robert Mussey, Milo Naeve, Dr. King Odell, Andrew Oliver, Jr., Daniel Oliver, Jess Pavey, Amelia Peck, Ronald Potvin, Jonathan Prown, Margaret Reasor, Betty Ring, Albert Sack, G. W. Samaha, Lesley and George Schoedinger, Nancy Shaw, Jim Tottis, Robert Trent, and Anne and Fred Vogel.

1. "The Country-Man's Answer to a Letter Intitled the Distressed State of the Town of Boston Considered," *Boston News-Letter,* April 14, 1720. In "A Brief Description of New England and the Severall Townes Therein, Together with the Present Government Thereof," Samuel Maverick referred to Boston as the "Metropolis of New England," *Proceedings of the Massachusetts Historical Society*, 2nd series, 1 (1884–1885): 237. Neil D. Kamil, "Hidden in Plain Sight: Disappearance and Material Life in Colonial New York," in *American Furniture,* edited by Luke Beckerdite (Hanover, N.H.: University Press of New England for the Chipstone Foundation, 1995), pp. 193–96. Thomas Fitch's letterbooks and account books are in the following collections: Letterbook, 1702–1711, New England Historic Genealogical Society; Letterbook, 1723–1733, Massachusetts Historical Society; Account book, 1719–1732, and Account Book, 1732–1736, Massachusetts Historical Society.

2. Roger Gonzales and Daniel Putnam Brown, Jr., "Boston and New York Leather Chairs: A Reappraisal," in *American Furniture,* edited by Luke Beckerdite (Hanover, N.H.: University Press of New England for the Chipstone Foundation, 1996), pp. 179–89. Benno M. Forman, *American Seating Furniture, 1630–1730* (New York: W. W. Norton for the Winterthur Museum, 1988), pp. 244, 286, 313. Leigh Keno, Joan Barzilay Freund, and Alan Miller, "The Very Pink of the Mode: Boston Georgian Chairs, Their Export and Their Influence," in *American Furniture,* edited by Luke Beckerdite (Hanover, N.H.: University Press of New England for the Chipstone Foundation, 1996), p. 269. Samuel Grant's account books and receipt book are in the following collections: Account Book, 1728–1737, Massachusetts Historical Society; Receipt Book, 1731–1740, Bostonian Society; Account Book, 1737–1760, American Antiquarian Society.

3. Keno, Freund, and Miller, "The Very Pink of the Mode," pp. 269–306.

4. Kamil, "Hidden in Plain Sight," pp. 192, 196. Boston leather chairs were undoubtedly inspired by British caned chairs and leather chairs. Like their New England counterparts, British leather chairs exported to the colonies were also adaptations of London cane chairs. In 1680, the Cane-Chair Makers Company noted that "about the year 1664, cane-chairs came into use." Such chairs were esteemed "for their Durable Lightness, and Cleanness from Dust,

Worms and Moths which inseparably attend Turkey-work, serge and other stuff chairs and couches, to the spoiling of them and all furniture near them" (Peter Thornton, *Seventeenth Century Interior Decoration in England, France & Holland* [New Haven and London: Yale University Press, 1978], p. 202; see also Gonzales and Brown, "Boston and New York Leather Chairs," p. 193, nt. 7). For references to Faneuil and his shipments of leather chairs to New York and Rhode Island, see Forman, *American Seating Furniture*, pp. 201, 204, 208, 243–44, 261–64, 271, 281–88, 292, 294–95, 297–99, 310, 313, 316, 323, 326, 335, 337–38, 340, 348, 351–52.

5. The first reference to chairs with crooked backs and molded stiles in Fitch's accounts is February 27, 1722/23 (Forman, *American Seating Furniture*, p. 262). Ibid., pp. 242, 284–85, 258–67.

6. Ibid., pp. 244, 250, 258–67.

7. Samuel Grant Account Book, October 14, 1729; November 21, 1730; and January 13, 1731/32. Thomas Phill sold chairs with sawn cabriole legs, described as "frames of ye newest fashion," to Edward Dryen of Canons Ashby in Northamptonshire in 1714 (see Nicholas Grindley, *The Bended Back Chair* [London: Barling, 1990]). One of the chairs from Canons Ashby is illustrated in Ralph Edwards, *The Shorter Dictionary of English Furniture* (London: Country Life), pp. 133, fig. 67. Edwards also illustrates another early cabriole leg chair made for Sir William Humphrey, Lord Mayor of London, about 1717 (ibid., p. 135, fig. 75). A suite of furniture possibly made for the Earls of Guilford, Sezincote, Gloucestershire, has carved details that suggest a date of production earlier than the Dryen and Humphrey suites (see Sotheby's *Important English Furniture,* London, July 10, 1998, p. 28, lot 6). For chairs attributed to the Roberts family, see Christie's, *Works of Art from Houghton*, London, December 8, 1994, lots 126 and 127. Two Boston side chairs with sawn cabriole legs not illustrated in this article are in a private collection in Newbury, Massachusetts. Both are made of maple and have a punched "I". Forman, *American Seating Furniture,* p. 286. On February 27, 1722/23, Fitch sold Edmund Knight "1 doz crook'd back chairs" for £16.4. On March 20, 1723/24, Fitch sold a dozen "Rushia newest fashion'd chairs" to Adam Powell of New York (ibid., p. 285).

8. Forman, *American Seating Furniture*, p. 301. The center stretcher on the chair shown in figure 6 is closely related to one on a Boston backstool dating about 1710–1720 and several leather chairs from the first quarter of the eighteenth century (see ibid., p. 361, no. 85).

9. Grant may have referred to backstools as "low chairs." His account book lists "1 Crimson Chainy Easy Ch:" and "1 Low chair horse bone foot cush^n seat" on January 25, 1731/32. Grant Account Book, pp. 360, 342–43. Although the history of the armchair shown in figure 9 is unknown, it resembles one that reportedly belonged to Reverend Theophilus Pickering (1700–1747), who graduated from Harvard College in 1719 and served as minister of Chebacco Parish in Ipswich, Massachusetts, from 1725 until 1747 (Forman, *American Seating Furniture*, p. 349). For the Remey reference, see Christopher Gilbert, "The Temple Newsam Furniture Bills," *Furniture History* 3 (1967): 21.

10. Forman, *American Seating Furniture*, pp. 298, 358. Gonzales and Brown, "Boston and New York Leather Chairs," pp. 175–80.

11. The other easy chairs are at the Winterthur Museum (see Forman, *American Seating Furniture*, p. 365, no. 89), Colonial Williamsburg, and the Chipstone Foundation. The Williamsburg chair has a partially replaced crest rail and has lost its carved Spanish feet. The Chipstone chair is virtually identical to the Williamsburg chair and the example shown in figure 13, with the exception of having a double-arched crest rail. For related easy chairs, see Forman, *American Seating Furniture*, pp. 364–69; nos. 88–92. The low chair is illustrated in ibid., p. 361, no. 85.

12. For the Oldmixon quote, see Esther Singleton, *Furniture of Our Forefathers* (New York: Doubleday, Page, & Co., 1908), pp. 372–73. Edmund Burke, *An Account of the European Settlements in America*, 2 vols. (1758; reprint ed., New York: Research Reprints, 1970), 2:172–73. The Speaker's chair made for the Virginia House of Burgesses and a small group of late baroque tables attributed to Williamsburg, Virginia, appear to date from the mid- to late 1720s (Wallace B. Gusler, *The Furniture of Williamsburg and Eastern Virginia, 1710–1790* [Richmond: Virginia Museum of Fine Arts, 1979], pp. 12–19). The dining table shown in figure 9 of Gusler's book descended in the Carter family of eastern Virginia. Oral tradition maintains that it came from King Carter's home, Corotoman, which burned in 1728 (conversations between Luke Beckerdite and members of the Carter family during a visit to Sabine Hall in 1997). The late baroque style may have been introduced to Williamsburg by cabinetmaker Peter Scott who was established there by 1722 (Gusler, *Furniture of Williamsburg*, pp. 25–27).

13. Nancy Richards and Nancy Goyne Evans, *New England Furniture at Winterthur: Queen Anne and Chippendale Periods* (Winterthur, Del.: Winterthur Museum, 1997), pp. 13–14. The authors thank Alan Miller for the information on spokeshaves.

14. *Boston Gazette*, April 4–11, 1726. Brock Jobe, "The Boston Furniture Industry, 1720–1740," in *Boston Furniture of the Eighteenth Century*, edited by Walter Muir Whitehill, Brock Jobe, and Jonathan Fairbanks (Boston: Colonial Society of Massachusetts, 1974), p. 28. As quoted in Alan Miller, "Roman Gusto in New England: An Eighteenth-Century Boston Furniture Designer and His Shop," in *American Furniture*, edited by Luke Beckerdite (Hanover, N.H.: University Press of New England for the Chipstone Foundation, 1993), p. 162. The tally of chairs was derived from customhouse clearances posted in the *Boston News-Letter* and *Boston Gazette*. The 1735 petition is quoted in Justin Winsor, ed., *The Memorial History of Boston, 1630–1880*, 4 vols. (Boston: Tickner and Co., 1886), 2:457, nt. 1.

15. The cane chair shown in figure 4 is one of the earliest Boston examples with a triple-swelled medial stretcher. Variations of this stretcher design persisted until about midcentury (see Keno, Freund, and Miller, "The Very Pink of the Mode," p. 258, figs. 29, 30). Joseph K. Ott, "Abraham Redwoods Chairs?" *Antiques* 119, no. 3 (March 1981): 672; Keno, Freund, and Miller, "The Very Pink of the Mode," p. 295; and Richards and Evans, *New England Furniture at Winterthur*, pp. 171–73.

16. For more on the influence of Ming furniture on London seating, see Grindley, *The Bended-Back Chair*. The Boston desk-and-bookcase is illustrated and discussed in Miller, "Roman Gusto in New England," pp. 167–70. For more on Welch's apprenticeship, marriage, and career, see Mabel M. Swan, "Boston's Carvers and Joiners, Part I," *Antiques* 53, no. 3 (March 1948): 199; Myrna Kaye, "Eighteenth-Century Boston Furniture Craftsmen," in Whitehill, Jobe, and Fairbanks, eds., *Boston Furniture of the Eighteenth Century*, p. 301; Barbara M. and Gerald W. R. Ward, "The Makers of Copley's Picture Frames: A Clue," *Old Time New England* 67 (summer-fall 1976): 16–20; Luke Beckerdite, "Carving Practices in Eighteenth-Century Boston," in *New England Furniture: Essays in Memory of Benno Forman*, edited by Brock Jobe (Boston: Society for the Preservation of New England Antiquities, 1987), pp. 123–62; Morrison H. Heckscher, "Copley's Picture Frames," in Carrie Rebora, Paul Staiti, et al., *John Singleton Copley in America* (New York: Harry Abrams for the Metropolitan Museum of Art, 1995), pp. 142–59; and Keno, Freund, and Miller, "The Very Pink of the Mode." Evidently, Robinson was very successful. His inventory included shop goods valued at £139.19.8 and a silver plate worth £58.10.1 (Forman, *American Seating Furniture*, p. 313).

17. Richards and Evans, *New England Furniture at Winterthur*, pp. 24–26. Sarah May's father, Samuel (b. Roxbury, February 17, 1723; d. Boston, August 9, 1794), was a Boston area carpenter. If the chair descended in his line, Samuel was probably the second owner. For more on the May family, see Rev. Samuel May, "Col. Joseph May, 1760–1841," *New England Historical Genealogical Register* 27, no. 2 (April 1873): 113–15. The Johnson history was given to Michigan dealer Jess Pavey, who sold the armchair to the Henry Ford Museum (Jess Pavey to Leigh Keno and Joan Barzilay Freund, August 9, 1996).

18. Another late baroque Boston easy chair with baluster-turned side stretchers and double-scrolled arms is illustrated in Richards and Evans, *New England Furniture at Winterthur*, pp. 142–44. This example also has rear legs with almost no rake, another feature that links it with the early examples illustrated in figures 13 and 14. The Winterthur chair probably dates from the late 1720s or early 1730s.

19. For more on Smibert, see Richard H. Saunders, *John Smibert, Colonial America's First Portrait Painter* (New Haven, Conn.: Yale University Press for the Barra Foundation, 1995), p. 174, no. 73. Grant Account Book, 1728–1733. On October 9, 1728, Fitch wrote, "Andrew Oliver Dr to Cash paid him towards his Wife Mary's portion One Thousand Pounds" (Fitch Account Book). On September 3, 1734, Fitch sold Smibert white lead and linseed oil (ibid.). Grant Account Book, April 29, 1732. Brock Jobe, "The Boston Furniture Industry, 1720–1740," p. 44, fig. 32. An identical chair with rounded stiles is illustrated in John Kirk, *American Chairs: Queen Anne and Chippendale* (New York: Alfred A. Knopf, 1972), p. 129, no. 161.

20. Grant Account Book, February 4, 1731/32. John Wainwright commissioned the painting in the summer of 1728. For more on *The Bermuda Group*, see Richard H. Saunders and Ellen G. Miles, *American Colonial Portraits, 1700–1776* (Washington, D.C.: Smithsonian Institution Press for the National Portrait Gallery, 1987), pp. 116–21. Christie's, *Works of Art from Houghton*, pp. 294–300. Two other Boston backstools from the same shop as figure 33 are known. One is in a private collection in the Midwest, and the other is owned by Leigh Keno, Inc. In London, chairs with low seats and upholstered backs became fashionable at the end of the seventeenth century and were often referred to as "dressing chairs," indicating that they were probably used in bedchambers. They were occasionally made en suite with easy chairs. On February 21, 1718, London upholsterer George Remey charged £5.5 for "two wallnut wood

veneired dressing chaire frames very handsomely made with stuft Backs & seats covered with your gold silk made all Compleat & Fashionable" (Gilbert, "Temple Newsam Furniture Bills," p. 21). An advertisement in the *Boston News-Letter* of January 9, 1746, listed goods to be sold at the house of Charles Paxon, including "Eight Walnut Tree Chairs, stuft backs and Seats covered with the same Damask."

21. For an Irish chair with a stretcher similar to the one on the backstool (fig. 33), see *Antiques* 57, no. 5 (May 1950): 336. Grant Account Book, February 3, 1741/42. The authors thank Jeanne Vibert Sloane for the reference to flat stretchers. A Boston or Portsmouth side chair at the Ipswich Historical Society has a carved crest rail, an India back, sawn cabriole legs with leaf-carved hoof feet, and flat stretchers. The authors thank Bob Trent for information on this chair.

22. For more on the Apthorp chairs and related seating, see Keno, Freund, and Miller, "The Very Pink of the Mode."

23. Samuel Grant Account Book, October 25, 1736. The chair tally was derived from Grant's Account Book.

24. Brock Jobe, "Boston Furniture Industry, 1725–1760" (M.A. thesis, University of Delaware, 1976), p. 83.

25. John R. Commons, "American Shoemakers, 1648–1895: A Sketch of Industrial Evolution," *Quarterly Journal of Economics* 24, no. 4 (November 1909): 48–50, as cited in Jeanne A. Vibert, "Market Economy and the Furniture Trade of Newport, Rhode Island" (M.A. thesis, University of Delaware, 1981), pp. 2–3. Vibert noted that "elaborate custom-order work comprised only one level of production in the pre-industrial economy. Expanding trade in the eighteenth century provided the craftsman with a wide market for his goods, so that he looked beyond his own neighborhood for customers. Colonial cabinetmakers, like other artisan-producers, manufactured goods of varying levels of quality and cost depending on the nature of the market."

26. Samuel Grant Account Book, 1728–1733.

27. Clifford K. Shipton and John L. Sibley, *Biographical Sketches of Those Who Attended Harvard College*, 17 vols. (1942; reprint ed., Boston: Harvard University Printing Office, 1962), 12:151. Anderson Galleries, *Colonial Furniture, The Superb Collection of Mr. Francis Hill Bigelow of Cambridge, Massachusetts*, New York, January 17, 1924, lot. 142. William Ellery, Jr., also attended Harvard (class of 1747) and roomed with Andrew Oliver, Jr., whose mother was Mary Fitch (see fig. 30). For more on the Ellery family, see Shipton and Sibley, *Biographical Sketches of Those Who Attended Harvard College*, 7:66–69, 12:134–52. Keno, Freund, and Miller, "The Very Pink of the Mode." A Boston chair similar to the example shown in figure 43 but with pad feet is illustrated in Edwin J. Hipkiss, *Eighteenth-Century American Arts: The M. and M. Karolik Collection* (Cambridge, Mass.: Harvard University Press for the Museum of Fine Arts, Boston, 1941), p. 142, fig. 79.

28. For more on Grendy, see Geoffrey Beard and Christopher Gilbert, eds., *Dictionary of English Furniture Makers, 1660–1840* (London: W. S. Maney and Son for the Furniture History Society, 1986), pp. 371–72; and Christopher Gilbert, *Furniture at Temple Newsam House and Lotherton Hall*, 2 vols. (London: National Art-Collections Fund and the Leeds Art Collections Fund, 1978), 2:79–80. A set of British side chairs related to the Boston example shown in figure 44 is illustrated in Sotheby's, *A Celebration of the English Country House*, New York, April 16–17, 1998, lot 802. For an illustration of Apthorp's bureau with cabinet, see Keno, Freund, and Miller, "The Very Pink of the Mode," p. 272, fig. 2.

29. For the Bromfield chairs, see Sotheby's American Furniture Department files. For the Huse history, see Richard H. Randall, Jr., *American Furniture in the Museum of Fine Arts Boston* (Boston: By the museum, 1965), pp. 170–71, no. 133.

30. Grant Account Books, April 13, 1739–March 21, 1747/48. Brock Jobe and Mryna Kaye, *New England Furniture, The Colonial Era: Selections from the Society for the Preservation of New England Antiquities* (Boston: Houghton Mifflin, 1984), pp. 362–64, no. 101.

31. For Grant's bill to Green, see Forman, *American Seating Furniture*, p. 358. As quoted in Jobe, "The Boston Furniture Industry," p. 34, nt. 58.

32. Grant Account Book, October 26, 1756. Morrison H. Heckscher, *American Furniture in the Metropolitan Museum of Art, Late Colonial Period: The Queen Anne and Chippendale Styles* (New York: Random House for the Metropolitan Museum of Art, 1985), pp. 122–24, no. 72. Telephone conversation with Amelia Peck, Associate Curator of American Decorative Arts, Metropolitan Museum of Art, May 19, 1998. Two other Boston easy chairs have their original Irish-stitch covers. They are in the Winterthur and Bayou Bend collections.

33. Although no bills, labels, or account books were mentioned in the sale catalogue, the set

was identified as the work of Job Townsend and "purchased in Warren, Rhode Island, from a descendant of the original owner." Anderson Art Galleries, *Philip Flayderman Collection*, January 4, 1930, lots 492, 493; Anderson Galleries, *One Hundred Important American Antiques*, January 9, 1932, lots 80, 81, 85. The Eddy chairs are in a private collection in California. Job Townsend Account Books, Newport Historical Society. Jeanne A. Vibert, "Rhode Island—Attributed Queen Anne Chairs," unpublished paper, University of Delaware, December 22, 1978, p. 6; and Oswaldo Rodriguez Roque, *American Furniture at Chipstone* (Madison, Wis.: University of Wisconsin Press for the Chipstone Foundation, 1984), p. 38, no. 17.

34. For example, on May 3, 1743, Eddy transported "30 Chairs Leather Back & Bottom @ 38/ [and] 6 Ditto Leather Bottoms @ 35/6" to John Banister of Newport (Banister Invoice Book, Rhode Island Historical Society). For more on Jeremiah Eddy, see Ruth Eddy, comp., *The Eddy Family in America* (1930; reprint ed., Ann Arbor, Mich.: Braun-Brumfield, Inc., 1990), p. 74.

35. Attribution of the Eddy chairs to Townsend became more entrenched following the publication of Ralph E. Carpenter, Jr.'s, *The Arts and Crafts of Newport Rhode Island 1640–1820* (Newport, R.I.: The Preservation Society of Newport, 1954), p. 39, nos. 13, 17. Charles Hummel's "Queen Anne and Chippendale Furniture in the Henry Francis du Pont Winterthur Museum" *(Antiques* 98, no. 6 [December 1970]: 900–9), questioned this attribution as cited by Carpenter in *The Arts and Crafts of Newport* and Joseph Ott in *The John Brown House Loan Exhibition of Rhode Island Furniture* (Providence: Rhode Island Historical Society, 1965), p. 4, no 4; however, Hummel also attributed the Eddy chairs to Rhode Island. "John Goddard and His Work," *Bulletin of the Rhode Island School of Design* 15, no. 2 (April 1927):15. The original letters from Brown to Goddard are at the Rhode Island Historical Society. When Ralph Carpenter included a chair from the set in *The Arts and Crafts of Newport*, he wrote that the set was "evidently the 'leather chairs' referred to in a letter from Moses Brown to John Goddard" (p. 37, no. 11). Frank Fuller, archivist at the Moses Brown School, confirmed that the Moses Brown School's attribution of the chairs to Goddard was based upon Carpenter's research (Fuller to Keno and Freund, August 16, 1996) and not upon any evidence provided by the Brown family at the time the chairs were donated. Vibert, "Rhode Island Chairs," p. 6. See The Museum of Fine Arts, Boston, *Collecting American Decorative Arts and Sculpture, 1971–1991* (Boston: By the museum, 1991), p. 35, pl. 8. For more on Barrett, see Jobe and Kaye, *New England Furniture*, pp. 154–55.

36. Brock Jobe, "The Boston Upholstery Trade," in *Upholstery in America & Europe from the Seventeenth Century to World War I,* edited by Edward S. Cooke, Jr. (New York, W. W. Norton, 1987), p. 78. The number of ships was derived from customhouse clearances posted in the *Boston News-Letter* and *Boston Gazette*. Thomas Fitch Account Books, 1719–1732 and 1732–1736. Boston figures taken from Myrna Kaye, "Eighteenth-Century Boston Furniture Craftsmen," 267–302. Newport figures taken from Wendell D. Garrett, "The Newport Cabinetmakers: A Corrected Check List," *Antiques* 73, no 6 (June 1958): 558–61; Joseph K. Ott, "Recent Discoveries among Rhode Island Cabinetmakers and Their Work," "More Notes on Rhode Island Cabinetmakers," and "Still More Notes of Rhode Island Cabinetmakers and Their Work," *Rhode Island History* 28, nos. 1, 2, 4 (winter, spring, and fall 1969): 18–24, 51–52, 116–21; and Vibert, "Market Economy of Newport," pp. 91–93. Joiners and cabinetmakers have been counted together due to the vagaries of eighteenth-century terminology. Vibert noted that at Newport both terms referred "to makers of case furniture as opposed to chairmakers, housewrights and ship joiners." Ronald Potvin is presently compiling a list of cabinetmakers and joiners in Newport and feels that current compilations include many craftsmen who simply did not make furniture.

37. John Banister to John Thomlinson, June 1, 1738, Banister Copy Book, 1730–1742, Newport Historical Society. Undated invoices between dated letters, Banister Copy Book.

38. Banister Papers, Newport Historical Society. "Invoice of sundrys recd of Capt. Powers as Letter of Advice of July 1, 1743," in John Banister Invoice Book, 1739, p. 134.

39. Port of Annapolis Entries, Maryland, vol. 1, ms. 21, Maryland Historical Society. Vibert, "Market Economy of Newport," p. 23.

40. "Invoice of Sundry's ship . . . on board ye Sheffield," Banister Invoice Book, 1739. John Banister to Thomas and James Hayward, May 28, 1739, Banister Copy Book, 1730–1742.

Charles L. Venable

Germanic Craftsmen and Furniture Design in Philadelphia, 1820–1850

▼ GERMAN CRAFTSMEN and styles contributed a great deal to the extraordinary complexity of American furniture design during the first half of the nineteenth century. A host of aesthetic ideas, including Germanic ones, competed in the marketplace for acceptance. Before 1830, the complete acceptance of Germanic impulses was rare. Most German workmen were forced either to adopt the prevailing American taste in consumer goods or to change professions. With the dramatic rise in German immigration beginning in the 1830s, however, this sublimation of German design aesthetics was less complete. Between 1830 and 1850, thousands of Germanic woodworkers found employment in America's urban centers. In introducing Germanic construction methods and stylistic details, these craftsmen played a vital role in transforming furniture design, particularly in the late classical and rococo revival modes.[1]

German Immigrant Cabinetmakers: The Continental Background
Although the colonies had attracted German immigrants from the very beginning, North America did not experience any great influx of Germans until 1683, when the first group of Palatinate Germans arrived in Pennsylvania. By the late eighteenth century, German immigration had slowed to a virtual standstill, but in 1816, the situation changed. Spurred by a series of bad harvests in southwestern Germany, an estimated 20,000 Germans emigrated to the United States between 1816 and 1817. This exodus, primarily from the area around Württemberg, soon ceased due to a temporary economic recovery. Throughout the 1820s, German immigration to America was slow. In the peak year 1828, only 3,443 Germans and Swiss crossed the Atlantic. The total number for the entire decade stood at 4,785 Germans and 3,117 Swiss.[2]

The years between 1830 and 1854 proved to be very different. As historian Mack Walker points out, "emigration was revived about 1830 by rising prices, the European revolutions [and] a more definite and more favorable view of America." Such factors, coupled with the severely depressed state of the German economy, especially with regard to agriculture, created a situation in which many Germans came to believe that their traditional, small-town way of life was slipping away. As a result, thousands of those who could afford to do so left—primarily for America. During the 1830s, 124,726 arrived in America, and 464,330 landed between 1840 and 1850 (inclusive). In 1854, the peak year for this great wave of immigration, 215,009 Germans left their homes to begin again in this country.[3]

The vast majority of Germans who came to America during the first half of the nineteenth century were members of the lower middle class rather than peasants. Most were small farmers, independent village shopkeepers, and skilled artisans from rural areas. The percentage of craftsmen was occasionally as great as 60 percent. As Walker notes, this era of immigration "probably included a higher proportion of prosperous and skilled, educated people than that of any other time, while the poorest and least valuable members of the society stayed behind."[4]

The reasons behind this large-scale exodus of highly skilled craftsmen and businessmen were manifold, but several factors seem particularly important. First, the collapse of the French Empire under Napoleon had a major impact on the rural craftsman. After French domination of the Continent ended and the British lifted their blockade of Continental ports, the German states (along with the rest of Europe) were flooded with cheap English exports, many of which displaced locally manufactured goods. This instability in Germany's regional economy was furthered by the creation of the *Zollverein* (Customs Union) in 1834. Under the stipulations of this union, many German states lifted tariffs on goods from other member states. Although designed to bring prosperity through increased trade, the *Zollverein* removed the legal barriers behind which regional economies had formed; consequently, many local products were replaced by less expensive goods from other parts of Germany. The situation deteriorated even more as the roles of the factory and middleman became more pronounced throughout the period, as Germany matured industrially.[5]

Another occurrence that ultimately forced craftsmen to leave their homes was the decline and stagnation of German agriculture during much of the early nineteenth century. Since most of the artisans who eventually came to America were from small rural towns, their livelihood ultimately depended on the strength of the agricultural sector. When farmers no longer were able to produce an agricultural surplus, orders for custom-made goods, like furniture, quickly declined and often ceased altogether.

Beyond these more purely economic factors, demographics also worked against the craftsman in early nineteenth-century Germany. As young men moved out of the depressed agricultural sector into the crafts, the number of apprentices and journeymen grew at an abnormally high rate. By the 1830s, the ratio of craftsmen to the general population was completely out of balance. This situation (which did not change until much later in the century when industrialization began to absorb the surplus) led directly to underemployment, lower wages (approximately 25 percent), and general hardship. In some professions, especially weaving, as many as one-quarter to one-half of the artisans lived on the edge of subsistence. This enormous increase in the number of apprentices and journeymen also meant that master craftsmen no longer dominated their trade. Between 1800 and 1850, the number of masters rose approximately 30 percent, while that of apprentices and journeymen increased 127 percent. In 1800, every third master had a journeyman; by 1819, every second master had a journeyman; and by 1861, there were more journeymen than masters. As a result, most journeymen could no longer look forward to becoming masters with full guild rights and their own shop.[6]

While economic and demographic shifts combined to make the craftsman's place in society less secure, changes in the way Germans perceived America aided individuals in making the final decision to leave their homeland. Though the image of "America" had appeared in German literature since the seventeenth century, it was not until the early nineteenth century that firsthand travel accounts began to surface with frequency. Initially, some of these works, such as Ludwig Gall's *My Immigration to the United States of North America* (1822), presented a very negative view of America, but this outlook soon changed. In 1829, Gottfried Duden published his far more positive and influential *Report on a Journey to the Western States of North America*. This book, which coincided with and to some degree initiated the revival of German immigration around 1830, spoke of America in glowing terms.[7]

Alongside the travel accounts, two other literary genres had a profound influence on German immigration. The first of these was the letter. By the 1830s, correspondence from relations and friends who had established themselves in America was pouring into Germany. Having experienced a horrific crossing from Baden to Baltimore in 1817, Chrisostomus Weis nevertheless wrote:

> Dearest brother what do you think will you come yes I advise you to come 100 times we have wished if only our brothers and sisters were with us and I advise all who are of a mind to come they must just come they will make better lives than in Germany. [America is] a free country, it is under no ruler every 4 years a cardinal is elected over the whole country, the country is divided into cantons and each canton has a president you pay no taxes and give nothing. . . . If you were in this country working as in Germany you would make a good future for your children.

The impact of letters such as Weis's was often magnified by their publication in German newspapers. Not suprisingly, they often sparked cluster immigration from the vicinity of the recipient.[8]

The *Auswanderungsratgeber* (immigrant advice book), which became increasingly popular during the 1830s, was another important catalyst for immigration. Advice books provided information on which route to take and where to settle. Most recommended that the "section of society which has money enough to make a new start in America will find it easy to begin a new life, but those who possess only 'naked life' should not emigrate in the first place." Expanding on this general rule, many advice books provided potential emigrés with very specific information on their prospects across the Atlantic. Alexander Ziegler's *German Immigrant to the United States of North America: A Guide for His Journey* (1849) noted that "those craftsmen who come to America can be divided into four groups: (1) those who always find work and profit; (2) those who have difficulty in finding employment; (3) those who fare especially poorly; (4) and those who must change professions." Among the first group, he listed forty professions including cabinetmakers, joiners, ship carpenters, clockmakers, lacquerers, and gilders.

Ziegler concluded that in general "the worker in America can, due to higher pay, obtain a higher standard of living, easily get married, provide a good upbringing for his children, and can put back a nest egg for his family." Such statements in advice books, along with letters from America, played a major role in helping individuals make that final and fateful decision to leave their homes for the New World.[9]

Once the decision had been made, questions remained regarding the best route to take and where to settle. Again, personal contact and advice books showed the way. Early in the century, the majority of Germans came to America by way of Le Havre, Antwerp, and the Dutch ports at the mouth of the Rhine. As time went on, however, increasing numbers of immigrants passed through the north German ports of Bremen and Hamburg. Initially, they left Europe as outward ballast on American-bound ships. This situation soon changed, as the number of emigrés rose in the 1830s and as shipowners realized they could profit from passenger service. Direct packet lines between German and American ports were thus established. As this transportation network developed, arrivals in Philadelphia, which had always been the traditional port of entry for incoming Germans, began to decline. New York emerged as the main port of entry for European immigrants due to its ice-free harbor and location. By 1814, New York equaled Philadelphia in volume of emigrés, and by 1825 it was firmly established as the leading immigrant port. Regardless of immigrants' place of arrival, coastal shipping lines carried them to their final destination if it was not inland.[10]

Naturally, the advice of friends and relatives already in America greatly influenced the choice of these "final destinations," but advice books also played an important role. Of particular interest are the published descriptions of American cities and regions. New England, for example, was portrayed as uninviting; thus, few Germans chose cities like Boston as their new home. New York was a different matter. In 1847, one author wrote:

> The city of New York has about 50,000 German immigrants. As soon as one crosses Bowery Street almost everything is German and as a rule one can always converse in German with those who are dressed more comfortably than fastidiously. If one takes into consideration the northern parts of the city which are mainly populated by Germans and excludes those Germans who live separately throughout the rest of the city, it appears that the Germans form at least one-eighth of the population of New York City. This number is probably more low than high. . . . Thus, approximately 80,000 Germans live in New York and its environs.

Though a myriad of factors influenced where a German craftsman settled in America, passages like this one must have been responsible for funneling thousands of highly skilled German craftsmen into the urban centers of New York, Philadelphia, Baltimore, and New Orleans.[11]

The New World
Although New York eventually became the main port of landing for immigrants, Philadelphia attracted a substantial number of Germans and Irish newcomers. In German immigrant literature, Philadelphia invariably received very good billing. In 1819, Ludwig Gall advised his countrymen to

immigrate there, for "there [were] a hundred opportunities to earn six to eight dollars a week." Nearly three decades later, the popular advice writer Traugott Bromme described Philadelphia as "one of the most well-planned and beautiful cities on earth," with many attractions and a strong economy. By concentrating on the positive aspects of urban life in Philadelphia and ignoring or distorting negative features like street violence and labor unrest, Bromme created an idyllic view that must have appealed to many prospective immigrants. Perhaps even more enticing were those descriptions of Philadelphia that stressed the Germanic background and character of the city. In his *History and Status of the Germans in America* (1847), Franz Löher expanded on what many advice books had been saying for years when he wrote that "over one-third of the population of Philadelphia is of German origin. Of these 80,000 still understand German, but only 40,000 speak it." Regardless of the negative comments that Löher occasionally made, his reference to Philadelphia's large Teutonic community was certainly what many Germans were looking for, given their unfamiliarity with the English language and American customs.[12]

Such descriptions of Philadelphia and the early presence of Germans in the city helped make it a major destination for new arrivals. Although numerous Germans probably came to Philadelphia during the late 1820s and early 1830s, early figures on immigrant landings there are unavailable. Beginning in the mid-1830s, a clearer picture emerges. In 1835, 1,890 immigrants arrived from Germany; 4,079 arrived in 1840; 5,767 arrived in 1845; and 10,515 arrived in 1850. The number of Germans and Irish who came to Philadelphia via New York is unknown, but it probably surpasses the number who arrived by direct routes. By 1850, Philadelphia's population was 29 percent foreign born. The Irish comprised 17.6 percent (71,787), and the Germans accounted for 5.6 percent (22,788).[13]

Many of the Germans who came to America before 1850 were highly skilled artisans. As a result, they tended to occupy jobs commensurate with their training. The furniture-making trades were particularly prominent. By 1850, there were 494 German cabinetmakers and 76 German turners working in Philadelphia. In all, over a third of the city's furniture makers (38.8 percent of cabinetmakers and 29.2 percent of turners) were German emigrés. The situation was even more skewed in New York where 61 percent of the furniture makers were German born by 1855.[14]

Although skill accounted for much of the success of these immigrant craftsmen, the establishment of a labor information network beginning in the early 1830s helped artisans find employment. The primary agents in this network were the various German aid societies in Philadelphia, New York, and Baltimore and German-language newspapers such as the Philadelphia-based *Die Alte und Neue Welt* (*The Old and New World*). As soon as immigrant ships landed, agents from one or more of the city's German aid societies generally went on board to advise the newcomers. A good example of such a group is Philadelphia's Hermann Unterstützungs Brüdershaft (Hermann Benevolent Brotherhood), which was founded in 1816 to assist immigrants (fig. 1). Aid societies helped maintain ledgers "in which the names of

Figure 1 Coffer for the Hermann Benevolent Brotherhood, Philadelphia, 1816. Mahogany, maple, and cherry with yellow poplar. H. 41⁵/₁₆", W. 77³/₁₆", D. 41⁵/₁₆". (Courtesy, Yale University Art Gallery, Mabel Brady Garvan Collection.)

those who seek work as well as those of employers who need workers, are recorded" and often kept them at the docks or in the business districts. Representatives from these groups also advised artisans to contact the various city workshops in person and warned them not to trust the deceptive agents of transport companies, who were far more interested in the immigrant's money than in his general welfare.[15]

Like benevolent societies, German-language newspapers also helped woodworkers find employment. J. G. Wesselhoeft, the owner of the nationally distributed *Die Alte und Neue Welt*, used his newspaper to support the "information network" he established in the early 1830s. At the center of Wesselhoeft's business was his "Address-und Nachfragungs Bureau" (address and inquiry bureau) at 471 Pearl Street in New York. As a complement to the New York office, he established a "Commissions Bureau" on the Place Louis-Philippe in Le Havre, France. For a fee, the Continental office provided Germans who were emigrating from French ports with information and advice to simplify their crossing and relocation and offered services such as letter and address forwarding. When the agency in New York received the specific requirements of an artisan, it provided that individual with "further information through which hand craftsmen and day laborers [could] obtain employment in most cases." The most amazing aspect of Wesselhoeft's operation is that it was national in scope and presumably gathered information on job opportunities in every city in which his newspaper had an agent. His papers also ran lists of jobs available. One published by Wesselhoft's German Intelligence Office in New York in June 1836 concluded: "All possible effort will be made to find a position for workers in other professions and crafts within eight days or less."[16]

Many American-born shopowners were anxious to hire German woodworkers, particularly if they would work for lower wages. In fact, the employment of Germans in previously all-Anglo shops became so common that nativists railed against the practice during the 1840s. In November of 1845, the *New York Daily Tribune* reported that journeymen's wages had fallen from $12 per week in 1836 to $5 in 1840 and speculated:

> The cause of the great decrease in the wages of Cabinet-Makers is in a great measure the immense amount of poor Furniture manufactured for the Auction-Stores. This is mostly made by Germans, who work rapidly, badly and for almost nothing. There are persons who are constantly on the watch for German emigrants who can work at Cabinet-Making—going on board the ships before the emigrants have landed and engaging them for *a year* at $20 or $30 and their board, or on the best terms they can make. The emigrants of course know nothing of the state of the Trade, prices, regulations, &c. . . . and become willing victims to any one who offers them immediate and permanent employment. This it is which has ruined the Cabinet-Making business, and the complaints on the part of the Journeymen are incessant. There is, however, no remedy for the evil, as we see.

Although this article appeared in a New York paper, the widespread employment of German cabinetmakers in Philadelphia and other American cities undoubtedly prompted similar responses.[17]

Expectations and Realities

The fact that hundreds of German furniture makers found employment in Philadelphia does not mean that their relocation was easy or that America fulfilled their expectations. According to Mack Walker, German immigrants came to America "less to build something new than to regain and conserve something old, which they remembered or thought they did: to till new fields and find new customers, true enough, but ultimately to keep the ways of life they were used to, which the new Europe seemed determined to destroy." In the case of the German cabinetmaker, this vision was doomed.[18]

Judging from the amount of space allocated to the topic in advice books, the fact that America maintained a highly competitive free trade system, as opposed to one dominated by guilds, presented a major problem for most immigrant craftsmen. With its myriad rules and regulations, the guild governed virtually every aspect of a craftsman's life in early nineteenth-century Germany. Guilds decided who could become a cabinetmaker and dictated the length of the apprentice's and journeyman's terms. Rules also prescribed exactly how furniture could and could not be made. Cabinetmakers, for example, were often forbidden to use nails of any kind. Some guilds even specified what type of wood and joinery techniques to employ. Master-journeyman relations were similarly controlled, and the number of apprentices and journeymen in a single shop was strictly regulated. In short, almost every facet of a cabinetmaker's life was ordered and protected by the cabinetmakers' guilds.[19]

Because the guild system ran counter to American free trade practices, advice books often described what it would be like to work without guilds. In 1846, German author Traugott Bromme wrote:

> It is important to acquaint the German craftsman with the fact that in [America] there are no guild privileges. Each man can work at any occupation he chooses. The consequence thereof has been an extraordinarily strong competition between workers. As a result many products are made either better or in a simpler manner requiring less time. The craftsman coming from [Germany] is thus initially at a disadvantage, since he neither speaks English nor is accustomed to working in the freer American manner. However, both problems are not insurmountable and an industrious craftsman, once having overcome these difficulties, can succeed well in this country.

"Skill, quickness, honesty, rectitude, and piety," he concluded, "are the conditions which form the basis of one's success and happiness" in America. In reality, however, the radical difference between German guilds and American free trade proved to be an insurmountable obstacle for some immigrant cabinetmakers, and the decision to change professions was common. In Philadelphia, furniture makers Charles Pommer (1780–1839) and Adolph Hoehling (1807–1893) temporarily became hotel and tavern proprietors. Similarly, Charles Dominique (b. 1804) worked as a grocer for several years, and Theobald Stockel (1806–1856) became a stovemaker. Some cabinetmakers advised their sons not to enter the craft. Frederick Gutekunst (1801–1890), for example, wanted his son, Frederick, Jr. (1831–1917), to become a lawyer. Although documentation for their relocation is scant, hundreds of German furniture makers probably left the city and moved inland. A fictional German glazier alluded to this negative aspect of urban American life in a popular novel of the day: "I, like all Germans, have fallen on hard times. The goldsmith is supposed to become a watchmaker, the cloth weaver a mechanical loom operator, the wallpaperer a cabinetmaker, and the cabinetmaker a painter—now what a glazier is supposed to become here I cannot determine." A large number of Germanic emigrés undoubtedly agreed with this perspective.[20]

Despite such disadvantages, many German cabinetmakers who stayed in Philadelphia survived. Most did not establish their own shops, however, even though they had come to America to do precisely that. According to the 1850 Census of Manufactures, Germans owned only thirteen of the 169 shops that produced goods worth $500 or more a year. Less than 10 percent of German-born cabinetmakers had their name and profession listed in the 1850 edition of *McElroy's Philadelphia Directory*. This rate, which is five times lower than that of the adult male population of Philadelphia in general, supports the hypothesis that most German furniture makers worked for other people, since journeymen had no need to advertise independently.[21]

The reasons why Germans did not establish their own shops in Philadelphia are not completely clear, but several factors are apparent. Advice books often cautioned immigrant craftsmen against working for themselves initially because most did not speak English or understand American business practices. A lack of proficiency in English was a great hindrance to the establishment of one's own shop, particularly if one's clientele was mostly English speaking. The extent of this problem is attested to by the frequent advertisements in German-language newspapers in which German craftsmen were seeking bilingual apprentices and journeymen. Such newspapers also abound with notices for English lessons and German-English dictionaries. A particularly revealing example of a contemporary language aid is *The American Interpreter/Der Amerikanische Dolmetscher*, which was printed in New Berlin, Pennsylvania, in 1831. Designed to be carried in the owner's pocket, this thin volume primarily consists of vocabulary words concerning the major crafts in which Germans were heavily concentrated, particularly woodworking, metalworking, and agriculture. It also outlines how orders, receipts, and bills should be written in the target language. With the help of such books and bilingual co-workers and friends, Germans and Americans managed to work and live together as best they could.[22]

Lack of capital also prevented many immigrant German cabinetmakers from establishing their own shops. Often immigrants had to sell virtually all their possessions to pay for their transatlantic crossing. Tools appear to be the principal exception to this rule. Although American tools were thought to be of higher quality, German craftsmen were consistently told not to sell their tools in Germany because comparable ones in America were "almost twice as expensive" and "a craftsman is usually more comfortable with his own tools, and new ones are never as handy."[23]

The fact that most Germans did not establish their own shops, as they had expected, pushed them into the mainstream of American life. For most,

America proved to be a land of both opportunity and disappointment. Not only did they have to adjust to working for someone else permanently, but they typically had to learn English and associate with native co-workers. American work routines were faster, and the need to cut labor costs meant that furniture was often less meticulously made than in Germany. Although this country's laissez faire craft system freed them from the often oppressive control of the guilds, it simultaneously exposed immigrant woodworkers to fierce competition and to work practices with which they were totally unfamiliar.

Some German cabinetmakers resisted these changes by joining their native-born counterparts in the re-organization of the Society of Journeymen Cabinetmakers. When founded in Philadelphia in 1806, this organization was basically a benevolent society. In 1829, however, the members revised the constitution, so that the main purpose of the society centered around labor relations. Unskilled labor was to be kept out of the craft, and wages were to be maintained at an acceptable level. Ultimately these efforts failed, and the journeymen opened their own cabinet warerooms in 1834 in order to bypass their masters' role as retailers. Although their Continental training had not prepared them for this form of political aggressiveness, the Society of Journeymen Cabinetmakers offered a type of guild protection that may have appealed to European craftsmen. This supposition is supported by the fact that at least four Danish-born cabinetmakers working in Philadelphia signed the Society's new constitution in 1829. These artisans were George Brown (b. 1798), Nicholas Dalhoff (b. 1802), Charles Holst (1798–1867), and Jacob Sievers.[24]

German Influence on Philadelphia and Its Furniture
Due to the early settlement of Germans in and around Philadelphia, the city traditionally had a strong Teutonic element. With the cessation of significant German immigration in the late eighteenth century, however, the German character of Philadelphia receded. Germans arriving in the early nineteenth century often found Philadelphians of German ancestry to be "dry, cold Americans," unaware of their origins. With the revival of immigration in 1816, this situation changed. The German nature of Philadelphia was not only renewed but enhanced. The simple fact that the approximately 23,000 Germans (5.6 percent of the total population) who lived in Philadelphia by 1850 did not settle within the confines of an ethnic ghetto meant that their presence was felt throughout the city.[25]

German was spoken widely within Philadelphia. Some native shopowners found it necessary to hire bilingual clerks to serve German-speaking customers. In 1844, cloth merchant George F. Smith advertised that German was spoken in his store. Besides reintroducing the German language, this new influx of immigrants altered the character of Philadelphia in other ways. Among the city's numerous libraries, for example, two were devoted to German language books and periodicals. The library of the Philadelphia German Society had 4,000 volumes in 1833, and Wesselhoeft's Lending Library contained 1,679 volumes when it opened in 1842. Arriving Germans also enhanced Philadelphia's musical and theatrical life. Contemporary German-language newspapers are filled with notices of performances by German singing societies and musical groups as well as dozens of concerts by central European soloists and concert artists. In addition, certain restaurants in the city specialized in German food and drink. In 1819, Kutter & Shuman opened their "New German Coffee House" at 75 Walnut Street, where an assortment of beverages including "good coffee, tea, chocolate, the best of liquors, wines, port, ale, cider, strong beer, etc." were "served up with exactness and prompt attention." During the first half of the nineteenth century, substantial quantities of wine and foodstuffs, particularly cured meat and fish, were imported into Philadelphia directly from central Europe.[26]

Even though these developments in libraries, music, and gastronomy were significant, they may not have affected the native population as directly as the burgeoning importation of German consumer goods during this period. Although American merchants were free to trade with any country they chose following the Revolution, the real expansion in German-American trade seems to have paralleled the influx of German shopowners and merchants in the 1830s and 1840s. The presence of such immigrants, coupled with the establishment of German business agents and trade councils in this country, meant that direct and often familial ties existed between central European producers and American consumers.[27]

Native-born and German-American merchants quickly took advantage of these connections, ordering either through German agents or directly from Europe. Trade manuals, like C. W. Rördansz's *Complete Mercantile Guide to the Continent of Europe* (1819), helped simplify the process. German-language manuals were also available through urban book dealers. J. G. Wesselhoeft stocked numerous trade and business aids, including "Exchange-Rate Guides" and the fourth edition of the *Complete Address Book for Merchants, Manufacturers, Apothecaries, Smelters, Glass Houses, and Hotels*. This multivolume set contained descriptions of 3,000 European cities and main marketplaces of the world, along with 80,000 business addresses, including foreign branches of firms. Along with the publication of business guides and directories, German banks sent agents to America to facilitate trade with Europe. Philipp Speyer, the New York agent for a banking house in Frankfurt am Main, advertised in 1842 that his direct connections with Germany and Europe as a whole enabled him "to handle any monetary exchange, including payments in any part of Europe to the satisfaction of his customers." Such agents enabled American merchants to carry out transatlantic business more safely and expeditiously.[28]

Using their personal contacts, trade manuals, and exchange tables, Philadelphia merchants imported a variety of German goods ranging from sheep shears to chessmen. German products that were especially prevalent included drugs and chemicals, textiles and clothing, table and mirror glass, base metal utensils, arms, and musical instruments. "Fancy goods" merchants were particularly dependent upon German products. Philadelphia directories between 1820 and 1850 abound with shops advertising German fancy goods, especially combs, baskets, brushes, and toys. In fact, the trade

Figure 2   Leaf no. 77 showing toy furniture from a trade catalogue, possibly G. G. Fendler and Company, Nuremburg, Germany, 1830–1840. Hand-colored lithograph. (Courtesy, Winterthur Museum Library.)

in German fancy goods was so substantial that retail book dealers sold German trade catalogues for such wares (fig. 2). From 1839 on, Wesselhoeft regularly advertised catalogues for items made in and around Nuremberg, the European center of production for many fancy goods and toys:

> Patternbooks for Nuremberg and Furth Manufacturers—one hundred half folio plates with texts and prices. $8. The plates are very neat and correct, painted in colors, and for Fancy ware merchants very useful. They contain, for example, boxes, mirrors, treenware, toys, brassware, writing pens, tin and wooden ware, etc.

Trade catalogues for other German products, such as furniture hardware and glassware, were also sent to America.[29]

Of all German products imported into America, the most significant for this study were clocks and musical instruments. In 1835, the New York firm of Hass and Götz advertised that it specialized in importing "Black Forest wall clocks, musical marble and alabaster clocks (*Stockuhren*), Viennese mantel clocks, high quality alarm clocks, and kitchen clocks (*Küche-Standuhren*)." This firm also sold clocks to dealers in other cities. During the 1840s, Philadelphia clock dealer J. G. Syz ran a similar business specializing in Black Forest musical clocks. Judging from newspaper advertisements and directories, musical instrument dealers similarly imported vast quantities of German products. In the 1819 Philadelphia directory, George Willig reported that "Grand and Square German Pianos [of] superior quality with Turkish Music [Janissary attachments]" and "Grand and Square English Pianos [of] superior quality" were available at his shop, the "Musical Magazine" on Chestnut Street. Similarly, the Philadelphia firm of A. W. Bolenius and Company offered a huge assortment of musical instruments "from various German manufacturers." Well over fifty types of instruments are enumerated in Bolenius's 1838 advertisement.[30]

Apparently, the large-scale importation of German and English pianofortes threatened American producers. In 1820, the Philadelphia piano-making firm of Loud & Brothers remarked that "business formerly was more thriving than it is at present owing to the Exertions that the Import-

Figure 3 Designs for fall-front secretaries by Frederick Gutekunst, Sr. (1801–1890), Württemberg, Germany, 1828. Ink and ink wash on paper. (Courtesy, Athenaeum of Philadelphia.) This sheet is one of fourteen brought to Philadelphia by Gutekunst in 1831. The images are variously dated from 1825 to 1828.

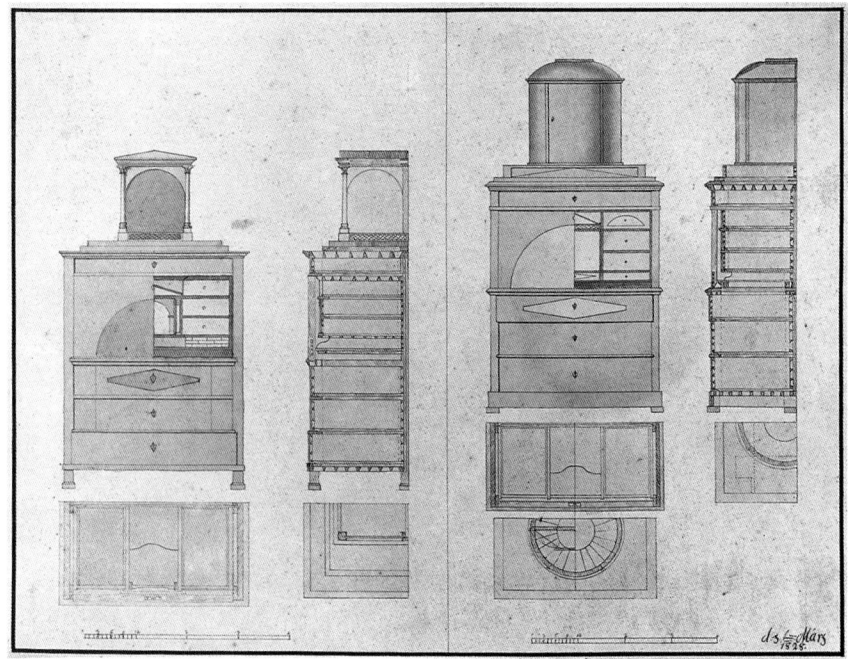

ing of Foreign Manufactures are making to crush (if possible) this rising manufacture of American Arts." Loud & Brothers believed that an increased tariff was needed to protect American piano makers.[31]

Given the wide variety of objects imported and consumed by both natives and German-Americans, clearly German-made or -processed goods had a definite appeal in this country. The attraction of such goods is particularly noticeable in the manner in which they were advertised. German products were regularly identified by dealers as such, alongside French and English merchandise. Although the connotation of "German" did not necessarily identify a product as better than its native counterpart or those of other countries, it nevertheless seems to have been associated with high-quality specialty and luxury items.

Design Accommodation, 1820–1830

If Philadelphians considered German items to be on a par with English and French goods, what effects, if any, did this opinion have on domestic products? Were Philadelphians familiar with German design in objects other than those they imported? If so, were Germanic characteristics accepted and encouraged in the production of Philadelphia-made goods? In the case of furniture, the answers to these questions are complex and change over time. First, some Philadelphia consumers were probably aware of German furniture design, at least tangentially. The simple fact that scores of highly skilled Germanic woodworkers poured into the city between 1816 and 1850 meant that there was a direct link between German and Philadelphia design aesthetics.

In furniture design, this connection was further strengthened by the presence of portfolios that immigrant craftsmen brought from Germany. Often used in preparation for their guild examinations, these portfolios contained furniture designs that were commonly saved for future use (see figs. 3, 22).

Figure 4 Fall-front secretary with musical works attributed to Johann Gottfried Kaufmann (1751–1818), Dresden, Germany, ca. 1804. Burled veneer with basswood; marble, paint, and gilded bronze. H. 84", W. 33 1/4", D. 20 1/8". (Stephen Girard Collection, Girard College, Philadelphia; photo, Gavin Ashworth.)

The aforementioned drawings reveal that most of the cabinetmakers who immigrated to Philadelphia during the 1820s and 1830s were well versed in the late classical design mode known today as Biedermeier. Their presumed familiarity with this style is supported by the fact that the mean age of a German immigrant cabinetmaker was 31.8 years in 1850. Having been born around 1818, most of these artisans grew up with and served their apprenticeships constructing Biedermeier furniture. By the time they became mature craftsmen (in the late 1830s and 1840s) and immigrated to America, they were familiar with the older Biedermeier style as well as the emerging rococo revival taste.[32]

The Biedermeier aesthetic that German cabinetmakers brought to Philadelphia, and to America in general, dominated German furniture production between 1815 and 1835. Originally developed in response to material shortages caused by the Napoleonic wars and as a reaction against the foreign French Empire style, Biedermeier furniture catered to middle-class tastes rather than to those of the aristocracy. Living in what were often small houses or apartments and desiring stylish yet functional furniture, middle-class consumers found the small scale, clean lines, and bold shapes of Biedermeier design appealing. Ornamentation generally relied on meticulously matched wood veneers as opposed to elaborate bronze mounts or gilding. Occasionally furniture makers used black paint as a decorative device to contrast with a light-wood veneer as in figure 4.[33]

The basic design of Biedermeier furniture was often conceived of in a highly imaginative manner. Generally, furniture was thought of as completely frontal in both ornamental and spatial orientation, the sides being totally subordinate to the facade. Within the overall structure of the design, forms were built up out of a series of rectangles or boards placed one atop the other, with little overall integration (figs. 3, 4). Within the context of this basic rectilinearity, a limited number of geometric shapes, such as the arch, diamond, and sphere, were used. Almost invariably, however, such elements were subordinate to the mass of the carcass. In chair design, the emphasis was also frontal, with elaboration generally occurring in the back and slightly canted legs (fig. 5). Only in the most opulent examples did chairs assume an assertive, three-dimensional, sculptural quality.

During the 1830s, this emphasis on planarity, frontality, and conservative ornamentation changed as rococo revival designs became popular. Increasingly, the rectilinearity of Biedermeier furniture was broken by curvilinear elements, while plain surfaces were covered with carving. Mahogany, which had been largely displaced by native, light-colored fruit- and nutwoods early in the century, reasserted itself along with rosewood. By 1850, most traces of Biedermeier design had vanished from German furniture, especially in urban centers (see figs. 30, 33, 34).

Although Biedermeier design drew most of its inspiration from the fashion centers of Vienna, Mainz, and Berlin, the style relied significantly on two other sources. The first and most important was the imagination of the craftsman. Unlike American cabinetmakers, German woodworkers had to prove their proficiency in drawing during their apprenticeships. For their final exam-

Figure 5 Designs for chairs and other furniture illustrated on plate 1 from G. J. Lipp, *Meubles-Zeichnungen für Tischler* (Berlin, 1835). (Courtesy, Winterthur Museum Library.)

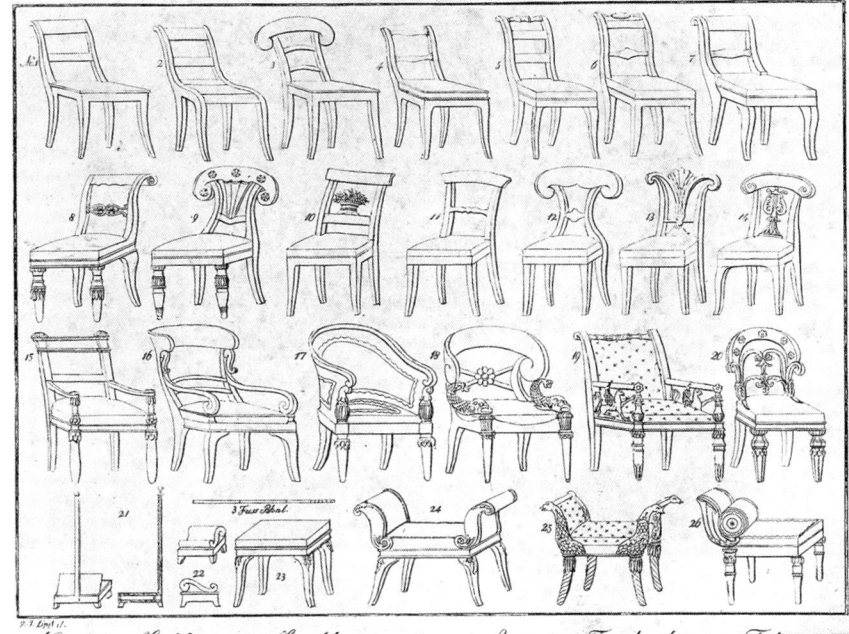

ination, they had to create a *Meisterstück* of their own design. This emphasis on individuality, coupled with the fact that few German patternbooks appeared before 1835, is reflected in the imaginative and often eccentric character of much Biedermeier furniture (see figs. 3, 6). Creative combinations of bold shapes are often employed, and architectural elements are sometimes incorporated in a nonarchitectural manner. Details such as concave drawer fronts and inverted feet appear frequently, enlivening the composition.[34]

French and English designs also inspired early nineteenth-century German furniture. Because French forces occupied large areas of central Europe during the Napoleonic wars, Germans were well aware of their styles and products. Much of the German aristocracy adopted the French Empire taste for their residences, often ordering directly from Paris or commissioning German craftsmen to execute French designs. Despite some affinities between the Biedermeier and French Empire styles, including appreciation of highly figured veneers, French late classical designs were primarily confined to the nobility in central Europe and thus were not ordered on a large scale in that part of the Continent.

The influence of English furniture on the Biedermeier style was probably more significant, particularly with regard to German design in America. Because English styles had been popular in Germany since the second quarter of the eighteenth century, patternbooks by designers such as Thomas Chippendale, George Hepplewhite, Thomas Sheraton, George Smith, and Rudolf Ackermann were relatively common in northern Europe. Sheraton's *The Cabinet-Maker and Upholsterer's Drawing Book*, for example, appeared in German in 1794. English furniture, much of which arrived in the northern port cities of Bremen, Hamburg, and Lübeck, was another important design source for German artisans. Although some German cabinetmakers used these sources to produce copies of English furniture, most simply

Figure 6 Fall-front secretary, Germany, 1820–1835. Mahogany with oak, pine, and basswood; gilding, pewter inlay, and gilded bronze. H. 72", W. 40¾", D. 20¼". (Private collection; photo, Gavin Ashworth.)

adopted specific details, such as swags and classical architectural elements, just as they had with French designs.[35]

It was this Biedermeier aesthetic, with its strange geometric core and French and English undercurrents, that German woodworkers brought to Philadelphia and other American cities between 1816 and 1850. Were these ideas accepted and encouraged, or were they rejected? During the first three decades of the nineteenth century, the complete acceptance of German designs in Philadelphia was rare. Given the slow pace of German immigration (compared to that of the 1830s and 1840s), it seems only logical that Teutonic designs would be subordinate to Anglo-French styles; however, exceptions do exist. As in other American cities, a small though potentially significant amount of German furniture arrived in Philadelphia during this period.[36]

Two fall-front secretaries are representative of these German imports. The example shown in figure 6 descended in the Oppenheimer family of Bedford, Pennsylvania. With its crowning architectural structure, unusual placement of sphinxes, and temple interior, it is totally Biedermeier in character. A Continental origin is suggested by the presence of a wide variety of woods, including oak for the drawer linings, and maker's marks in German. Secretaries like this example could have arrived with German immigrant families or have been purchased from a Philadelphia importer.[37]

Stephen Girard (1750–1831) purchased the musical fall-front secretary illustrated in figure 4 from Simon Chaudron in 1804. Despite its having been sold by a French immigrant, this secretary has always been considered a German product. Its history and strong adherence to Biedermeier design,

Figure 7 Fall-front secretary, Philadelphia, 1820–1830. Mahogany and rosewood with pine, yellow poplar, and chestnut; gilded bronze. H. 61", W. 49 3/4", D. 26 1/2". (Smithsonian Institution, Washington, D.C.; photo, Gavin Ashworth.)

Figure 8 Pianoforte by Emilius N. Scherr (1794–1874), Philadelphia, ca. 1830. Mahogany with unrecorded secondary woods; ivory and basemetals. H. 36", W. 68", D. 28". (Courtesy, Philadelphia Museum of Art, gift of Mrs. George L. Rush.)

Figure 9 Pianoforte by Loud & Brothers (fl. 1825–1833), Philadelphia, ca. 1830. Mahogany with unrecorded secondary woods; ivory and basemetals. W. 68⁵/₁₆". (Courtesy, Metropolitan Museum of Art.)

evident in the secretary's highly figured, light wood veneers, contrasting black reserves, and eccentric architectonic quality, supports this conclusion. The fact that it cost $650 and was owned by America's wealthiest individual makes the secretary particularly noteworthy, since many of Philadelphia's elite must have seen it in Girard's home.[38]

In addition to importing a small amount of Biedermeier furniture early in the century, Teutonic craftsmen also produced some isolated but typical examples of German late classical furniture. The coffer from the Hermann Benevolent Brotherhood is a fine example (fig. 1). Made in 1816, just as German immigration to the United States revived, this chest displays the Biedermeier predilection for visually compartmentalized space in its use of light wood banding and a layered top. With their white color and bold shape, the spherical ivory feet add to the diversity of the design. The fall-front secretary illustrated in figure 7 also attests to the Teutonic presence in Philadelphia. Although Germanic in every detail, including its use of geometry, outward curving bottom drawer front, eccentric rectangular feet, and decorative use of the wood grain, its yellow poplar secondary wood and history point to a Philadelphia origin.[39]

Despite the existence of imported and American-made Germanic furniture in and around Philadelphia, the complete acceptance of German design was rare before 1830. The question must therefore be asked—What were the German cabinetmakers of Philadelphia producing? Although this query may never be answered conclusively, it is likely that German craftsmen drew upon those aspects of Biedermeier design that were closest to contemporary American taste in order to produce furniture virtually indistinguishable from that of native-born cabinetmakers. This aesthetic assimilation could have been achieved in several different ways. An immigrant furniture maker could, for example, have taken a Biedermeier design and eliminated its distinctive German features. The addition of locally popular details, such as carving and mahogany veneers, would have resulted in a product that melded into the furniture mainstream. The more complicated chairs illustrated in figure 5, for example, may not have appealed to Philadelphia consumers; however, the simpler forms are quite close to popular regional designs.

This process of design synthesis and accommodation is evident in Philadelphia piano cases of the period. A square pianoforte case by the Danish-born and German-trained artisan Emilius N. Scherr (1794–1874) is virtually identical to those produced by Loud & Brothers of Philadelphia (figs. 8, 9). In building or commissioning a case that so closely approximates that of a well-established Anglo-American firm, Scherr relied upon the basic similarities between the German and English traditions of square pianoforte case design to produce a saleable product. The addition of carving typical of American pianos but foreign to Germanic ones was a clear concession to local tastes; however, it did not significantly alter the maker's mental image of what a piano should look like or affect the design of the musical works. The fact that Philadelphia pianos almost invariably follow popular English designs, even though 50 percent of the piano makers in the city were German born by 1850, attests to the success of this process.[40]

Immigrant craftsmen also maintained continuity with their Continental training by producing Germanic forms derived from French and English designs rather than from purely Biedermeier ones. Two pier tables in the French style—one Philadelphian and the other German (figs. 10, 11)—have similar shaped bases, scrolled supports with leaf decoration, concave cornices, marble tops, and veneered surfaces. English-style card tables made in Philadelphia and Germany illustrate similar parallels in their overall form, composition, and decoration (see figs. 12, 13). As these examples suggest, many German furniture makers arrived in Philadelphia with a stylistic vocabulary sympathetic to local tastes.

Figure 10 Pier table attributed to Anthony Quervelle, Philadelphia, ca. 1830. Mahogany with yellow poplar, white pine, and yellow pine; marble and glass. H. 37^1/$_2$", W. 41", D. 30". (Courtesy, Dallas Museum of Art, Faith P. and Charles L. Bybee Collection, gift of Mr. and Mrs. Willard E. Brown, III—The Bolton Foundation, Governor and Mrs. William P. Clements, Jr., Mr. and Mrs. Gerald C. Johansen, George and Schatzie Lee, Mr. Irving L. Levy, Mr. and Mrs. Ronald L. McCutchin, the Stanley and Linda Marcus Foundation, Mr. Frederick R. Mayer, and the Frederick M. Mayer Memorial Fund.)

Figure 11 Pier table, southern Germany, 1820–1830. Materials and dimensions not recorded. (Former collection of L. Brenheimer, Munich, Germany; image from Hermann Schmitz, *Deutsche Möbel des Klassizismus* [Stuttgart: Hoffmann, 1923], p. 202.)

Figure 12 Card table by Anthony Quervelle (1789–1856), Philadelphia, 1830–1840. Mahogany with unrecorded secondary woods. H. 29³⁄₄", W. 36⁷⁄₈", D. 18¹⁄₂". (Private collection; photo, Gavin Ashworth.) This table bears Quervelle's label for his 126 South Second Street shop. He was active there between 1829 and 1849.

Figure 13 Card table, possibly Altona, Germany, ca. 1830–1835. Mahogany. Secondary woods and dimensions not recorded. (Courtesy, Städtisches Museum, Flensburg, Germany.)

The Fall-Front Secretary: A Case Study in European Influences

Of all the furniture forms produced in Philadelphia, none reveals how Germanic artisans accommodated local tastes more clearly than the fall-front secretary. Having obtained its mature form in the work of Jean-François Oeben (ca. 1721–1763), a German cabinetmaker working in Paris, the fall-front secretary soon became popular on the Continent. During the first half of the nineteenth century, the form was especially fashionable in countries dominated by Biedermeier design—Germany, Austria, and Scandinavia. When required to design and build a piece of furniture for their guild examinations, apprentices almost invariably chose a fall-front secretary.[41]

Since this form was not popular in England, its appearance in Philadelphia is probably the result of Continental influence. As Stephen Girard's secretary (fig. 4) shows, some Continental imports were present in Philadelphia during the early nineteenth century. In fact, the designs that German craftsmen (and perhaps French immigrants as well) brought to America were generally dominated by this particular furniture form (see figs. 3, 22).

The fall-front secretary was very fashionable among the upper class of Philadelphia, even though it never displaced the secretary-bookcase. Besides Girard, the Gratz, Kuhn, and Gilpin families owned examples. The form was also included in *The Philadelphia Cabinet and Chair Makers' Union Book of Prices for Manufacturing Cabinet Ware* (1828). According to this book, the labor cost for building a fall-front secretary (described as a "French Secretary") was $22. The survival of more than a dozen early examples further attests to the form's acceptance in Philadelphia. Although cabinetmakers in other American cities also produced fall-front secretaries, the form appears to have been more popular and more varied in Philadelphia. Boston secretaries, for example, almost invariably have strong French overtones, whereas those from Philadelphia have English, French, and/or Germanic details.[42]

The striking diversity within the Philadelphia group reflects the various foreign influences present in that city. Several of these secretaries are extremely French in character. The one shown in figure 14 relates to a design by French cabinetmaker Pierre de la Mésangère (1761–1831) in having classical columns, capitals, bases, and arches that are architectural rather than purely representative. Like their Continental counterparts, these Philadelphia secretaries in the French style have restrained, unified designs and classical proportions. Most have columns that extend from the feet to the cornice, framing the facade and supporting the marble top. The use and placement of ormolu mounts further unifies the composition, those at the top echoing those at the bottom.[43]

The Philadelphia Biedermeier secretary illustrated in figure 7 provides an interesting contrast to the preceding examples. Despite having flanking columns, its visual emphasis is on individual parts rather than on unity. The columns, curved bottom drawer, square feet, multilayered cornice, and escutcheon-shaped recess function as distinct parts, competing for attention. The repeated use of horizontal bands such as those between the drawers and in the cornice further compartmentalizes the facade.

Figure 14 Fall-front secretary, Philadelphia, 1815–1830. Rosewood with pine and tulip poplar; marble, gilding, paint, brass, and gilded bronze. H. 60", W. 40", D. 19". (Private collection; photo, Sotheby's.)

Several other Philadelphia secretaries also have a strong affinity with German design. Similarities in proportions and construction indicate that eight are from the same unidentified shop (see fig. 15). As with the example illustrated in figure 7, all of the pieces in this group reflect the Germanic propensity for imaginative design in which the facade is an amalgamation of parts, not a unified whole. On the secretary shown in figure 15, the columns do not extend from base to cornice, as in a typical French example, but rather stop halfway. The use of columns over pilasters, the orientation of the fall (horizontal) and doors (vertical), the contrasting burl-veneers, and the emphatic horizontal banding at the top, middle, and bottom all serve to compartmentalize the facade. Beyond this lack of unity, the relationship of these secretaries to German aesthetics is further revealed in the imaginative use of an

Figure 15 Fall-front secretary, Philadelphia, 1815–1830. Mahogany, hard maple, ebony, and cherry with yellow poplar and eastern white pine; gilded bronze. H. 62⁷⁄₈", W. 35⁷⁄₈", D. 21¹⁄₈". (Courtesy, Dallas Museum of Art, Faith P. and Charles L. Bybee Collection, anonymous gift in memory of Frederick Miller Mayer; photo, Tom Jenkins.)

Figure 16 Design for a fall-front secretary illustrated on plate 3, figure 19 of Marius Wölfer, *Der Bau- und Meubel-Schreiner, eine bildliche Anweisung zur antiken und moderne Architecktur* (Illmenau, Germany, 1828). (Courtesy, Metropolitan Museum of Art, Watson Library.)

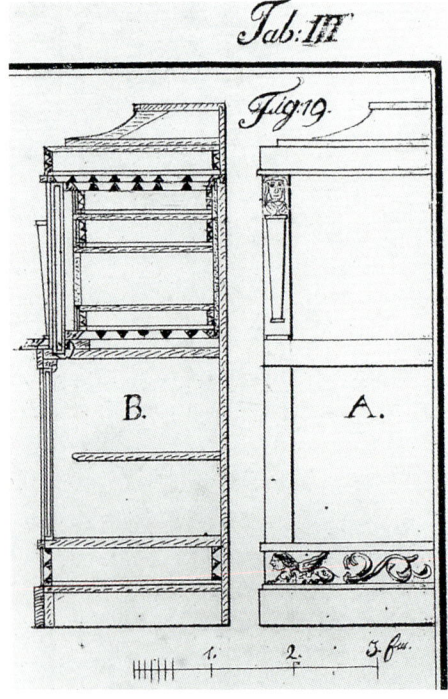

Figure 17 Rear view of the fall-front secretary illustrated in fig. 15.

Figure 18 Fall-front secretary with wings, Philadelphia, 1817–1825. Mahogany with white pine and tulip poplar; ebony, brass, and glass. H. 63³⁄₄", W. 73³⁄₄", D. 28¹⁄₂". (Philadelphia Museum of Art, donated by Simon Gratz in memory of Caroline S. Gratz; photo, Eric Mitchell.)

Figure 19 Interior view of the fall-front secretary illustrated in fig. 18.

architectural structure at the top. The secretary shown in figure 15 is one of the more conservative examples, featuring a stepped plinth that was likely meant to support a clock. Others in this group are crowned with more elaborate devices, including temple-like forms with recessed lunettes in their facades. As surviving German secretaries and patternbooks (see fig. 16) demonstrate, the placement of such structures on a sloping base is in keeping with Biedermeier taste. Another Germanic trait is the frequent use of light burl-veneers on both interior and exterior surfaces (see fig. 20). Light-wood furniture was especially prevalent in northern Germany and Scandinavia (see fig. 4). The back construction of these Philadelphia secretaries (see fig. 17) also relates to central European work. All have two vertical panels separated by a wide muntin. The panels are not framed by rails or stiles but are nailed to the top and into rabbets in the sides. This structure was dominant in Germany during the period.[44]

The shop that made these eight secretaries must have been a significant one given the sophistication of its products. It either influenced or produced some of the most elaborate case pieces ever made in Philadelphia, including a brass-inlaid sideboard with knifeboxes, a fall-front secretary, and a secretary with wings (fig. 18) created for the Gratz and Kuhn families between 1815 and 1825. Traditionally, scholars have attributed these pieces to Joseph B. Barry (ca. 1757–1839), a prominent Philadelphia cabinetmaker who advertised brass-ornamented furniture and operated a large shop that employed European journeymen. Regardless of whether these objects came from his shop, they may well represent the work of a German cabinetmaker.[45]

As with the preceding group of Germanic secretaries (see fig. 15), the secretary with wings (fig. 18) has a beveled horizontal fall and two beveled ver-

Figure 20 Interior view of the fall-front secretary illustrated in fig. 15.

tical doors below. The facades of the Germanic secretaries and case pieces in the Gratz and Kuhn group are also compartmentalized in related ways. On the latter pieces, strong horizontal bands divide the surface into upper and lower halves, while vertical pilasters break in the middle. Invigorating the surface are cut brass panels and stringing inlaid into ebony or mahogany. A similar effect is achieved in the previous group with lightwood burl-veneer (see fig. 15). The interiors of the Gratz and Kuhn secretaries are closely related to those of the eight secretaries (see figs. 19, 20). Both feature banks of drawers surmounted by pigeonholes arranged on either side of a central space consisting of a lower open compartment, central section with banded columns, and crowning arch.

The construction of the Gratz and Kuhn case furniture is related but not identical to that of the Germanic secretaries (see fig. 15). All of these objects have mahogany drawer linings and case sides that are flat (except for the continuation onto the sides of the three horizontal bands from the facades); however, the backs of the Gratz and Kuhn pieces have framed-in horizontal panels. Given these structural differences, it would be premature to attribute the Germanic secretaries to Barry's shop or to dismiss him as a possible maker. These secretaries and the Gratz and Kuhn furniture do not, furthermore, negate the possibility that other European traditions influenced them. Not only was brass inlay used both on the Continent and in England, but furniture historian Deborah Ducoff-Barone has identified English and French parallels with the Gratz and Kuhn secretary and secretary with

Figure 21 Design for a fall-front secretary illustrated on plate 101 of Pierre de la Mésangère, *Collections des Meubles et Objects de Goût* (Paris, 1804). (Courtesy, Winterthur Museum Library.)

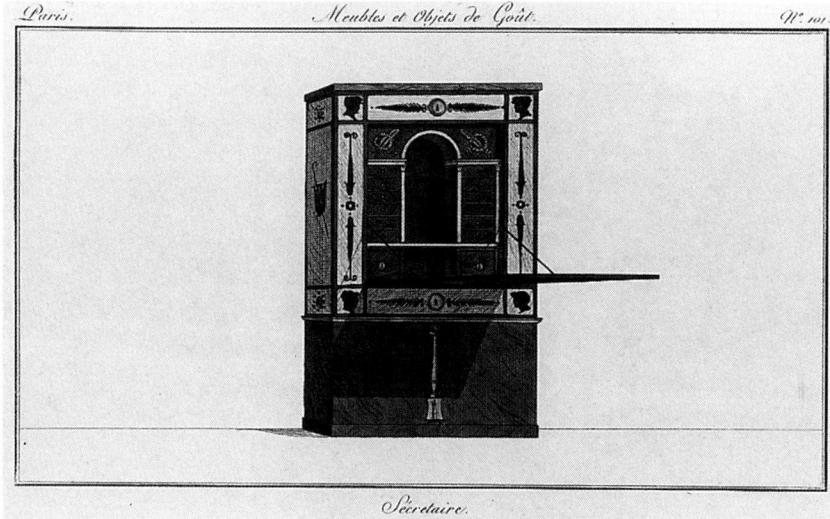

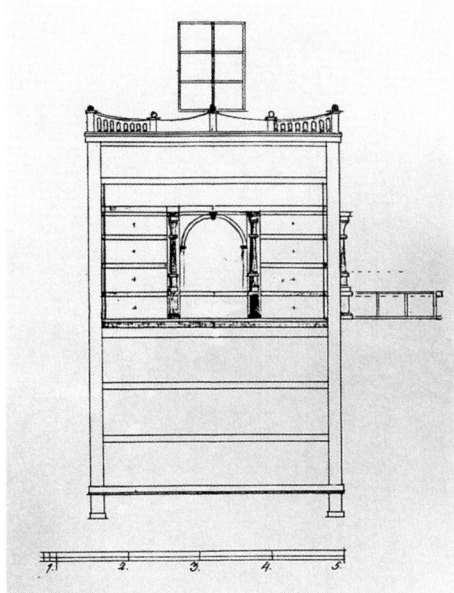

Figure 22 Design for a fall-front secretary by Joseph Fiedler, Württemberg, Germany, 1800–1810. Ink on paper. (Courtesy, Historical Society of York County, York, Pennsylvania; photo, Charles Venable.)

wings. The latter example relates to a Mésangère design for a secretary with wings as well as to one for a fall-front secretary with similarly organized interior (fig. 21).[46]

With its undercurrents of English and French design, central European late classical furniture may also have inspired the Germanic secretaries and Gratz and Kuhn pieces. German immigrants clearly introduced related designs for secretary interiors. Cabinetmaker Joseph Fiedler had a sketch of a secretary with an interior similar to Stephen Girard's when he arrived in Pennsylvania in 1819 (figs. 4, 22). Both interiors feature banks of drawers, banded columns, an arch, and a space between the lower two drawers. It is, therefore, entirely possible that the design of the Germanic secretaries and Gratz and Kuhn furniture owe more to their maker's imagination and training than to printed patternbooks or European prototypes.[47]

Other Philadelphia fall-front secretaries have Germanic features, but they are only tangentially related to the group of eight secretaries and the brass-inlaid pieces. The secretary illustrated in figure 23 has been attributed to the French immigrant cabinetmaker Michel Bouvier (1792–1874) for years. Although no conclusive evidence for this attribution is known, the secretary appears to have been made by an artisan trained on the Continent. One of the interior drawers is numbered "7" in the Continental fashion, and the basic unity of design and paired, full-length columns are very French in character. The presence of contrasting burled maple veneer in the interior and a pedimented top, however, links this piece to German design. Only rarely do such pediments occur in French furniture, as opposed to central European work. If Bouvier did make this secretary, his pediment may have been influenced by the popular Biedermeier forms of rival Philadelphia shops.[48]

This survey of fall-front secretaries made before 1830 reveals the complicated nature of furniture design in early nineteenth-century Philadelphia. Because the city supported a variety of foreign- and native-born cabinetmakers and because customers accepted or rejected culturally specific design elements in the marketplace, Philadelphia craftsmen produced a wide range of forms. At the ends of this spectrum were quintessentially French and German pieces. In between were forms featuring German, French, and English details in varying degrees and combinations. After 1830, the picture becomes clearer, at least where German influence is concerned.

Late Classical Design

The late classical style of the 1830s and 1840s, known today as "pillar and scroll," is often characterized by designs that stress the compartmentalization of decoration and an eccentric mixture of curvilinear and rectilinear shapes. In this late phase of neoclassicism, the emphasis is on the wood itself and on solid, heavy forms. Carving is de-emphasized, and gilded decoration appears infrequently. The sources for this style were undoubtedly interna-

Figure 23 Fall-front secretary, Philadelphia, 1815–1830. Mahogany and maple with yellow poplar and pine; gilded bronze. H. 65", W. 43½", D. 21¾". (Courtesy, Athenaeum of Philadelphia; photo, Gavin Ashworth.)

Figure 24 Work table, Philadelphia, 1820–1840. Mahogany with ash and other unidentified secondary woods. Dimensions not recorded. (Courtesy, *Antiques*.)

Figure 25 Chest of drawers, Philadelphia, ca. 1840. Mahogany with pine and yellow poplar. H. 45½", W. 43½", D. 20¾". (Private collection; photo, Tom Jenkins.) The chest is inscribed: "Bought from the / D. Pine Estate of Whitford, Pa. / by Justen Warren (?) / West Chester, Pa. / March 1912".

Figure 26 Pier table, Philadelphia, 1830–1840. Mahogany and unidentified secondary woods; marble and glass. Dimensions not recorded. (Courtesy, Decorative Arts Reference Library, Winterthur Museum.)

tional. So-called "Regency" and "French Restoration" styles both played a role, but perhaps the most important influence was late Biedermeier design from Germany.

Common German conventions that appear in Philadelphia furniture of the period include an emphasis on veneered surfaces, the use of various geometric motifs, and overall lack of visual unity. Specific decorative motifs such as large lunettes and diamonds (often in conjunction) are found on both Philadelphia and northern European furniture of the period. In the case of the Philadelphia work table shown in figure 24, the compartmentalization of the carved, veneered, and applied ornaments (gadrooning, leaves, fans, diamonds, and bosses) and of the lyre and components of the base is analogous to German and Danish work (see fig. 3). Furniture in which flat and curved, and projecting and recessive surfaces are dramatically juxtaposed is also found in both of these countries. A Philadelphia chest of drawers reflects this Germanic aesthetic (fig. 25) by having a facade that is divided into distinct horizontal bands unified solely by the grain of the wood. The upper drawers are convex, whereas the molding above them is concave. The middle drawers recede, and the bottom one protrudes below another curved molding. This same aesthetic is apparent in contemporary Philadelphia pier tables. The example illustrated in figure 26 has several visually distinct parts—marble top, scrolled supports, back, marble shelf, feet—unified solely by mahogany veneer. Although the plinth feet seem odd, they are fairly common in German work (see fig. 3).

As a contemporary plate from Wilhelm Kimbel's *Journal for Cabinetmakers and Upholsterers* (1835–1853) suggests (fig. 27), the secretary shown in figure 28 is strikingly close to German prototypes. Not only is the arrangement of the three lower drawers and fall the same but the cornice profile, concave framing molding, and rounded corners are virtually identical. Both facades also feature highly figured veneer.

Besides making furniture that emphasized veneered surfaces, bold and often eccentric shapes, and a lack of visual unity, German craftsmen probably encouraged the use of native light woods in Philadelphia. The rather sudden popularity of light-wood furniture occurred around 1830, just as German woodworkers began to enter the city in large numbers. In that year, Walter Pennery received an "honorary mention" at the Franklin Institute for a light-wood bureau he made in the shop of John Jameson (fig. 29). The judges described the piece as "a very beautiful specimen of maple work." Four years later, the judges commended a Loud & Brothers upright piano "for its good tone, and truly tasteful and splendid exterior, the case being made of American bird's eye maple." Encouraged by such awards, some Philadelphia shops began to specialize in light-wood furniture. The most notable was that of native-born cabinetmakers J. and A. Crout. From the founding of their shop in 1833 through the 1840s, they repeatedly received accolades for their "American-wood furniture" from the Franklin Institute. In the 1841 issue of the *Public Ledger,* they advertised a "splendid assortment of furniture, manufactured from a selection of American wood, such as has never before been introduced to the American public, and which, for beauty

Figure 27 Design for a fall-front secretary (1837) illustrated on plate 2 of Wilhelm Kimbel, *Journal für Möbelschreiner und Tapezierer*, vol. 1 (Mainz, 1835–1853). (Courtesy, Cooper-Hewitt, National Museum of Design.)

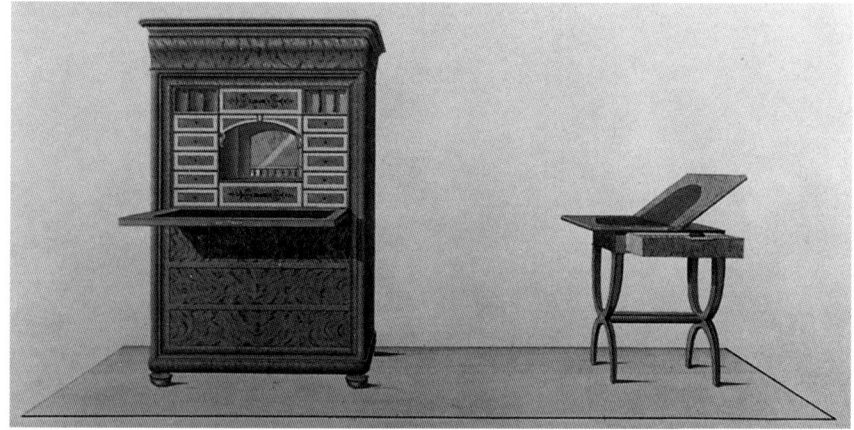

Figure 28 Fall-front secretary, probably Philadelphia, 1835–1850. Mahogany with yellow poplar; glass. H. 65 1/2", W. 42 3/4", D. 22 1/4". (Courtesy, Historical Society of York County, York, Pennsylvania; photo, Gavin Ashworth.)

Figure 29 Dressing bureau made by Walter Pennery in John Jameson's workshop, Philadelphia, 1830. Maple with tulip poplar; glass, brass, and iron. H. 87 3/8", W. 43 3/8", D. 24 1/2". (Courtesy, Winterthur Museum.) The bureau is inscribed: "The year of our lord one thousand eight hundred / and thirty / Philadelphia June 11th 1830 / Walter Pennery".

Figure 30 Design for a desk and chairs illustrated on plate 11 of D. Freudenvoll, *Neuestes Mainzer Moebel-Journal* (Mainz, 1846–n.d.). (Courtesy, Athenaeum of Philadelphia.)

and design, cannot be surpassed by any cabinet ware manufactured from Imported Wood." By 1850, the Crout shop was producing $10,000 worth of light-wood furniture annually.[49]

Although light-wood furniture was made in France and England during the early nineteenth century, it was more prevalent in Germany and Scandinavia. In Germany, it was seen as a nativist statement distinguishing German taste from that of France, where mahogany dominated. Some of the German cabinetmakers who came to Philadelphia probably worked with native American light woods in their homeland. In 1841, Frankfurt am Main lumber merchant Carl Küchler advertised that his warehouse contained "foreign furniture woods—including Mahogany, Palisander (or Jacaranda), Lemon, Zebra, American Maple, Amaranth, veined Amboina, veined Swedish, wild and high-quality Cedar, Ebony, Palmwood, Boxwood, and Pocked wood, etc. in blocks, planks, and veneers." American woods were so esteemed that a Viennese piano maker named Schneider imported American maple to cover the grand piano he sent to the Crystal Palace in 1851. In view of the wood trade between America and central Europe, the continuation of a tradition of light-wood furniture using American wood would have been a logical step for many immigrant German cabinetmakers.[50]

Although the sudden popularity of light-wood furniture in Philadelphia around 1830 may also have stemmed from the rarer English and French usage, surviving furniture usually points to a Germanic connection. For example, the outward sweeping base and overall lack of visual unity of the dressing bureau by Walter Pennery suggests that he was influenced by an immigrant German craftsman (compare fig. 29 to figs. 25, 26).

Figure 31 Sofa, New York City, ca. 1849–1850. Rosewood with ash. H. 43", W. 74", D. 34". (Courtesy, Dallas Museum of Art, gift of the Friends of Decorative Art; photo, Tom Jenkins.) The back is constructed from seven layers of laminated wood. The newspaper fragments found in this sofa are dated 1849.

Figure 32 Advertisement for Charles H. L. Goehmann (d. 1866) on page 27 of *O'Briens Philadelphia Wholesale Business Directory* (Philadelphia, 1850). (Photo, Charles Venable.) Goehmann is listed in Philadelphia directories from 1849 to 1866. He was at the 15th Street address noted here in 1850 and 1851. He was well known for his fancy twist work, for which he was cited by the Franklin Institute in 1844.

The Rococo Revival Style

In America, the introduction of the rococo revival style paralleled that of the late classical style. Although Parisian designers first revived this mid-eighteenth-century taste, immigrant German craftsmen were largely responsible for introducing rococo revival designs and construction techniques in this country. By the early 1830s, curvilinear, florid carving began to appear on rectilinear Biedermeier forms. Within a decade, much of the furniture produced in central Europe was fully rococo revival in style (figs. 30, 33). As a result, those hundreds of cabinetmakers and carvers who immigrated to America in the late 1830s and 1840s must have contributed significantly to the emergence of the style in this country. Not only were they familiar with French and other Continental design sources, but they knew how to execute them. German cabinetmaker Johann Heinrich Belter (1804–1866), for example, arrived in New York around 1840 and built a thriving business making furniture in the rococo revival style. Many contemporary products from other American shops also reveal a German hand. Pages from a New York, German-language newspaper found under the rear upholstery panels of a late 1840s rococo revival sofa (fig. 31) suggest that it came from a shop with German workers skilled in laminating and carving wood. In Philadelphia, several immigrants such as Charles H. L. Goehmann (d. 1866) worked in the rococo revival style at mid-century (fig. 32).[51]

Along with the ever-increasing waves of craftsmen who immigrated to America during the 1830s and 1840s, the rise of German patternbooks provided yet another avenue for the transfer of designs (especially rococo revival and, to a lesser extent, Gothic revival) to America. Although furniture designs had been published in Germany before 1830, the number of publications increased dramatically during the 1840s and 1850s. Simultaneously, the ability of German publishers to distribute their books throughout Europe and overseas improved markedly as Germany strengthened its international trade ties during the early nineteenth century.[52]

The United States was particularly receptive to German books, including patternbooks and trade catalogues. In Philadelphia, more than fifty dealers advertised as "Foreign and American Booksellers and Publishers" in the early 1840s. Several of these, including George S. Appleton, J. Dobson, George W. Mentz, J. W. Moore, J. G. Ritter, and L. A. Woollenweber, stated that they specialized in German books. Newspaper advertisements also reveal that New York importers had established strong connections with German publishing centers, especially Leipzig and Stuttgart, by the early 1830s. In 1843, New York importer William Radde (whose Philadelphia agent was C. Rademacher) announced that he was associated with the prominent book clearinghouse of Cotta in Stuttgart and could supply a wide variety of books.[53]

Judging from their frequent appearance in advertisements, patternbooks and technical treatises were a significant part of many dealers' businesses. In 1850, the Philadelphia firm of Zeitz and Company reported that they "import to order and have constantly on hand a very large assortment of goods.... BOOKS in German, Latin, Greek, Hebrew, French, Italian, Span-

Figure 33 Designs for chairs illustrated on plate 3 of J. W. Hanke, *Neues Journal für Möbelschreiner* (Frankfurt am Main, 1841). (Courtesy, Winterthur Museum Library.)

ish and other languages; Classics, Dictionaries, Grammars, Vocabularies, School, Juvenile, Picture, Drawing and Model Books for Architects, Cabinet, Carriage, and other manufacturers." J. G. Wesselhoeft, perhaps the largest German book importer in the country, regularly advertised design and technical books in his newspaper, *Die Alte und Neue Welt,* throughout the 1830s and early 1840s. In 1840, he described the technical works kept in stock as "a large collection of highly useful works for merchants, manufacturers, artists, craftsmen, farmers, and housekeepers."[54]

Although the subjects covered in Wesselhoeft's advertisements ranged from vinegar to porcelain production, most of the technical books he imported pertained to architecture, textile dyeing, metalworking, and woodworking. In addition to stocking inexpensive, multivolume technical books by J. C. Leuchs (Nuremberg), Carl Matthaey (Weimar), and Marius Wölfer (Leipzig), Wesselhoeft advertised Leuchs's *Recipes for Preparing Cabinetmaker's Glue* (1839) and *Stone Veneer: Its Preparation and Advantages Over Wood Veneer* (ca. 1839) and Matthaey's *Designs and Descriptions of the Newest Styles for Artists and Craftsmen* (3 vols., 1831–1835) and *The General Polytechnical and Trade Newspaper* (1834–1840). Along with these works, Wesselhoeft probably had other companion volumes, such as Matthaey's *The New Teaching, Pattern, and Ornament Book for Cabinetmakers and Carpenters* (1840), *New Patternbook for Wood, Horn, and Bone Turners* (1841), and *New Idea Magazine for Luxury, Furnishings, and Draperies* (1841). Wesselhoeft also advertised Wölfer's treatises on house and barn building, and he may have carried the same author's *The Carpenter and Cabinetmaker* (1828) (fig. 16), *Newest London, Parisian, Viennese and Berlin Window, Bed, and Furniture Decorations* (1829), and *Model and Patternbooks for Carpenters and Cabinetmakers* (1832).[55]

In addition to those titles that are known to have been imported, internal evidence in other German patternbooks indicates that they were marketed in America. The *Neues Journal für Möbelschreiner (New Journal for Cabinetmakers)* by J. W. Hanke (1841) (fig. 33) contains advertisements in German and English. The German one lists woods and other materials available at Carl Küchler's warehouse in Frankfurt am Main, whereas the English one concerns steel pins and uses an Anglicized version of Küchler's name (Kuchler). Some of Küchler's "portrait pins," furthermore, had likenesses of Lafayette and Washington on them, proving that the advertisement, and hence Hanke's furniture designs, were intended for an America audience.[56]

The patternbook that most clearly demonstrates a connection between German and American design between 1830 and 1850 is D. Freudenvoll's *Neuestes Mainzer Moebel-Journal (New Mainz Furniture Journal)* (1846–n.d.) (figs. 30, 34). Freudenvoll's son Charles (Carl) (b. 1812) came to Philadelphia in the late 1830s and was active for at least a decade. Charles's records and the title pages of *Neuestes Mainzer Moebel-Journal* indicate that he sold his father's lithographic designs at his shop at 9 Gaskill Street. D. Freudenvoll also distributed his designs in Mainz, Paris, Brussels, and London. By 1847, his success in Philadelphia induced him to send his other son, John,

Figure 34 Designs for fall-front secretaries illustrated on plate 12 of D. Freudenvoll, *Neuestes Mainzer Moebel-Journal* (Mainz, 1846–n.d.). (Courtesy, Athenaeum of Philadelphia.)

to Boston to oversee the journal's distribution there (John's cabinet shop was at 10 Middlesex Street). The fact that the Boston distribution center opened the same year that the London one closed suggests that Americans embraced German rococo revival designs more closely than did the English.

Given the trilingual nature of the journal (marketed in America and England as the *New Magazine for Cabinet-makers and Upholsterers*) and its fashionable plates, Freudenvoll's book probably had an impact on rococo revival design in this country. Unfortunately, so little is known about early rococo revival furniture in America that the extent of the journal's influence is hard to evaluate. Some parallels are apparent, however, since several fall-front secretaries from Philadelphia are closely related to Freudenvoll's designs (see fig. 34).[57]

Conclusion

By the 1850s, the links between German and American furniture design were firmly established. Virtually every major urban center in America had large numbers of German-trained artisans working in the furniture industry. Over a third of the cabinetmakers in Philadelphia were German born by 1850, and nearly two-thirds of those in New York were of German origin by 1855 (2,153 German cabinetmakers and upholsterers). In addition, the importation of patternbooks, most of which were trilingual, meant that native-born furniture makers had access to central European design regardless of their language capabilities or the nationality of the journeymen they employed.

German immigrants and imported furniture influenced Philadelphia furniture design during the first quarter of the nineteenth century. Although halting and incomplete before 1830, the acceptance of German design increased dramatically during the decades that followed. The shift from "Empire" design to the often more eccentric shapes of American late classical furniture owes much to the Germanic predilection for highly figured veneers and visually compartmentalized spaces, just as the introduction of the rococo revival style in the United States is greatly indebted to both the skill of German woodworkers and their patternbooks.

1. For the purpose of this article, the term "Germanic" is used to describe people, objects, and furniture styles from areas as far south as Austria and as far north as Sweden and Denmark. Parts of northern Italy and Russia produced furniture of a closely related nature as well. For clarity, I refer to the late neoclassical style emanating from these parts of Europe during the first half of the nineteenth century as Biedermeier, even though this term is most properly used for objects originating in Germany, Austria, and the Czech Republic. Furniture from areas surrounding this central European core is stylistically related, however.

2. Mack Walker, *Germany and the Emigration, 1816–1885* (Cambridge, Mass.: Harvard University Press, 1964), p. 35. This is the best work in English on the subject. U.S. Bureau of the Census, *Historical Statistics of the United States, Colonial Times to 1957* (Washington, D.C.: Government Printing Office, 1960), p. 57. Totals for Swiss immigrants are listed separately in Anges Bretting, *Soziale Probleme deutscher Einwanderer in New York City 1800–1860* (Wiesbaden, Germany: Steiner, 1981), pp. 76–77.

3. Walker, *Germany*, p. 42. Bureau of the Census, *Historical Statistics*, p. 57.

4. Walker, *Germany*, pp. 47, 51.

5. Walker, *Germany*, p. 46; for a discussion of factors affecting immigration, see pages 42–69.

6. The term "master" is used in the European guild sense and does not merely denote shop ownership. Craftsmen earned the rank of master only after they had passed a series of guild examinations, completed their apprenticeships, and worked as a journeyman. Thomas Nipperdey, *Deutsche Geschichte 1800–1866: Bürgerwelt und Starker Staat* (Munich: Beck, 1983), pp. 210–13.

7. For a discussion of the theme of America in German culture, see Sigrid Bauschinger, et al., *Amerika in der deutschen Literatur* (Stuttgart, Germany: Reclam, 1975). Ludwig Gall, *Meine Auswanderung nach den Vereinigten Staaten in Nord-Amerika*, 2 vols. (Trier, 1822). Gottfried Duden, *Bericht über eine Reise nach den westlichen Staaten Nordamerikas . . . in Bezug auf Auswanderung und über Völkerung*, 2nd ed. (Bonn, 1834). For a discussion of the impact of this book, see Walker, *Germany*, p. 60.

8. Quoted in Walker, *Germany*, pp. 34–35; for a discussion of personal letters describing America, see pages 62–64.

9. As Walker, *Germany*, p. 62, notes, the popularity of such books is reflected in the fact that by 1858 at least 100 were in print. Alexander Ziegler, *Der deutsche Auswanderer nach den Vereinigten Staaten von Nordamerika: Ein Lehrbuch auf seinem Weg* (Leipzig, 1849), pp. 108, 111, 109.

10. The scholarly material on the various routes and ports is substantial. Two of the best general sources are Walker, *Germany*, pp. 70–102; and Birgit Gelberg, *Auswanderung nach Übersee* (Hamburg, Germany: Christians, 1973). Bretting, *Soziale Probleme*, p. 1. Eventually Baltimore would also surpass Philadelphia as a trading center with Germany, owing to the demand for Chesapeake tobacco in north Germany. For information on Baltimore and its trade ties with North Germany, see David Ward, *Cities and Immigrants: A Geography of Change in Nineteenth Century America* (New York: Oxford University Press, 1971), p. 28; and Walter Struve, *Die Republik Texas, Bremen und das Hildesheimische* (Hildesheim: Lax, 1983), p. 64.

11. Traugott Bromme, *Rathgeber für Auswanderungslustige: Wie und Wohin Sollen Wir Auswandern* (Stuttgart, 1846), p. 26. Franz Löher, *Geschichte und Zustände der Deutschen in Amerika* (Cincinnati and Leipzig, 1847), p. 298.

12. Gall, *Meine Auswanderung*, 2:100. Traugott Bromme, *Hand- und Reisebuch für Auswanderer nach den Vereinigten Staaten von Nordamerika*, 5th ed. (Bayreuth, 1848), pp. 159–60. Löher, *Geschichte*, p. 303.

13. Bruce Laurie, "Nothing on Compulsion: Life Styles of Philadelphia Artisans, 1820–1850," *Labor History* 15, no. 1 (winter 1974): 338. Sam Bass Warner, Jr., *The Private City: Philadelphia in Three Periods of Its Growth* (Philadelphia: University of Pennsylvania Press, 1968), pp. 137–38. *Philadelphia: Work, Space, Family, and Group Experience in the Nineteenth Century*, ed. Theodore Hershberg (New York: Oxford University Press, 1981), p. 180.

14. Hershberg, ed., *Philadelphia*, p. 180. For a complete breakdown of the furniture industry

by nationality, see Elizabeth Page Talbott, "The Philadelphia Furniture Industry, 1850–1880" (Ph.D. diss., University of Pennsylvania, 1980), table I-3A. Robert Ernst, *Immigrant Life in New York City, 1825–1863* (New York: King's Crown, Columbia University), table 27.

15. For a discussion of this coffer, see Gerald W. R. Ward, *American Case Furniture in the Mabel Brady Garvan and Other Collections at Yale University* (New Haven, Conn.: Yale University Art Gallery, 1988), pp. 77–78. Bromme, *Hand- und Reisebuch*, p. 498. Ziegler, *Der deutsche*, p. 108.

16. For a discussion of Wesselhoeft, see Robert C. Cazden, *A Social History of the German Book Trade in America to the Civil War* (Columbia, S.C.: Camden House, 1984), pp. 82–89. *Die Alte und Neue Welt* [Philadelphia], November 19, 1836, p. 4; February 17, 1838, p. 4. This German-language newspaper was Philadelphia's most important and is hereafter referred to as *ANW*. The Morris Library at the University of Delaware has a run on microfilm. The national scope of this operation is inferred from the national character of Wesselhoeft's newspaper and bookstores. *ANW*, June 18, 1836, p. 3.

17. *New York Daily Tribune*, November 11, 1845, p. 2.

18. Walker, *Germany*, p. 68.

19. For a discussion of German guilds, see Fritz Hellwag, *Die Geschichte des Deutschen Tischlerhandwerks vom 12. bis zum 20. Jahrhundert* (Berlin: Deutscher Holzarbeiter-Verband, 1924). This book is the only major work on the history of German cabinetmaking guilds.

20. Bromme, *Hand- und Reisebuch*, pp. 494, 416. Ellis P. Oberholtzer, *Philadelphia: A History of the City and Its People*, 4 vols. (Philadelphia: Clarke, 1912), 4:333. Ferdinand Kürnberger, *Der Amerika-Müde, Amerikanisches Kulturbild* (Frankfurt am Main, 1857), p. 124. Quoted in Bretting, *Soziale Probleme*, 94.

21. This figure was obtained by comparing the Philadelphia Social History Project's computerized "1850 Census of Manufacturing" data against the population census in order to check the shop owner's place of birth. The remaining records from the now defunct Philadelphia Social History Project (hereafter referred to as PSHP) are at the Van Pelt Library, University of Pennsylvania. This rough estimate of the percentage of German cabinetmakers who were listed in the directory was obtained by checking a sample of 389 German-born cabinetmakers on the PSHP's "1850 Census of Population" against *McElroy's Philadelphia Directory, for 1850*. Thirty-five Germans were in the directory (9 percent of the total). Although this estimate may be faulty due to misspelled names, clearly most Germans did not have themselves listed in directories. As noted in Hershberg, ed., *Philadelphia*, p. 509, 43.8 percent of the adult male population is included in the 1850 directory.

22. Ziegler, *Der deutsche*, pp. 108–9. *ANW* contains dozens of such advertisements. G. Gundrum, *The American Interpreter/Der Amerikanische Dolmetscher* (New Berlin, Penn., 1831).

23. Bromme, *Hand- und Reisebuch*, p. 480.

24. For a discussion of the Society of Journeymen, see Kathleen M. Catalano, "Cabinetmaking in Philadelphia, 1820–1840" (M.A. thesis, University of Delaware, 1972), pp. 42–48. *The Constitution of the Pennsylvania Society of Journeymen Cabinet-Makers, of the City of Philadelphia* (Philadelphia, 1829), p. 11. For more information on these cabinetmakers, see Charles L. Venable, "Philadelphia Biedermeier: Germanic Craftsmen and Design in Philadelphia, 1820–1850" (M.A. thesis, University of Delaware, 1986), p. 235ff.

25. Löher, *Geschichte*, p. 303. Hershberg, ed., *Philadelphia*, pp. 179–88.

26. *ANW*, March 30, 1844, p. 3. *Philadelphia As It Is, and Citizens Advertising Directory* (Philadelphia, 1833), pp. 72–74. *ANW*, October 15, 1841, p. 3. *Philadelphia Directory and Register* (Philadelphia, 1819), front matter. Numerous advertisements by Philadelphia, New York, and Baltimore merchants for imported wine, meat, cheese, and chocolate appear in *ANW* between 1834 and 1844. The "Index to U.S. Customs House Papers, Philadelphia, Pennsylvania, 1790–1869," Downs Manuscript Collection, Winterthur Museum, lists a wide variety of imported German goods, including foodstuffs.

27. See Struve, *Die Republik*, p. 11, for a discussion of German business agents and branches in America. The following central and northern European countries or cities had consuls in Philadelphia in 1820: Denmark, Sweden, Norway, Prussia, and Hamburg. *McElroy's Philadelphia Directory*, p. 500, shows a significant increase by 1850. By that time Austria, Bavaria, Bremen, Denmark, Württemberg, Hamburg, Hanover, the Netherlands, Prussia, Saxony, Sweden and Norway, and Switzerland had consuls in Philadelphia. For an account of a Philadelphia merchant attending the Leipzig trade fair and traveling throughout central Europe, see "Charles N. Buck Memoirs, 1791–1841," Pennsylvania Historical Society. Buck served as consul general of Hamburg in Philadelphia, even though he was a naturalized citizen.

28. *ANW*, July 11, 1840, p. 4, and November 21, 1840, p. 4. The correct German titles for these works are "Abbildungstafel von 56 Goldmünzen aller Länder, mit Angabe des Werthes" and *Grosses Adressbuch der Kaufleute, Fabrikanten, Apotheker, Berg und Hüttenwerke, Gasthöfe, u. von 3000 Städten von Europa* ($7.00). *ANW*, August 7, 1842, p. 4.

29. *ANW*, January 26, 1839, p. 3, and July 11, 1840, p. 4. For examples, see Unidentified German Firm, "Furniture Mounts and Jewelry Catalogue" (ca. 1820), Mesker Iron Co., Collection, Missouri Historical Society; and Unidentified Bohemian Firm, "Gardner Island Glass Catalogue" (ca. 1800–1810), Downs Manuscript Collection, Winterthur Museum Library.

30. *ANW*, June 13, 1835, p. 3. *ANW*, May 4, 1844, p. 3. *Philadelphia Directory and Register* (1819), front matter. *ANW*, March 3, 1838, p. 3.

31. U.S. Bureau of the Census, "1820 Census of Manufactures," Philadelphia County, p. 553. National Archives.

32. This Biedermeir style had its precursors in German neoclassical furniture, and it lingered on until midcentury, especially in rural areas. Hellwag, *Die Geschichte*, pp. 194–95. Talbott, "Philadelphia," p. 36.

33. For a thorough discussion of the Biedermeier style, see Georg Himmelheber, *Biedermeier Furniture* (London: Faber, 1973); and Himmelheber, *Die Kunst des deutschen Möbels: Dritter Band, Klassizismus/Historismus/Jugendstil*, 2nd ed. (Munich: Beck, 1983), pp. 72–128.

34. See Himmelheber, *Die Kunst*, pp. 105–7.

35. For a discussion of the influence of English design in Germany, see Jörn Bahns, *Biedermeier-Möbel: Entstehung-Zentren-Typen* (Munich: Keyser, 1979), pp. 17–18; and Himmelheber, *Biedermeier Möbel*, pp. 50–51.

36. For an example of German furniture being imported into New Orleans, see Stephen G. Harrison, "Furniture Trade in New Orleans, 1840–1880: The Largest Assortment Constantly on Hand" (M.A. thesis, University of Delaware, 1997), p. 42ff.

37. German immigrants frequently brought substantial amounts of personal property with them to America. For examples, see Charles van Ravenswaay, *The Arts and Architecture of German Settlements in Missouri: A Survey of a Vanishing Culture* (Columbia, Mo.: University of Missouri, 1977), pp. 81–104. Establishing the exact provenance of the Oppenheimer secretary has not proven a simple task. According to a 1984 auction catalogue entry, the secretary reportedly descended in the "Oppenheimer Family, Bedford County, Pennsylvania" (Sotheby's, *Important American Furniture*, New York, January 26, 1984, lot 769). The desk was billed as being from Philadelphia, but its oak secondary woods, paneled drawer bottoms, pewter inlay, and German construction suggest that it was made in central Europe and imported to America. Research on the Oppenheimer family of Bedford County suggests that most of its members came there from Germany during the second half of the nineteenth century. Other Oppenheimers lived in Philadelphia and Dauphin Counties by 1850. It is possible that one of the latter families eventually moved to Bedford County, taking the desk in question with them (Gwen Morral, Bedford County Historical Society, to Charles Venable, March 24, 1986).

38. Windy C. Wick, "Stephen Girard: A Patron of the Philadelphia Furniture Trade" (M.A. thesis, University of Delaware, 1977), pp. 84–86. Clearly, the desk was considered German during the period because German craftsmen were repeatedly hired to repair the piece and because a late nineteenth-century newspaper article noted that the secretary was made by a specific German cabinetmaker. This newspaper account is noted in ibid. An 1804 bill for "1 bureau" valued at $650 is in the Girard Papers (Phyllis Abrams, Girard College, to Charles Venable, September 5, 1986). This amount is the most paid for any of the Girard furnishings and most likely is for this elaborate musical secretary.

39. Joseph G. Fledman gave the Smithsonian this desk in 1975. He purchased it from Peter Hill, who recalls that he acquired it on Pine Street in Philadelphia in the 1960s (Peter Hill to Charles Venable, February 21, 1985). For a closely related German example, see Bahns, *Biedermeier Möbel*, p. 100, fig. 86.

40. Laurence Libin, Metropolitan Museum of Art, to Charles Venable, December 2, 1985. Talbott, "Philadelphia," p. 31.

41. See Rosemarie Stratmann, "Design and Mechanism in the Furniture of Jean-François Oeben," *Furniture History* 4 (1973): 110–13; and John Flemming and Hugh Honor, "Oeben," *The Penguin Dictionary of Decorative Arts* (London: Penguin, 1977), p. 571. Biedermeier design was strongest in German- and Czech-speaking areas and highly influential in Scandinavia. The style also impacted other parts of Europe, including Russia, Hungary, and northern Italy. The spread of Biedermeier design to these areas was partially due to the movement of German-trained cabinetmakers within Europe. See Bahns, *Biedermeier Möbel*, pp. 91–108.

42. The Gratz and Kuhn examples are the subject of Deborah Ducoff-Barone, "Design and Decoration in Early Nineteenth Century American Furniture: A Case Study of a Philadelphia Secretary Bookcase," *The Decorative Arts Society Newsletter* (Philadelphia Museum) (March 1983): 1–8. An inventory for Thomas Gilpin lists "1 mahogany French Secretary," which was being sent to Wilmington, Delaware, for sale at auction in 1839 (Inventory of Thomas Gilpin, Philadelphia, 1817–1845, Downs Manuscript Collection, no. 2606, Winterthur Museum Library). *The Philadelphia Cabinet and Chair Maker's Union Book of Prices of Manufacturing Cabinet Ware* (Philadelphia, 1828), pp. 38–39. For an example by the Boston firm of Isaac Vose & Son, see Page Talbott, "Boston Empire Furniture: Part I," *Antiques* 107, no. 5 (May 1975): 880.

43. For an illustration of Mésangère's plate 563 (1823), see Wendy Cooper, *In Praise of America: American Decorative Arts, 1650–1830* (New York: Knopf, 1980), p. 264.

44. Besides the eight examples cited, several fall-front secretaries exhibiting Germanic traits have appeared in recent years. See Sotheby's, *The Andy Warhol Collection*, New York, April 29, 1988, lot 3229; Sotheby's *Fine American Furniture*, New York, June 27, 1990, lot 487; Sotheby's, *Fine Americana*, New York, January 23, 1992, lots 1098 and 1157. The example sold as lot 1157 is made of bird's-eye maple and fitted with a bookcase (for another illustration, see *Maine Antique Digest*, June 1989, p. 38-D). The design of this secretary and of a pedimented example formerly in the collection of James M. Goode (see Oscar Fitzgerald, *Three Centuries of American Furniture* [New York: Gramercy Publishing, 1982], p. 129) relates to the core group of eight discussed here; however, they appear to be from a different shop. According to Robert C. Smith, a secretary similar to the example sold as lot 1157 bears a label of Philadelphia cabinetmaker and furniture retailer Anthony Quervelle. See Robert C. Smith, "The Furniture of Anthony G. Quervelle, Part IV," *Antiques* 105, no. 1 (January 1974): 180. Unfortunately, this labeled example has never been located by the author. For more on the example at the Dallas Museum of Art (fig. 15), see Charles L. Venable, *American Furniture in the Faith P. and Charles L. Bybee Collection* (Austin: University of Texas Press, 1989), pp. 100–103; a privately owned secretary featuring a rectangular section with spherical finials on top is shown on page 102. For the other examples, see J. Michael Flanigan, *American Furniture from the Kaufman Collection* (Washington, D.C.: National Gallery of Art, 1986), pp. 222–23; Christie's, *Fine American Furniture,* New York, May 23, 1985, lot 183; Christie's, *Important American Furniture,* New York, October 21, 1989, lot 297; Sotheby's, *Important Americana,* New York, January 28, 1989, lot 1478; Christie's, *Important American Furniture,* New York, January 22, 1993, lot 546; and Northeast Auctions, *New Hampshire Auction,* Portsmouth, New Hampshire, March 1, 1997, lot 586. For an early example (ca. 1800) of a design for a secretary with a sloping top, see *Sammlung von Zeichnungen der neusten Londoner und Pariser Meubles als Muster für Tischler* (Leipzig, 1796–n.d.), pt. 4, pl. 9. A copy of this work is at the Winterthur Museum Library. Although the title to this work states that it reproduces the latest designs from London and Paris, the one for this secretary is very Germanic. Georg Himmelheber, Bavarian National Museum, to Charles Venable, August 13, 1985.

45. The fall-front secretary is illustrated in Ducoff-Barone, "Design," cover. The sideboard and knifeboxes are shown on p. 4.

46. Ducoff-Barone, "Design," pp. 1–2. For examples of early nineteenth-century English pieces with brass inlay, see Margaret Jourdain, *Regency Furniture* (London: Country Life, Ltd., 1965), pp. 41–43. For the design with wings, see Pierre de la Mésangère, *Collections des Meubles et Objects de Goût* (Paris, 1804), pl. 125. That plate is illustrated in Ducoff-Barone, "Design," p. 2. In 1823, Mésangère published designs for more typical French examples in plate 563.

47. A set of unpublished mechanical drawings and a diary fragment from 1819 by Fiedler are at the Historical Society of York County, Pennsylvania. These documents have been translated by Drs. Sylvia M. and Charles Venable.

48. See note 44 for citations of several Philadelphia secretaries exhibiting Germanic qualities. James Francis Dallett, "Michael Bouvier, Franco-American Cabinetmaker," *Antiques* 81, no. 2 (February 1962): 198–200.

49. *Journal of the Franklin Institute* (Philadelphia), 1st series, October 1830, p. 274; and January 1834, p. 25. For examples that descended in the Markoe family of Philadelphia, see Sotheby's, *Fine American Furniture,* New York, June 27, 1990, lot 395. For a discussion of the Crout

shop, see Talbott, "Philadelphia," pp. 209–11. Advertisement from the *Public Ledger* (Philadelphia), May 10, 1841, as quoted in Talbott, "Philadelphia," p. 210. U.S. Bureau of the Census, "1850 Census of Manufactures," Philadelphia County, p. 196, line 4.

50. Himmelheber, *Biedermeier,* p. 39. J. W. Hanke, *Neues Journal für Möbelschreiner* (Frankfurt am Main, 1841), back matter. *The Crystal Palace, and Its Contents* (London, 1852), p. 202.

51. For the best discussion to date of Belter's career, see Marvin D. Schwartz, Edward J. Stamek, and Douglas K. True, *The Furniture of John Henry Belter and the Rococo Revival* (New York: E. P. Dutton, 1981).

52. For a discussion of German patternbooks, see Himmelheber, *Die Kunst*, pp. 106–8 and 121–32. For an overview of the German book trade, see "The Book Trade of Germany," *Hunt's Merchant's Magazine,* November 1843, pp. 399–418; and Cazden, *A Social History*.

53. For extensive lists of Philadelphia book dealers, see *O'Brien's Philadelphia Business Directory, for 1844* (Philadelphia, 1844), pp. 50–51; and *O'Brien's Philadelphia Business Directory, for 1845*, pp. 62–63. Advertisements for Mentz and Dobson are in the *Philadelphia Circulating Business Directory, of 1838* (Philadelphia, 1838), pp. 13 and 20. *ANW,* May 20, 1843, p. 4.

54. *O'Brien's Philadelphia Business Directory, for 1850,* p. 62. *ANW,* May 16, 1840, p. 3.

55. Advertisements for such works appear in *ANW* periodically between 1836 and 1842.

56. Hanke, *Neues Journal*, back matter.

57. For a Philadelphia example on cabriole legs, see Neal Auction Company catalogue, New Orleans, April 27, 1991, lot 600.

Philip D. Zimmerman

Labeled Randolph Chairs Rediscovered

▼ PHILADELPHIA FURNITURE maker and carver Benjamin Randolph (1721–1791) attracted considerable interest among early American furniture dealers, collectors, and scholars in the 1960s and early 1970s. Historian Nicholas Wainwright advanced Randolph's name as maker of some of the most ornate Philadelphia furniture in the rococo style in his otherwise excellent study of the house and furnishings of John and Elizabeth (Lloyd) Cadwalader. Art historian Robert C. Smith linked Randolph's name to the grand traditions of eighteenth-century European classicism in his 1971 article on Philadelphia furniture busts and subsequently to a very ornate desk-and-bookcase.[1]

Two studies published in the 1970s contributed to replacement of Randolph's name in the number one position with that of Philadelphia cabinetmaker Thomas Affleck. In his influential and valuable book *American Chairs: Queen Anne and Chippendale* (1972), John Kirk argued that a chair bearing a Randolph label and its mate—both in the Karolik Collection at the Museum of Fine Arts, Boston—were out-of-period (see figs. 1, 2). As a consequence of this analysis, both objects were removed from exhibition and have remained in storage since. Kirk also hypothesized that the design of these chairs, heretofore associated with Randolph, was more likely the work of Affleck. Seven years later, an article titled "A Methodological Study in the Identification of Some Important Philadelphia Chippendale Furniture" revised prevailing opinion about Randolph's involvement with a group of furniture commissioned by Philadelphia merchant John Cadwalader, again replacing Randolph's name with Affleck's. Historical arguments advanced in the aforementioned article were reinforced by new scientific technologies applied to furniture scholarship in a 1989 study at Winterthur. More recently, the focus on cabinetmakers such as Affleck and Randolph has yielded to interest in individual carvers and carving schools.[2]

Trends and preferences exist in furniture history scholarship and influence how physical and written evidence is evaluated and interpreted. These scholarly currents respond at least partially to certain published works and unpublished discoveries that enter the mainstream of generally accepted opinion. As the corpus of American furniture history grows, it is useful to revisit earlier works upon which today's scholarship continues to build. On occasion, intervening research may substantially challenge and change earlier findings. When such information comes to light, it seems appropriate to correct distortions of the historical record so that errors are not compounded in further research.

Figure 1 Side chair (one of a pair) labeled by Benjamin Randolph, Philadelphia, 1765–1775. Mahogany. H. 38 3/8", W. 23 3/4", D. 19". (Courtesy, Museum of Fine Arts, Boston, M. and M. Karolik Collection.)

Figure 2 Detail of the label applied to the inside rear rail of the chair illustrated in fig. 1.

In the case of the Randolph labeled chair, the bibliographical record began with its feature publication in Edwin J. Hipkiss's, *Eighteenth-Century American Arts: The M. and M. Karolik Collection* (1941). A decade later, Albert Sack described the chair as "the ultimate of this type and one of the greatest of the Philadelphia chairs" in *Fine Points of Furniture: Early American*, his popular guide to evaluating early American furniture. John Kirk's detailed argument that the chairs are out-of-period stands in sharp contrast. He did not express doubts about the authenticity of the printed label, but he advanced a modest argument that it was fraudulently applied, a circumstance that must follow logically if the chair is not period.[3]

Patricia E. Kane's catalogue of the chair collection at the Yale University Art Gallery, published in 1976, acknowledged the doubt cast by Kirk's analysis but did so in a noncommittal fashion. She stated that "the authenticity of that label has been questioned" but provided no references to her sources and supplied no opinion of her own. She also noted that "the present whereabouts of another labeled example is not known, leaving the Randolph attribution somewhat in doubt." This second chair, illustrated in Joe

Kindig, Jr.'s, advertisement in the January 1943 issue of *Antiques*, appears to be identical to the Karolik chair. Without adequate explanation, the reader must infer that Kane's reluctance to state an opinion was related to a concern that the label of the Kindig chair may have been removed and applied to the now problematic Karolik chair.[4]

The Karolik chair reappeared as "one of the most controversial pieces of American furniture" in an exhibit of art fakes and alterations at Yale in 1977. Francis J. Puig's catalogue entry for the chair increased the uncertainties surrounding this object by placing it in a "questionables" category and offering several possible interpretations: The chair is fraudulent, but the label is authentic; the chair is an altered revival form; or the chair is a genuine Philadelphia example by another maker. His reference to Kirk's book to document all of these possibilities is inaccurate. Kirk developed a single argument—the chair is fraudulent, but the label is authentic.[5]

This study revisits the controversy to lay uncertainty to rest. It offers yet another point of view—that both the chair and its label are genuine. Misunderstandings of the chair stem from misinterpretation of physical evidence partially altered and obscured by restorations. Although reinstatement of this documented example of Randolph's work may interest only some students of early American furniture, the causes of these erroneous interpretations have broad application.

Kirk's argument that the labeled Randolph chairs are out-of-period relied upon his comparisons of the pair to other Philadelphia examples in the rococo style. More specifically, he used five similar chairs at Yale as a "control group" and the primary base of comparison. Kirk expressed his argument as sixteen points of difference from the control group and from other contemporary Philadelphia chairs and chairmaking practices. His points, which combined objective and subjective observations of physical evidence, do not appear to follow any particular logic; but, in total, they are daunting. His objective evidence focused on details of construction; the subjective observations addressed issues of design. Several points identified apparent departures from all known practices, whereas others cited practices that are merely infrequent.[6]

Generally, objective or quantifiable evidence is more persuasive and comprehensible than subjective or qualitative evidence. Although the majority of Kirk's observations belong in the objective category, several addressed condition issues of only modest importance. He noted, for example, that the corner blocks on the chairs are of "new stained pine" and their seat frames "are of oak, not nearly as common as pine," suggesting that they too may be replacements. The carved brackets for each of the front legs were also called into question because they have wooden plugs covering nails or screws rather than exposed, wrought nails. Although each of Kirk's observations represents a fair and accurate assessment of condition, none casts doubt upon the age of the chairs. Replacement of all corner blocks and resecuring of all brackets indicates that each chair must have been partially disassembled at some time. Even so, there is no indication that the knee brackets or other chair parts are replacements.

Certain construction features of the front rails are more worrisome. Their decoration incorporates an important detail that deviates from known Philadelphia furniture-making practices. The front rails have C-scroll appliqués set opposite one another to create a serpentine line, and they are undercut below. Undercutting preserved the structural advantages of large tenons while providing a lighter appearance. On Philadelphia rococo side chairs, the front and side rails are typically undercut in a straight line ending in decorative hollows (quarter rounds) or ogee curves, whereas rear rails are seldom undercut. Although many of these chairs have ornaments on their front rails—shells, scrolls, leafage, flowers, cartouches—the designs are either carved in relief or applied. Kirk objected to the Randolph chairs because their decoration features both techniques; the C scrolls are applied, and their upper edges are accentuated with a groove cut into the rail. Moreover, additional small pieces of wood are glued to the backs of the scroll volutes to reinforce them where they drop below the bottom edge of the front rail. Although eighteenth-century furniture makers often glued wood to achieve required dimensions, these tiny laminations have no known parallel in Philadelphia chairmaking. They suggest that wood-dimension deficiencies occurred *after* assembly rather than as an intentional step.[7]

Another problematic feature, not described by Kirk but noted by others, is the presence of small veneered fills or repairs at the extremities of the C scrolls (fig. 3). These repairs, whose purpose is not immediately apparent,

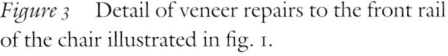

Figure 3 Detail of veneer repairs to the front rail of the chair illustrated in fig. 1.

are identical on both sides of each chair. They also appear on the labeled Randolph chair advertised by Kindig and on its mate (see figs. 4, 5). Kindig purchased both chairs from Francis P. Garvan (the pioneer collector who gave part of his collection to Yale in honor of his wife, Mabel Brady Garvan) and subsequently sold them to another important collector, Reginald Lewis. The present owner acquired the chairs at the Lewis sale in 1961.[8]

These additional chairs shed virtually no light on Kirk's argument. Since

Figure 4   Side chair (one of a pair) labeled by Benjamin Randolph, Philadelphia, 1765–1775. Mahogany. H. 38 3/8", W. 23 3/4", D. 19". (Private collection; photo, Gavin Ashworth.)

Figure 5   Detail of the label applied to the inside rear rail of the chair illustrated in fig. 4. (Photo, Gavin Ashworth.)

Figure 6   Detail of the rear corner block of the chair illustrated in fig. 4, showing screw holes and impressions of an angle-iron plate. (Photo, Gavin Ashworth.)

they are so nearly identical to the ones in the Karolik Collection, they merely extend the number of chairs in question. All four examples are constructed exactly the same. Their overall dimensions and component dimensions also match, indicating that they were laid out with the same templates. The Kindig chairs are stamped "I" and "II" on the inside tops of the front rails; the Karolik chairs are numbered "III" and "IIII" in the same location, suggesting that they may all be from the same set. Similarly, the condition of each pair, including the problematic front rail decoration, is the same with the exception that the Kindig chairs were refinished more recently. Subsequent to their manufacture, all four chairs had their seat rail joints reinforced with iron braces and screws. Although the evidence on all four chairs

Figure 7 Armchair, Philadelphia, 1765–1775. Mahogany. H. 37", W. 29½", D. 24". (Private collection; photo, Gavin Ashworth.)

is partially obscured by the replacement corner blocks—all of which are stained in the same manner—the screw holes are visible on the Kindig examples (fig. 6) and filled on the Karolik ones.

Comparison of the two pairs of Randolph chairs to contemporary Philadelphia examples resolves all of the front rail questions. An armchair and a side chair that differ slightly from the Randolph chairs and from each other indicate that the front rails of the Randolph chairs were merely restored incorrectly and are not evidence of out-of-period workmanship (figs. 7, 8). Collectively, these objects demonstrate unequivocally that the original front rail design of the Randolph chairs consisted of incised C scrolls (fig. 9). Not only are the present appliqués and small glued backings incorrect additions but the enigmatic veneer repairs cover the ends of the original incised design. The outer volutes of the replaced appliqués direct the eye to the knee brackets flanking them, whereas the original incised decoration passed over the leaf tips of each front bracket.[9]

Figure 8   Side chair, Philadelphia, 1765–1775. Mahogany. H. 33³⁄₈", W. 24¹⁄₄", D. 22". (Private collection; photo, Gavin Ashworth.)

To question why a restorer interpreted this evidence differently, added unnecessary carving, and covered up other decoration is futile. Unlike the revealing patterns of workmanship and design that establish a sound foundation for describing "what," the information needed to judge "why" is simply insufficient. To project today's standards of design and restoration

Figure 9   Detail of the front rail of the armchair illustrated in fig. 7. (Photo, Gavin Ashworth.)

Figure 10 Detail of the rear end of the side rail shaping and through-tenon of the chair illustrated in fig. 1, showing two-piece construction.

back to the time of this repair invites the same error of which the chairs' repairer is accused, namely, using contemporary approaches to solve problems presented by furniture of an earlier period.

Kirk's other objections to the Karolik chairs were increasingly dependent upon personal opinion and preference. He noted that the height of the rear through-tenons was almost an inch less than the height of the side rails from which they are cut. These dimensions, he continues, usually are nearly the same. Kirk's statement is factually correct, but it implies an aberrant practice that reinforced suspicions about the age of the chairs. If typical is defined as a frequency of more than 50 percent, or even 60 or 70 percent, then this feature is atypical; however, viewing eighteenth-century craft traditions in such a dualistic manner introduces the likelihood of misinterpretation. Two different practices, such as using through-tenons or blind tenons, may have existed within a specific furniture-making community; thus, although mid-eighteenth-century Philadelphia chairs with blind rear tenons are rare, they are no less authentic. Similarly, through-tenons cut to a shorter height than the average are no less acceptable in terms of period workmanship.

Another instance where Kirk's personal preferences adversely affected his interpretation was his analysis of the laminated rear brackets of the side rails (fig. 10). This construction detail, which appears on all four Randolph chairs, has no eighteenth-century parallel. Neither eighteenth-century chairmakers nor modern reproducers or fakers would derive any advantage from gluing up the side rails and rear tenons in this manner: It does not save materials or time. Since all of the chair frames have been taken apart, however, it is reasonable to suggest that this structural anomaly results from a restoration campaign. If the original brackets had been damaged during disassembly, they may have been planed down and replaced with the present laminations. In any event, Kirk's assertion that the curve of the brackets is "uninspired" diverts attention from more objective considerations—namely, that these elements are probably repairs. The "subtle curve" of the brackets on two of the "control-group" chairs cited by Kirk may be visually more appealing, but their shape does not represent the only "correct" design. Philadelphia chairmakers used a variety of shapes for rear brackets, including both filleted and unfilleted ogees and quarter-rounds (or "hollows"). The laminated brackets on the Randolph chairs may thus imitate the shape of the integral ones that were there originally.

Character of line, liveliness of carving, and other subjective observations are problematic in determining age or authenticity. Surely, such judgments have their place, but they often express personal preferences rather than period tastes and furniture-making practices. In his book, Kirk used his well-trained and highly developed eye to great advantage in many instances, but he failed to enlighten in the case of the Randolph chairs. In support of his belief that these chairs are not period, he stated unequivocally that the "loose, serpentine [front seat rail] line . . . depends for effect upon the applied carving, [and] lacks character. The chair legs lack spring and strength of line." The front rail "line" has not been altered, and its serpentine shape has parallels on several other eighteenth-century Philadelphia chairs. The notion that this design "lacks character" has nothing to do with the chairs' age. Similarly, the profiles of the front legs match those of contemporary Philadelphia examples, some of which are considered exemplars of the rococo style. In fact, one can easily agree with Albert Sack's assessment that "the cabriole legs achieve a perfect curve" by looking past the incorrect repairs and by not allowing hasty and incomplete conclusions to discolor the "magnificence of this example." Kirk's analysis of the carving also centered around observations that were more subjective than objective. He stated that "the carving is not alive" and, although "correct in detail, [it is] spiritless in execution, like the work of a copyist." Whereas Kirk erred in suggesting that the carving is not period, his assessment may have been influenced by surface qualities stemming from previous restoration of the chairs.[10]

An armchair and a side chair in the Winterthur Museum shed light on Kirk's perspective by showing how our observations can be affected by the changes and alterations that furniture experiences over time. In *American*

Figure 11 Armchair, probably Delaware, 1760–1780. Mahogany. H. 39 1/2", W. 24 3/8". (Courtesy, Winterthur Museum.) The armchair is from the same set as the side chair illustrated in fig. 12.

Figure 12 Side chair, probably Delaware, 1760–1780. Mahogany. H. 38¹¹/₁₆", W. 23¹³/₁₆". (Courtesy, Winterthur Museum.) This chair has a history of ownership in the Crowe family of Odessa, Delaware.

Furniture: Queen Anne and Chippendale Periods (1952), Winterthur curator Joseph Downs described the armchair as one of the fullest expressions of the Gothic style in Philadelphia (fig. 11). He also noted that the chair lacked through-tenons and was "an exception to the rule of construction." Its splat design draws directly from English prototypes, although it appears more rigid and lacks some carved detail.[11]

In 1976, Winterthur was offered a set of three side chairs with the same splat design as a gift (see fig. 12). Most of the collections staff agreed that the chairs were out-of-period and cited one or more of the following reasons: their splats were too big, and the feet were too small; they lacked through-tenons; their corner blocks were made of mahogany or walnut rather than less expensive local secondary woods; their carving was flat and not representative of the

Figure 13 Detail of the inside rear rail of the armchair illustrated in fig. 11.

period. Poor finish and bleached color only exacerbated the physical evidence, but no reference was made to the armchair already in the collection.

Comparison of the side chairs to the armchair, however, reveals identical and distinctive construction practices. Shared features include mahogany corner blocks, blind rear tenons, unpinned seat rail joints, and an extra strip of mahogany applied to the inside rear rail below the shoe (fig. 13). This curious addition, presumably intended to stop the back of the slip seat, is constructed of two pieces of wood, joined in the center with a diagonal glue line. The splats of the armchair and side chairs were also laid out with the same splat template, a circumstance that accounts for the slightly oversized proportions of the side chair backs. Their splats were shortened at the base to accommodate their smaller dimensions. Slight variations between these patterns disappear when the template is reversed, indicating that the chairmaker must have flipped the template between tracing each splat.[12]

In *Grandeur on the Appoquinimink* (1959), John Sweeney reported the provenance of the side chairs and tied them to a document that in turn associates them with the armchair. An 1845 "List of the Residue of the Household Goods of Wm. Corbit, decd., which belongs to his daughter Sarah C. Spruance & Danl. Corbit" recorded "6 best Mahogany chairs & 2 arm chairs—divided—each took 4 of these chairs." This set must have had special meaning for the two siblings. It was divided equally, but all of the other furnishings were valued so that Daniel could buy out Sarah's share. The three Winterthur side chairs descended directly from Daniel to the donor. They are numbered "II," "IIII," and "V" on the inside top of the front seat rails. The armchair is similarly numbered "VII," establishing a sequence that supports its identification as part of the William Corbit furnishings divided in 1845.[13]

Further comparisons show how different histories of use and repair have affected the physical properties of the side chairs and armchair. Several repairs executed in a darker mahogany mar the appearance of the side chairs. Their crest rails also reveal that the repairer not only cleaned certain details

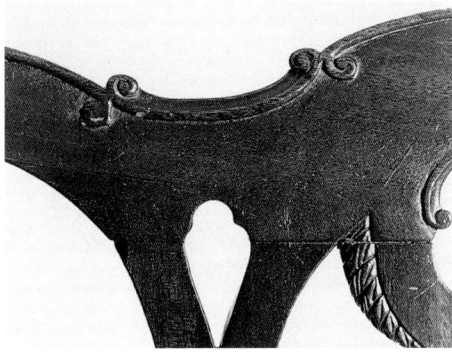

Figure 14 Detail of the crest rail of the armchair illustrated in fig. 11, showing the carved volutes.

Figure 15 Detail of the crest rail of the side chair illustrated in fig. 12, showing evidence of removed volutes.

but removed some of them completely. Although outlining cuts document their presence in the original carved design, small volutes that transform outlining beads into distended C scrolls have been removed from the inside edge (figs. 14, 15).

In comparison to the armchair, the side chair carving appears flat and lacking in richness of detail (figs. 16, 17). Criticism of the Randolph chair carving as "not alive . . . correct in detail but spiritless in execution, like the work of a copyist" fits the Corbit side chairs exactly. As with the Randolph chairs, the Corbit chairs tell a different story. Although the carving on the Corbit side chair is flatter and less detailed than that of the armchair, these qualities do not express the spiritlessness and misunderstanding of a copyist; rather, they probably result from harsh abrasion of the surface. This abrasion, which may have occurred at the same time as the aforementioned repairs and carving alterations, removed texture from the highlights, resulting in some loss of detail.

The precise nature of physical losses on the Randolph chairs is more difficult to assess. Perceptions of carving can be influenced by finish coatings applied to the wood. Subtle shifts in color and texture accentuate the topography of carving by reflecting light differently. Altering finishes changes the visual qualities of carving, which may result in the impression that wood has been lost as well. None of the Randolph chairs has its original finish. The Karolik chairs display a heavy, black, textured coating in crevices and carving recesses. The localized application of this finish and the abrupt transitions between coated and uncoated surfaces suggest that it did not erode naturally but was applied to recapture the appearance of age. Unfortunately, the sharp contrast in surface colors between the dark coating and cleaned areas has the opposite effect and makes the chairs look raw and abraded.

The Randolph chairs advertised by Kindig had their artificially blackened surface removed when they were refinished in the mid-1980s. Although the carving now has a relatively bright, homogenous surface, few would consider it "spiritless" or question its authenticity. In time, the finish on these chairs will age and become more subtle. Similarly, the finish on the Karolik chairs has softened and darkened noticeably over the twenty-five years since they were removed from exhibition.

Criticism of the labels on the Karolik and Kindig chairs must follow if the furniture is deemed to be out-of-period. In support of his claim that a genuine label was applied fraudulently, Kirk noted the lack of color variation on the wood where portions of the label had been lost and the presence of stain, presumably to simulate different oxidation patterns. In raising this issue, Kirk drew attention to an area of furniture connoisseurship that has received too little study. Despite the soundness of his assumptions—that shifts in the color of the wood should mark the original outline of the label—the wood around and underneath the edges of some other eighteenth-century labels fails to yield the expected patterns. Sometimes deep oxidation runs within the boundaries of period labels. The Randolph label on a side chair at Yale is one of several such examples. Also, the extent and

Figure 16 Detail of carved ornament on the splat of the armchair illustrated in fig. 11.

Figure 17 Detail of carved ornament on the splat of the side chair illustrated in fig. 12, showing abraded carving.

rate of color change caused by oxidation itself, which vary with changing environmental conditions and materials, are not well established. The staining on the inside rear rail of the Karolik chair, if it was applied to deceive, does not appear on the labeled example sold by Kindig. Some other cause may have resulted in this staining.[14]

Kirk's remaining comments regarding the Karolik chairs addressed broader issues of furniture history and interpretation. Citing three other chairs of "stripped-down quality," he stated that the Karolik examples do not resemble other Randolph labeled chairs and that the "super-refinement of [their] decoration" is out of character. He makes no mention of the labeled mate advertised by Kindig nor of the elaborate, labeled Randolph card table at Winterthur. Manuscript evidence, such as carving bills rendered to John Cadwalader, indicates that Randolph's shop produced some of the most elaborate work in Philadelphia. The implication that an eighteenth-century shopmaster such as Randolph could not supply furniture of different styles and tastes is at odds with Kirk's own observation that London-trained Thomas Affleck responded to consumer demands by supplying ornate and simple furniture in the rococo style after his arrival in Philadelphia in 1763.[15]

Rather than standing as contrary evidence, the labeled chairs are physical documents of Randolph's work and capabilities. They reflect a sense of immediacy that manuscript documentation can only approximate. Who today could describe the mahogany desk-and-bookcase for which Randolph charged Col. George Vaughan the substantial amount of £30 (far more than any single piece of furniture sold by Affleck to John Cadwalader) in 1765? And despite the many obvious differences between the design of the Karolik chairs and the simpler labeled Randolph chair at Yale, further study may one day reveal commonalities. One such shared feature is the unusual pronounced bead that encircles the upper part of the shoe at the base of the splat.[16]

Kirk concluded his discussion of the Randolph chairs with an analysis of their design that led him to suggest that other (authentic) chairs with these same backs should be attributed to Thomas Affleck. This point contributed nothing to the question of age and authenticity but introduced a new element of confusion. Kirk's reasoning centered around the English qualities of the chair back, the fact that Affleck trained in London, and the existence of similar crest rails on two other chairs attributed to Affleck. Whatever argument is advanced becomes moot upon acceptance of the Randolph chairs as authentic. Regardless of that outcome, however, the argument itself assumes that individual designs or motifs are emblematic of specific makers. Ample scholarship, including Kirk's own opinion expressed elsewhere, identifies the substantial weaknesses in this approach. Comparing the backs of the Randolph chairs with those having Affleck associations becomes yet another demonstration of the sharing of particular features of chair design—whether proportion or carved motif—throughout the Philadelphia furniture-making community.[17]

The physical evidence of early furniture is at once overtly real and covertly problematic. Detailed analysis of the Randolph chairs underscores how the structure of furniture history is dependent upon subjective observation. The physical evidence that survives today is the accumulation of actions starting from the time of original manufacture through all subsequent changes, intentional and unintentional. Although the layers of activity and their effect on the object can be separated in theory, sorting through whatever physical evidence remains is formidable and uncertain. Is carved work "lifeless" because it has lost its highlights through abrasion or because it was executed by someone copying, and not fully understanding, earlier work? How do surface qualities—altered years ago by refinishing, newly applied but intended to look older, or left undisturbed—influence comprehension of design attributes that lead to authenticating or rejecting a piece of furniture?

Furniture study, as with material culture studies in general, relies on a fundamental premise that made things are shaped and conditioned by people and are therefore expressive of those people's experiences and thoughts. Furniture and material culture scholars turn this formula around in the practice of history: Because people determine the physical properties of things, these same physical properties can be "read" to investigate the makers and users. Despite the beautiful symmetry of this theory, the language of objects is inexact and ambiguous. One of the many challenges facing students of early American furniture is to dissect the reasoning processes that transform a mute piece of furniture into a set of descriptions and evaluations.

1. Nicholas B. Wainwright, *Colonial Grandeur in Philadelphia: The House and Furniture of General John Cadwalader* (Philadelphia: Historical Society of Pennsylvania, 1964), pp. 19–20, 38–39, 116–19, 122–23. Robert C. Smith, "Finial Busts on Eighteenth-Century Philadelphia Furniture," *Antiques* 100, no. 6 (December 1971): 900–905; Robert C. Smith, "A Philadelphia Desk-and-Bookcase from Chippendale's *Director*," *Antiques* 103, no. 1 (January 1973): 128–35.

2. John Kirk, *American Chairs: Queen Anne and Chippendale* (New York: Alfred A. Knopf, 1972), pp. 172–74. Philip D. Zimmerman, "A Methodological Study in the Identification of Some Important Philadelphia Chippendale Furniture," in *American Furniture and Its Makers: Winterthur Portfolio 13*, edited by Ian M. G. Quimby (Chicago: University of Chicago Press, 1979), pp. 193–208. The appearance on the market and record-breaking performance of several pieces of Cadwalader furniture reinforced the cachet of Affleck's name during the 1980s. Mark Anderson, Gregory Landrey, and Philip D. Zimmerman, *Cadwalader Study* (Winterthur, Del.: Winterthur Museum, 1995). See, for example, Luke Beckerdite, "Philadelphia Carving Shops, Part I: James Reynolds," *Antiques* 125, no. 5 (May 1984): 1120–33; "Philadelphia Carving Shops, Part II: Bernard and Jugiez," *Antiques* 128, no. 3 (September 1985): 498–513; and "Philadelphia Carving Shops, Part III: Hercules Courtney and His School," *Antiques* 131, no. 5 (May 1987): 1044–63.

3. Edwin J. Hipkiss, *Eighteenth-Century American Arts: The M. and M. Karolik Collection* (Cambridge, Mass.: Harvard University Press for the Museum of Fine Arts, Boston, 1941), pp. 152–53, no. 89; and Albert Sack, *Fine Points of Furniture: Early American* (New York: Crown Publishers, 1950), p. 37. Sack dropped the reference to the Randolph labeled chair in his revised edition of 1993.

4. Patricia E. Kane, *300 Years of American Seating Furniture: Chairs and Beds from the Mabel Brady Garvan and Other Collections at Yale University* (Boston, Mass.: New York Graphic Society, 1976), p. 106, no. 90; *Antiques* 43, no. 1 (January 1943): inside front cover.

5. Francis J. Puig, "Questionables" and nos. 124–25 in *The Eye of the Beholder: Fakes, Replicas and Alterations in American Art* (New Haven, Conn.: Yale University Art Gallery, 1977), pp. 86–88.

6. Kirk, *American Chairs*, p. 172. He identified only three of the five chairs as those included in his book (nos. 80–82). Kane published a likely fourth, namely no. 92, in *300 Years*. The fifth chair is not identified. Objective and subjective observations parallel "intrinsic" and "extrinsic" evidence discussed in Zimmerman, "A Methodological Study," pp. 194–95.

7. A small group of case pieces from an anonymous Philadelphia cabinetmaking shop have carved appliqués that are intermittently outlined with gouge or parting tool cuts (see William McPherson Hornor, *Blue Book, Philadelphia Furniture* [Philadelphia: By the author, 1935], pp. 112–13, pls. 141, 145). A somewhat similar instance of in-filling after the fact that seems to be original work occurs in a dressing table discussed in Philip D. Zimmerman, "The Art and Science of Furniture Connoisseurship," *Antiques* 152, no. 1 (July 1997): 98–99.

8. Parke-Bernet Galleries, *Important American Eighteenth Century Cabinetwork, Decorative Objects, Notable Currier & Ives Prints: Property of the Estate of the Late Reginald Lewis*, New York, March 24–25, 1961, lot 248.

9. This conclusion makes moot Kirk's point "8" that construction of the front rail decoration indicates attempts to save wood, which he maintained is not an eighteenth-century practice in American furniture making. See below for further comment.

10. Sack, *Fine Points*, p. 37.

11. Joseph Downs, *American Furniture: Queen Anne and Chippendale Periods* (1952; reprint, New York: Viking Press, 1967), no. 44. For an English example, see Christie's, *Fine English Furniture*, London, Thursday, November 14, 1991, sale 4652, lot 47.

12. Philip D. Zimmerman, "Workmanship as Evidence: A Model for Object Study," *Winterthur Portfolio* 16, no. 4 (winter 1981): 300 n. 43, figs. 19–20.

13. The chairs descended from William Corbit to Daniel Corbit in 1845, to Daniel Wheeler Corbit in 1877, to Sara Corbit Levis, and to Mrs. Earle R. Crowe. John A. H. Sweeney, *Grandeur on the Appoquinimink: The House of William Corbit at Odessa, Delaware* (Newark, Del.: University of Delaware Press, 1959), pp. 101, 110–12. One of the chairs is illustrated as plate 4, Appendix I. Although the side chairs may be among the "6 Mahogany chairs" valued at $12.00 in William Corbit's 1818 estate inventory, no appropriate listing appears for the armchairs (see pp. 102–5).

14. Illustrated as fig. 108a in Kane, *300 Years*, p. 129. Dozens of labeled looking glasses afford other examples.

15. *Antiques* 47, no. 1 (January 1943), inside front cover. The card table was first published in Charles F. Hummel, "Queen Anne and Chippendale Furniture in the Henry Francis du Pont Winterthur Museum, Part III," *Antiques* 99, no. 1 (January 1971): 106, figs. 16, 17. Kirk may not have known about the card table at Winterthur until after writing his book. Wainwright, *Colonial Grandeur*, see index. Kirk, *American Chairs*, p. 166.

16. Benjamin Randolph to Col. George Vaughan, April 2, 1765, photostat, Downs Manuscript and Microfilm Collection, Winterthur. Visible in fig. 108a in Kane, *300 Years*, p. 129.

17. For English and other regional expressions of this chair back design, see John T. Kirk, *American Furniture and the British Tradition to 1830* (New York: Alfred A. Knopf, 1982), figs. 948–58; and Brock Jobe, *Portsmouth Furniture: Masterworks from the New Hampshire Seacoast* (Boston, Mass.: Society for the Preservation of New England Antiquities, 1993), nos. 82–83, pp. 310–12. For the Affleck-attributed chairs, Kirk cites Hornor, *Blue Book*, pls. 260 and 265. Kirk, *American Chairs*, pp. 14 nos. 6, 166.

Appendix

For ease of reference, each of Kirk's points are summarized and presented in the order they appear in *American Chairs*. Original wording is set off in italics; my comments follow.

1. *On both chairs all corner blocks are of new stained pine.* Corner blocks on all four chairs are replacements. These replacements partially cover screw holes and surface evidence that indicate that iron braces once reinforced the joints. Any evidence of original or early corner blocks is covered by the present replacements.

2. *Both seat frames are of oak, not nearly as common as pine.* None of the seat frames may be original. Original slipseat frames get separated from the chairs for which they were made for a variety of reasons. Repeated upholsterings and insertion of metal straps or wood boards to reinforce sagging seats are among several actions that accelerate damage to old slip seats. Antiques collectors and dealers occasionally reuse eighteenth-century seat frames from other chairs or merely make new ones.

3. *The knee brackets are not applied with large-headed, hand-made nails as was standard in Philadelphia, but show wooden pegs, which are perhaps plugs covering screws (these may be original, not a later addition).* Wedge-shaped, hand-forged nails lose their holding ability once they have been loosened. Upon removal of these brackets for other restoration purposes, another fastener, most likely a screw, was used in place of the ineffective nails. The restorer opted to hide the screw head with a wooden plug.

4. *The C-scroll carving on the front seat rails is applied, rather than carved from the solid as is standard in Philadelphia.* This applied carving is an improper restoration.

5. *The outside ends of the C scroll, where they fall below the seat rail, are backed by applied pieces rather than by the extension of the rail itself, not a Philadelphia practice.* As with the C-scroll tips that these applied pieces support, they are later and improper restorations. This applied backing was never installed on one side of one of the chairs sold by Kindig.

6. *There is a groove carved above the carved scroll edging to make it appear deeper, an unusual practice for the eighteenth century.* Originally, this groove did not enhance a decorative motif, rather it functioned alone as the decorative motif. The groove is filled with bits of mahogany where it extends horizontally toward the sides of the chair beyond the present applied C scroll.

7. *The rear shaping of the side rails is a separate piece of wood and is an uninspired curve.* The present construction of the rear end of each side rail, being made of two pieces of wood, is not original and makes no structural or design sense. For some reason, unknown and perhaps unknowable, the restorer reattached all of the side rails to the rear stiles using this two-piece technique. Determining whether the curve of this inconsequential element is

inspired and using that judgment as an indicator of period workmanship is not persuasive reasoning.

8. *Points 5 through 7 show an attempt to save wood not customary in Philadelphia or indeed in American work of the eighteenth century.* Since points 5 through 7 represent later and improper restorations, they cannot be held to a standard of eighteenth-century practices.

9. *The height of the through tenons is 3/4 of an inch less than the side seat rail, whereas usually they are nearly the same depth.* Indeed, the majority of through-tenons are approximately as high as the seat rails from which they are cut, but exceptions are common enough that they cannot be used to suggest out-of-period work.

10. *The rear of the horizontal shaping, which is a separate piece like a bracket respond, is applied with a through tenon—not normal on Philadelphia eighteenth-century Chippendale chairs.* This observation essentially duplicates point 7.

11. *The carving is not alive; that is, it is correct in detail but spiritless in execution, like the work of a copyist.* Words like "alive," "spirited," "inspired," and "lacking in character" are judgmental labels that may result from detailed analysis. On their own merits, however, they do not convey specific information or values and are not effective in communicating a clear argument or set of reasons that can lead the reader from one level of understanding to another.

12. *The front seat rail is shaped to a loose, serpentine line, with its higher corners rather flat, and depends for effect upon the applied carving. The line itself lacks character.* This point represents a classic error in subjective reasoning, an approach that projects values onto the object or issue in question. The serpentine line Kirk criticized is a product of eighteenth-century, high-style Philadelphia chairmaking. If the line lacks character, then character cannot be a measure of eighteenth-century work.

13. [In comparison to the Karolik high chest] *the legs lack spring and strength of line and the carving is far less inspired; for example, all the leafage springs from one point.* This point, as with point 12, is a statement of personal design preference. Aesthetic judgments and comparisons have their place in furniture history and appreciation, but they may lead to incorrect results if they are the sole or primary basis for identification and authentication. The statement about leafage springing from one point, for example, seems undermined by the fact that one of Kirk's "control" chairs of a similar design also employs this general pattern (see Patricia E. Kane, *300 Years of American Seating Furniture: Chairs and Beds from the Mabel Brady Garvan and Other Collections at Yale University* [Boston, Mass.: New York Graphic Society, 1976], no. 91; no. 90 is another variant).

14. *No variation in oxidation appears in areas where the label has worn or torn off, and stain appears to have been applied with the intent to deceive.* Authenti-

cating original application of a label on an object is an inexact process. Several other labels on furniture also lack oxidation patterns that outline the original label size. The need to argue that the label was attached fraudulently disappears if the chair is accepted as eighteenth-century work. Although the rear rail has stain on it, the presence of the stain is not sufficient to discredit the label. Intent to deceive is not inherent in the pattern of staining.

15. *In approach to design, the chairs do not resemble the other known labeled Randolph chairs.* [Other Randolph labeled chairs are of] *"stripped-down quality"*; [the] *"super-refinement of decoration"* [of this chair is out of character]. Eighteenth-century furniture makers supplied customers with a variety of designs. Other documented furniture as well as ample written evidence establish that Randolph was capable of making chairs as ornate and well proportioned as these. Despite the obvious differences in design, the Karolik and Yale labeled chairs share the same unusual beaded shoe design.

16. *The back design of the Garvan and Boston chairs is English in its breadth and general treatment and corresponds to the Affleck-Penn chair shown in plate 260 of Hornor, . . .* [making] *it natural to attribute* [chairs of this design] *tentatively to Affleck.* This point contributes little if anything to the question of age and authenticity. The observation is predicated on the assumption that individual designs or motifs are emblematic of specific makers. Ample scholarship indicates that most designs, these among them, were used by more than one maker or shop.

Nancy Goyne Evans

The Christian M. Nestell Drawing Book: A Focus on the Ornamental Painter and His Craft in Early Nineteenth-Century America

The Life and Career of Christian M. Nestell

Christian Michael Nestell was eighteen years old when he attended an unidentified school or academy in New York City for three semesters in 1811–1812 to obtain instruction in ornamental painting. A drawing/copy book of pencil and watercolor ornament that bears his name survives from this period and is the subject of this study (fig. 1).[1]

Nestell was born to Christian I. and Mary (Swan) Nestell on February 10, 1793. The elder Nestell is listed variously as a baker, grocer, flour inspector, or flour merchant in city directories before his death in 1822 or 1823. Many years later, he was identified as being of German birth in the death record of Christian Michael. Records of the Nestell (also Nestle) family in America are few. A Michael Nestell (d. 1772) and family emigrated from Germany, probably Wittenburg, sometime between 1753 and 1756, although a direct link between that family and Christian I. Nestell has yet to be established.[2]

The United States census for 1790 describes the Christian I. Nestell household as containing two males sixteen years or older, a male under sixteen years, and a female. The second adult male likely was an apprentice or journeyman in the family bakery, and the male child probably was an older brother of Christian Michael. Early twentieth-century Masonic records identify a John J. Nestell as a nephew of Christian Michael and the donor of his uncle's Masonic "jewels, papers, and other . . . relics" to the Nestell Lodge, No. 37, A.F. and A.M., of Providence, Rhode Island, about 1916–1917. During his lifetime, John may also have been the keeper of his uncle's drawing book. The document was offered at auction in 1982 from an unknown consignor.[3]

Handwritten notations in Nestell's drawing book describe a period of instruction extending from June 1, 1811, to March 9, 1812, the time divided into three, three-month semesters. Nestell had his nineteenth birthday during this period. Whether other notebooks and related papers once accompanied this document is unknown, although it seems unlikely that a notebook of later date ever existed. A brief biographical sketch of Nestell in an

Figure 1 Detail of the front cover of the Christian M. Nestell *Drawing Book*, New York City, 1811–1812. Ink on paper boards with leather. 15⁵⁄₁₆" × 10". (Courtesy, Winterthur Museum Library.)

early twentieth-century Masonic publication states that he "served in the War of 1812 in New York when 19 years old."[4]

New York was a leading American seaport in 1811–1812 and supported a large craft community, as confirmed in city directories published annually. The population of the urban center was 96,000 by 1810, rising to almost 124,000 in another decade. During a visit to New York in 1811, Timothy Dwight, president of Yale College, described the city's superiority as a trade center:

> The advantages of a commercial nature possessed by New York are unrivaled on this side of the Atlantic. . . . The harbor . . . is capable of containing the greatest number of ships which will ever be assembled in one place, with sufficient depth of water and good anchorage. . . . There are between three and four hundred vessels . . . employed continually on [the] Hudson River throughout the mild season. The quantity of property floating on this stream exceeds beyond comparison that which moves on any other river in the eastern section of the United States. New York is fast becoming . . . the market town for the whole American coast from St. Marys [Georgia] to Cape Cod. The foreign commerce of this city is carried on with every part of the world. . . . The bustle in the streets, the perpetual activity of the carts, the noise and hurry at the docks which on three sides encircle the city; the sound of saws, axes, and hammers at the shipyards; the . . . numerous buildings rising in almost every part of it, and the multitude of workmen employed upon them form as lively a specimen of "the busy hum of populous cities" as can be imagined.[5]

Potential candidates for Christian M. Nestell's instructor are numerous and represent several related occupations, as identified principally in city directories for 1811 and 1812: chair, coach, ornamental, or sign painter; gilder; japanner; miniature and portrait painter; watercolorer; artist; picture maker; and proprietor of a drawing or painting academy or school. Some artisans retitled their occupation from year to year, and others appeared and disappeared in the listings on an annual basis. Seventy-seven candidates who emerged from the records were identified on a facsimile map of lower Manhattan dating from the early nineteenth century. Only a few are located north of the residence and business site maintained from 1811 to 1814 by Nestell's father on Fourth Street (probably now Allen Street) near Hester, a location just east of the Bowery Road and south of the present-day approach to the Williamsburg Bridge to Brooklyn. From 1808 to 1810, the Nestell family had resided nearby at 68 Harman Street.[6]

Slightly fewer than half the instructor candidates on the list resided within a fifteen-block walk of the Nestell residence. All the occupations noted are represented except that of japanner. Only one academy falls within the boundaries of this region, and it is located on the fringe. By contrast, thirteen gilders plied their trade in the neighborhood. Nestell also could have trained beyond the general vicinity of his home with an artisan residing at the tip of Manhattan or in a neighborhood along the Hudson River. The existence of a drawing book suggests that the young man enjoyed the formality of academy training, yet the nature and quality of the designs suggest the influence of a sign and/or ornamental painter.

Nestell's possession of a drawing book raises questions other than the identity of his instructor: Was this the only training the future ornamental

Figure 2 Advertisement of Christian M. Nestell, *Providence Patriot*, Providence, Rhode Island, February 26, 1820. (Courtesy, University of Delaware Library.)

painter and gilder received? Did he pursue this training every day during the period described? Did he train earlier or concurrently in another, possibly a complementary, craft, such as chairmaking? Providing some insight into the conduct of academy training (if such was the route taken by Nestell) are early nineteenth-century advertisements of Archibald Robertson, proprietor of the Columbian Academy of Painting and Drawing on Liberty Street, a location on Manhattan's tip near City Hall and the well-known Tontine Coffee House. Robertson offered classes on Tuesdays, Thursdays, and Saturdays. Ladies attended in the afternoon, and gentlemen, from 6 PM to 8 PM. Private tuition at home also was available.[7]

Following his training in ornamental painting, Nestell dropped from sight in the records. Army enlistments covering the period of the War of 1812 are silent on the subject of his supposed military service, although at best the records are incomplete. More important is the young artisan's whereabouts following the war and before 1820 when he settled in Providence, Rhode Island. Perhaps Nestell remained in New York and practiced the trade of ornamental painter as a journeyman or assisted his father in the flour business. Residing with his employer or his family could explain the absence of Nestell's name from city directories. About 1820, the elder Nestell suffered financial reverses, as documented in a creditor agreement dated January 8, 1821. If young Nestell was still in the city, this circumstance may have prompted his relocation to Providence.[8]

The first reference to Christian M. Nestell in Providence, which was for payment of $15 for "Quarter Shop Rent" to the Proud brothers on February 17, 1820, almost coincides with his earliest newspaper notice of February 26 stating that he had "taken the Store formerly occupied by Samuel and Daniel Proud, nearly opposite the Rev. Mr. Wilson's meeting-house" on Broad Street (fig. 2). Nestell's merchandise consisted of "a general assortment of painted and gilt Windsor CHAIRS." Whether the craftsman both framed and applied finish to his stock or purchased framed chairs "in the wood" to paint, ornament, and gild is unclear, as is Nestell's arrangement with the Prouds, who were turners and chairmakers. The brothers' accounts record "Shop Rent," suggesting that Nestell occupied part of their manufacturing facility, whereas the advertisement describes a store vacated by the brothers. Although the shop and store addresses appear to be the same (replace "nearly opposite" in the advertisement with "set over nearly against"), the Prouds still actively pursued their trade. When their Broad Street structure was erected in the 1790s next to the Abbot Parade, which in turn was adjacent to the meetinghouse, it was described as a house and shop (fig. 3). Apparently, in 1820 the Prouds continued to work in a freestanding shop on the property and rented the first floor of the house to Nestell. Houses in this period frequently served dual functions as work/retail and dwelling spaces. Notable also is the absence of charges for finished or unfinished chairs, except for a few odd purchases, in the Prouds' accounts with Nestell. Instead, the records describe minor repairs, adding rockers to eight chairs, bottoming a few rush-seat chairs, fabricating three "high seats," and Nestell's purchase of "a narrow ax."[9]

Figure 3 Detail of the Daniel Anthony map of Providence, Rhode Island, 1823. Engraving on paper. 23 1/2" × 33 5/8". (Courtesy, Rhode Island Historical Society Library.)

Nestell Main Street shop
Proud house and shop
Abbot Parade
Rev. Wilson's church
Nestell residence
New Market

Figure 4 Advertisement of Christian M. Nestell, *Providence Patriot*, Providence, Rhode Island, August 28, 1822. (Courtesy, University of Delaware Library.)

The second, and possibly last, Nestell advertisement dates more than two years later to August 28, 1822, and announces the removal of his "Chair Ware Room and Shop" to 112 South Main Street, an address on the opposite side of the Providence River (figs. 3, 4). Again, interpretation is open to speculation. Both the old and the new facility appear to have had an area set off for use as a work space—possibly a chairmaking shop, a painting room, or both. Like the first notice, this one is illustrated with a woodcut of a Windsor armchair bearing the craftsman's initials on the top of the seat. By 1822 Nestell had expanded his stock to include both fancy and Windsor chairs. The "common" chairs identified in the notice heading were either cheap Windsors or rush-bottom slat-back chairs, a type still used at that date in kitchens. A further term—"high back"—appears to describe slat-back seating. The wood-seat rocking chair, another item, was soaring into popularity in this period.

The population of Providence when Nestell moved there about 1820 was just under 12,000. The Providence River divided the community into two almost equal parts connected by a bridge. Main Street lies close to the eastern side of the river and runs parallel with it (fig. 3). Brown University (established 1770) and the First Baptist Meeting House were prominent structures on the rising land above the river. Samuel Breck, visiting from Philadelphia in 1826, also observed that "some of the handsomest houses in the United States are in the town of Providence." Two years earlier, Anne Newport Royall, an inveterate traveler, commented on the flourishing state of the community and noted its extensive trade with the East Indies. Other foreign destinations, as reported in newspapers of the period, included Europe, Africa, the West Indies, South America, and the Orient. Domestic trade existed from Penobscot Bay to New Orleans, and passenger steamboats connected the community with New York, Boston, New London, Norwich, and Fall River. The Blackstone Canal, linking the inland town of

Figure 5 Windsor side chair, Christian M. Nestell, Providence, Rhode Island, 1820–1822. Woods unknown. H. 33 1/4", W. 17 3/4" (crest), D. 15" (seat). (Private collection; photo, Winterthur Museum.)

Figure 6 Detail of the label on the bottom of the chair illustrated in fig. 5.

Figure 7 Windsor side chair by Christian M. Nestell, Providence, Rhode Island, 1825–1835. Woods and dimensions unknown. (Private collection; photo, Winterthur Museum.)

Worcester, Massachusetts, with Providence, was begun in 1825. Considerable capital had been diverted to manufacturing by this date, with the production of cotton and woolen cloth as a substantial industry. Other leading manufactures were machinery for the textile mills, jewelry, metalwares, and leather products.[10]

Windsor side chairs of two patterns are documented as coming from the shop/store of Christian Nestell. The earliest pattern, represented by three chairs from a set produced when the craftsman was located on Broad Street, has a slat back framed with three arrowlike spindles known during the period as "flat sticks" (fig. 5). The chairs retain their original peach-colored surface paint and leafy ornament executed in red and dark green. A paper label on the bottom of one plank is embellished with the same cut of a slat-back, flat-spindle armchair that appears in Nestell's advertisements (fig. 6). The shield-type seat is better modeled than the plank in a later Nestell slat-back chair framed at the back with ball-type spindles (fig. 7). Painted pencilwork and heavy banding were required to give definition to the relatively shapeless, flat-sided seat of the second pattern. The bamboo-work of the legs in the two designs is about the same. The stenciled identification of the maker within a large oval border on the plank bottom of the ball-spindle chair includes an address on Main Street (fig. 3).

The few manuscript references that identify the nature of business at Nestell's shop/store after his relocation to Main Street describe basic activity in the painting and ornamenting trade. His known customers were individuals of prominence. For Richard Ward Greene, Esq., United States district attorney for Rhode Island and later chief justice of the state, Nestell varnished a bureau and repaired a "large wash Table" in 1827. Other recorded activity focuses on chairwork. Edward Carrington, a merchant in the China trade, sought Nestell's services several times between 1824 and 1826 for repairs, painting, and gilding. Another China-trade merchant, Sullivan Dorr, had chairs painted in 1826. When the work was completed, Nestell arranged for their delivery to Dorr's mansion on Benefit Street.[11]

Nestell sought the patronage of other merchants, noting in his second advertisement that he could provide shippers with any quantity of chairs for export. He also was able to supply cabinetwork, although the wording of this item suggests he acted in the capacity of a broker rather than as a craftsman (fig. 4). Ornamental painting and gilding appear to have been Nestell's principal focus when not retailing furniture.

A survey of advertisements by other Providence craftsmen in the ornamental painting trade during the 1820s is enlightening. As a companion activity to ornamental and plain painting, many craftsmen offered oil and water gilding. Surfaces finished by the first method could be burnished to a high luster. Picture and looking glass frames were the usual products, and re-gilding was as brisk a business as new gilding. In a directory advertisement of 1830, Samuel J. Bower added another dimension to the business: "Vanes and ball for Churches and Factories, and Spires for Lightning-Rods gilded in a superior style and with the best of gold."[12]

Ornamental painting encompassed a variety of tasks and mediums. Nestell's principal focus, understandably, was painting and ornamenting new furniture. When wood surfaces became worn or marred, families could have "their Chairs re-painted and gilt upon fair terms" (fig. 4). Samuel Bower and others in the trade paid "particular attention to the painting of Military Standards," which appear to have been in considerable demand by local militia groups. Bower also was a source for "Ships' Colours made and Painted in the best manner, and at short notice." Since Providence was a thriving, moderate-sized seaport, requests for these colorful ensigns must have been brisk. Another substantial arm of the business was the supply of Masonic banners and aprons and "other symbolic representations of masonry." As a dedicated, lifelong member of the brotherhood, Nestell likely enjoyed good patronage in this branch of his trade.[13]

Another principal thrust in ornamental painting was the production of signs. Given the flourishing economy and population growth of early nineteenth-century Providence, the constantly changing arrangements in business, and the toll extracted by weather conditions on outdoor fixtures, demand must have been constant. Craftsmen offered "signs of every description"—ornamental, plain, and gilded—"executed in the neatest manner and at short notice." To guarantee timely delivery, William M. Pitman stocked an assortment of semi-finished boards "of almost any pattern." For his part, Samuel Bower counseled potential customers to look around them, since "specimens of his work may be seen on almost every building in town." One of the principal uses of gilding on signs was for lettering.

Bower also offered "smalted" signs. In his comprehensive series on "House Paints in Colonial America," Richard M. Candee ascertained that this powder blue pigment was used primarily "by strewing it on any ground of oil-paint; where it makes a bright warm blue shining surface." A popular use was over gilded lettering.[14]

Other applications of the ornamenter's art in the daily life of Providence include a miscellany of items. William Pitman advertised that he painted fire buckets. The name of the fire company, the date, and the initials or name of the owner could be accompanied by an appropriate decorative device or scene. In 1829, Henry Wilder Miller of neighboring Worcester billed that town for "Painting and Figuring 16 Fire Buckets." Painters also stood ready to supply cloth bags stenciled with identification for the removal of valuables from the home in the event of fire. In another medium, John S. Barrow executed "Coats of Arms . . . in the best stile" for framing and hanging on the wall. These symbols of family status were popular in Boston during the first quarter of the nineteenth century, just as they had been decades earlier when George Davidson painted "a Coate of arms Complete" for a member of the Oliver family. To celebrate special events, community groups and private organizations often requested the ornamental painter to fabricate one or more transparencies for illumination. Samuel Bowers painted "Transparenc[i]es of all descriptions, on silk or linen." Either cloth was finely woven so that when light passed through it the scene, ornament, or device was displayed to advantage.[15]

Ornamental painters produced glass mats for many types of pictures, including watercolors, drawings, prints, and needlework. Borders were enameled in an opaque color and "lettered in Gold or Bronze," as requested. In addition, some decorators such as Kinsley C. Gladding were prepared to supply "Magic Lantern Glasses, transparent or opaque," and "Timepiece and Looking-Glass Tablets in gold, silver, or colors." Householders called for a variety of items to be varnished to preserve the surface. Gladding varnished and framed prints and watercolors. In 1824, William Pitman offered the community "maps of the town of Providence neatly varnished." The following year he suggested to customers that he varnish the "trimmings on furniture . . . to prevent tarnishing and getting soiled."[16]

It is unknown whether Christian Nestell ever decorated coaches, wagons, and other vehicles, as did Whipple and Low at their shop on Andrews' wharf; however, New York directory listings of 1811–1812 indicate that the trades of coach painter and ornamental painter usually were separate. Nestell was more likely to have practiced the art of wood graining, particularly on furnishings, front doors, and interior woodwork. In 1826, William Pitman offered "Mahogany, Satin wood, Rose wood, Oaks, and Marble neatly imitated." Several ornamental painters broadened their services. Kinsley Gladding provided customers with "Views of Country Seats and other Buildings" and offered "Mourning pieces painted in India ink or colors." Both Gladding and Sanford Mason also had equipment to produce profiles. Gladding cut his figures "with exactness," whereas Mason painted his profiles on glass or paper.[17]

From time to time craftsmen from outside the community provided competition for local painters. Two artisans whose work is well known today are cases in point. John Ritto Penniman, an accomplished artist, advertised a full range of services, from ornamenting military standards to painting landscapes, in a Providence newspaper notice of June 1822. He gave his address as Orange Street, Boston, "at the sign of the Painter's Arms." Rufus Porter visited Providence the same year and took up residence at Wesson's Coffee House, where he showed a specimen of his work. He offered "to paint walls of rooms in elegant *full colors,* Landscape Scenery, at prices less than the ordinary expense of papering." He pointed out that "spending the gloomy winter months amidst pleasant groves and verdant fields" would be uplifting.[18]

Providence directories beginning with the first volume in 1824 through 1836 locate Nestell's store at 111 (1824) or 109 South Main Street. His residence remained on the opposite side of the river. The sixteen years from 1820 to 1835–36 may define the extent of Nestell's career as an independent ornamental painter and gilder. Beginning in 1837, city directories refer to him as a bank clerk; from 1847 he is listed without an occupation. Masonic records describe Nestell as "a diligent and successful worker at his trade, that of painter and gilder," without mention of another occupation. Nestell's death record of 1880 also describes him as a chair painter. Perhaps beginning in the mid-1840s the craftsman returned to his trade, working as a journeyman in the shop of another master.[19]

Nestell apparently never owned land. He evidently built his "chair establishment," described as a "building measuring eighteen feet front by forty back," on land that he leased on Main Street. On October 20, 1835, Nestell sold the shop to one William Haslett for $350. (Nestell is listed as proprietor of the shop in the 1836 directory; however, the survey for the directory probably occurred before he sold the building to Haslett.) The only other deed located for Nestell is dated April 18, 1831, describing his purchase of three shares in the Providence New Market Association. The association owned a piece of land containing a building called the New Market, located at the juncture of Pawtuxet and High Streets. This site probably was less than a block from Nestell's first chair store on Broad Street.[20]

As indicated, Nestell became a resident of Providence early in 1820, if not during the last months of 1819. He quickly joined the Masonic fraternity and through this connection likely met his wife, Betsey Horton Bosworth, daughter of Asa Bosworth, "a prominent and respected Mason." Nestell married in 1821, although his happiness was short-lived. Betsey died on October 30, 1822, leaving one son. Nestell never remarried. Providence municipal records dating from 1827 to 1852 show that he was taxed on personal property that ranged in value from $500–1,000 in the early years and from $2,000–2,500 beginning in 1843. The amounts are respectable for a man with a trade who owned no real estate. Nestell's family obligations were also minimal. The craftsman held at least one public office, that of clerk of Ward No. 5 in 1832. He appears to have remained outside the ranks of the popular Providence Association of Mechanics and Manufacturers whose

Figure 8 Photograph of Christian M. Nestell. Frontispiece of *Nestell Lodge, No. 37, A.F. and A.M., Providence, Rhode Island, Fiftieth Anniversary Celebration, 1880–1930* (Providence: By the lodge, 1930). (Courtesy, Rhode Island Historical Society Library.)

notices appeared regularly in local newspapers, usually accompanied by the device of a workman's upraised arm grasping a hammer. The craftsman died on February 26, 1880, age 87 years, 16 days. He was survived by his son and two married granddaughters.[21]

Nestell had a long and respected association with Freemasonry in Rhode Island. He was admitted to Mount Vernon Lodge, No. 4, of Providence in September 1820. Three years later he became both a Royal Arch Mason and a Knight Templar. In 1826, Nestell was elected Worshipful Master of the Mount Vernon Lodge where he served for a term of two years. Over the years other degrees and offices followed as he continued to rise in the American Rite. Nestell remained a staunch supporter of the tenants of Freemasonry during the difficult years of the anti-Masonic movement in America in the late 1820s and early 1830s. At the craftsman's death, the Grand Chaplin conducted the church service, and later the Templar burial service was read. Attendance at the funeral was large, the numbers swelled by the presence of many members of the fraternity. Nestell's death occurred at a time when a new local lodge was forming in Providence. On March 4, 1880, it was constituted as the Nestell Lodge, No. 37, "to perpetuate the memory of . . . brother Christian M. Nestell." In 1930 the lodge celebrated its fiftieth anniversary and marked the occasion by publishing a commemorative booklet. A photograph of Nestell forms the frontispiece (fig. 8).[22]

The Christian M. Nestell Drawing Book: Design Sources
The Nestell drawing book is a modest volume bound in plain paper boards with a leather spine and corners. The owner's name is penned in black ink on the front cover (fig. 1) and on several pages. The pagination includes eighty-two numbers, the first two forming a double-page format, the rest identifying the right-hand page only. The inside back cover is numbered 83. The laid paper that forms the leaves is watermarked with two devices: a fleur-de-lis within a cartouche surmounted by a crown, the date "1802" below the cartouche, and the word "IPING" above the date "1802." The first mark is a type referred to in the trade as a "Strasburg Lily." The second mark identifies the name of the mill and its location in Sussex, England.[23]

Pencil and watercolor is the medium of the eighty ornaments comprising the body of the drawing book. (Page 66 was removed at an unknown date; another page was "lost" in misnumbering.) Slightly more than half the ornaments (forty-one in number, or 51 percent) are represented by two complete or nearly complete drawings—the instructor's original and the student's competent copy. Another group of fifteen ornaments (19 percent) is incomplete; the student copy is executed fully or partially in pencil without color. As many as twenty-four ornaments (30 percent) are single units representing the work of the instructor only. Perhaps copies of some of these ornaments were made originally on loose sheets of paper now lost. The sequence of designs in the drawing book gives little hint of a structured progression from elementary to complex work. Several drawings that rely on perspective, detail, and shading as critical elements appear at the beginning of the sequence, whereas simple, flat, two-dimensional border patterns

Figure 9 Page 4 (top) of the Nestell *Drawing Book*. Pencil and watercolor on laid paper.

are intermixed throughout the book. Subject matter covers a broad spectrum: land and water scapes; animals, birds, and insects; floral forms and fruits; shells; geometric borders; trophies; classical, mythological, and patriotic subjects; and grained grounds.

Publications dealing with the arts, from theory and practical instruction to material preparation and technique, were common in the late eighteenth and early nineteenth centuries. Some popular titles achieved many editions. Among prominent spokesmen was Thomas Sheraton, whose books of furniture design were consulted widely. He and others advised students of ornamental drawing to obtain a good grounding in perspective—the art of representing natural objects as they appear to the eye in respect to their relative distance and positions—and in geometrical drawing—the management of straight lines, curved lines, and angles. Proficiency in ornamental drawing was achieved through extensive copywork to master line and shade and to become acquainted with a broad range of subjects.[24]

Many drawing and needlework schools that flourished in federal-era America had a collection of visual materials that instructors and students consulted for inspiration or used for copywork. Prints were a popular medium, the subject matter often drawn from Biblical, allegorical, mythological, literary, and historical sources. Imported engravings by George Morland and by Francesco Bartolozzi after paintings by Angelica Kauffmann were especially sought. Drawings along with illustrations in books imported from England and France were available to students at the academy of Mrs. Saunders and Miss Beach in Dorchester, Massachusetts. Miss Beach likely inherited the library from her father, who had emigrated from Bristol, England, about 1793. The Reverend William Bentley of Salem had an opportunity to examine one of the library's volumes of natural history and found it "ornamented with figures highly coloured."[25]

Alexander Robertson, proprietor of a painting and drawing academy in New York, had a London correspondent in 1802 who was "particularly attentive in sending every publication of merit tending to the improvement of the young pupil or interesting and valuable to the scholar more advanced." Robertson also had a collection of sketches that he had made during "various tours through the United States and Canada." The same year his brother, Archibald Robertson, who directed the Columbian Academy

Figure 10 Page 54 (top) of the Nestell *Drawing Book.*

Figure 11 Page 5 (top) of the Nestell *Drawing Book.*

Figure 12 Illustration from William Enfield, *Elementary View of the Fine Arts,* London, 1809, following p. 280. (Courtesy, Winterthur Museum Library.)

of Painting in the city, announced that he would spare "no pains or expense . . . to procure new and elegant additions to his collection of patterns." He had "greatly increased" his collection two years later "by the very particular exertions of friends and correspondents in the chief countries of Europe," including Italy, France, and England. Among the selection were landscapes. Nestell's drawing master apparently owned some visual materials, for figure 11 is based closely on a published source (see fig. 12).[26]

Thatched-roof buildings are common in European pictorial sources, and they were part of the design repertory drawn upon by American needleworkers and ornamenters. The Nestell drawing book contains three scenes with thatched structures (figs. 9, 10). Each scene has two images—the instructor's drawing at the top and the student's copy at the bottom. The trees, which are similar in all the landscape views, are rendered in a distinctive, horizontally layered manner with clumps of foliage, a technique recommended in an ornamental painters' guide of the early nineteenth century: "The trees need not be painted in strokes, but dabbed with . . . great freedom. They will have a much better effect than if great care was used in bringing up the foliage, which would be quite lost in this style of painting." In figure 9 a waterwheel is prominent in the foreground and a peasant with a sack of grain walks in the middle ground. Waterwheels appear in some European scenes; they also occur in other American views. This wheel is delineated in basic terms and appears detached from its building and improperly oriented to the water source. The thatched building in figure 10 is accompanied by a pair of beehives elevated on a platform, the subject of another drawing in the book. Nestell's drawing master inscribed the view in a sure, sophisticated hand; the student added a signed inscription in a less polished style.[27]

The landscape scene on page 5 of the drawing book (fig. 11) is distinctly different in layout from those discussed above and those that follow, and for good reason. The drawing master adapted the view directly from an illustration in a printed source, a volume titled *Elementary View of the Fine Arts* published at London in 1809 (fig. 12). The changes are minor: the addition of a figure on the winding road in the foreground and the substitution of a fence for the small buildings behind the church. On the subject of composition, in general, the author commented:

> The principal figure should strike the eye most, and stand out, from among the rest. This may be effected various ways, as by placing it in the centre of the piece; by exhibiting it, in a manner, by itself; by making the principal light fall upon it; by giving it the most resplendant drapery, or, indeed, by several [or all] of these methods.

Another noteworthy feature of the view is the crossed tree trunks in the right foreground. This unusual configuration may be noted in another printed source, an allegorical mezzotint engraving of Charity by P. Stampa,

Figure 13   Page 1 of the Nestell *Drawing Book.*

Figure 14   Page 60 of the Nestell *Drawing Book*.

published at London in 1802. A church stands in the distance behind the trees in the print. The scene is one that was copied closely by young needleworkers in the Misses Patten's school at Hartford, Connecticut, a few years later. Crossed tree trunks were also a prominent feature in the work of Samuel Folwell (1764–1813) and his students at Philadelphia, although the church was replaced by a tomb. In their crossed form the trees would seem to embody Christian symbolism, knowingly or otherwise.[28]

Four views contain a body of water as a principal focus (figs. 13–15,17). Figure 13, the lead design in the drawing book, is accompanied by a pencil sketch drawn by Nestell and an ink inscription penned by the master. Small boats, often with fishermen, were a common fixture in water scenes. Ruins of buildings, such as appear faintly in the background, were current in European art from the seventeenth century. A more picturesque rendering is the castellated style of figure 14.[29]

Hannah Robertson, when commenting on landscape drawing in 1777, had advice for amateur artists:

> Express a fair horizon, shewing the heavens cloudy or clear, more or less according to the occasion. . . . Take great care to augment or lessen every object, proportionably to its distance from the eye; and also to express them stronger or weaker. . . . If the landscapes are drawn in colours, the farther you go, the more you must heighten it with a very thin and airy blue, to make it appear as if farther off. . . . Let every site have its proper adjuncts . . . as the farm-house, windmill, woods, cattle, travellers, ruins of temples, castles, and monuments.

Nestell's drawing master appears to have been well acquainted with this advice, although his scenes reveal a considerable lack of technical skill.

Figure 15   Page 57 (top) of the Nestell *Drawing Book*.

Figure 16   Detail from William Faden, *A Map of the Inhabited Part of Canada,* London, 1777. Engraving on paper. 23⁵/₈" × 34⁷/₁₆". (Courtesy, Winterthur Museum.)

Figure 17   Page 58 of the Nestell *Drawing Book.*

"Proper adjuncts" to figure 15 include the sailing vessels and the small ruin standing in the background. An unusual feature is the waterfall at the right, the water seeming to appear out of nowhere. The delineation has a close parallel in a vignette accompanying a 1777 map of the northeastern American-Canadian border (fig. 16). Another notable element in figure 15 is the penciled grid that divides the drawing into small squares, a technique used to produce an "enlarged" or "contracted" facsimile of an original image. Given the small size of this view, the drawing master probably reduced a larger scene. The elements in each square of the copy would have replicated those of the original, making "the one exactly correspond with the other in due Symmetry and Proportion." Figure 17, the most accomplished landscape scene, may represent a view taken directly from a printed source. The knarled tree in the foreground provides a strong focus, although one held in check by the subtle colors of the scene and the use of a panel border.[30]

Two landscape vignettes are enhanced with human figures of simple form clothed in the rough dress of wanderers or itinerant traders (figs. 18, 19). The man with a walking stick in his hand and a dog on a lead carries his possessions or trading goods in a bundle on his back (fig. 18). Although travelers with walking sticks are relatively common in contemporary views (fig. 11), individuals with both a stick and a dog on a lead are rare. A catalogue of pictures exhibited in the gallery of the silhouettist Master Hubard, probably at

Figure 18 Page 73 (top) of the Nestell *Drawing Book*.

Figure 19 Page 82 (top) of the Nestell *Drawing Book*.

Figure 20 Detail of the inside back cover of the Nestell *Drawing Book*.

Liverpool, twice lists *A Blind Man and His Dog*. Concealment of the eyes of the figure adds weight to this identification. The dog, as drawn, probably represents a hound.[31]

The seated man of figure 19 appears to be preparing a simple meal. He too has a walking stick but no dog. Nestell made a simple pencil sketch of this scene below that of the drawing master. The exercise, which is the last one in the numbered pages of the drawing book, may have inspired the young student to sketch a related scene on the inside of the back cover (fig. 20). Three figures, two smoking pipes, idle upon the ground while waiting for a pot to boil. The poses appear to better describe vagabonds than wanderers. The spontaneity of the scene suggests it may have been drawn from life or remembrance, although printed sources with related scenes likely were available. One such vignette in a country setting with castle ruins appears in a two-volume work on *The Antiquities of Ireland* published in the 1790s. A rural scene in an 1807 London publication devoted to landscape drawing also includes as a prominent feature a tall tripod frame with a large kettle suspended over a fire in the manner of the Nestell sketch.[32]

The author of The Art of Drawing and Painting in Water-Colours (1778) advised young artists that "in the Imitation of Beasts, Fowls, Fishes, &c. it is requisite not only to be perfect in laying down the exact Proportions, but, before you proceed to the shadowing and trimming your Work, to be well acquainted in the general outward Lines."[33]

Four pages in the Nestell drawing book are devoted to illustrations of animals—rabbits, squirrels, and a fox with a bird—each placed in a vignette-like setting containing foliage, a background considered appropriate "to show the figures to advantage." The two illustrations of rabbits are appre-

Figure 21 Page 11 (top) of the Nestell *Drawing Book*.

Figure 22 Page 12 of the Nestell *Drawing Book*.

Figure 23 Page 50 (top) of the Nestell *Drawing Book*.

ciably different in their interpretation of anatomy. The animals of figure 21 are solid and muscular, much like the "Cony" illustrated in Edward Topsel's *History of Four-Footed Beasts and Serpents* (1658). The term "cony," a now archaic spelling, once identified animals of "the third rank . . . among the divers kinds of Hares." "Cony" is also a term used in heraldry. The "hare" depicted in the Topsel volume is lean and sprightly in appearance, closer in type to the second pair of rabbits illustrated in the drawing book which are distinguishable from squirrels only in the short length of their tails.[34]

Squirrels appear less frequently than hares in artists' source books. Their prominent, long bushy tails resemble the appendage of the squirrel at the left in figure 22. The posture of this animal also approximates that of a squirrel illustrated in reverse in a volume titled *A Booke Containing Such Beasts As Are Most Usefull For Such As Practice Drawing, Graveing, Armes Painting, [and] Chaseing,* which was probably published in the late seventeenth century. Nestell's drawing master may have had an original copy of this volume or a later edition. Pet squirrels are depicted with some regularity in American portraits of children and even those of adults, an indication of public interest in the small animal.[35]

The fox was almost as popular as the hare among purveyors of ornament. It too is depicted in a leaping or springing attitude (fig. 23). Topsel illustrated a fox in his *History of Four-Footed Beasts* (1658), and the animal was well known to readers of *Aesop's Fables* in one or more of its many editions. The story depicted here, "The Fox and the Divining Cock" (the cock portrayed as a goose), moralizes on the subject of a fool swayed by flattery. The fox has coaxed the cock out of a tree by praising its faculties as a great prophet. By seizing the bird by the neck and carrying it to the woods, Reynard muses "upon vain Fools": "For this So[r]t of a *Cock* (says he) to take himself for a *Diviner,* and yet not foresee at the same time, that if he fell into my Clutches, I should certainly make a Supper of him."[36]

Figure 24 Page 9 (top) of the Nestell *Drawing Book.*

Figure 25 Page 72 (top) of the Nestell *Drawing Book*.

Figure 26 Page 10 (top) of the Nestell *Drawing Book*.

The birds of figures 24 and 25 are more noteworthy for their decorative appeal than for their ornithological merit. Species identification was not a goal of the painter. Natural settings add dimension to the vignettes, and touches of bright color enhance the visual appeal of the compositions. The foliage of the trees is in the style of this drawing master.

Aviculture became a popular pastime among the wealthy during the Renaissance, and the appetite for birds seems never to have abated. As new trade routes opened around the world, opportunities increased for collecting exotic species. The Portuguese introduced the canary to Europe, and Columbus returned to Barcelona from the New World with a pair of parrots. Parrots appear to have caught on quickly because of their brilliant plumage and ability to imitate the human voice (fig. 26).[37]

American sailors brought parrots back from voyages to the southern hemisphere, although, closer to home, parakeets of green plumage ranged throughout the Carolinas into the early nineteenth century. Shopkeepers made the colorful birds available to householders. As early as 1759 and 1762, metalworkers in New York City offered "Wire Cages for Parrots." The craze for parrots and parakeets was not confined to large cities however. George Pottie of Louisa County, Virginia, ordered a parrot cage in 1772. Pet parrots were often released from their cages to roam about the house, much to the delight or dismay of guests.[38]

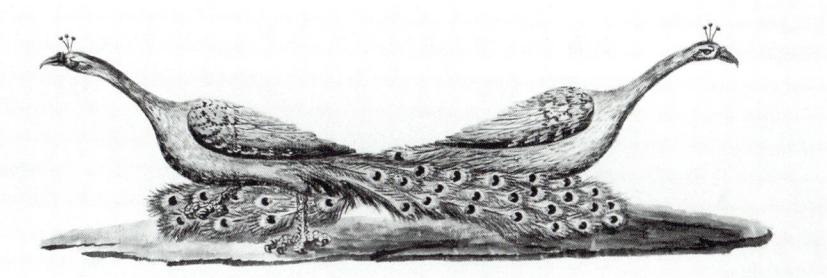

Figure 27 Page 29 (top) of the Nestell *Drawing Book*.

The peacock first became a bird of status among aviculturists during the Tudor period (fig. 27). Ages earlier its original home was India. The bird was a favorite with illustrators, thus books on ornithology frequently include specimens with lavish plumage. The bird also figures in fable and rhyme. Juno gave the proud peacock its train, but when it attempted to fly, it found it had "sacrificed all [its] *activity* to *ostentation*"; nevertheless, as reported in a book of rhyme for children published at New York in 1817, "No bird there is beneath the sky, That with the peacock's plumes can vie." In the Nestell drawing book, the master has carefully delineated the bird's principal features—the distinctive crest and the colorful flowing train composed of feathers that sometimes extend more than four feet. Each feather ends in a flat vane decorated with an "eye," described as "a brilliant spot, enamelled with the most enchanting colours." A fanciful border also captures some of the brilliance of this feature (fig. 28). Thomas Hope, an English designer of classical and exotic ornament, made good use of fanlike sprays of painted peacock feathers in the tympanums of the barrel-vaulted ceiling of his London drawing room, as illustrated in *Household Furniture and Interior Decoration* (1807).[39]

Figure 28 Page 34 (top) of the Nestell *Drawing Book*.

Figure 29 Page 67 (top) of the Nestell *Drawing Book*.

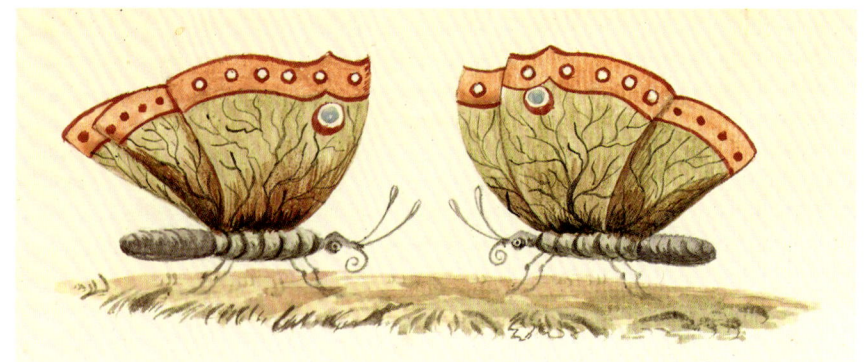

The insect kingdom is represented in the Nestell drawing book by bees and butterflies. A lone drawing of two hives on a platform is similar to that detailed in figure 10. The bee and hive were emblematic of industry, thus a moral lesson frequently was intended, especially for children. The beehive was also a Masonic symbol, and printers often used it as a decorative device. As illustrated, hives usually were made of straw, sometimes woven with vertical ridges, although more commonly formed of horizontal coils.[40]

Representations of butterflies appear just twice in the drawing book—as wispy, principal motifs in figure 29 and as an ornament of secondary rank in figure 24. These lepidopterous creatures are pervasive in the decorative arts, appearing in textiles, prints, ceramics, and wallpaper. Artists' manuals also provided models for copying.[41]

John Cart Burgess in a *Practical Essay on the Art of Flower Painting* (1811) expressed the opinion that "choice of subjects in flower-drawing simply consists of a happy selection of the finest and most beautifully picturesque flowers." The rose is one of the most prominent floral forms in the Nestell drawing book (figs. 30–36). The cabbage rose with its compact, rounded

Figure 30 Page 16 (top) of the Nestell *Drawing Book*.

shape probably is the variety depicted, although buds of the moss rose seem indicated in figure 34. Flower books frequently illustrate the moss rose with fuzzy stems and buds. American interest in this flower is denoted in the siz-

Figure 31   Page 19 (top) of the Nestell *Drawing Book*.

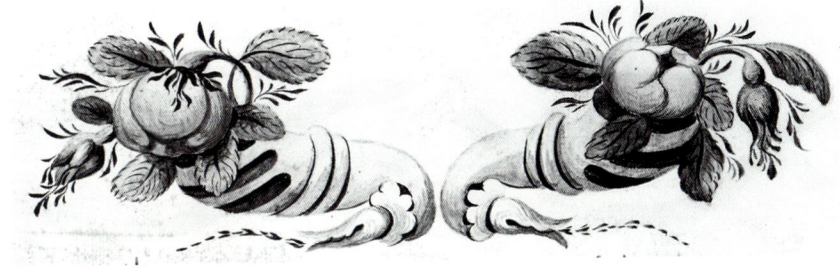

Figure 32   Page 21 (top) of the Nestell *Drawing Book*.

Figure 33   Page 65 of the Nestell *Drawing Book*.

Figure 34   Page 41 of the Nestell *Drawing Book*.

Figure 35   Page 53 (top) of the Nestell *Drawing Book*.

Figure 36   Page 52 (top) of the Nestell *Drawing Book*.

able number of federal-period portraits painted with women and children holding or wearing moss rose buds. Floral subjects, including the rose, also were considered appropriate for ladies' tambour work and other pictures wrought with the needle.[42]

The acknowledged favorite of painters, roses were considered the most difficult flowers to draw. In the drawing book the blossoms have been reduced to their basic lines, and simple shading with color molds the form. A composition probably related to that in figure 30 is the subject of comment in a young ladies' handbook of the arts published in 1777. In discussing symbols, the author describes the white rose as "the emblem of purity and love, and the red of beauty and grace." The decorative form is varied in figure 31 with the addition of cornucopias, symbols of abundance.[43]

Although artfully laid out, the composition of figure 32, unlike that of figure 34, shows little of the chiaroscuro, or "disposition of . . . lights and shadows," considered essential to imparting "force and distinction" to an ornament. Thus in the opinion of Burgess, the "outline is seen to great disadvantage." The artist has chosen several noteworthy subjects, however. The large rose at the left is balanced on the right by an equally prominent blossom of the type seen in figure 43. The central figure, a ram's head, was a decorative motif much admired by architects and designers of the neoclassical period and earlier. Thomas Chippendale designed a ram's head and swag ornament for the frieze of a marble-slab frame, and in fact figure 32 is so similar in layout and motif that the drawing master may have adapted his design from the third edition of *The Gentleman and Cabinet-Maker's Director* (1762). Another example occurs in a pedestal for a sideboard published by George Smith in 1808.[44]

Figure 37   Page 24 (top) of the Nestell *Drawing Book*.

The simple border design of cabbage roses in figure 33, although rendered in a basically flat style, gains a certain forcefulness of composition from repetition. Strangely, this ornament appears on page 65 of the drawing book rather than as an introductory exercise.

Burgess's comments on composition in flower painting seem appropriate when considering the bow-tied bouquet in figure 34. Taste, elegance, and simplicity are the elements addressed in his short essay. Color and form were deemed complementary in tasteful arrangements, and irregularity was "considered a peculiar beauty." The choice of graceful forms and their careful placement in the bouquet introduced elegance. Simplicity was equated with restraint—limiting the bouquet to a few flowers and "those mostly of a large size and such as are without a great multiplicity of colors." Nestell, the student, made a competent copy of the master's arrangement. Supplementing the rose are carnations, the subjects of figures 40 and 41, and heart's ease, or the wild pansy. Carington Bowles, writing in the *Florist,* provided instructions for coloring the heart's ease that describe perfectly the illustrated blossoms: "The two upper Petals of this Flower are a rich Purple; the other three Yellow, or Straw Colour, edged and otherwise stained with Purple, or Olive Colour, with very fine Lines of deep Purple, beginning at the Base and spreading delicately over each Petal. The Stalk and Leaves are a pleasant Green."[45]

In matters of shading, flower painters were advised that "light should generally descend in an oblique direction . . . from the left," a dictum the drawing master applied to his work. The basket of flowers in figure 35 is bathed in light at the left, causing the container to cast a shadow at the right. The flowers of the composition show good variety in size and form, and a liberal infusion of green leaves has "relieved" the mass of any "gaudy and confused effect." Burgess instructed that "red flowers . . . be allowed to predominate in a group," although he would have preferred a few yellow or white blossoms as an accompaniment to lighten the color mass. Blue and purple, he cautioned, "produce [a] Coldness of effect," and he recommended limited use. The small red blossoms may be flowers of the primrose family. The basket appears to have been the popular container for floral arrangements among designers of ornament. Handled vases, glass bottles, and other vessels were chosen occasionally. Nestell marked the end of his second semester with a short pencil notation in the upper right corner of the drawing.[46]

The drawing master has captured in figure 36 that season of flower growth in which the blossoms "blow in their greatest perfection." The full rose, "the pride of the garden," is accompanied by mature tulips of magenta and crimson "streaked according to nature." The crossed twigs below the rose have tips cut in an elongated spatulate form, a feature that is a convention in flower painting of the period (fig. 38). The tulip of figure 37 differs

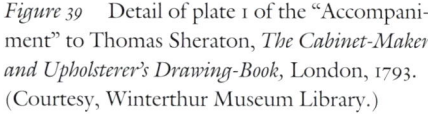

Figure 38 Page 76 (top) of the Nestell *Drawing Book*.

little in general form, although it is flanked by boldly scrolling leaves and stems that make a strong statement. The effect is heightened by sharp contrasts in color.[47]

The flower depicted in figure 38 is the convolvulus, also called bindweed and, today, morning glory. The artist has taken liberties in rendering the plant—the highly stylized form of the blossom, the coloring of the bloom, and the substitution of elongated leaves for the plant's usual foliage, a cordate or heart-shaped leaf. In some publications centering on drawing instruction or plant identification, the stamens of the blossoms are prominent, as depicted. The blue pigments recommended for painted blossoms were smalt and Prussian blue. Lake was the red used to tinge the petals. The American variety of convolvulus was apparently more colorful in this respect than the closest European plant.[48]

Figure 39 Detail of plate 1 of the "Accompaniment" to Thomas Sheraton, *The Cabinet-Maker and Upholsterer's Drawing-Book,* London, 1793. (Courtesy, Winterthur Museum Library.)

The foliage accompanying the convolvulus in figure 38 is of two types. One is a long leaf with a slightly serrated edge and a bend near the tip that gives the ornament a three-dimensional quality. The other leaf, one closely related to the foliage in figure 37, acquires its vitality from a prominent center line and deep indentations at the edges, which produce fingerlike projections called raffles. In a guide to drawing foliage published in London in the 1740s, Mathias Lock delineated in four steps the "simple Principle" upon which "all kind of Foliage is formed," proceeding from a plain looped outline to an "enriched" flowing design with shading and tips bent over in tiny lips. Thomas Sheraton included complex finished examples in the "Accompaniment" at the back of the *Cabinet-Maker and Upholsterer's Drawing-Book* of 1793 (fig. 39). The page is titled "Specimens of Ornament for the Exercise of Learners." The first and third leaves from the top, identified in the text as a thistle leaf and a parsley leaf, respectively, are closest in design to the raffled leaves of figure 38. The ornaments of the Nestell drawing book indicate that the young student learned his technique from drawing finished specimens.[49]

The carnation, or pink, a member of the dianthus family, appears to have been close in popularity to the rose among ornamental painters and amateur artists. This flower is the lone subject in figures 40 and 41 and provides variety in the mixed bouquets of figures 34 and 35. Carington Bowles of

Figure 40 Page 35 (top) of the Nestell *Drawing Book*.

London, who published several books for the instruction of young artists in the late eighteenth century, commented on the carnation as a subject for flower painters: "There is such a variety of *Carnations,* that a particular Description of them would be endless. . . . Any student may take the Liberty of his Fancy, without the Danger of deviating from what may happen in Nature." Some variety is demonstrated in the Nestell drawing book. The pinks of figure 40 are bold, brilliant, and colorful in their interpretation, and the swirling foliage appears to be adapted from the work of Sheraton or another late eighteenth-century designer of neoclassical ornament. By contrast, figure 41 is a delicate composition in color, size, and stem.[50]

Figure 41 Page 33 (top) of the Nestell *Drawing Book.*

Figure 42 Page 17 (top) of the Nestell *Drawing Book.*

Of lavender tint shading to pinkish purple, the tiny five-petal blossoms of figure 42 may represent violets. A London publication, *The Art of Painting in Water Colours* (1797), describes briefly the coloring technique for violets, and a volume of the *Botanical Magazine* identifies and illustrates the cut-leaved plant from Virginia. The elliptical-shaped leaves of figure 42 are common to other varieties. This delicate, undulating border pattern is given stability and substance by introducing a stick, or baton. Thomas Chippendale delineated several border patterns with rods and foliage in the *Director* under the title "Designs of Borders for Damask or Paper Hangings." Sheraton illustrated a related design in the *Drawing-Book* and commented on the use of straight lines in ornament: "Some continuance of a right [straight] line is beautiful; but it ought quickly to be broken in . . . compositions, whether perpendicular or horizontal." A remarkably similar, delicate composition appears as a panel ornament in the posts of an elaborate bedstead designed and dated by George Smith in 1804.[51]

The repeating flower design of figure 43 appears at first inspection to be an artist's whimsy. The prominent pincushion-like center and brilliant orange-red and yellow coloring suggest a more definite inspiration, however. The sunflower (helianthos) is one possibility. A London publication of 1759 illustrates a specimen, and emblem books of the period picture and describe the plant as a symbol of gratitude. Other identifications have merit. The helenium and gaillardia also are similar in appearance to figure 43, and both are native American plants. The helenium was illustrated and described

Figure 43 Page 56 of the Nestell *Drawing Book*.

in the *Flora of North America* in 1821; the name originated in Greek mythology. The gaillardia commemorates an eighteenth-century French botanist.[52]

The graduated, lobelike fingers of the blossoms rising from leafy beds in the border design of figure 44 represent the blooms of the honeysuckle plant before the flowers have acquired their typical trumpet-shaped form. To color the flower, an early nineteenth-century publication suggested that the ornament be "washed over with a light tint of Gamboge," a reddish yellow pigment, followed by a second tint of lake red. Dark touches were added using a mixture of lake and sepia. Sap green, a color used in flower painting and print coloring, was recommended for the foliage. Nestell's drawing master followed this plan in coloring the design. The honeysuckle, a popular subject in flower painting, achieved considerable status as an ornament among architects and designers, to whom it was known as the anthemion.[53]

Figure 44 Page 37 of the Nestell *Drawing Book*.

Figure 45 is an unusual composition among the designs in the drawing book because it is formed principally of feathers. Two flower stalks and a large, centered bow-knot complete the design. The pastel colors are delicate yet forceful: The large white feathers are edged in pinkish red with pale blue shafts, the small feathers are pale yellow edged with medium green to harmonize with the stems and leaves of the foliage, the flower stalks are white shaded with gray, and the bow is golden yellow. In a book of ornament published in 1764, Pouget fils of Paris illustrated headdresses for women made of feathers, flowers, and bow-knots. The bow-knot became a popular

Figure 45 Page 79 (top) of the Nestell *Drawing Book*.

Figure 46 Page 23 of the Nestell *Drawing Book*.

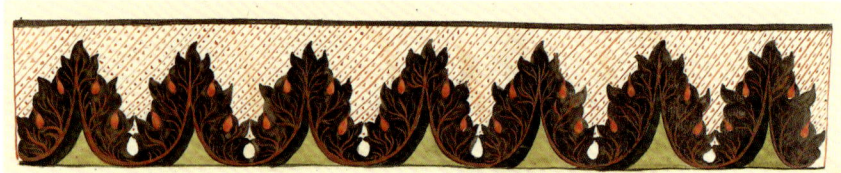

motif in rococo ornament in Europe before the reign of Louis XVI and remained prominent during the neoclassical period. Thomas Chippendale designed furnishings from chair backs to crests for pier glasses with bow-knot motifs. Ornamental bouquets are frequently accompanied by bow-knots, as illustrated in figures 45 and 34. The loops of the bow usually are large and open, the ribbon, frequently crinkled.[54]

Borders figure prominently in the Nestell drawing book. They comprise about one-quarter of the ornaments and include several subject categories. Of the eight border patterns illustrated with floral and leaf forms, four contain reasonably identifiable plant motifs (figs. 33, 42–44). Four others employ stylized leaf forms as decorative units (figs. 46–49). Figure 46 is bold in color and design. The ruled and stippled background provides a striking contrast to the dark leafage highlighted by spots of bright red. In "reading" the design, it is the inverted, V-shaped peaks anchored with green at the bottom rather than the broad, U-shaped valleys that form the principal units. A strong light source is directed from the left. Leaf motifs of this type appear in architectural borders as early as the Romanesque period, although it was the eighteenth century before the pattern achieved its greatest popularity in architecture and as a border for picture frames.[55]

Figure 47 Page 55 (top) of the Nestell *Drawing Book*.

Figure 47 is a whimsy without an apparent prototype. The delicate red-colored upper element, which appears to be a feather, is balanced by pendent buds of tassel form. A more abstract version of this diagonal leaf-and-volute motif forms the basic pattern of figure 48. The ruled ground gives sharp definition to the bold, wavelike, scrolling elements of the design. The pattern was popular in the neoclassical period in one variation or another. Michelangelo Pergolesi, an Italian engraver who resettled in London, occasionally used delicate plant forms for ornamental borders of this general type in designs issued between 1777 and 1801. A closer interpretation appears as a border decoration in a Grecian-style jar illustrated by Thomas Hope in 1807 in his trendsetting volume on interior decoration. Another pertinent illustration in the book is the cyma-curved back of an avant-garde

Figure 48   Page 28 (top) of the Nestell *Drawing Book*.

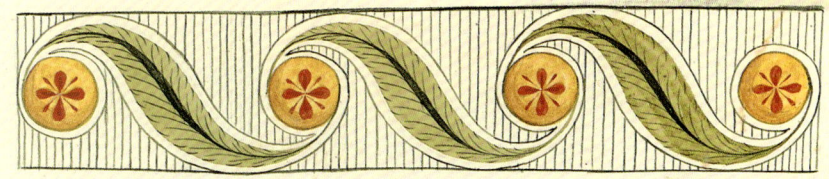

Grecian seating piece with a volute top, which exhibits much of the character and forcefulness of the scrolling element in figure 48.[56]

The border elements in figure 49 are essentially the same as those in figure 48—a cyma-curved leaf terminated by volutes—although the attributes are wholly different: The arches are close to the vertical and more compact; the slender leaves are of two types, and the volutes are oval; the background is

Figure 49   Page 15 (top) of the Nestell *Drawing Book*.

Figure 50   Detail of plate 3 of the "Accompaniment" to Thomas Sheraton, *The Cabinet-Maker and Upholsterer's Drawing-Book,* London, 1793. (Courtesy, Winterthur Library.)

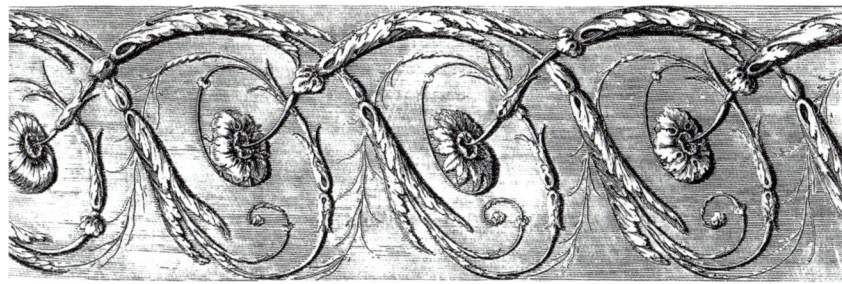

plain. Sheraton, Pergolesi, and other designers of the neoclassical period produced many variations of this general pattern, some of great delicacy. Sheraton's design in figure 50 employs realistic plant material, including blossoms for volutes instead of ovals with stylized ornament. The author identifies the design only as a border for japanning or inlaying. An inscription at the top of the page in the drawing book notes the commencement of the second quarter of instruction on September 1, 1811.[57]

Baskets and other vessels filled with fruit are less frequent subjects of ornamental work than containers of flowers (figs. 51, 52). The selection in the drawing book includes bunches of grapes, strawberries, cherries, plums, peaches, and pears or apples. The lobed form left of center in figure 51 is

127   THE NESTELL DRAWING BOOK

Figure 51 Page 7 (top) of the Nestell *Drawing Book*.

either a small melon or a gourd. A pear-shaped form in the upright basket of figure 52 may be another gourd, as the irregular surface is wartlike. The drawing master has introduced green leaves to both compositions to vary the texture and color and perhaps to address a shortcoming described by one author as the "great sameness in the form of fruit." The author, in acquainting "the learner with the study of fruit," carefully instructed that "to give roundness . . . a strong light must be left in the centre." The grapes, and to a lesser extent the strawberries, of figure 51 have been highlighted in

Figure 52 Page 59 (top) of the Nestell *Drawing Book*.

this manner. Drawing manuals generally provide instructions for coloring fruit. Lake red frequently supplied the bloom, or rosy tint, on the surfaces of light-colored fruit, such as pears, peaches, and apples. Artists achieved a realistic effect in strawberries by stippling the surface with white and "thin Lake."[58]

The design sources of the bundlelike ornaments in the Nestell drawing book are uncertain (figs. 53, 55), although figure 53 may be adapted from an element in a book of furniture designs. The turned and carved arms of a bed stool or window stool illustrated in an early nineteenth-century volume published at Rome are similar and suggest the relevance of this type of

Figure 53 Page 43 (top) of the Nestell *Drawing Book*.

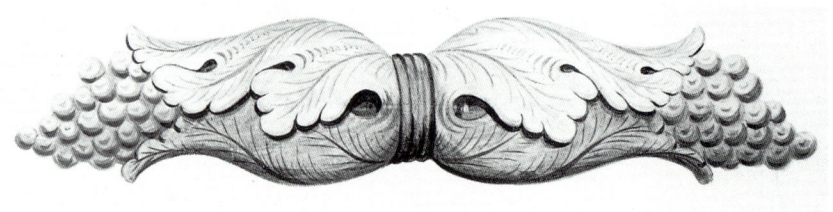

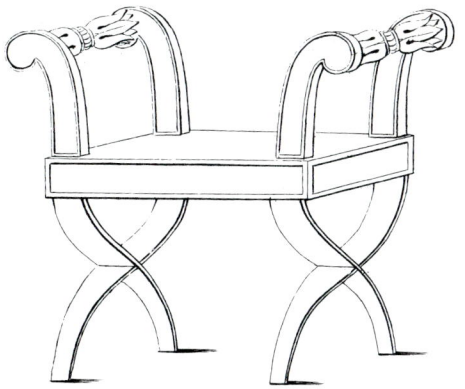

Figure 54   Detail of plate 27 from Lorenzo Roccheggiani, *Invenzioni Diverse di Mobili ed Utensilj Sacri e Profani,* Rome, ca. 1806. (Courtesy, Winterthur Museum Library.)

Figure 55   Page 36 (top) of the Nestell *Drawing Book.*

Figure 56   Page 77 of the Nestell *Drawing Book.*

source (fig. 54). Of contemporary date is a plate from George Smith's *A Collection of Designs for Household Furniture and Interior Decoration* (1807) that delineates a footstool designed with roller ends of comparable form. In the drawing book a central knot secures ogee-profile leaf clusters to which the imaginative painter has introduced grapes at the tips. The colorful leaves of figure 55, the stems cut in the elongated spatulate form of figures 36 and 38, provide a casing for the brilliant pinkish red seedpod. The ornamenter's careful use of highlighting has created a surface iridescence.[59]

Nuts and leaves of two patterns painted yellow and green form a compact border design in figure 56. A subtle detail is the loss of one nut from its shell. Rather than botanically correct, the leaves are principally ornamental. Reasonably close prototypes for a decorative pattern of the type exist in several branches of the arts. Architectural moldings are one important source, and metal mounts for furniture are another. Printers used variant designs as ornaments, and Rudolph Ackermann offered an embossed pattern of leaves and acorns, possibly for use in what is termed today craft activity. Printed

textiles may also have had some influence on the design. A dense pattern with trees, titled "Royal Oak and Ivy" and produced at Bannister Hall, Lancashire, England, in 1799, has acorns of similar character, and the scalloped-border oak leaves are similar to the green foliage in this composition. Berries sometimes replace acorns in the general design.[60]

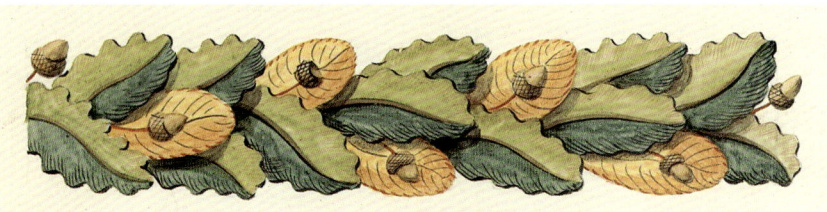

Of all the fruits used for ornament, the grape was the most common (figs. 57–59). The undulating vine of figure 57 with its large leaves and bunches of fruit is the type of pattern encountered most frequently. Thomas Hope used a related border in the neck of a vase he "ornamented with Bacchanalian masks, vine wreaths, and other emblems of Bacchus," the Greek god of wine. The grape motif was common in Roman architecture, and its use continued into the Byzantine period. During the late eighteenth century Chippendale employed a running vine occasionally in carved decoration, and a similar design appears in an early nineteenth-century Italian book of orna-

Figure 57 Page 20 of the Nestell *Drawing Book*.

Figure 58 Page 71 (top) of the Nestell *Drawing Book*.

Figure 59 Page 70 (top) of the Nestell *Drawing Book*.

mental patterns for furnishings. Ackermann offered an embossed example. The compositions of figures 58 and 59 are variations on the same decorative scheme. Rather than borders, the ornaments are self-contained units designed to fill specific spaces. The C-scrolled elements of figure 59 have a shell-like quality without actually having conchological validity.[61]

The six pineapples lined up soldier fashion in figure 60 form an unusual border design. The term pineapple originally identified the fruit of the pine tree, that is, the pine cone. Because of its resemblance to the pine cone, the fruit of the tropical American bromeliad was named *pineapple*. The drawing master has ably recorded the salient characteristics of the exotic food: the color, the segmented skin, the tuft of stiff leaves at the top, the radiating bed of elongated leaves at the base. The cohesiveness of the border is assured by the leaf-formed, swagged rope that links the fruit. Inspiration for the design could have sprung from many sources.

As early as 1657 Richard Ligon drew attention to the pineapple in his history of Barbados. The Dutch may already have been cultivating the fruit in Surinam, and before the end of the century pineapple culture had been introduced to the hothouses of Europe. Among the gentry in early eighteenth-century Virginia, the pineapple was sufficiently well known to be incorporated into the interior or exterior architecture of several colonial mansions built along the James River. Knowledge of the pineapple was disseminated even more broadly as the century advanced through importa-

Figure 60 Page 26 (top) of the Nestell *Drawing Book*.

Figure 61 Page 27 of the Nestell *Drawing Book*.

tions of the fruit, publication of new treatises, circulation of botanical prints containing images of the fruit, and use of the motif on a variety of household objects. Josiah Wedgwood's factory even produced a line of representational pineapple creamware in the third quarter of the century. Before 1800 John Hewson, a calico printer of Philadelphia, produced a block-printed linen handkerchief with a bold pineapple border; in the early nineteenth century the fruit sometimes appeared as a decorative element in schoolgirl needlework. As summed up by one modern author: "The fruit was, again and again, imprinted, impressed, painted onto, or sculpted on all manner of objects, buildings, fabric, wallpaper, and momentoes."[62]

The wreath was a favorite ornament of designers, judging by the frequency of its use (fig. 61). The circular band of interwoven leaves or flowers served in ancient classical cultures as a mark of honor when worn on the head as a chaplet. The chaplet also is borne as a charge in a shield of arms; as a heraldic ornament for the head, it was "granted to gallant knights for acts of courtesy." The late eighteenth-century Italian designer of ornament,

Michelangelo Pergolesi, frequently employed the wreath, to which he added bow-knots, berries, and acorns as accompaniments. The Nestell drawing master chose similar embellishments, adding a leafy frond and augmenting the circular arrangement by crossing the frond and a stem of oak leaves and acorns to form a base. The elongated spatulate tips of the stems are a typical artistic convention of the period. Thomas Hope's *Household Furniture*, another potential design source, circulated in America shortly after its publication in London in 1807. Of the sixty plates in Hope's work, ten contain a wreath motif. In 1809 Rudolph Ackermann, a contemporary of Hope's, began publication of his popular journal, *The Repository,* which contains hand-colored plates of furniture. Early issues promoted the Grecian style and included the wreath motif.[63]

The subject of shells is appropriately introduced by a pair of mermaids, imaginary sea creatures that were the sirens of classical mythology and also appear in heraldry (fig. 62). Interest in collecting shells was already well established internationally when L. D. Chapin advertised at Providence in 1825 that he had received "from the Pacific Ocean, a large collection of rare and elegantly variegated Shells, consisting of numerous specimens of multivalves, bivalves, and univalves." Many artists' instruction books of the neoclassical period devote a section to the topic of drawing shells, and a few technical publications deal with the study of conchology.[64]

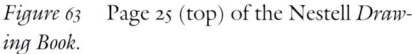

Figure 62   Page 49 (top) of the Nestell *Drawing Book*.

Five pages in the Nestell drawing book are devoted to shells, underscoring the claim by one author that "shells are so rich and varied in form and colour, that all persons that have a taste for drawing Flowers, have a desire to depict these beautiful marine productions." The Nestell drawings offer limited variety, however. The shell supported by the mermaids appears to be a univalve of the genus *Murex,* identified by its spiral top and egg-shaped body with an opening on one side. The hairy material is seaweed.[65]

The shells of figure 63 consist of two fancifully drawn conical specimens, probably representing what one author termed the "spotted Murex," flanking a scallop shell. Shading for shells, which are opaque, was "required to be much stronger than [for] Flowers." Whereas students were advised that "the colouring on the scallop is very delicate," the same tint used for creating shadow was used to form the ribs of the shell. In coloring the shells of figure 63, the master selected a bright palette: pale yellow with pink interiors for the conical specimens; white, shaded gray with a pink scroll at the base for the scallop shell; red and green for the seaweed. Another drawing book ornament with a *Murex* at the center is more gaily colored.[66]

Figure 63   Page 25 (top) of the Nestell *Drawing Book*.

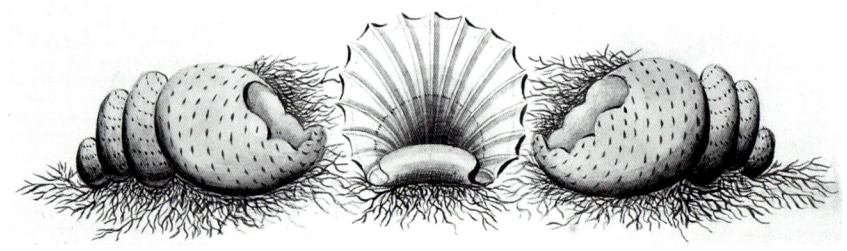

Figure 64 Page 32 (top) of the Nestell *Drawing Book*.

The handsomely drawn spotted shell at the center of figure 64 appears to be a cowrie, although the artist has taken liberties with the shape. The form may be a stylized representation common to ornamental design of the period, because a printed textile dating a few years later is adorned with similar shells. A small, spotted *Murex* is at either side, the color slightly more intense than that of figure 63. The foliage also shows more imagination and, by its use of seedpods, adds considerable vitality to the ornament. The large shell is one the author of the *Conchologist* (1834) likely would have recommended for "a conspicuous place in public collections." By contrast, the

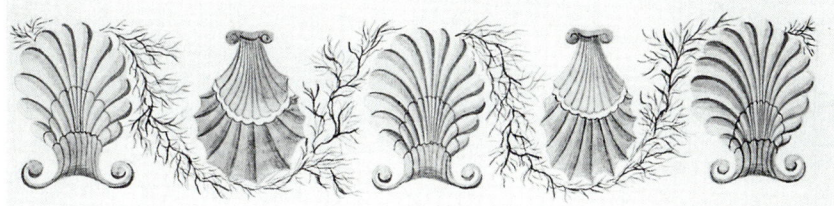

Figure 65 Page 30 (top) of the Nestell *Drawing Book*.

border composition of figure 65 is conceived of as a purely fanciful ornament with little attempt at reality. The stylized scallop shells are colored either in bright pink with light brown or in shades of blue with pink. An undulating vine of seaweed ties the isolated elements together.[67]

Writing more than a century ago, F. Edward Hulme commented on "the influence that geometrical forms have at all times exercised in decorative art." Without question, one of the most common ornaments of this genre through the ages has been a border popularly called a Greek key (fig. 66). The key, which in its many variations is part of a larger body of open designs called frets, is composed principally of short, straight bars. The bars in a Greek key are placed at right angles to one another. The drawing book key,

Figure 66 Page 38 of the Nestell *Drawing Book*.

one of two of the same simple form, has a light, patterned ground of vermiculated, or wormlike, design. Modest shading creates a three-dimensional figure.[68]

The easiest way to lay out a key, or fret, is to use a grid. The patterns are endless, as first demonstrated in the cultures of the Greeks and Romans. Further variation is achieved by patterning the ground or the bars. One special effect simulates a raised molding. Many late eighteenth- and early nineteenth-century designers of ornament and furnishings employed the key border: Rudolph Ackermann, Robert and James Adam, C. A. Busby, John Crunden, Thomas Hope, Michelangelo Pergolesi, and George Smith, to name a few. Key borders also played an important role in typography.[69]

Figure 67 Page 18 (top) of the Nestell *Drawing Book*.

Figures 67 and 68 are guilloche borders, defined as ornamental designs formed of loosely interlaced bands, or ribbons. These examples are just two of the many patterns available. The pointed ellipses of figure 67, which are rare, are interwoven with a second band to form a double guilloche. Guilloches composed of circular or oval loops are the most common pattern. Figure 68 illustrates additional choices: variation in loop size, a textured band—this one simulating a rope—and ornament introduced to the loop centers.

Figure 68 Page 42 of the Nestell *Drawing Book*.

The circular guilloche, which has strong roots in ancient cultures and reappears in Renaissance art, is the one later architects and designers looked to principally for ornamental embellishment. An eighteenth-century French sourcebook for artists illustrates several guilloche patterns, among them one composed of "Roses and Ribbons." Thomas Chippendale employed the guilloche in some of his executed commissions, and similar borders in wood and plaster were offered in English trade catalogues of the late eighteenth century. Both Thomas Hope and Rudolph Ackermann made extensive use of the star, a feature of figure 68, although as an ornament independent of the guilloche. Floral forms were the popular choice for the interstices of this border, as demonstrated in various sources.[70]

The ornament of figure 69 is an unusual one, appearing principally in printers' borders and architectural moldings. The figure in the drawing book appears to represent two tubes of printed cloth twisted together to form a ropelike band. The design may have a direct source in heraldry. There, one side of a twisted wreath serves as a support for a crest, an ornament placed above a coat of arms. The heraldic wreath is further described as "a

Figure 69 Page 22 (top) of the Nestell *Drawing Book*.

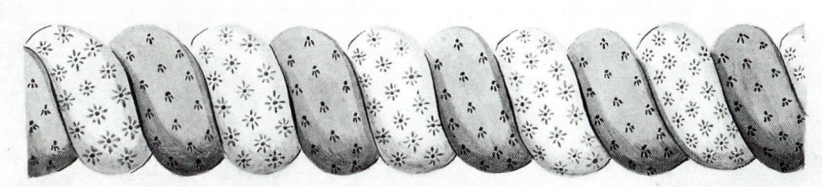

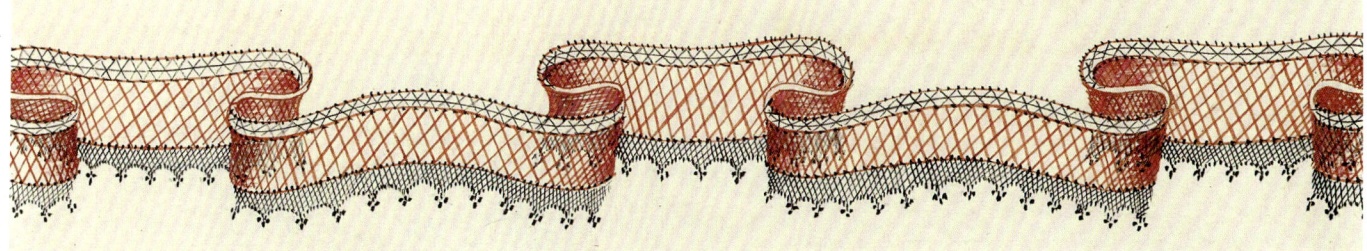

Figure 70 Page 40 (top) of the Nestell *Drawing Book*.

chaplet of two different-coloured silks wound round each other." Continuing in the vein of textile arts as inspiration for the Nestell drawing master, figure 70 appears to have its source in the upholstery trade. This delicately colored ribbon of netting is a type used in the late eighteenth and early nineteenth centuries principally to trim window and bed hangings. Thomas Hope and George Smith illustrated examples of the same general pattern.[71]

The trophy, a collection of objects forming an ornament usually based on a single theme, was a popular embellishment in the arts during the eighteenth century and later, although its roots lie in earlier periods (figs. 71–73). Many themes were fashionable, including love, war, agriculture, the sciences, and the theater. The subjects illustrated in the Nestell drawing book—music and the hunt—are represented by some of the most colorful and prominent accouterments found in these thematic groups. Principal designers of the period included the trophy in their published engravings, among them Ackermann, Chippendale, Hepplewhite, Hope, and Pergolesi. Designs for trophies also appear in English trade catalogues, and the French produced other examples. Trophies occur with some regularity in printed textiles.[72]

Figure 71 Page 74 of the Nestell *Drawing Book*.

135   THE NESTELL DRAWING BOOK

The trophy of music is one of the most carefully drawn and colorful designs in the Nestell drawing book (fig. 71). A survey of more than a dozen published contemporary examples sheds light on object selection. Horns are almost always present, although four is a large number. By contrast, the tambourine is uncommon. A book of music appears in about half the compositions, and a garnish of leaves is a frequent choice.[73]

The wreath as a unifying element in the trophy is particularly effective when combined with the slender accouterments of the hunt (fig. 72). A bow and quiver of arrows are usual selections; the bludgeon is a rarity. The typ-

Figure 72 Page 61 (top) of the Nestell *Drawing Book*.

ical quiver is a tapered rectangular container with paneled sides, often terminated by a leafy cup and button at the base. The stylized hunting bow is a double ogee with a straight midsection. The drawing master likely made a selection of elements from several sources and combined them to suit his fancy. Circulating European design materials were supplemented in 1809 by a specimen book of letters and ornament issued by the Binny and Ronaldson type foundry of Philadelphia. One of the ornaments in the volume is a trophy with a rectangular quiver. The drawing book instructor's masterstroke was the addition of a red ribbon to the composition.[74]

The wreath and a crossed quiver and bow are elements in a second trophy centered in the hunt (fig. 73). The composition is different from that of figure 72 because it is dominated by a lion's mask contained within the

Figure 73 Page 78 of the Nestell *Drawing Book*.

wreath. The lion's mask, sometimes interpreted as a leopard's face, was part of the ornamental baggage of architecture and the decorative arts in ancient Roman culture, and use of the motif continued through the Byzantine, Romanesque, and Renaissance periods. Renewed interest in the ancient classical cultures in the late eighteenth century brought the mask again to the attention of designers—Chippendale, Pergolesi, Hope, Smith, and

Ackermann. The ornament was interpreted in several mediums: carved wood, cast plaster, cast or stamped metal, and paint on wood. Ornaments from any of these mediums or from a published source could have caught the attention of the drawing master. Of particular note is the design of furniture hardware after 1800. Lion's-mask drawer pulls, sometimes combined with cast lion's-paw feet, adorned some of the finest case furniture, especially that made in New York City, where Christian Nestell attended drawing school.[75]

The neoclassical theme is a prominent one in the Nestell drawing book, although some motifs occur in ornaments dominated by other subjects or are better studied in different categories. Several motifs, in particular, can be cited: the cornucopia (fig. 31); the ram's head (fig. 32); the wreath (figs. 61, 72, 73); the honeysuckle, or acanthus (fig. 44); and the key and guilloche borders (figs. 66, 68). Neoclassicism had its genesis in the mid-eighteenth century when reawakened interest in classical architecture and activity at archaeological sites in Europe began to impact the arts. The neoclassical style held sway for almost a century both in Europe and America.[76]

The griffin, a mythological creature with the head and wings of an eagle and the body of a lion, is the subject of figure 74. The beast in its several variations was employed in ancient Greek and Roman art, following which interest waned until revived during the Italian Renaissance. Griffins and

Figure 74   Page 44 of the Nestell *Drawing Book*.

related beasts became popular motifs for architectural friezes and tablets in the neoclassical period. One such design illustrated by Thomas Sheraton in *The Cabinet-Maker and Upholsterer's Drawing Book* (1793) appears to have had widespread influence, particularly among ornamental painters in America. Sheraton also commented on the griffin, identifying it as a figure "employed by the antiques in their decorations. . . . They suppose it to watch over golden mines and hid treasures." He added, perhaps with tongue in cheek, "These, if you please, may be introduced into subjects intended to represent covetousness; or they may be placed over cabinets where treasure is kept." Doubtless, such symbolism was lost on most American consumers of furniture and furnishings, as it was on their suppliers.[77]

The seated, occasionally standing, figure of the griffin usually is depicted as one of a facing pair and placed amid lush, scrolling foliage (fig. 74). An urn or other ornament is a central feature in the composition. The foliage in the drawing book design is restrained, confined to the base of the urn, although frequently the beasts' tails are replaced by oversized leafy scrolls containing floral forms. Compositions of this type fall within a class of ornament called arabesques. These collections of "foliage, fruits, beasts of every species, and imaginary creatures, intermingled" were the subject of comment by a nineteenth-century English author of a guide to drawing. Balance of composition was essential "that the heavier parts may sustain the lighter." Unity of design, lightness, and grace were other attributes of a good composition. The author warned that "foliage . . . ought to be drawn from nature" and advocated the use of "long . . . volute scrolls" eminating "from each side of a reeded and cupped pedestal." On the subject of color he advised "that in ancient decorative painting of this description, the beauty existed by the balance of colour being strictly attended to." The Nestell drawing master has heightened the effect of his composition by choosing a monochromatic color scheme.[78]

Rather than an imitation of a section of column or a reeded bedpost, the ornament in figure 75 seems based on an ancient Roman fasces, a bundle of rods bound together and containing an axe. The fasces, borne upright on a

Figure 75   Page 81 of the Nestell *Drawing Book*.

stick, was a badge of authority for Roman magistrates, and examples are found in Roman art and architecture. A French book of designs for ornaments and moldings dating to the 1750s or slightly later illustrates a horizontal figure described as a "bundle of sticks with intertwined leaves" that has the basic features of figure 75, including bands of raffled leaves. The leaves of the Nestell ornament include both lightly serrated and raffled examples and can be compared to the foliage in figure 38. Textiles present another possibility as a design source. Shortly after 1800 a new textile pattern called a "pillar print" came onto the market in England. Although the simulated columns of these printed fabrics do not taper, they are punctuated by bunches of flowers rather than spiraling leaves. Another potential source is published furniture designs. Ackermann's *The Repository*, for example, included large fasces at the front corners of a pier table suitable for "an officer of high rank" or a "military gentleman"; however, that particular design dates several years later than the Nestell drawing book.[79]

Thomas Sheraton was anything but reticent in expressing his views on the appropriateness of mythological subjects in painted ornament. Commenting on the story of Diana and Endymion, he noted the vast number of other

Figure 76 Page 63 of the Nestell *Drawing Book*.

such tales and proclaimed them "merely the fabrication of ancient poets and idolators forming to themselves innumerable gods, according to their vain imaginations, and which now, only serve to try the painter's skill in decorating our walls." The female image of figure 76, which clutches a trident and rides across the waves in a dolphin-drawn, shell-like chariot, appears to be Amphitrite, wife of Neptune. Neptune's symbol is the trident, and he paid court to Amphitrite riding on a dolphin. A subtle feature is the use of trident heads as spokes in the chariot wheels.[80]

The chariot of the sun god Apollo is the likely subject of figure 77. The disarray of the horses supported on clouds may be an indirect reference to the story of Apollo's son Phaethon, who was granted permission to drive the chariot for one day. Phaethon was an inept charioteer and lost control of the horses, threatening the world with fire. Jupiter stepped in and hurled him into the River Po.[81]

The nature of the material in figures 76 and 77 suggests that the drawing master had explicit models from which to copy or adapt his ornaments. Potential sources are broad and varied, since public interest in classical subjects was intense in the early nineteenth century. Printed textiles and block-printed papers for bandboxes sometimes display mythological subjects as do design books of the period. Sheraton, for example, designed a tablet with a representation of Diana and Endymion. Diana as huntress also charges

Figure 77 Page 80 of the Nestell *Drawing Book*.

139   THE NESTELL DRAWING BOOK

across a panel scene in Pergolesi's book of ornament. Books of emblems and devices provided vignettes appropriate for copying. Phaethon is the subject of one. In a modest-sized catalogue of embossed ornament numbering ten pages, Ackermann illustrated four figures from mythology riding in chariots; figures in the vignettes include Neptune and Juno.[82]

The American constitution was ratified by a majority of the original thirteen states in 1788 and placed into effect the following year. One of the emblems soon associated with the new country was the American bald eagle, a distinct species of bird from the heraldic eagle of prominence in European art. The eagle and the motto "E Pluribus Unum" were adopted for the official seal of the United States. In 1790 engraver Amos Doolittle depicted the American eagle—complete with shield body, talons clutching arrows and olive branches, and beak with banner and motto—in the pediment of the old City Hall building in New York to mark the inauguration of George Washington as president the previous year. The bird took flight quickly, and it soon appeared "in all sorts of unofficial places as a decorative device."[83]

Pewterers were among the earliest American craftsmen to employ the eagle as a device to mark their work. Some examples date from the early 1790s. When Charles Cotton Hayward, a chairmaker of Charlestown, Massachusetts, ordered a trade card advertisement sometime between 1803 and 1811, he chose a design with a large, spread eagle perched on the back of a long settee. Merchants also used the eagle as an advertising device. About 1812 Peter Bauduy of Wilmington, Delaware, designed a label for the woolen mill of Victor du Pont, his partner's brother. Above frolicking cherubs and the family's merino ram, an eagle surveys the scene while supporting a banner bearing the company name. By this date American type

Figure 78   Page 6 (top) of the Nestell *Drawing Book*.

Figure 79   Page 45 (top) of the Nestell *Drawing Book*.

Figure 80   Page 14 of the Nestell *Drawing Book*.

founders, including Binny and Ronaldson of Philadelphia, produced eagles as part of a broad selection of ornament for commercial use. The eagles in the Nestell drawing book are representative of the many variations that circulated in the public sector, some with patriotic accompaniments—a shield, the balance of justice, a banner with a motto (figs. 78, 79).[84]

Cherubs, also known as cupids, boys, putti, and amorini in the annals of art and decoration, are the subject of two ornaments with patriotic overtones in the Nestell drawing book (figs. 80, 81). Contemporary published manuals provided instructions for drawing the human form and examples to copy, including some for the infant figure. Directions provided by Thomas Sheraton correspond exactly with the images in the drawing book:

> As boys or cupids are frequently introduced in ornaments, it is proper that the learner should take notice of their proportions and general appearance [and] the general cast of these figures; the head is large and round; the neck scarcely distinguishable between the head and shoulders; no joints appearing in the arms or legs scarcely; the ankle covered with flesh, and the whole leg thick and massy.[85]

The floral swag in figure 80 relates to that in figure 32, the rose again a prominent flower. The urn commemorating George Washington, a popular theme in all mediums during the federal period, may be based in profile on a ceramic or metal form. George Hepplewhite illustrated a similar urn

Figure 81   Page 13 of the Nestell *Drawing Book*.

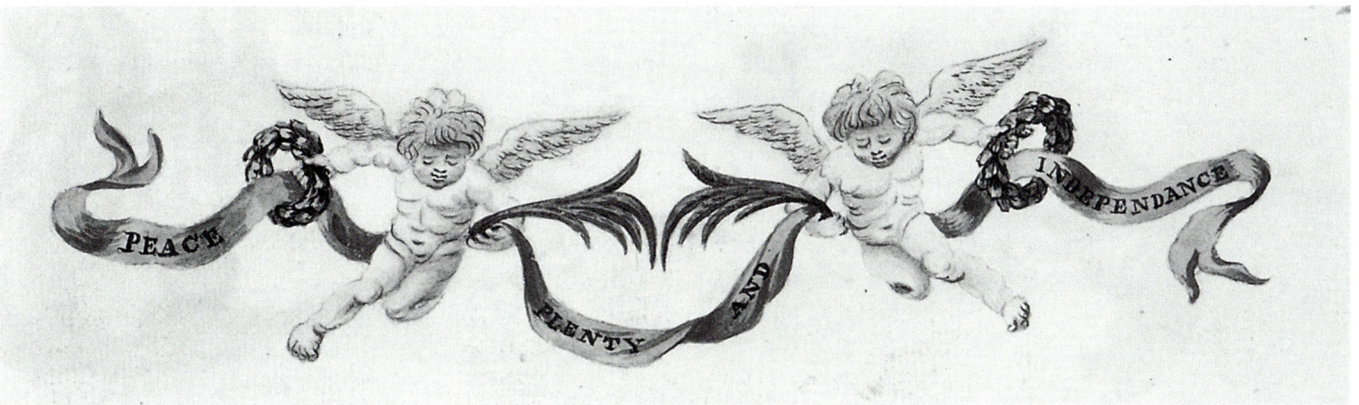

as an ornament for a tea caddy, and related shapes were delineated in trade catalogues of ornament. The floating cherubs of figure 81 are linked by a bright red banner with a patriotic motto extolling "INDEPENDENCE." As the spelling in the banner and in that of figure 79 clearly demonstrates, the word has challenged orthographers in all ages.[86]

The art of imitating the grain and color of natural substances is represented in the Nestell drawing book; however, except for determining that one image represents wood (fig. 82) and the other marble (fig. 83), a more precise identification is elusive. Regarding the imitation of fancy woods, Nathaniel Whittock, author of an early nineteenth-century guide for painters, advised the practitioner to "apply to nature herself," although clearly that is not the case here. In the absence of original material, Whittock provided instruc-

Figure 82   Page 48 (top) of the Nestell *Drawing Book*.

tions and sample illustrations. The color of the work in figure 82 best follows that described for maple or oak. The workman started with a light straw-colored ground, then worked the figure in shades varying from yellow to brown. As advised in other subject areas of ornamental painting, practice was a requisite to developing good technique. The quarter-fans in the corners of the panel, which represent inlay, provide a striking contrast.[87]

The center panel of figure 83 most clearly approximates sienna marble in coloring but not in veining. The ground, which consists of straw yellow shaded to light mustard, is contrasted with splashes of light brownish red and muted green accented by subtle, medium brown veining. Whittock advised starting with pure yellow ochre for the ground and then introduc-

Figure 83   Page 46 of the Nestell *Drawing Book*.

ing burnt sienna for the red and Prussian blue, which produced green when it interacted with the yellow ground. The side panels, which contain a golden star, are mottled in shades of light and medium blue-green. The color varies from Whittock's descriptions for painting green marble—verd antique, Egyptian green, and serpentine—which all start with a black ground. The three marbleized panels are effectively displayed on a background of raffled white leaves penciled in a dark color and placed, in turn, on a dark green ground.[88]

Upon reflecting on the diverse variety of subject matter contained in the Nestell drawing book, a statement by Thomas Sheraton seems appropriate: "To be fully qualified for ornamental decorations is to be acquainted with every branch of drawing."[89]

The Christian M. Nestell Drawing Book: Design Application

> Ornament in decorative art is [that] element which adds an embellishment of beauty in detail. [It] is in its nature accessory; . . . it does not exist apart from its application. . . . Ornament belongs to the very inception of [a] thing [and] is good only in so far as it is an indispensable part of something. . . . The test of ornament is its *fitness*. It must occupy a space, fulfill a purpose, be adapted to the material in which and the process by which it is executed.

The ornaments in the Nestell drawing book have a potentially broad range of application, and many are fully suited for use on various materials. A principal emphasis in this study is the embellishment of furniture and wooden objects, since when training as an ornamental painter the eighteen-year-old Nestell likely had his craft objectives in sight. His known activity in Providence in the 1820s revolves primarily around the sale, repair, painting, and ornamenting of furniture—principally chairs—and around gilding. In exploring the various ways the designs in the drawing book functioned as ornament, the discussion will focus on records and objects of contemporary date, although neither will be specific necessarily to the place, date, or exact content of the Nestell document given the limitations of resource materials.[90]

Newspaper notices of the early nineteenth century provide an initial focus on the use of painted scenes in the decoration of furniture. As early as January 1803, Hugh and John Finlay of Baltimore offered local residents furniture "with or without views adjacent to the city." By November 1805, customers had a broader choice between "real Views" and "Fancy Landscapes." The Finlay brothers' list of furniture suitable for receiving this embellishment is impressive: card, pier, dressing, writing, shaving, and work tables; wash and candle stands; cane- and rush-bottom fancy chairs, Windsor chairs, settees, and window seats; fire and candle screens.[91]

Chairmakers in New York were quick to note the novelty and suitability of landscape scenes for furniture, and they began to incorporate them into their work. One design in the Nestell drawing book is framed in a tablet-style crest piece copied directly from a Baltimore chair (fig. 17). Within the banded and penciled border surrounding the distinctive panel, a central landscape contains buildings of notable European character. The eight-pointed stars at either end appear in another drawing book design (fig. 68). Baltimore chairmaking remained a strong influence on New York design for several decades, as indicated in the accounts of Benjamin Branson who in 1835 prepared Baltimore "stuff" (chair parts) for sale to other chairmakers and paid to have Baltimore-style chairs ornamented. Landscape vignettes enhance several New York fancy chairs that have survived with their original decoration intact. New York chairmakers Stephen Wheaton and Robert Davies further confirmed local interest in this type of decoration in June 1817 when advertising "an elegant assortment of Curl'd Maple, Plain Painted and Ornamented, [and] Landscape . . . Chairs . . . all of the newest fashion."[92]

The painted panel in the center back of a New York fancy chair, one from a set of six with a Van Renssalaer family history (fig. 84), relates in general composition and features to two waterscapes in the drawing book (figs. 14, 15). In all these scenes a course of water flows toward the viewer, and in two views a wooden bridge crosses a waterfall. The chair back and figure 15 share common elements in a rocky outcropping supporting a tree and other foliage and the presence of small human figures in the view.

Figure 84 Detail of the back panel of a fancy side chair, New York City, 1815–1820. Maple, cherry, yellow poplar, and hickory. H. 32³⁄₄", W. 19", D. 16¹⁄₂". (Courtesy, Winterthur Museum.)

Landscapes occasionally appear on other wooden household objects, such as large lidded storage chests and small boxes for sewing equipment or trinkets. Talented schoolgirls sometimes ornamented the personal items. Other surfaces bearing landscape decoration were part of interior architecture or closely associated with it—overmantels, fireboards to close the hearth in warm weather, and window cornices. The shade that hung within a window frame provided another surface for decoration. Artist and ornamenter Ezra Ames painted "3 pair of window Shades" in 1792 for Daniel Waldo while working in Worcester, Massachusetts, although the nature of the decoration is unknown. A brisk business for a number of ornamental painters was the preparation of reverse-painted glass tablets for use in looking glasses and timepieces, primarily the shelf clock and the banjo clock. Occasionally a tall case clock exhibits a small landscape vignette in the arch above the dial.[93]

Representations of the animal kingdom are uncommon in the decorative arts of the federal period except as adjuncts to other ornament, the landscape in particular. Rufus Porter, a prolific itinerant New England mural artist, painted some landscapes with grazing horses or cattle. Other artists included grazing sheep in their pastoral scenes. Several Windsor chairs retaining original decoration include animals as part of a landscape scene in the crest. A hunter and horse are a feature of one. A horse-drawn wagon and a farmer driving cattle are illustrated in two chairs from a suite of seating furniture.[94]

Several manuscript references broaden the picture. In 1800 Ezra Ames, then a resident of Albany, New York, charged a customer for "painting a Lion," although both the form and purpose of the ornament are unknown. Possibly the figure was for a signboard. More explanatory are the records of Daniel Rea, Jr., an ornamental painter of Boston whose accounts for 1788 describe a sizable job of "painting a Room and Entry Floor Cloth 35 yd." The decoration was "a Poosey Cat on One Cloath and a Leetel Spannil on ye other." George Davidson, a fellow member of the ornamental painting community in Boston, included coach painting among his customer services. After painting Isaac Tapley's chaise a "Dark Colour," he added a landscape to the back and a "haire" to each side.[95]

Figures of birds appear with frequency in printed textiles and wallpapers; however, they are rare in painted ornament, except for the eagle, which is treated here as a patriotic symbol. Painted feathers embellish some furniture, although carving is the usual medium. An example of painted feather decoration occurs in the work of chairmaker Samuel Gragg of Boston who patented a classic bentwood chair in 1808. A peacock plume reminiscent of those in a Nestell border design (fig. 28) provides a strong center-back focus (fig. 85). The pair of back-to-back peacocks in another drawing book design (fig. 27) is conventionally posed, as indicated in other sources. An overmantel from the John Peterson house in Duxbury, Massachusetts, painted about 1800 by Rufus Hatheway, contains naively drawn peacocks in a similar attitude. The pose is repeated on a paper-covered bandbox ornamented with a pair of grouse. In a quick flight into the insect world, it can be noted that the beehive as a decorative feature for furniture probably was more common than it appears today. A New York fancy chair, possibly dating as early as 1815, has a gold-leaf beehive flanked by cornucopias as a crest ornament (see fig. 10).[96]

Figure 85 Detail of the center back of a bentwood side chair by Samuel Gragg, Boston, ca. 1809–1812. Birch, white oak, and beech. H. 34 3/8", W. 18", D. 25 1/8". (Courtesy, Winterthur Museum.)

A floral figure was by far the most popular subject for ornamenting all types of utilitarian and fancy furnishings in the federal period. The list of objects embellished in this manner is not unlike that noted for landscape ornament. Seating pieces and tables are again the principal furniture forms, added to which are bedposts with spiral decoration and pianos with ornamented name boards. The glass tablets in looking glasses and wall and shelf clocks often have floral decoration, as do the enameled dials of tall case clocks. Architectural features enriched with floral ornament were prominent, the previous list augmented by wall painting in imitation of paper. Extending the range of small decorated items are tea boards and wooden equipment for the hearth, including brushes and hand bellows.[97]

At best, manuscript and other references to floral work are brief and often indefinite; yet, there are clues to build on. The Finlay brothers of Baltimore offered a range of furniture forms embellished with "Flowers" as an alternative to their landscape views, including "Flower Borders of entire new patterns" for bed and window cornices. At Boston affluent customers had other options. Daniel Rea, Jr., painted "a sett of Bed Cornices in Imitation of the Copperplate" in 1793 for 24s., the equivalent of four days' pay for a working man with a trade. George Davidson followed suit and was also prepared to paint "Window Cornices in imitation of Calico." Both copperplate and calico were popular printed cotton fabrics used for bed and window hangings and furniture covers. Floral patterns were the principal and most popular designs.[98]

Silas Cheney, a cabinetmaker who worked in Litchfield, Connecticut, in the early nineteenth century, made several references in his accounts to "sprigged" dining Windsors, which he priced substantially above the average cost of Windsor chairs. A sprig is defined as "a stemmed flower" or "a spray of a plant." The decoration enriched either the turned work of the chairs or the cross slats used as crest pieces after 1800. Titus Preston of Wallingford, Connecticut, was more specific when identifying the striping on a group of Windsor chairs as "a vine on the front of the bow & legs." Work tables, chamber tables, and washstands occasionally have leafy vines spiraling up the legs.[99]

The rose was the popular choice in floral decoration for painted furnishings, as even a brief survey will confirm. George Davidson, who did a brisk business in coach painting, filled the request of one customer for a "shais [chaise] Body Painted Green, Curtain on Back and Rose on sides." Although Davidson's roses may have been single blossoms only, swags, sprays, bouquets, clusters, compositions, and borders were equally common options. The swagged rose decoration on the top of a circular card table of Connecticut origin (fig. 86) interrelates with elements in several rose designs from the Nestell drawing book. One is the double-swag ornament with ram's

Figure 86 Detail of the top of a card table, Middletown area of Connecticut, 1795–1810. Maple with white pine. H. 29", W. 38", D. 18⅝". (Courtesy, Winterthur Museum.)

head in figure 32, its rings substituting for bows. The rose composition in the left swag and the blossoms on the card table are similar in character, an affinity shared also by figure 30, the central element in figure 36, and the roses in the cornucopias of figure 31.[100]

A composition of cornucopias and roses is the principal decoration on the crest of a Windsor chair made in New York City a few years after Nestell

Figure 87 Detail of the back of a Windsor armchair, New York City, 1814–1820. Yellow poplar, and maple. H. 34½", W. 16⅞" (crest), D. 16⅞" (seat). (Courtesy, Winterthur Museum.)

completed his drawing book (fig. 87). Although the ornament of the chair is more stylized than that of the drawing (fig. 31), the horns in both have twisted bodies marked by prominent ridges. The ribbon, large rose, and general organization of the ornament in figure 34 have their counterparts on the lid of a maple box assigned to Salem, Massachusetts, and dating to the early nineteenth century. Another visual link exists between figure 35 and a display of flowers in a woven basket painted on the fall of a drop-leaf table of Connecticut origin. A floral composition on the drawer front is an expansion of the design in figure 30.[101]

Tulips appear in several drawing book ornaments (figs. 36, 37), although they are rare on painted furniture dating to the early nineteenth century. An unusually detailed Boston advertisement suggests that the flower had more currency as decoration than present evidence indicates. In early December 1810, Nolen and Gridley "received from one of the first manufactories at New-York—300 Fancy CHAIRS, of different patterns." Among them was a pattern identified as "Tulip Top." The term could describe a shaped crest; however, there are no candidates among surviving chairs. Since other patterns on the list were created with paint, such seems to have been the intent of the description. Most contemporary floral patterns are described in records in general terms only, as for instance the "12 Slat Back (Flower)" chairs made in the Newark, New Jersey, shop of David Alling in 1817.[102]

Considerably more popular were chair patterns containing the convolvulus, or morning glory, although most are of simpler design than figure 38. An exception is the chair crest of figure 88, an example of uncommon vitality. A three-dimensional quality is achieved through the use of modeled elements, twisted leaves, and background shading. The effect is heightened by a monochromatic color scheme accented in gold.

The feather pattern of figure 45 also may have been intended for the crest piece of a chair; however, it would have served equally well on the skirt or drawer front of a table. One of the workmen employed occasionally in the

Figure 88 Detail of the upper back of a Windsor side chair by Silas Buss, Sterling, Massachusetts, 1820–1827. White pine and other woods. H. 34⁷⁄₈", W. 16½" (crest), D. 15¾" (seat). (Courtesy, Marblehead Historical Society, Marblehead, Massachusetts; photo, Winterthur Museum.)

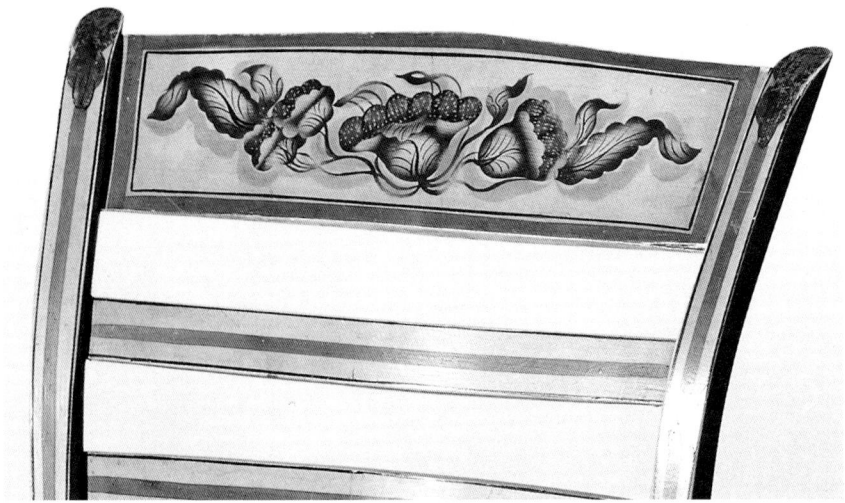

chairmaking facility of Thomas Boynton at Windsor, Vermont, in 1814–1815 concentrated on decorating and varnishing chairs. One of his tasks was "Ornamenting feathers."[103]

Linear designs as principal features on furniture are rarer than self-contained compositions. The running border of figure 49 is well suited, however, because the design has a definite start and finish. When transferred to a chair back (fig. 89) and defined by a penciled frame, it has the character of a composition. Several chairs retain decoration of this type, suggesting that the pattern was relatively common. The design in one crest without a penciled border ends in twisted cones, the points directed outward. The chair in figure 89, made and decorated in New York City, is contemporary with the Nestell drawing book.[104]

Second to floral decorations, fruit, usually accompanied by leaves, was the most common ornament on painted objects in the early nineteenth century. Fruit was also a popular subject in the medium of stenciling. Grapes are depicted most frequently, followed by melons. The range of forms and surfaces ornamented with fruit basically is that described for floral decoration.

Figure 89 Detail of the upper back of a Windsor side chair, New York City, ca. 1809–1815. Yellow poplar and other woods. H. 34¾", W. 16³⁄₈" (crest), D. 14¼" (seat). (Private collection; photo, Winterthur Museum.)

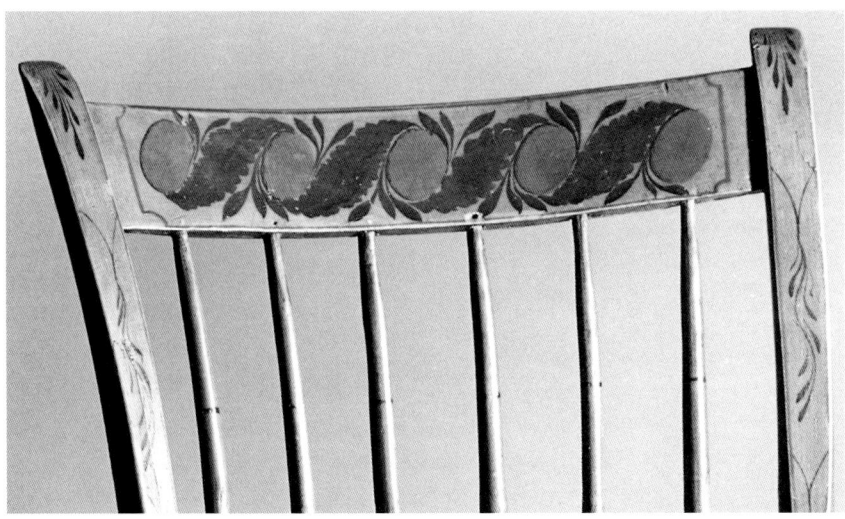

Figure 90 Detail of the right crest panel of a fancy settee, probably northeastern Massachusetts, 1810–1820. Maple, mulberry, ash, birch, and hickory. H. 34", W. 66½", D. 19". (Courtesy, Winterthur Museum.)

Six years before Nestell began his studies with a drawing master, John and Hugh Finlay of Baltimore offered their customers furnishings "enriched with Gold and Painted Fruit." Fancy chairs of "Grape Leaf" pattern were among those imported from New York in 1810 by Nolen and Gridley of Boston. Chairs of grape pattern were particularly important to David Alling whose shop in Newark, New Jersey, was just across the bay from New York. The chairmaker noted two types of grape decoration in his accounts—one painted "Natural Color," the other "Bronzed," or stenciled. All the chairs had slat backs (see fig. 89).[105]

Grapes with leaves, vines, and tendrils are the subject of three ornaments in the drawing book (figs. 57–59). Figure 57, a running vine, is representative of the open pattern introduced first in the early nineteenth century. A simpler version appears on the crest tablets of a Massachusetts settee of this date (fig. 90). The more complex design of figure 58, which has the character of a composition, is one that became popular for chair crests, including the rocking chair, in the 1820s. By that date an oak-leaf and acorn pattern was fashionable for borders on tables. David Alling noted in 1815 that he had ornamented a set of bed cornices with "Oak Wreaths." The central wreath in figure 61 relates to that description, although berries are substituted for acorns. A comparable vine flanking a wreath of a different pattern is illustrated on the tablet of the fancy chair in figure 93.[106]

Pineapples are the subject of several craftsmen's accounts (see fig. 60). As early as 1796, George Davidson of Boston painted a pineapple on a customer's shop sign. John Doggett and David Alling of Boston and Newark, respectively, recorded their work in gilding three-dimensional pineapples, although the purpose of the ornaments is unknown. Alling also employed the pineapple in his fancy chair work. Part of a furniture consignment shipped to New Orleans in 1819 consisted of "one doz rose wood Couler [chairs] pine apple in back." Occasionally, a pineapple is part of a larger composition of fruit that fills the slat or tablet of a chair back.[107]

The selection of fruit in the tray and basket illustrated in figures 51 and 52 includes the peach, a fruit noted by David Alling in chair accounts dating to 1817: "Bronzing 12 Scroll Backs (Peaches)." Although Alling used stencils to produce his design, freehand brush strokes created the ornament in the cross slat of the New York chair illustrated in figure 91. The use of natural coloring enhances the ornament.[108]

Ornamental painters and schoolgirl artists alike exhibited considerable interest in shell decoration. The best-known composition, a work of art in

Figure 91 Detail of the upper back of a Windsor side chair, New York City, 1820–1825. Yellow poplar, maple, and other woods. H. 34³/₁₆", W. 15⁷/₈" (crest), D. 15¹/₄" (seat). (Private collection; photo, Winterthur Museum.)

its own right, is one painted by John Ritto Penniman for the top of a satinwood and mahogany commode made in 1809 by Thomas Seymour for Elizabeth Derby (West), daughter of the Salem merchant Elias Hasket Derby. One of the prominent shells is a cowrie. By contrast, a border of shells edging the lid of a sewing box painted by schoolgirl Jane Otis Prior for a friend in 1822 is naively drawn but nevertheless captivating. The three naturalistically rendered shell ornaments in the drawing book fall closer in quality to the work of Jane Prior than to that of Penniman (figs. 62–64).[109]

Shells appear to have been very popular when Penniman and the Nestell drawing master painted their ornaments. Cabinets and mantel shelves were common repositories, and ornamented furniture carried out the theme. By 1815 a chair decorator in Thomas Boynton's shop at Windsor, Vermont, was "[Ornamenting] shells." Boynton had relocated to Vermont from Boston in 1811–1812, thus he was familiar with developments in the coastal market. Before he left the city, Nolen and Gridley were importing chairs described as "White and gold double shells and green Tops." The white and gold chair of New York origin shown in figure 92 has neatly executed double shells in the crest and on the seat casing and may well identify the imported pattern.[110]

The basic function of the border is to enhance, supplement, contain, or enclose decorative material of greater prominence or significance to a design. Borders occur on fixed architectural elements and movables alike. The Greek key border of figure 66, with its many variants, probably appeared in the American furniture market about 1800 and likely in the form of japanned furniture imported from England. Within a decade the decorative element had been absorbed into the vocabulary of American furniture design, as suggested by the border pattern in the Nestell drawing book and confirmed by Nolen and Gridley of Boston, who in 1810 imported from New York chairs of coquelicot, or red poppy, color with "gold Grecian Border."[111]

The guilloche border of rounded loop, represented by figure 68, appears to have been a more frequent choice of cabinetmakers and chairmakers and predates popular use of the key border in England by at least several decades. The Finlay brothers of Baltimore offered furniture with "Scroll . . . Borders" by November 1805. A guilloche is a prominent feature in the front stretcher

Figure 92 Fancy armchair, New York City, 1810–1820. Maple and yellow poplar. H. 35", W. 20", D. 16". (Courtesy, Winterthur Museum.)

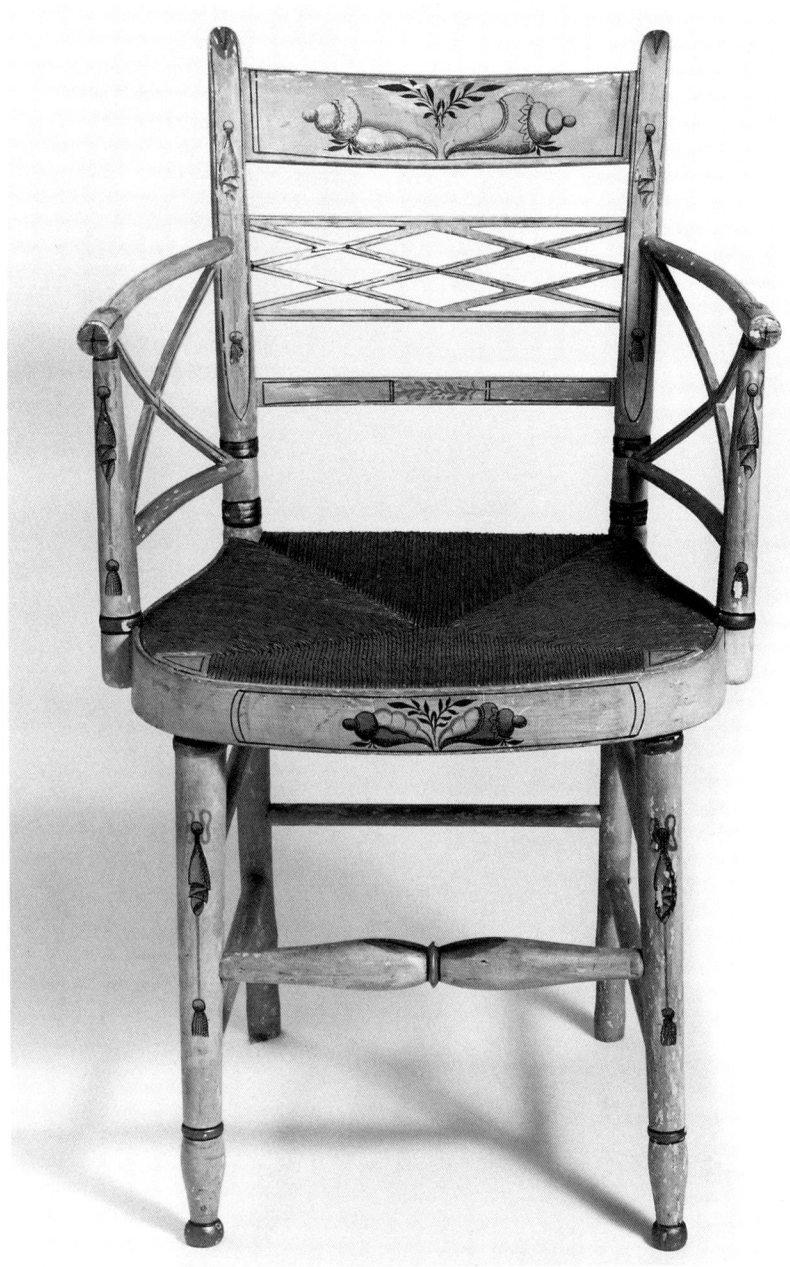

of figure 93, a chair from a set made by the Finlays in 1815 for the Hagerstown, Maryland, merchant Richard Ragan. The brothers were well aware of developments in the English furniture market even before Hugh made an extended trip abroad in 1810 to collect engravings and drawings of European designs.[112]

The stars that fill the loops of the Nestell guilloche border (fig. 68) probably are conscious substitutions for the small florets often found in English ornament. Stars are part of the decoration of figure 87, a New York chair dating to the period of the Nestell drawing book. Benjamin Henry Latrobe used the star as a motif in furniture he designed in 1809 for the White House, although use of stars in American decorative painting dates even earlier. At Boston in 1794, a patron engaged George Davidson "to [paint]

Figure 93 Fancy side chair by John and Hugh Finlay, Baltimore, 1815. Yellow poplar, maple, and walnut. H. 32 1/2", W. 17 3/4", D. 20". (Courtesy, Winterthur Museum.)

his Coach with Silver stars." The star-painted chair illustrated in figure 87 also exhibits another motif found in the drawing book—a heraldic wreath. The twisted band on the lowest cross rail of the chair back is merely a simplification of the ornament in figure 69.[113]

Trophies abound in ornamental painting of the federal period, and nowhere were they more popular than in Baltimore. The Finlay brothers offered "Trophies of Music, War, Husbandry, Love, &c.," to which can be added the hunt, based on its appearance on Baltimore furniture. The most common choice everywhere was the trophy of music, although from ornament to ornament considerable variation existed in composition and the selection

Figure 94   Detail of the center panel on the skirt of the card table illustrated in fig. 86.

Figure 95   Detail of the left front panel on the skirt of a pier table, Baltimore, 1810–1820. White pine, poplar, and cherry; marble. H. 34¼", W. 53½", D. 24¼". (Courtesy, Winterthur Museum.)

of elements. The principal furniture forms decorated with trophies are tables, seating pieces, and looking glasses. A painted Connecticut card table with a floral swag on the top (fig. 86) has a trophy of music centered at the front of the skirt (fig. 94) that relates to the ornament in figure 71. Based on technological accomplishment and composition, the example in the drawing book is the more successful of the two.[114]

Of greater prominence than a trophy of music on a Baltimore pier table is a second trophy representing the hunt, which occurs four times on the skirt (fig. 95). The ornament again bears a remarkable similarity to one in the Nestell drawing book (fig. 72), although the trophy on the table has been painted with greater skill and assurance, particularly the wreath. John Doggett of Roxbury, Massachusetts, noted a related use of elements common to the two trophies in his accounts for December 1808 when recording a job of "Gilding Bed cornise Bows Darts Quivar arrows &c." for client Elizabeth Derby (West). The 67½-inch cornice, which still exists, consists of a long bow, duplicating the shape of the one in the drawing book, crossed at the center by a square, tapered quiver and a torch. The latter element shifts the theme from that of the hunt to love.[115]

The wreath of leaves in figures 72 and 73 is an infrequent element of the trophy. Its principal application as a furniture ornament is to frame a centered device, as illustrated in the crest of the chair shown in figure 93. The wreath as a frame was popular with ornamental painters in Baltimore. Architect Benjamin Henry Latrobe centered a striped shield within a large wreath on the end faces of a Grecian-style sofa when designing the White House furniture in 1809. David Alling identified "Oak Wreaths" specifically in his 1815 accounts in connection with ornamenting a set of bed cornices at Newark.[116]

The griffin was a popular motif among ornamental painters at Baltimore, more so than elsewhere in the American furniture market. The influence that led Nestell's master to include a design with griffins in the drawing book (fig. 74) likely came from that city, a suggestion underscored by the selection of a Baltimore-style chair crest to illustrate the landscape scene in figure 17. Despite the fascination of Baltimore consumers with the griffin, local records are silent on the subject of these beasts. The well-traveled Robert Gilmor, Jr., wrote home to Baltimore in 1800, commenting on the lion's heads and sphinxes he had seen on furnishings in Paris. During his travels in Europe in 1810, Hugh Finlay undoubtedly encountered the griffin, and the beast likely figured as an ornament in some of the furniture engravings and drawings he collected to bring home. The motif appears principally on seating furniture and tables. The tablet-type crest of a Baltimore fancy chair suggests something of the endless possibilities for varying the motif (fig. 96). The luxuriant scrollwork that is part of the chair design is only suggested in the central scrolls of figure 74.[117]

The leaf-bound bundle of rods in figure 75, which suggests the fasces motif, had several applications as an ornament. A popular one was as a stenciled, handpainted, or printed-paper border for walls. One paper with a fasces-like continuous border is documented to a Boston manufactory and can be dated between 1811 and 1817. A hand-painted fasces border above a dado figures in the background of a self-portrait of an unidentified artist seated on a rush-bottomed fancy chair, paint brush in hand. As expected, Baltimore craftsmen occasionally chose the true fasces motif as a painted ornament for their classically inspired chairs, and the ornament even appears as a carved figure on the crests of mahogany chairs made in New York during the 1810s.[118]

The two drawing book vignettes that illustrate mythological-type scenes probably were intended as subjects for reverse-painted glass plates, or

Figure 96 Detail of the crest tablet of a fancy upholstered-seat side chair, possibly John or Hugh Finlay, Baltimore, 1815–1825. Cherry, maple, and yellow poplar. H. 31⁵⁄₈", W. 20¹⁄₈", D. 21¹⁄₂". (Courtesy, Winterthur Museum.)

tablets (figs. 76, 77). Glass tablets are found commonly in the waist and base sections of wall, or banjo, clocks and in the top panels of looking glasses. Occasionally glass tablets embellish high-style tables and case pieces. The heavy border that "panels" the image in figure 76 reinforces its presumed use as a tablet. The most common mythological motif in wall-clock tablets is the female figure riding through the clouds in a chariot drawn by a pair of horses or winged horses. Some figures are identified as Aurora, and the torch is a frequent attribute. Figures drawn across a body of water in shell-like chariots, as illustrated in figure 76, are uncommon, and the animals usually are horses instead of dolphins.

Unlike mythological subjects, patriotic symbols embellish many surfaces and objects—from interior walls to exterior signs, from household furniture and furnishings to firefighting and militia equipment. On May 3, 1796, George Davidson of Boston billed a Mr. Hayman, "Tavern Keeper" of Cambridge, for "Painting his Sine With flag." A spread eagle was another popular subject, given the evidence of surviving signboards.[119]

In 1810 the Boston firm of Nolen and Gridley itemized "Eagle Top" chairs in their long list of painted seating furniture imported from New York. Baltimore painters also chose the eagle as a motif for chair backs, as indicated by the chair illustrated in figure 93, one from a set made by the Finlay brothers in 1815. The same year, Thomas Boynton of Windsor, Vermont, employed John Patterson to ornament a large number of chairs. Boynton also credited the workman with "Lettering National Emblems" (see figs. 79, 81), although the nature of the job is unspecified. The account entry falls between listings for chairwork, suggesting that movables of some type were involved, perhaps militia equipment. A spread eagle on a nineteenth-century drum from Connecticut is painted with a banner bearing the national motto. Daniel Rea, Jr., of Boston recorded "Painting a Drum Shell Blue Ground & Spread Eagle" for a "Connecticut Man" in 1792.[120]

Painted busts of national figures occasionally adorn chair backs and the surfaces of other movables. Tombs and urns were popular motifs, with Washington a prominent subject (see fig. 80). When Daniel Rea, Jr., painted "the burst figure of General Washington" for Boston carver and cabinetmaker John Skillin, he probably identified a figure in the round. Ezra Ames included "Cherubs" in his portfolio of figures while painting in Worcester, Massachusetts, in 1791 (see figs. 80, 81).[121]

References to painted imitations of natural materials in documents contemporary with or slightly earlier than the Nestell drawing book are ambiguous at best (see figs. 82, 83). The most common references are to mahogany, red cedar, and marble. The usual terminology includes the word "color" in relation to the named material, although pricing appears to support painting in a plain color rather than special manipulation of the surface. Thus, when Daniel Rea, Jr., of Boston painted a "short post Bedstead mehagony Colour" in 1791, he may simply have applied a coat of reddish brown paint. Rea was more specific about other tasks, such as painting a set of bed cornices "in Imitation of the Copperplate" or painting a room and entry floor cloth "in Straw Work & Borders." Further confusing the picture is Hezekiah Reynolds's *Directions for House and Ship Painting* (1812), which provides instructions for mixing oil colors for outside work. His recipe for "chocolate color" describes plain brown paint; the one for "mahogany color" outlines the entire graining process. The range of objects and surfaces painted "mahogany color" in this period, whatever the process, is broad. Outdoor work focused on window shutters and front doors. Furniture included bedsteads, bookcases, "buros," chairs, cradles, desks, and tables.[122]

References by painting specialists to "marble" or "marble color" are as uncertain as those for wood colors, with a few exceptions. On July 13, 1790, Daniel Rea, Jr., filled a custom order by painting a "Cooler in Imitation of marble." Seven years later, Samuel Barrett, Esq., engaged the craftsman to paint a part of his parlor in "Mahogany & Marble work." References to marble-colored furniture center on tables. A few entries describe combinations of materials, as for example one in the accounts of William Gray of Salem, Massachusetts, who in 1796 painted "a Table Mohog'y & Marble." Hezekiah Reynolds provided directions for painting "marble color," which again describe a graining process. The ground was white, and the shading, Prussian blue "in imitation of marble."[123]

The Christian Nestell drawing book probably is the most complete document of its type for the federal period. Although many questions remain unanswered about the actual creation of the book, the range of visual material contained within its covers documents popular interest in ornamented surfaces. As suggested, painters drew from a broad range of patterns in bright, vibrant colors.

ACKNOWLEDGMENT   The author acknowledges support for initial work on this project from a Winterthur Research Fellowship awarded by the Winterthur Museum, Library, and Garden, Winterthur, Delaware.

1. The Christian M. Nestell Drawing Book is in the Joseph Downs Collection of Manuscripts and Printed Ephemera (hereinafter cited as DCM), Winterthur Museum Library, Winterthur, Del.

2. *Nestell Lodge, No. 37, A.F. and A.M., Providence, Rhode Island, Fiftieth Anniversary Celebration, 1880–1930* (Providence: By the lodge, 1930), n.p.; Rhode Island Death Records, 1877–1880, microfilm roll 48, pp. 1264–65, Rhode Island Historical Society (hereinafter cited as RIHS), Providence, R.I. For information on Michael Nestell, see "Notes and Queries," *New York Genealogical and Biographical Record* 8, no. 1 (January 1877): 44.

3. *Nestell Lodge Fiftieth Anniversary Celebration*, n.p.; Sotheby's, *Americana*, March 13, 1982, lot 43.

4. *Nestell Lodge Fiftieth Anniversary Celebration*, n.p.; "Register of Enlistments in the U.S. Army, 1798–1815," National Archives, Washington, D.C. (microfilm, DCM).

5. For New York population figures, see Henry Tudor, *Narrative of a Tour in North America*, 2 vols. (London: James Duncan, 1834), 1:22. Timothy Dwight, *Travels in New England and New York*, 4 vols., edited by Barbara Miller Solomon (Cambridge, Mass.: Belknap Press, 1969), 3:326–27, 330.

6. *Elliot and Crissy's New-York Directory, for the Year 1811* (New York: Elliot and Crissy, 1811); *Longworth's American Almanac, New-York Register, and City Directory* (New York: David Longworth, 1811); *Elliot's Improved New-York Double Directory* (New York: William Elliot, 1812); *Longworth's American Almanac, New-York Register, and City Directory* (New York: David Longworth, 1812); George L. McKay, comp., *A Register of Artists, Engravers, Booksellers, Bookbinders,*

Printers, and Publishers in New York City, 1633–1820 (New York: New York Public Library, 1942); Mr. Cottu in *New-York Evening Post* (New York), January 2, 1811.

7. Archibald Robertson in *New-York Evening Post,* April 26, 1802, as quoted in Rita Susswein Gottesman, comp., *The Arts and Crafts in New York, 1800–1804* (New York: New-York Historical Society, 1965), pp. 10–11, and *New-York Evening Post,* November 4, 1811.

8. "Register of Enlistments"; Christian I. Nestell Creditor Agreement, January 8, 1821, with Nestell Drawing Book, DCM.

9. William, Daniel, and Samuel Proud Ledger, 1770–1825, and Daniel and Samuel Proud Daybook and Ledger, 1810–1834, RIHS; Henry R. Chace, *Owners and Occupants of the Lots, Houses, and Shops in the Town of Providence, Rhode Island, in 1798* (Providence: By the author, 1914), p. 20; William Mitchell Pillsbury, "The Providence Furniture Making Trade, 1772–1834" (M.A. thesis, University of Delaware, 1975), p. 92.

10. John Hayward, *The New England Gazetteer* (Boston: By the author, 1839), s.v. "Providence, R.I."; "The Diary of Samuel Breck, 1823–1827," *Pennsylvania Magazine of History and Biography* 103, no. 1 (January 1979): 105; [Anne Newport Royall], *Sketches of History, Life, and Manners in the United States* (New Haven, Conn.: By the author, 1826), pp. 368–69.

11. Christian M. Nestell Bill to R. W. Greene, April 3, 1827, A. C. and R. W. Greene Collection, RIHS; Joseph K. Ott, "Still More Notes on Rhode Island Cabinetmakers and Allied Craftsmen," *Rhode Island History* 28, no. 4 (November 1969): 118; Jane L. Cayford, "The Sullivan Dorr House in Providence, Rhode Island" (M.A. thesis, University of Delaware, 1961), p. 141.

12. Samuel J. Bower in *The Providence Directory* (Providence, R.I.: H. H. Brown, 1830), p. 3.

13. Samuel J. Bower in *Providence Gazette* (Providence, R.I.), June 4, 1820; Samuel E. Brown in *Providence Patriot* (Providence, R.I.), May 30, 1821.

14. Kinsley C. Gladding in *Providence Patriot and Columbian Phenix* (Providence, R.I.), May 16, 1827; William W. Pitman in *Providence Patriot,* November 4, 1820, and January 31, 1824, and *Rhode-Island American and General Advertiser* (Providence), March 30, 1821; Samuel J. Bower in *The Providence Directory* (Providence, R.I.: H. H. Brown, 1828), p. 2, and *Providence Patriot,* January 4 and August 9, 1823; Richard M. Candee, "Housepaints in Colonial America: Their Materials, Manufacture, and Application," *Color Engineering* 5, no. 2 (March/April 1967): 37.

15. William W. Pitman in *Rhode-Island American and General Advertiser,* March 30, 1821; Henry Wilder Miller Account Book, 1827–1831, Worcester Historical Museum, Worcester, Mass.; John S. Barrow in *Manufacturers' and Farmers' Journal, Providence and Pawtucket Advertiser* (Providence, R.I.), February 28, 1820; Betty Ring, *Girlhood Embroidery: American Samplers and Pictorial Needlework, 1650–1850,* 2 vols. (New York: Alfred A. Knopf, 1993), 1:75; George Davidson Waste Book, 1793–1799, Old Sturbridge Village, Sturbridge, Mass.; Samuel J. Bower in *Providence Patriot,* August 9, 1823.

16. Samuel J. Bower in *Providence Directory* (1830); Kinsley C. Gladding in *Providence Patriot and Columbian Phenix,* May 16, 1827; William M. Pitman in *Providence Patriot,* January 31, 1824, and *Rhode-Island American and Providence Gazette* (Providence), December 30, 1825.

17. Whipple and Low in *Providence Patriot,* July 15, 1820; William W. Pitman in *Rhode-Island American and Providence Gazette,* May 12, 1826; Kinsley C. Gladding in *Rhode-Island American and General Advertiser,* August 14, 1822, and *Providence Patriot and Columbian Phenix,* May 16, 1827; Sanford Mason in *Rhode-Island American and General Advertiser,* January 15, 1822.

18. John R. Penniman in *Rhode-Island American and General Advertiser,* June 8, 1822; Rufus Porter in *Providence Patriot,* November 20, 1822.

19. Henry W. Rugg, *History of Freemasonry in Rhode Island* (Providence: E. L. Freemen and Son, 1895), p. 371, reference courtesy of Robert P. Emlen; Rhode Island Death Records.

20. Christian M. Nestell Deed to William Haslett, October 20, 1835, Record of Deeds Book 70-A, p. 15, City Hall Archives, Providence, R.I.; Christian M. Nestell Deed for Shares in Providence New Market Association, April 18, 1831, Registry of Deeds, Providence, R.I.

21. *Nestell Lodge Fiftieth Anniversary Celebration,* n.p.; *A List of Persons Assessed in the Town Tax of Forty Thousand Dollars Voted by the Freemen of Providence, June 1827* (Providence, R.I.: Hutchens and Cory, 1827), and continuing through 1832 with various publishers; *A List of Persons Assessed in the City Tax of Forty Thousand Dollars Ordered by the City Council, June 1833* (Providence, R.I.: J. S. Ham and S. R. Weeden, 1833), and continuing through 1852 with various publishers and title changes to reflect new tax bases, City Hall Archives, Providence; *List of Freemen with the City Officers of Providence* (Providence, R.I.: H. H. Brown, 1832), p. 23; Rhode Island Death Records; Christian M. Nestell Will, written April 19, 1876, presented in court March 9, 1880, Registry of Probate, Providence, R.I.

22. Rugg, *History of Freemasonry*, pp. 371–73; *Nestell Lodge Fiftieth Anniversary Celebration*, n.p.

23. Thomas L. Gravell and George Miller, *A Catalogue of Foreign Watermarks Found on Paper Used in America, 1700–1835* (New York: Garland Publishing, 1983), p. 221, item 12.

24. Thomas Sheraton, *The Cabinet-Maker and Upholsterer's Drawing-Book* (1793; reprint, New York: Dover Publications, 1972).

25. Jane C. Nylander, "Some Print Sources of New England Schoolgirl Art," and Betty Ring, "Mrs. Saunders' and Miss Beach's Academy, Dorchester," *Antiques* 110, no. 2 (August 1976): 296, 301, 307.

26. Alexander Robertson in *New-York Evening Post*, April 19 and 26, 1802, and Archibald Robertson in *Morning Chronicle* (New York), December 11, 1804, as quoted in Gottesman, comp., *Arts and Crafts in New York, 1800–1804*, pp. 9–13.

27. For European sources with thatched buildings and/or waterwheels, see Johns Burtons, *Landschafts Maler nach der Natur* (Leipzig: Baumgaertner, 178?), n.p.; David Cox, *The Young Artist's Companion* (London: S. and J. Fuller, 1825), pls. 17, 37; Florence M. Montgomery, *Printed Textiles: English and American Cottons and Linens, 1700–1850* (New York: Viking Press, 1970), figs. 254–55; William Orme, *The Rudiments of Landscape Drawing and Perspective* (London, 1801), n.p.; George C. Williamson, *George Morland, His Life and Works* (London: George Bell and Sons, 1907), pls. facing pp. 10, 20, 26, 86, 118. For American needlework with thatched building, see Ring, *Girlhood Embroidery*, 2:384. Nathaniel Whittock, *The Decorative Painters' and Glaziers' Guide* (London: Isaac Taylor Hinton, 1827), pp. 321–22.

28. William Enfield, *Elementary View of the Fine Arts* (London: Thomas Tegg, 1809), p. 76; Ring, *Girlhood Embroidery*, 1:206, 2:380–82.

29. For delineations of small boats, see W. H. Pyne, *Picturesque Views of Rural Occupations in Early Nineteenth-Century England* (1808; reprint 1824 ed., New York: Dover Publications, 1977), pl. 63; *The Artist's Vade Mecum, Being the Whole Art of Drawing* (London: R. Sayer, 1762), pls. 87, 98. For European scenes with ruins, see Joshua Bryant, *Progressive Lessons in Landscape* (London: R. Ackermann, 1807), pls. 13, 16; Cox, *Young Artist's Companion*, pl. 50; Orme, *Rudiments of Landscape*, n.p.

30. Hannah Robertson, *The Young Ladies' School of Arts* (York, England: By the author, [1777]), pp. 22–23; *All Draughtsmen's Assistant, or Drawing Made Easy* (London: R. Sayer and J. Bennett, 177? [Engraved plates in the book are dated between 1770 and 1777; the title page is inscribed in ink "January 16, 1781."]), p. 14 and pl. 5, figs. 4, 5.

31. For examples of rough dress, see Pyne, *Picturesque Views*, pl. 100; John Thomas Smith, *The Cries of London* (London: John Bowyer Nichols and Son, 1839), pl. 16. For a figure with a walking stick, see Enfield, *Elementary View*, facing p. 281. *A Catalogue of the Subjects Contained in the Hubard Gallery* (New York: D. Fanshaw, 1824), nos. 21, 25.

32. Francis Grose, *The Antiquities of Ireland*, 2 vols. (London: S. Hooper, 1791[–1795]), 1: pl. 101; Bryant, *Progressive Lessons in Landscape*, pl. 28.

33. *The Art of Drawing and Painting in Water-Colours* (Dublin: J. Potts, 1778), p. 10.

34. Edward Topsel, *The History of Four-Footed Beasts and Serpents* (London: G. Sawbridge et al., 1658), pp. 86, 207; *The Manual of Heraldry*, edited by Francis J. Grant (Edinburgh: John Grant, 1962), p. 68; Whittock, *Painters' Guide*, p. 320.

35. Francis Barlow, *A Booke Containing Such Beasts As Are Most Usefull for Such as Practice Drawing, Graveing, Armes Painting, Chaseing, and for Severall Other Occasions* (London: Henry Overton, [before 1704]), pl. 8; Topsel, *History of Four-Footed Beasts*, p. 508. For representations of squirrels in American portraits, see Albert Ten Eyck Gardner and Stuart P. Feld, *American Painting: A Catalogue of the Collection of the Metropolitan Museum of Art, Painters Born by 1815* (New York: Metropolitan Museum of Art, 1965), pp. 44–45; Jules David Prown, *John Singleton Copley* (Washington, D.C.: National Gallery of Art, 1965), pp. 40–41; *American Naive Paintings from the National Gallery of Art* (Washington, D.C.: National Gallery of Art, 1985), p. 52; Beatrix T. Rumford, ed., *American Folk Portraits: Paintings and Drawings from the Abby Aldrich Rockefeller Folk Art Center* (Boston: New York Graphic Society for the Colonial Williamsburg Foundation, 1981), p. 42.

36. Topsel, *History of Four-Footed Beasts*, p. 173; Roger L'Estrange, *Fables of Aesop and Other Eminent Mythologists with Morals and Reflections* (3d ed.; London: R. Sare et al., 1669), fable 424.

37. Sonia Roberts, *Bird-Keeping and Birdcages: A History* (Newton Abbot, England: David and Charles, 1972), pp. 28–31, 38.

38. Alan Feduccia, *Catesby's Birds of Colonial America* (Chapel Hill: University of North Carolina Press, 1985), pp. 64–67; Rita Susswein Gottesman, comp., *The Arts and Crafts in New York, 1726–1776* (1938; reprint, New York: Da Capo Press, 1970), pp. 194, 254; Jane Carson,

Colonial Virginians at Play, Williamsburg Research Series (Williamsburg, Va.: Colonial Williamsburg Foundation, 1965), p. 101; Elisabeth Donaghy Garrett, *At Home: The American Family, 1750–1870* (New York: Harry N. Abrams, 1990), pp. 73, 92.

39. Roberts, *Bird-Keeping,* p. 33; Francis Barlow, *Aesops Fables with His Life* (London: By the author, 1687), pp. 95, 155; R. Dodsley, *Select Fables of Esop and Other Fabulists* (Philadelphia: Mathew Carey, 1811), fable 29; *Juvenile Sketches of Natural History of Birds* (New York: Samuel Wood and Son, 1817); *A History of British Birds,* 2 vols. (Newcastle, England: T. Bewick, 1805), 1:301–4; Joseph Kastner, *The Bird Illustrated, 1550–1900* (New York: New York Public Library, 1988), p. 99; Montgomery, *Printed Textiles,* figs. 217–19, 221; Thomas Hope, *Household Furniture and Interior Decoration* (1807; reprint, New York: Dover Publications, 1971), pl. 6.

40. George Wither, *A Collection of Emblems, Ancient and Moderne* (London: John Grismond, 1635), p. 250; Barbara Franco, *Masonic Symbols in American Decorative Arts* (Lexington, Mass.: Museum of Our National Haritage, 1976), p. 48; *A Specimen of Metal Ornaments Cast at the Letter Foundry of Binny and Ronaldson* (Philadelphia: Fry and Kammerer, 1809), no. 67, as printed in facsimile in *The Specimen Books of Binny and Ronaldson, 1809–1812* (New Haven, Conn.: Yale University Press, 1936); *Specimen of Printing Types from the Boston Type and Stereotype Foundry* (Boston: Samuel M. Dickinson, 1832), p. 102, no. 113, as printed in facsimile in Stephen O. Saxe, ed., *Old-Time Advertising Cuts and Typography,* (New York: Dover Publications, 1989); Ring, *Girlhood Embroidery,* 2:437; *A Complete Guide for the Management of Bees through the Year* (Worcester, Mass.: Isaiah Thomas, 1792), facing title page; Thomas Mouffet, *The Theater of Insects* (London, 1658), front cover.

41. *Artist's Vade Mecum,* p. 71; *The Young Artist's Assistant, A New Drawing Book* (London, 1826), fig. 28.

42. John Cart Burgess, *A Practical Essay on the Art of Flower Painting* (London: D. Jacques, 1811), p. 16; Kilburn and Dodd, *A New Book of Sprigs of Flowers* (London: R. Sayer and J. Bennett, 1776), n.p.; *The Botanical Magazine, or Flower-Garden Displayed,* 2 vols. (London: W. Curtis, 1787), Vol. 1: pl. 69; John Edwards, *A Collection of Flowers Drawn after Nature* ([probably London], 1786), s.v. "Moss Province Rose Buds" and "Cabbage Province Rose"; Rumford, ed., *American Folk Portraits,* pp. 38–39, 73–74, 211, 213, 215–16.

43. Robertson, *Young Ladies' School of Arts,* p. 28.

44. Burgess, *Practical Essay,* pp. 12–13; Thomas Chippendale, *The Gentleman and Cabinet-Maker's Director* (1762; reprint of 3d ed., New York: Dover Publications, 1966), pl. 176; George Smith, *A Collection of Designs for Household Furniture and Interior Decoration* (1808; reprint, New York: Praeger Publishers, 1970), pl. 96; Arthur T. Bolton, *The Architecture of Robert and James Adam,* 2 vols. (London: Country Life, 1922), 1:265, 2:61.

45. Burgess, *Practical Essay,* pp. 22–23; Carington Bowles, *Bowles's Florist: Containing Sixty Plates of Beautiful Flowers* (London: Carington Bowles, 1777), p. 18, pl. 49.

46. Burgess, *Practical Essay,* pp. 13, 19, 20, 27; James Andrews, *The Art of Flower Painting* (London: Tilt and Bogue, 184?), pls. 6, 20. For flowers in containers, see *Specimens of Printing Types and Ornaments Cast by Alexander Robb* (Philadelphia, 1846), metal ornaments, nos. 66–68, 182; *Artist's Vade Mecum,* pl. 81; *A Drawing Book of Flowers* (London: R. Marshall, [ca. 1770–1800]), n.p. (flowers in vase and tall basket); A. Heckle, *The Florist, or an Extensive and Curious Collection of Flowers* (London: John Bowles and Son, [1759]), pls. 23, 24.

47. Burgess, *Practical Essay,* p. 19; Robertson, *Young Ladies' School of Arts,* p. 59.

48. *Botanical Magazine* (1787), vol. 1, pl. 27; *Curtis's Botanical Magazine, or Flower-Garden Displayed* (London: T. Curtis, 1803), vol. 8, pl. 732; *The Young Ladies' Drawing Book, or Complete Instructor in Drawing and Colouring Flowers, Fruits, and Shells* (London: E. Wallis, [1832]), pl. 11; *The Art of Painting in Water Colours* (London: Robert Laurie and James Whittle, 1797), p. 29.

49. Mathias Lock, *The Principles of Ornament, or the Youth's Guide to Drawing Foliage* (London: Robert Sayer, 174?), pp. 2–5; Sheraton, *Drawing-Book,* "Accompaniment," pl. 1.

50. Bowles, *Bowles's Florist,* p. 14, pl. 33; *Botanical Magazine* (1787), vol. 1, pl. 25; Edwards, *Collection of Flowers,* s.v. "Pinks Royal," "Carnation," "Indian Pinks."

51. *Art of Painting,* p. 46; *Botanical Magazine* (1787), vol. 1, pl. 89; Chippendale, *Director,* pl. 195; Sheraton, *Drawing-Book,* "Accompaniment," pl. 3; Smith, *Designs for Household Furniture,* pl. 26.

52. Heckle, *The Florist,* p. 19; J. H. Wynne, *Choice Emblems, Natural, Historical, Fabulous, Moral, Divine* (London: G. Riley, 1777), pp. 33–34; William P. C. Barton, *A Flora of North America* (Philadelphia: Mathew Carey and Sons, 1821), pl. 26.

53. *Young Ladies' Drawing Book,* pp. 21–22, pl. 10; Heckle, *The Florist,* pls. 14, 24; A. Heckle,

The Lady's Drawing Book (London: T. Bowles, 1753), pl. 17; *Curtis's Botanical Magazine* (1803), vol. 8, pl. 781.

54. Designs from Jean Henri Prosper Pouget fils, *Nouveau Recueil de Parures et Joaillerie* (Paris, 1764), as illustrated in Alexander Speltz, *The Styles of Ornament* (1906; reprint of 2d ed., New York: Dover Publications, 1959), p. 557, nos. 7, 8; Chippendale, *Director,* pl. 15; Christopher Gilbert, *The Life and Works of Thomas Chippendale* (New York: Tabard Press, 1978), pp. 162–63; *Drawing Book of Flowers,* n.p. (flowers tied with bowknots); Edwards, *Collection of Flowers,* "Indian Pinks"; Trade catalogue of ornaments probably made of wood or plaster, England, ca. 1780, pp. 17, 25, Victoria and Albert Museum, London (microfilm, DCM).

55. Speltz, *Styles of Ornament,* pp. 141 (no. 1), 577 (no. 3); Trade catalogue of ornaments, pp. 1, 2, 5, 6.

56. *Classical Ornament of the Eighteenth Century Designed and Engraved by Michelangelo Pergolesi* (1792; reprint, New York: Dover Publications, 1970), pl. 48, nos. 275, 289; Hope, *Household Furniture,* pls. 31, 59. For a related wavelike border, see F. Edward Hulme, *Principles of Ornamental Art* (London: Cassell Petter and Galpin, 1875), fig. 250, the source given as a Greek vase in the British Museum, London.

57. *Classical Ornament Designed by Pergolesi,* pl. 14, bottom, pl. 48, nos. 283, 288.

58. *Young Artist's Assistant,* pl. 27; *Young Ladies' Drawing Book,* pp. 11, 17; *Art of Painting,* pp. 23–24.

59. Smith, *Designs for Household Furniture,* pl. 49, lower right. See also Hope, *Household Furniture,* pls. 12 (no. 4), 22 (no. 4), 29 (no. 1).

60. Trade catalogue of ornaments, p. 7, left center; Giocondo Albertolli, [*Ornamenti Diversi*] (Milano?: 1781–1787), pl. 12, bottom; Speltz, *Styles of Ornament,* p. 602, no. 5; Thomas Sheraton, *The Cabinet Dictionary,* 2 vols. (London: W. Smith, 1803), vol. 1, pl. 9, no. 3; Saxe, ed., *Old-Time Advertising,* p. 129, no. 320; Rudolph Ackermann, *Pattern Card of Embossed Ornaments in Gold or White* ([probably London], ca. 1810), p. 4, no. 153; Montgomery, *Printed Textiles,* fig. 127, pl. 6.

61. Hope, *Household Furniture,* pls. 35, 36, 52; Speltz, *Styles of Ornament,* p. 78, nos. 2, 3, p. 135, no. 1; Gilbert, *Thomas Chippendale,* p. 190, fig. 345; Lorenzo Roccheggiani, *Invenzioni Diverse di Mobili ed Utensilj Sacri e Profani* (Rome, ca. 1806), pl. 42; Ackermann, *Pattern Card,* p. 4, no. 125.

62. Michael Olmert, "The Hospitable Pineapple," *Colonial Williamsburg* 20, no. 2 (winter 1997–1998): 46–57; Montgomery, *Printed Textiles,* fig. 59; Ring, *Girlhood Embroidery,* 2:494, 496.

63. Grant, ed., *Manual of Heraldry,* p. 64; *Classical Ornament Designed by Pergolesi,* pls. 5, 6, 16, 56a, 58 (no. 375); Hope, *Household Furniture,* pls. 2, 7, 9, 11, 19, 20, 25, 45, 47, 60; Pauline Agius, *Ackermann's Regency Furniture and Interiors* (Marlborough, England: Crowood Press, 1984), pls. 4, 9, 17, 20, 24. For other contemporary publications illustrating the wreath, see C. A. Busby, *A Collection of Designs for Modern Establishments* (London: J. Taylor, [1808]), pl. 24; George Smith, *A Collection of Ornamental Designs after the Manner of the Antique* (London: J. Taylor, [1812]), pls. 8, 22.

64. L. D. Chapin in *Providence Patriot and Columbian Phenix,* July 13, 1825.

65. *Young Ladies' Drawing Book,* p. 19. For illustrations of specimen shells, see *Artist's Vade Mecum,* pl. 84; Elizabeth Mayo, *Lessons on Shells* (New York: Peter Hill, 1834), pls. 4, 7, 9.

66. Mayo, *Lessons on Shells,* pl. 4; *Young Ladies' Drawing Book,* p. 19.

67. Montgomery, *Printed Textiles,* fig. 383; John Warren, *Conchologist* (Boston: Russel, Odiorne, and Metcalf, 1834), p. 5.

68. Hulme, *Principles of Ornamental Art,* p. iv.

69. James Page, *Guide for Drawing the Acanthus and Every Description of Ornamental Foliage* (London: Atchley, 184?), pp. 169–71; Speltz, *Styles of Ornament,* pp. 55, 60, 79; Agius, *Ackermann's Regency Furniture,* pls. 32, 49; Bolton, *Robert and James Adam,* 1:84; Busby, *Collection of Designs,* pls. 2, 25; John Crunden, *The Joyner and Cabinet-Maker's Darling, or Pocket Director* (London: A. Webley, 1770), pl. 20; Hope, *Household Furniture,* pls. 9, 20, 24, 26, 29, 43; *Classical Ornament Designed by Pergolesi,* pls. 25 (no. 78), 33 (nos. 158, 165, 166), 58 (nos. 374, 377, 381), 61 (no. 402); Smith, *Designs for Household Furniture,* pls. 4, 158.

70. Hulme, *Principles of Ornamental Art,* nos. 115–20; *Dessins de Divers Ornemens et Moulures Antiques et Modernes* (Paris: Jombert, [after 1751]), pl. A, center; Gilbert, *Thomas Chippendale,* fig. 125; Trade catalogue of ornaments, pp. 3, 5; Hope, *Household Furniture,* pls. 14, 16, 20, 28, 30, 38, 39, 42, 44; Agius, *Ackermann's Regency Furniture,* pls. 3, 43 (rope), 74; *Ornaments Displayed on a Full-size for Working Proper for All Carvers, Painters, &c.* (London: L. and J. Taylor,

ca. 1800), pl. 20, bottom; *Classical Ornament Designed by Pergolesi,* pls. 22 (nos. 96, 99), 58 (no. 382).

71. Saxe, ed., *Old-Time Advertising,* p. 78, bottom, 129; Robb, *Specimens of Printing Types,* pp. 4, 9; Trade catalogue of ornaments, p. 2, center right; Grant, ed., *Manual of Heraldry,* pp. 55, 71, 133; Florence M. Montgomery, *Textiles in America, 1650–1870,* (New York: W. W. Norton, 1983), p. 33, fig. 22; Abbott Lowell Cummings, comp., *Bed Hangings: A Treatise on Fabrics and Styles in the Curtaining of Beds, 1650–1850* (Boston: Society for the Preservation of New England Antiquities, 1961), figs. 5, 33, 43; Hope, *Household Furniture,* pl. 19, no. 6; Smith, *Designs for Household Furniture,* pls. 2, 8, 26.

72. Ackermann, *Pattern Card,* p. 4, nos. 142–44; Agius, *Ackermann's Regency Furniture,* pl. 3; Chippendale, *Director,* pls. 24, 25, 45, 84, 92, 150, 183, 185–88; George Hepplewhite, *The Cabinet-Maker and Upholsterer's Guide* (1794; reprint of 3d ed., New York: Dover Publications, 1969), pls. 9, 12; Hope, *Household Furniture,* pl. 45; *Classical Ornament Designed by Pergolesi,* pls. 6, 16; Trade catalogue of ornaments, p. 17; J. Dumont Le Romain, *Livre de Nouveaux Trophez* (Paris: Huquier, ca. 1740–1770), pl. 5; Alexandre Le Noir, *Nouvelle Collection D'Arabesques* (Paris: Treuttel and Würtz, [1800]), pl. 2; Montgomery, *Printed Textiles,* figs. 9a, 290, 421.

73. For the survey trophies, see *Classical Ornament Designed by Pergolesi,* pl. 16; Ackermann, *Pattern Card,* p. 4, no. 144; Unidentified *cahier* of ornament engraved by Berthault ([probably Paris], ca. 1730–1770), pp. 3, 4; Le Noir, *Collection D'Arabesques,* pl. 2; William Caslon, *A Specimen of Cast Ornaments* (London: C. Whittingham, 1795), nos. 72, 75; Robb, *Specimens of Printing Types,* metal ornaments, no. 53; Saxe, ed., *Old-Time Advertising,* metal ornaments, nos. 70, 399, 400; Trade catalogue of ornaments, p. 17.

74. For trophies with bows and square quivers, see *Classical Ornament Designed by Pergolesi,* pl. 6; Le Romain, *Nouveaux Trophez,* pl. 5; Unidentified French *cahier,* p. 3, upper left; Edwards, *Collection of Flowers,* n.p.; Caslon, *Specimen of Cast Ornaments,* no. 76; *Binny and Ronaldson Specimen Book of 1809,* no. 72.

75. Speltz, *Styles of Ornament,* pp. 74, 127, 152, 171, 261, 291, 308, 360, 366, 391, 419, 432, 490, 499, 571, 601; Chippendale, *Director,* pl. 84; *Classical Ornament Designed by Pergolesi,* pl. 56a; Hope, *Household Furniture,* pls. 11, 23, 58; Smith, *Designs for Household Furniture,* pls. 8, 45; Smith, *Ornamental Designs after the Antique,* pl. 20; Agius, *Ackermann's Regency Furniture,* pls. 13, 14, 38; Ackermann, *Pattern Card,* p. 6; Trade catalogue of ornaments, p. 20; Unidentified trade catalogue of ornaments (France, ca. 1800), pl. 6, no. 223. For lion's-mask furniture hardware, see Charles F. Montgomery, *American Furniture: The Federal Period* (New York: Viking Press, 1966), cats. 408, 415.

76. For other classical motifs in the Nestell Drawing Book, see the star (fig. 68), the urn (fig. 80), the lion's mask (fig. 73), the quiver and bow (figs. 72, 73), the cherub (figs. 80, 81), the quarter-fan (fig. 82), the grapevine (figs. 57–59), the acorn and leaf (fig. 56), the continuous open-loop scroll (figs. 48, 49), and mythological subjects (figs. 76, 77).

77. Speltz, *Styles of Ornament,* pp. 48, 51, 56, 80, 82, 90, 345; Ackermann, *Pattern Card,* p. 9, nos. 1, 2; Robert Oresko, ed., *The Works in Architecture of Robert and James Adam* (London: St. Martin's Press, 1975), p. 98; Albertolli, [*Ornamenti Diversi*], pl. 16, top; G. Richardson and Son, *A Collection of Ornaments in the Antique Style* (London, 1816), pl. 30, center; A. Pierretz, *Rechezches de Plusieurs Beaux Morceaux D'Ornemens Antiques et Modernes* (Paris: Pierre Mariette le fils, ca. 1740–1780), pl. 22, bottom; Bolton, *Robert and James Adam,* 2:38; Hope, *Household Furniture,* pl. 15, no. 4; Gilbert, *Thomas Chippendale,* figs. 32, 33; Roccheggiani, *Invenzioni Diverse,* pl. 42; Sheraton, *Drawing-Book,* facing p. 430 and "Accompaniment," pp. 15–16.

78. Page, *Guide for Drawing the Acanthus,* pp. 173–77.

79. Speltz, *Styles of Ornament,* p. 80; *Dessins de Divers Ornements,* p. 3, left center; Montgomery, *Printed Textiles,* p. 131, fig. 103; Agius, *Ackermann's Regency Furniture,* pl. 98.

80. Sheraton, *Drawing-Book,* p. 228; Thomas Bulfinch, *The Age of the Fable, or Beauties of Mythology* (Boston: S. W. Tilton, 1855), pp. 210–11.

81. P. G. Woodcock, *Short Dictionary of Mythology* (New York: Philosophical Library, 1953), pp. 15, 95–96.

82. Montgomery, *Printed Textiles,* figs. 293, 294; Wendy A. Cooper, *Classical Taste in America, 1800–1840* (New York: Abbeville Press, 1993), pp. 86–91, 142–54, fig. 153; Sheraton, *Drawing-Book,* "Accompaniment," pl. 11; *Classical Ornament Designed by Pergolesi,* pl. 35; F. Knight, *Knight's Gems, or Device Book* (London: J. Williams, 183?), pl. 41, center; Ackermann, *Pattern Card,* pp. 4, 5, 7, 8, 10.

83. For Doolittle's *Inauguration of George Washington,* see Marshall B. Davidson, *Life in*

America, 2 vols. (Cambridge, Mass.: Houghton Mifflin, 1951), 1:153; Marcus Cunliffe, *The Nation Takes Shape: 1789–1837,* Chicago History of American Civilization (Chicago: University of Chicago Press, 1959), p. 126.

84. For the Hayward trade card, see Nancy Goyne Evans, *American Windsor Chairs* (New York: Hudson Hills Press, 1996), fig. 7–26. For the du Pont label, see Betty-Bright Low and Jacqueline Hinsley, *Sophie du Pont: A Young Lady in America* (New York: Harry N. Abrams, 1987), p. 21. *Binny and Ronaldson Specimen Book of 1809,* no. 70.

85. *Young Artist's Assistant,* pl. 31; Mr. Lens, *A New and Compleat Drawing-Book* (London: B. Dickinson, 1751), n.p.; Sheraton, *Drawing-Book,* "Accompaniment," p. 13.

86. Hepplewhite, *Guide,* pl. 58; Trade catalogue of ornaments (England), p. 17.

87. Whittock, *Painters' Guide,* p. 20; Orson Campbell, *Treatise on Carriage, Sign, and Ornamental Painting* (De Ruyter, New York: Russel R. Lewis, 1841), p. 111.

88. Whittock, *Painters' Guide,* pp. 55–63.

89. Sheraton, *Drawing-Book,* "Accompaniment," p. 16.

90. *Encyclopaedia Britannica,* 11th ed., s.v. "ornament."

91. Stiles Tuttle Colwill, *Francis Guy, 1760–1820* (Baltimore: Maryland Historical Society, 1981), pp. 23–24; Finlay brothers in *Federal Gazette and Baltimore Daily Advertiser* (Baltimore, Md.), January 31, 1803, and November 8, 1805, as quoted and discussed in William Voss Elder III, *Baltimore Painted Furniture, 1800–1840* (Baltimore: Baltimore Museum of Art, 1972), pp. 10–11.

92. For New York chairs with landscape scenes, see Montgomery, *Federal Furniture,* cats. 469, 470. Benjamin W. Branson Accounts, 1831–1835, appended to Probate Records, DCM; Wheaton and Davis (Davies) in *New-York Evening Post,* June 14, 1817, reference courtesy of Michael K. Brown.

93. Ezra Ames Account Book, 1790–1797, New-York Historical Society (hereinafter cited as NYHS), New York.

94. Jean Lipman, *Rufus Porter Rediscovered: Artist, Inventor, Journalist, 1792–1884* (New York: Clarkson N. Potter, 1980), pl. 11; Jean Lipman, "Rufus Porter: Yankee Wall Painter," *Art in America* 38, no. 3 (October 1950): fig. 24; Nina Fletcher Little, "Painted Scenes on Country Furnishings," *American Art Journal* 9, no. 2 (November 1977): fig. 3. For the chair with hunter and horse, see Nancy Goyne Evans, *American Windsor Furniture* (New York: Hudson Hills Press, 1997), fig. 1–44. For one chair from the suite of seating furniture, see Evans, *American Windsor Chairs,* fig. 3–159.

95. Ezra Ames Account Book, 1797–1802, NYHS; Daniel Rea, Jr., Daybook, 1772–1800, Baker Library (hereinafter cited as BL), Harvard University, Cambridge, Mass.; Davidson Waste Book, work billed on May 22, 1797.

96. Nina Fletcher Little, *American Decorative Wall Painting, 1700–1850* (New York: Studio Publications, 1952), figs. 36, 37; Zilla Rider Lea, ed., *The Ornamented Chair* (Rutland, Vt.: Charles E. Tuttle, 1960), p. 53, fig. 39.

97. For wooden hearth equipment and tea boards, see James E. Kilbourn, *Norwalk Gazette* (Norwalk, Conn.), April 8, 1823.

98. Finlay brothers in *Federal Gazette and Baltimore Daily Advertiser,* November 8, 1805, as quoted in Elder, *Baltimore Painted Furniture,* p. 11; Daniel Rea, Jr., Daybook, 1789–1793, BL; Davidson Waste Book, work billed on December 21, 1793, and March 18, 1795.

99. Silas Cheney Account Book, 1802–1807, Litchfield Historical Society, Litchfield, Conn. (microfilm, DCM), work billed between December 1804 and October 1806; Titus Preston Ledger, 1795–1842, Sterling Memorial Library, Yale University, New Haven, Conn., work billed ca. 1811.

100. Davidson Waste Book, work billed on June 13, 1799.

101. For the decorated box, see *American Antiques from Israel Sack Collection,* 10 vols. (Washington, D.C.: Highland House Publishers, 1969 to present), 6:1524. For the decorated drop-leaf table, see Robert Bishop, *Folk Painters of America* (New York: E. P. Dutton, 1979), p. 55.

102. Nolen and Gridley in *Columbian Centinel* (Boston), December 12, 1810; David Alling Ledger, 1815–1818, New Jersey Historical Society (hereinafter cited as NJHS), Newark, N.J. (microfilm, DCM).

103. Thomas Boynton Ledger, 1810–1817, Dartmouth College Library, Hanover, N.H. (microfilm, DCM).

104. For the chair with twisted cones in the crest decoration, see Lea, ed., *Ornamented Chair,* p. 68.

105. Finlay brothers in *Federal Gazette and Baltimore Daily Advertiser,* November 8, 1805, as

quoted in Elder, *Baltimore Painted Furniture,* p. 11; Nolen and Gridley in *Columbian Centinel,* December 12, 1810; Alling Ledger, work billed 1815–1816.

106. For chairs with grape composition ornament, see Evans, *American Windsor Chairs,* figs. 7–64, 7–118. Alling Ledger.

107. Davidson Waste Book; John Doggett Daybook, 1802–1809, DCM, work billed in July 1805; Alling Ledger, work billed in 1815; David Alling Invoice Book, 1819–1820, NJHS. For chair with pineapple in crest, see Dean A. Fales, Jr., *American Painted Furniture, 1660–1880* (New York: E. P. Dutton, 1972), p. 206.

108. Alling Ledger.

109. For the Seymour commode and Prior sewing box, see Fales, *American Painted Furniture,* pp. 94, 182–83.

110. L. D. Chapin in *Providence Patriot and Columbian Phenix,* July 13, 1825; Boynton Ledger; Nolen and Gridley in *Columbian Centinel,* December 12, 1810.

111. For an English chair with key border, see Lea, ed., *Ornamented Chair,* p. 28, fig. 13. Nolen and Gridley in *Columbian Centinel,* December 12, 1810. A key border is present in a set of neoclassical chairs thought to have been designed about 1808 by Benjamin Henry Latrobe for William Waln of Philadelphia; see Cooper, *Classical Taste,* p. 116. The key border also appears in Baltimore furniture and possibly dates as early as 1805; see Gregory R. Weidman, *Furniture in Maryland, 1740–1940* (Baltimore: Maryland Historical Society, 1984), cat. 54; Fales, *American Painted Furniture,* p. 141.

112. For use of the guilloche border in English furniture, see Maurice Tomlin, *Catalogue of Adam Period Furniture* (London: Victoria and Albert Museum, 1982), pp. 11, 44, 66. Finlay brothers in *Federal Gazette and Baltimore Daily Advertiser,* November 8 1805, as quoted in Elder, *Baltimore Painted Furniture,* p. 11. For a discussion of the Finlays and their work, see Gregory R. Weidman, "The Painted Furniture of John and Hugh Finlay," *Antiques* 143, no. 5 (May 1993): 745–48.

113. For a guilloche border with florets in English furniture, see Tomlin, *Adam Period Furniture,* p. 4. Weidman, "Painted Furniture of John and Hugh Finlay," p. 746, pl. 4, center; Davidson Waste Book.

114. Finlay brothers in *Federal Gazette and Baltimore Daily Advertiser,* November 8, 1805, as quoted in Elder, *Baltimore Painted Furniture,* p. 11.

115. Doggett Daybook. For an illustration of the cornice, see Fales, *American Painted Furniture,* p. 117.

116. Weidman, "Painted Furniture of John and Hugh Finlay," pl. 4, right; Alling Ledger.

117. Gregory R. Weidman, "The Furniture of Classical Maryland, 1815–1845," in *Classical Maryland, 1815–1845,* edited by Gregory R. Weidman and Jennifer F. Goldsborough (Baltimore: Maryland Historical Society, 1993), p. 93.

118. For wallpaper borders, one documented, see Janet Waring, *Early American Stencil Decorations* (1937; reissue, Watkins Glen, N.Y.: Century House, 1968), figs. 27, 28. Richard C. Nylander, Elizabeth Redmond, and Penny J. Sander, *Wallpaper in New England* (Boston: Society for the Preservation of New England Antiquities, 1986), p. 13. For artist self-portrait, see Paul S. D'Ambrosio and Charlotte M. Evans, *Folk Art's Many Faces* (Cooperstown, N.Y.: New York State Historical Association, 1987), cat. 112. Elder, *Baltimore Painted Furniture,* p. 61; Israel Sack, *Celebrating Our 90th Anniversary* (New York: By the firm, 1993), p. 101.

119. Davidson Waste Book; Helene Smith, *Catalogue: Tavern Signs of America* (Greensburg, Pa.: McDonald/Swärd Publishing, 1988), pp. 17, 28; Mable M. Swan, "Early Sign Painters," *Antiques* 13, no. 5 (May 1928): 403, 405.

120. Nolen and Gridley in *Columbian Centinel,* December 12, 1810; Boynton Ledger. For the Connecticut drum, see John Tarrant Kenney, *The Hitchcock Chair* (New York: Clarkson N. Potter, 1971), p. 89. Rea Daybook, 1789–1793.

121. Daniel Rea, Jr., Daybook, 1778–1798, BL, work billed in January 1786; Ames Account Book, 1790–1797.

122. Rea Daybook, 1789–1793, work on cornices and floor cloth billed in 1791; Hezekiah Reynolds, *Directions for House and Ship Painting* (1812; facsimile ed., Worcester, Mass.: American Antiquarian Society, 1978), pp. 18–19. For additional references to objects painted mahogany color, see William Gray Ledger (Salem, Mass.), 1774–1818, Peabody Essex Museum, Salem, Mass. (microfilm, DCM); Davidson Waste Book; Ames Account Book, 1790–1797.

123. Rea Daybooks, 1789–1793 and 1772–1800; Gray Ledger; Reynolds, *House and Ship Painting,* p. 20.

Figure 1 Desk-and-bookcase in an advertisement by C. W. Lyon, Inc., 1945. (Illustrated in *Antiques* 47, no. 5 [May 1945]: 249; photo, Winterthur Museum Library.) For a current view of the desk-and-bookcase, see fig. 32.

*Brock Jobe and
Clark Pearce*

Sophistication in
Rural Massachusetts:
The Inlaid Cherry
Furniture of Nathan
Lombard

▼ IN 1945, ANTIQUE DEALER Charles Woolsey Lyon described the desk-and-bookcase illustrated in figure 1 as "without exception, the finest cherry secretary desk recorded." In this case such hyperbole was warranted. The intricate, pierced pediment, distinctive floral inlays, and flamboyant shield and eagle marquetry set the piece apart from contemporary New England work. The desk-and-bookcase attracted great interest, and within months the country's leading collector, Henry Francis du Pont, had purchased it for his home at Winterthur. Charles Montgomery, the Winterthur Museum's first director, selected it for the cover of his landmark catalogue, *American Furniture, The Federal Period in the Henry Francis du Pont Winterthur Museum*, and described the desk-and-bookcase as being "among the first rank of furniture in the Federal period." Despite its prominence, the desk-and-bookcase has remained an enigma. Montgomery could not pinpoint its origin, suggesting either Connecticut or Rhode Island as possible places of manufacture. Recent research, however, has tied the Winterthur desk-and-bookcase to a group of nearly forty closely related objects, one of which bears the inscription of its maker, Nathan Lombard (1777–1847), of Sutton, Massachusetts. This article explores the characteristics of this group and chronicles the career of this little-known cabinetmaker.[1]

The route that led the authors to Lombard has been a meandering one, with many detours along the way. In his 1945 advertisement, Lyon associated the Winterthur desk-and-bookcase with the noted East Windsor, Connecticut, cabinetmaker Eliphalet Chapin (1741–1807). Lyon had purchased the piece from a Boston client who believed that Chapin had made it as a wedding present for his daughter. It reportedly descended through her family to a Miss Wheelwright of Commonwealth Avenue in Boston, where it was photographed before 1940. Though interesting, the story is spurious, for Chapin's documented work bears little resemblance to the desk-and-bookcase either in design or construction. Montgomery alluded to a more promising connection when he compared the piece to a desk-and-bookcase bearing the label of Adrian Webb (1790–1840) and Charles Scott (1795–1851) of Providence, Rhode Island (fig. 2). Both objects were made of cherry and had similar desk interiors, comparable chevron stringing on the drawers, and bold, inlaid paterae. Unfortunately, Montgomery was unable to examine the labeled example. Sold at auction in 1930, its location remains unknown. Other furniture by Webb and Scott survives and sheds light on the careers of the artisans and their firm. They moved to Providence from

Figure 2 Desk-and-bookcase with a label of Webb and Scott, southeastern Massachusetts or northern Rhode Island, 1790–1805. (Illustrated in American Art Association, *The Collection of the Late Philip Flayderman*, New York, January 2–4, 1930, lot 431; photo, Winterthur Museum Library.)

Figure 3 Desk-and-bookcase attributed to Nathan Lombard, southern Worcester County (possibly Sutton), Massachusetts, 1800–1805. Cherry, cherry veneer, mahogany banding, and light- and darkwood inlays with white pine. H. 80 1/2", W. 44", D. 18 3/4". (Courtesy, Milwaukee Art Museum, Layton Art Collection; photo, Gavin Ashworth.)

neighboring Massachusetts communities during the second decade of the nineteenth century and worked together from 1816 to 1819. In all probability, the Webb and Scott label on the desk-and-bookcase documents a repair or secondhand sale rather than its manufacture.[2]

In 1962, Lyon advertised the flat-top desk-and-bookcase illustrated in figure 3. Although clearly from the same shop as the Winterthur example, it provided little new information regarding the place of origin or the maker of

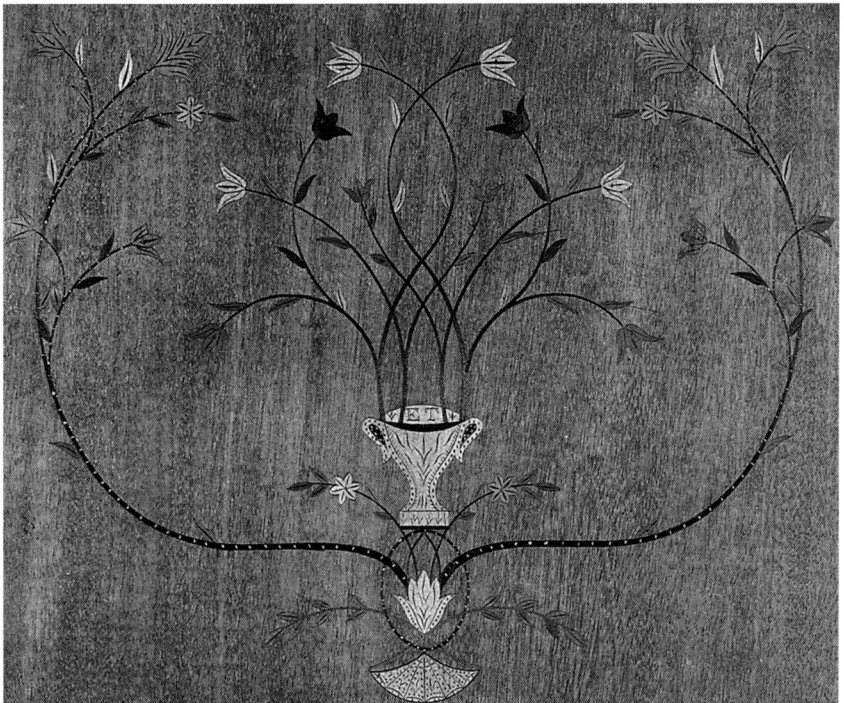

Figure 4   Detail of the initials "ET" scratched into the inlaid decoration on the door of the desk-and-bookcase illustrated in fig. 3. (Photo, Gavin Ashworth.)

either piece. Lyon purchased it from Dr. Harlan Angier, who had recently found it in a house in Brookfield, twenty miles north of the Connecticut border. The initials "ET" incised into the urns on the doors provided a tantalizing clue to the identity of the maker or original owner, but the inscription could not be linked to a specific name (fig. 4); nevertheless, to many collectors, the desk-and-bookcase looked "Connecticut." The dramatic impact of the decoration captured the eye of antiquarian Frederick Barbour, who purchased the desk-and-bookcase and shortly afterward donated it to the Connecticut Historical Society. The society exhibited the piece for nearly thirty-five years, until it was deaccessioned and sold at auction in 1996.[3]

New research had prompted the sale. In the December 1991 issue of *Antiques*, William Short compared the desk-and-bookcases at Winterthur and the Connecticut Historical Society to a striking group of furniture with histories of ownership in central Massachusetts. The group, which included a firescreen (see fig. 54) and two serpentine chests of drawers (see fig. 15), shared many details. The chests and desks had similar serpentine profiles, drawers faced with thick, vertical-grained cherry veneer, and feet outlined with chevron stringing. Additionally, most of the feet had a distinctive spur at the lower inside corner. The urn and flower inlay on the firescreen was

Figure 5 Chest of drawers by Nathan Lombard, southern Worcester County (possibly Sutton), Massachusetts, 1800. Cherry, cherry veneer, mahogany banding, and light- and darkwood inlays with white pine. H. 37 1/2", W. 41 3/8", D. 21 3/4". (Private collection; photo, Gavin Ashworth.) The brasses are replaced, and the beaded strip on the back edge of the top is missing.

Figure 6 Detail of the foot of the chest of drawers illustrated in fig. 5. (Photo, Gavin Ashworth.)

Figure 7 Detail of the foot of the desk-and-bookcase illustrated in figs. 1 and 32.

strikingly similar to that on the fallboard of the Winterthur desk-and-bookcase, and both objects featured fretwork. Short suggested that all of the pieces may have originated in one shop and "hoped that further research, or perhaps the appearance of other pieces from the group . . . [would] someday identify the maker of this extraordinary furniture." Although he could not attribute the group to a specific artisan, Short presented a compelling argument that they originated in rural Massachusetts, not in Connecticut or Rhode Island as many had believed.[4]

Short's article not only precipitated the sale of the flat-top desk-and-bookcase but also placed it and the Winterthur example within a larger context. These distinctive desk-and-bookcases joined other case furniture, tables, and stands as the products of a single shop. A picture of a talented but idiosyncratic artisan with a penchant for inventive inlays began to emerge. Unknown to Short, the artisan's identity lay in a chest of drawers offered by the New England Gallery in 1987 (fig. 5). Its serpentine facade, chevron stringing, cherry veneer, and mahogany banding tie it to one of the chests illustrated by Short (see fig. 15), and its feet virtually match those on the Winterthur desk-and-bookcase (figs. 6 and 7). The bottom of the chest shown in figure 5 is inscribed "Made by Nathan Lombard Apl 20 1800" (fig. 8).[5]

Born in Brimfield, Massachusetts, in 1777, Lombard (fig. 9) was the fourth of ten children. His parents, Joseph and Mary, had married a decade earlier. Local records describe Joseph as a yeoman with a modest farming operation who seems to have been well respected within the community.

Figure 8 Detail of the inscription, "Made by Nathan Lombard Apl 20 1800/ Repaired by Enoch Pond March 21th 1837," on the bottom of the chest of drawers illustrated in fig. 5. (Photo, Gavin Ashworth.)

Figure 9 Portrait of Nathan Lombard attributed to Zedekiah Belknap, possibly Sutton, Massachusetts, 1802–1815. (Private collection; photo, Gavin Ashworth.) The current location of this portrait is unknown; this illustration was copied from a photograph of the portrait in the collection of the Sutton Historical Society.

Figure 10 Detail of *A Map of the Most Inhabited Part of New England*, published by Tobias Conrad Lotter, Augsburg, 1776. (Private collection; photo, Winterthur Museum.)

He apprenticed Nathan's older brother Ariel to Abner Allen of neighboring Sturbridge to learn the trade of tanning and may have apprenticed Nathan to a local cabinetmaker. Presumably, Nathan began to work on his own by 1798, when he reached the age of twenty-one. Four years later, he married Delight Allen in Sturbridge, but within the year they had moved to Sutton, sixteen miles to the east. Lombard chose his new home wisely. A well-traveled route linking Worcester and Providence passed through the town, and Boston was accessible by road just forty miles away (see fig. 10). A prosperous farming community, nascent manufacturing center, and convenient crossroads, Sutton was in the midst of significant growth. By 1800 its population had reached 2,642 and was ranked second among Worcester County communities. Farming remained the primary occupation of residents, and, like many regional artisans, Lombard supplemented his income with agricultural activities. Cabinetmaking became increasingly important as population growth spurred local demand for household furnishings. The presence of turnpikes to Worcester, Providence, Boston, and westward toward Sturbridge and Brimfield facilitated the shipment of goods to a wider area. A highly skilled tradesman with strong commercial or family connections could find a sizable quantity of work. Lombard apparently had both, judging from the quality and design of his furniture and his extensive network of relatives. His wife's family, the Allens, were particularly numerous and undoubtedly secured many commissions for Lombard. The firescreen, chest of drawers, and set of chairs illustrated and discussed in Short's article belonged to Ezra Allen, a second cousin of Lombard's wife. His home in Holland, Massachusetts, abutted Brimfield, the town where Lombard grew up.[6]

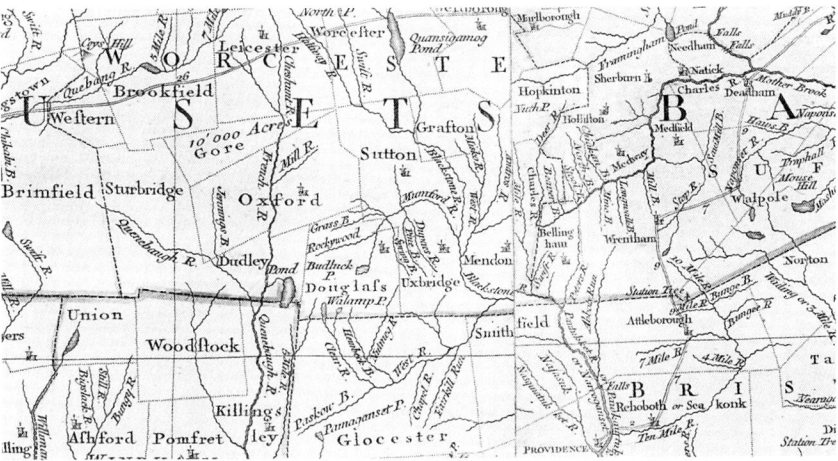

Such a widespread network of customers assured Lombard of business and probably kept him engaged in cabinetmaking for most of the year. To heighten productivity, he occasionally hired journeymen. In 1805, the Worcester *National Aegis* reported:

> *A Journeyman Cabinet-Maker.* Wanted immediately a good workman that understands all branches of the business well enough to do Mahogany work of the best kind. Such a one will find constant employ and as good wages as they can get in *Boston,* by applying to NATHAN LUMBARD . . . . April 30, 1805. N. B. No other but a good work-man need apply.

William Benedict and Hiram Tracy's *History of the Town of Sutton, Massachusetts* (1878) also noted that "Mr. Lombard['s] . . . shop stood where Mr. Mitchell's new house stands. He employed journeymen and apprentices. One of the latter, Clark Dalrimple, married Prudence Putnam, daughter of Aaron, and went to Providence, Rhode Island, where he became a wealthy broker."[7]

Lombard's oldest son, Alanson A. Lombard, assisted his father and later acquired his shop. An 1832 report of manufactures records the value of Alanson's cabinetwares at $1,250, the largest total for any furniture maker in Sutton. In 1834 alone he sold merchant Jonathan Dudley twenty-three bedsteads for one dollar each. His trade also included more ornate work. According to town lore, he and his father built the pulpit for the First Congregational Church in about 1830.[8]

Nathan Lombard died on September 4, 1847. By all accounts, his career had been solid and successful. He attained sufficient wealth to purchase several properties in Sutton, maintain a pew in the First Church (termed the Center Meetinghouse in his will), and pay for portraits of both himself and his wife. He clearly had the respect of his peers, serving as town selectman on numerous occasions during the 1810s and 1820s. His tombstone is modest and reflects the middle-class standing that Lombard had secured for his family. Although both his house and cabinet shop are mentioned in his will, no inventory was taken of Lombard's shop goods, lumber, tools, or personal possessions.[9]

Additional evidence of Lombard's trade lies in the signed chest of drawers and thirty-five other pieces associated with him. All fall within the early neoclassical style and most date from the first decade of the nineteenth century, when Lombard was still in his twenties or early thirties. His designs reveal the influence of English sources such as George Hepplewhite's *The Cabinet-Maker and Upholsterer's Guide* (1st ed., 1788), as well as traditional rococo forms. Collectively, this furniture suggests that Lombard was a clever and imaginative artisan who produced useful and often flamboyant pieces for a prosperous rural clientele. The contrasting woods and inlaid birds, eagles, flowers, and urns that adorn much of his work undoubtedly appealed to his customers, judging from the number of surviving examples.

The furniture associated with Lombard includes six desk-and-bookcases, thirteen chests of drawers, seven sideboards, two card tables, five stands, a clock, a pembroke table, and a firescreen. All are related in design, ornament, or construction. In addition, several objects have historical connections to Lombard: the signed chest (fig. 5); a chest of drawers (fig. 15), a sideboard (fig. 37), and a firescreen (fig. 54) owned in the nineteenth century by Ezra Allen of Holland, Massachusetts; and a card table (fig. 45) and two stands (figs. 52, 53) that descended with portraits of Nathan and Delight Lombard (fig. 9). The latter items belonged to Abijah Woodward (1811–1895) of Sutton, who married Lombard's daughter, Julia Ann, in 1837. They were later passed to descendants living in California and Massachusetts.

The signed chest of drawers (fig. 5) offers an appropriate starting point for the study of Nathan Lombard's work. Its serpentine facade conforms to popular New England patterns, but many other details are more idiosyncratic. For example, Lombard chose to veneer the drawer fronts with thick, vertical-grained cherry rather than the more typical mahogany. He surrounded the veneer with chevron stringing and mahogany "featherbanding" (banding cut at an angle). Afterwards, he trimmed the drawers with cherry cockbeading. He also nailed a narrow strip of cherry, much like cockbeading, along the back edge of the case top. Similar strips occur on many examples of Lombard's work (see fig. 20). Lombard further enhanced the chest with decorative inlay. Along the edges of the top, he sandwiched a broad band of mahogany between chevron stringing and at the base outlined the front brackets (but not the sides) with additional stringing. The feet are one of the most distinctive attributes of Lombard's furniture (see fig. 6). On the signed chest, he used his most complex pattern. This design features a sharp spur on the lower inside edge and combines details commonly found on the feet of Boston rococo case pieces—cusp and bead shaping—and early neoclassical chests—inner C-scroll shaping. Lombard sometimes simplified this design by eliminating the cusp and occasionally the spur (see fig. 15).[10]

The construction of the case and feet follows a standard Massachusetts formula (fig. 11). The frame consists of solid cherry sides dovetailed to a pine bottom and sub-top. For the latter, Lombard chose three pine slats rather than a single board and dovetailed them to the case about four inches apart (fig. 12). He used screws and small glue blocks to attach the slats to the finished cherry top. Occasionally, Lombard varied the arrangement by inserting two broad slats rather than three narrower ones. The drawers of the signed chest have shallow dividers and supports that are glued and nailed into dadoes in the case sides. At the back of the case, he glued pine stops to the sides to prevent the drawers from pushing out the backboards. He planed the base moldings on relatively wide cherry boards, which he glued and nailed to the underside of the frame (fig. 13). These cove-molded boards are mitered at the front corners, as are the foot facings. The front facings are backed with vertical stumps flanked by horizontal blocks. At the back of the case, large triangular supports, reinforced with vertical and horizontal blocks, butt against the bracket feet (fig. 14). Each rear unit—consisting of foot facing, triangular support, and blocks—is glued to the base molding and a pine board of matching thickness.

Lombard built his drawers in a manner typical of his time and place.

Figure 11   Detail of the interior of the chest of drawers illustrated in fig. 5. (Photo, Gavin Ashworth.)

Figure 12   Drawing showing the three pine slats that form the sub-top of the chest of drawers illustrated in fig. 5. (Artwork, Wynne Patterson.)

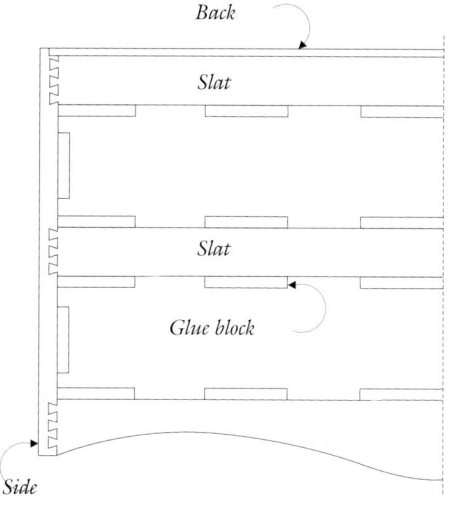

Figure 13   Detail of the bottom of the chest of drawers illustrated in fig. 5. (Photo, Gavin Ashworth.)

Figure 14   Detail of the rear foot of the chest of drawers illustrated in fig. 5. (Photo, Gavin Ashworth.)

Figure 15 Chest of drawers attributed to Nathan Lombard, southern Worcester County (possibly Sutton), Massachusetts, 1800–1805. Cherry, cherry veneer, mahogany banding, and light- and darkwood inlays with white pine. H. 37", W. 41⁷⁄₈", D. 21¹⁄₂". (Private collection; photo, Gavin Ashworth.)

Dovetails of average quality bind the corners. The sides, back, and bottom are solid pine, and the veneered front is glued to a horizontally laminated core formed of one-inch-thick pine strips. Each drawer bottom is made of a single board set into grooves in the front and sides and nailed to the back with four cut nails. A series of small, widely spaced glue blocks reinforces the joint along the sides and front. Remarkably, all of the original glue blocks remain. In design, construction, and condition, this chest is the rosetta stone of Lombard's work.

Five serpentine chests are closely related to the signed example. The best documented one (fig. 15) belonged to Ezra Allen (1773–1866) and presumably stood in a chamber of the farmhouse built by his father in the 1770s. The chest may date to 1802, the year of Ezra's marriage to Mary Needham. It differs from the signed example in only one significant detail—the shape of the foot. This simpler design matches the feet of the desk-and-bookcase illustrated in figure 3. Another chest in a private collection has identically shaped feet and features lightwood banding, possibly of butternut rather than mahogany. A third chest sold at auction in 1987 omits the banding altogether. Instead, vertical-grained cherry veneer faces the entire drawer front, and chevron stringing is set into the veneer. This chest displays other economies as well. The edges of the top have a single line of chevron stringing rather than the customary two, and the feet lack any chevron stringing. Even in this basic model, however, the essential characteristics of Lombard's work are clearly visible.[11]

The final two chests (see fig. 16) are the most ambitious of the group. Rather than having squared corners, these chests are fitted with concave col-

Figure 16 Chest of drawers attributed to Nathan Lombard, southern Worcester County (possibly Sutton), Massachusetts, 1800–1805. Cherry, cherry veneer, mahogany banding, and light- and darkwood inlays with white pine, butternut, and basswood. H. 37 1/8", W. 44 7/8", D. 21 1/2". (Private collection; photo, Winterthur Museum.) The feet are modern replacements.

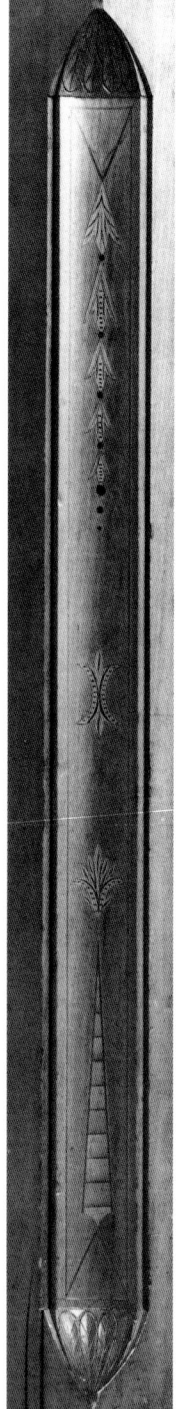

Figure 17 Detail of the corner column on the chest of drawers illustrated in fig. 16.

Figure 18 Detail of the top of the chest of drawers illustrated in fig. 16.

umns ornamented with inlay and capped with carved leaves. On the plainer example, a meandering vine surrounded by chevron stringing extends up the column. The other chest displays a more complex arrangement, with husk and dot inlay at the top, an inverted icicle at the bottom, and leaves at the center (fig. 17). The base and capital of each column are scooped to form pointed arches and carved in low relief with stylized leaves. The corner treatment on both chests defies popular tradition; rather than use conventional, convex quarter-columns, Lombard reversed the curve and added inlay. His inventiveness extended to other areas as well. On the top, an inlaid diamond frames a swirling paterae (fig. 18), whereas on each drawer a central leaf resting on crossed sprigs surrounds the keyhole (fig. 19). The latter detail is fur-

Figure 19   Detail of the decorative inlay surrounding the keyhole on the chest of drawers illustrated in fig. 16.

Figure 20   Detail of the applied strip along the upper back edge of the chest of drawers illustrated in fig. 16.

Figure 21   Detail of the interior of the chest of drawers illustrated in fig. 16.

ther enhanced with multicolored inlays and shallow chip cuts filled with a colored wax or resin. Similar features appear on Lombard's grandest items—the desk-and-bookcases shown in figures 3 and 32. The presence of these inlay details and the convex corners on the chest clearly place it among his finest works. The chest retains many original features, including the brass hardware and applied bead along the back edge of the top, one of Lombard's signature traits (fig. 20).[12]

The construction of the chests with concave columns varies in one noticeable detail from plainer versions attributed to Lombard. On the signed chest (fig. 5), the drawers run on narrow supports glued and nailed into dadoes in the case sides. The addition of the concave columns required much broader drawer supports. To provide adequate reinforcement, Lombard created a frame for the drawer by tenoning the supports into the drawer divider and into a rail at the back of the case (fig. 21). The frame is secured to the case at two points: The dividers are tenoned into stiles along the inner edge of the columns, and the supports are glued into dadoes in the case sides. Lombard employed this technique on every case piece with convex columns. The technique was successful, for the frames remain securely in place nearly two centuries after he installed them.

Two other types of chests can be attributed to Lombard. For the first, he modified a common federal form—the bowfront—by grafting the case onto straight bracket feet instead of onto the usual French feet. On the chest shown in figure 22, Lombard applied his characteristic chevron stringing to the top, drawers, and feet and placed a narrow beaded strip along the back edge of the

Figure 22 Chest of drawers attributed to Nathan Lombard, southern Worcester County (probably Sutton), Massachusetts, 1800–1810. Cherry, cherry veneer, mahogany banding, and light- and darkwood inlays with white pine. H. 33 7/8", W. 33 7/8", D. 20 3/4". (Private collection; photo, Gavin Ashworth.)

top. With one exception, his construction methods match those of the signed chest; for bowfront chests Lombard chose horizontal-grained veneer for the drawer fronts, and on serpentine examples he used vertical-grained veneer. The four known bowfronts by Lombard conform far more closely in design than do his serpentines. Other than size, the two examples illustrated here (figs. 22, 23) are virtually identical. Apparently, he perfected a single model and found sufficient demand to repeat it for a number of clients.[13]

His last type of chest falls into a far more unusual category. On three chests (and a desk-and-bookcase) he employed a swelled facade (see fig. 24). This distinctive shape has traditionally been linked to cabinetmaker George Stedman of Norwich, Vermont, on the basis of a signed example at the Winterthur Museum. Stedman began working on his own in 1816 and made the signed chest soon afterwards. Lombard's swellfronts, however, were built much earlier, probably about 1800. On the swellfront example shown in figure 24, a complex swirling paterae in the top matches one on Lombard's most ornate serpentine chest (figs. 25, 18). The distinctive concave columns with lamb's tongue caps have corresponding details on the serpentine chests (see fig. 17) and the desk-and-bookcases illustrated in figures 3 and 32. Chevron stringing edges the top and outlines the drawers. Here, however, the stringing arcs in a quarter circle at the corners of the drawer, a favorite motif of neoclassical furniture makers but one rarely employed by Lombard. On the two related swellfront chests, Lombard used his more typical formula of chevron stringing framed by bands of mahogany. The case construction of the swellfront chests echoes that of his serpentine models. The methods for fastening the top and installing the framed drawer support system repeat similar treatments on Lombard's signed chest (see fig. 12) and

Figure 23 Chest of drawers attributed to Nathan Lombard, southern Worcester County (probably Sutton), Massachusetts, 1800–1810. Cherry, cherry veneer, mahogany banding, and light- and darkwood inlays with white pine. H. 35", W. 40¼", D. 22½". (Private collection; photo, Thomas Jenkins.)

Figure 24 Chest of drawers attributed to Nathan Lombard, southern Worcester County (probably Sutton), Massachusetts, 1800–1810. Cherry and light- and darkwood inlays with white pine. H. 36", W. 43⅝", D. 21". (Courtesy, Henry Ford Museum & Greenfield Village.)

Figure 25 Detail of the top of the chest of drawers illustrated in fig. 24.

his most ambitious serpentine example (see fig. 21). Although the feet of the chest shown in figure 24 are replaced, the original support blocking remains intact. The pattern of the blocking conforms to that of the other chests, reinforcing the link between these unusual swelled chests and the rest of Lombard's case furniture.[14]

Figure 26 Desk-and-bookcase attributed to Nathan Lombard, southern Worcester County (probably Sutton), Massachusetts, 1800–1810. Cherry, mahogany and cedrella banding, and light- and darkwood inlays with white pine and yellow poplar. H. 102 1/16", W. 46 3/4", D. 32". (Private collection; photo, Gavin Ashworth.) The pediment is a modern replacement based on the one on the desk-and-bookcase shown in fig. 32.

Figure 27 Detail of the interior of the desk-and-bookcase illustrated in fig. 26. (Photo, Gavin Ashworth.)

Figure 28 Detail of the inlaid decoration on the corner column of the chest of drawers illustrated in fig. 24.

The swellfront desk-and-bookcase illustrated in figure 26 is without question Lombard's most commanding case piece. Although the scroll moldings and tympanum are replacements, the lower section of the removable pediment has a slot to receive a tympanum like that on the Winterthur desk-and-bookcase (fig. 32). This slot and evidence of braces guided the restoration. The design of the swellfront desk-and-bookcase has parallels in other desk-and-bookcases and chests attributed to Lombard. The paterae within diamonds on the fallboard and bookcase doors relate to similar features on the tops of several chests. In addition, the presence of chevron stringing and a single band of feathered mahogany on the doors and fallboard echoes the treatment of drawer fronts on the chests. The desk-and-bookcase interiors (fig. 27) are similar to those of the other examples (see figs. 3, 32), and the concave columns at the corners match those on the two swelled chests. The decorative motifs differ, however. On the chests, vertical strands of light and dark stringing intersect a floral sprig at the center of the column (fig. 28). On the swellfront desk-and-bookcase, the decoration is limited to a border of lightwood stringing and a central diamond flanked by smaller ones (fig. 29).[15]

Given the immense weight of the secretary, the base molding and feet are surprisingly diminutive (fig. 30). The molding is the standard cove profile seen on virtually all of Lombard's work. The foot, however, differs from others in its restrained outline and flaring outer edge. Presumably Lombard sought to incorporate the sweep of the French bracket foot within his established vocabulary of traditional straight brackets.

Figure 29 Detail of the inlaid decoration on the corner column of the desk-and-bookcase illustrated in fig. 26. (Photo, Gavin Ashworth.)

Both the swellfront chests and desk-and-bookcase differ in one distinctive detail from Lombard's other work. Like his counterparts throughout New England, Lombard typically used a solid bottom for his cases. Often made of one or two broad pine boards, the bottom is usually dovetailed to

Figure 30 Detail of the foot of the desk-and-bookcase illustrated in fig. 26. (Photo, Gavin Ashworth.)

Figure 31 Detail of the bottom of the desk-and-bookcase illustrated in fig. 26. (Photo, Gavin Ashworth.)

the case sides. On his swelled cases, he fabricated the bottom much like the sub-tops on his chests. Three slats, each set about four inches apart, are dovetailed to the bottom edge of the case sides (fig. 31). It is a peculiar arrangement rarely seen in early neoclassical furniture but more common on case furniture from the 1820s and 1830s.

Although slightly smaller than the swellfront example, the desk-and-bookcase at Winterthur is Lombard's most impressive achievement (fig. 32). It is his only major case piece retaining its original pierced tympanum and central urn finial. Both are affixed to the pediment, which is comprised of a dovetailed frame that slips down over the outer edge of the bookcase top. Just one-quarter-inch in thickness, the tympanum consists of two laminations of cross-grained cherry veneer (fig. 33). This fragile component fits

into a slot in the pediment and is backed by a series of support blocks at the base. The urn follows a standard neoclassical formula, but the carving is shallow and stylized. At the top of the urn, a husk and dot substitute for the more common flame.

Dramatic inlays on the doors of the desk-and-bookcase elevate it above its counterparts. The patriotic emblem of the eagle and shield command immediate attention (fig. 34). In this case, Lombard borrowed a motif that often appears in urban inlays in smaller form—for example, as a center tablet on Boston and Newport card tables. Lombard's version is bold and individualistic. The shield is fashioned of vertical strips much like those used for the paterae of his best serpentine chests (see fig. 18). The sprigs below the shield are reminiscent of details on the fallboard and doors of the desk-and-bookcase shown in figure 3. Lombard's skill is evident in the narrowing of the stem of the sprig as it extends to the tip. His eagles are carefully rendered, yet not complex. They are made of only three pieces: Two form the wings, and one serves as the body. Feathers are suggested by incised lines, and the illusion of depth results from shading with hot sand. The remaining inlays echo details on other case furniture attributed to Lombard. The urn and vine motif on the fallboard relates to that on the desk-and-bookcase illustrated in figure 3, and the escutcheon inlays on the drawers are more ambitious versions of those on his chests of drawers (see fig. 19). Lombard

Figure 32 Desk-and-bookcase attributed to Nathan Lombard, southern Worcester County (possibly Sutton), Massachusetts, 1800–1805. Cherry, cherry veneer, mahogany banding, and light- and darkwood inlays with white pine. H. 92 1/2", W. 41 1/4", D. 20 1/2". (Courtesy, Winterthur Museum.)

Figure 33 Detail of the cherry laminates that form the tympanum of the desk-and-bookcase illustrated in fig. 32.

181   NATHAN LOMBARD CHERRY FURNITURE

Figure 34 Detail of the eagle inlay on the door of the desk-and-bookcase illustrated in fig. 32.

Figure 35 Detail of the corner column of the desk-and-bookcase illustrated in fig. 32.

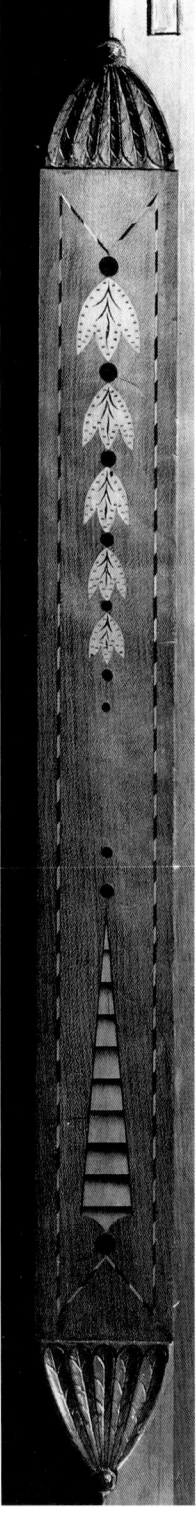

did, however, alter one design element on the Winterthur desk-and-bookcase. Unlike the other case pieces associated with his shop, which have either straight or concave corners, the Winterthur example has canted corners. The cants are embellished with a standard array of inlays, however. These include husks and dots at the top and an inverted icicle at the bottom (fig. 35).[16]

Four other desk-and-bookcases—the one shown in figure 3 and three plainer variants sold at auction—constitute the remaining examples of this stately form. As a group, they illustrate several consistent traits in addition to those already mentioned. All have steeply angled fallboards and waist moldings attached to the upper case, a feature more typical of Rhode Island furniture than that made in Massachusetts. The bookcases of the serpentine examples shown in figures 3 and 32 are anchored with two pins that extend up from the top of the desks and engage holes in the bottom of the upper case. On the swellfront example, the arrangement is reversed; pins in the bookcase slip into holes in the desk (fig. 36). Lombard used two pins that extend from the top of the desk section into holes in the bottom board of the bookcase. On the serpentine desk-and-bookcases, there is an awkward transition between the curved facade and straight fallboard.[17]

Lombard's shop produced at least two other case forms—sideboards and clock cases. The sideboards display an eye-catching array of bold inlays. The exact combination of details varies on each example yet many distinctive motifs occur with sufficient regularity to warrant an attribution to Lombard. Three sideboards are most similar in form and decoration. All have rectangular cases that project slightly in the middle, bowed center doors flanked by convex panels, outer doors that are rectangular rather than square, and drawers and doors with chevron stringing and featherbanding. Pictorial inlays adorn the doors, and differing arrangements of paterae, ici-

Figure 36 Detail of the pins that anchor the upper and lower cases of the desk-and-bookcase illustrated in fig. 26. (Photo, Gavin Ashworth.)

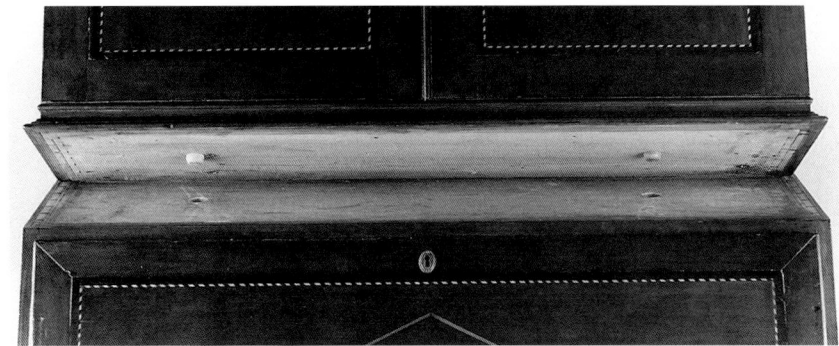

cles, and husks decorate the legs. The best-documented sideboard (fig. 37) belonged to Delight Lombard's cousin Ezra Allen. Allen may have been the second owner. The upper left drawer is inscribed in pencil, "Daniel Lis[t or d]el Brimfield." A Daniel Laisdell (Lasdell) of Brimfield married Betsy Lilley in 1801. Although Laisdell's relationship to Allen is unknown, the sideboard is clearly a product of Lombard's shop. The paterae on the outer doors compare with those on his desk-and-bookcases (see figs. 26, 27), and the legs feature his typical husks and unusual oval leaves. This distinctive leaf also appears on a tall clock case (fig. 42) and two card tables (see fig. 45), one of which may have descended from Nathan Lombard's daughter (fig. 44).[18]

A second sideboard (fig. 38) parallels the Allen example in size and shape but displays more flamboyant inlays. Eagles resembling those on the Winterthur desk-and-bookcase (fig. 32) embellish the outer doors, two-handled

Figure 37 Sideboard attributed to Nathan Lombard, southern Worcester County (probably Sutton), Massachusetts, 1800–1810. Cherry, cherry veneer, mahogany banding, and light- and darkwood inlays with white pine. H. 40", W. 73 1/2", D. 28 1/4". (Private collection; photo, Gavin Ashworth.)

Figure 38 Sideboard attributed to Nathan Lombard, southern Worcester County (probably Sutton), Massachusetts, 1800–1810. Cherry, cherry veneer, mahogany banding, and light- and darkwood inlays with white pine. H. 40", W. 73 1/2", D. 28 1/4". (Private collection; photo, Gavin Ashworth.)

Figure 39 Detail of the urn and flower inlay on the door of the sideboard illustrated in fig. 38. (Photo, Gavin Ashworth.)

urns with flowers decorate each inner door (fig. 39), and smaller floral bouquets grace the narrow quarter-round panels on either side. The dark stems and light petals of the floral arrangements lend a colorful contrast to the ornament. On the stems, punchwork filled with white pigment accentuates the contrast. Similar punchwork also occurs on the dark, sawtooth inlays on the feet. The construction of the sideboard relates to that of the Allen example. The sides and back are joined to the legs; the two-part cherry top is attached to the frame with glue blocks; and full dustboards separate the tier of drawers from the doors. The doors are made in two ways. The outer ones have horizontal cherry veneer on a cherry core, whereas the inner ones have vertical cherry veneer on a laminated white pine core. The case bottom consists of two pine boards beneath each section. These boards are secured with nails driven up into the partitions and through the back boards into the rear edge of the bottom. Lombard's construction is adequate but not exceptional. It lacks the precision characteristic of the best neoclassical work from New England urban centers such as Boston, Salem, Providence, and Newport.

The third sideboard (fig. 40) has a history of ownership in Uxbridge, a town neighboring Sutton. It incorporates many of the elements seen on the aforementioned examples. Paterae and eagles dress the doors, and Lombard's typical husk and icicle inlays decorate the legs. The fleur-de-lis on the quarter-round panels flanking the center doors resemble leafage on the concave columns of the chest shown in figure 16. This sideboard, however, differs from its counterparts in having drawers outlined with ash banding rather than chevron stringing and mahogany featherbanding.[19]

Figure 40 Sideboard possibly by Nathan Lombard, southern Worcester County (probably Sutton), Massachusetts, 1800–1810. Cherry, cherry veneer, ash banding, and light- and darkwood inlays with white pine. H. 39¼", W. 69⅜", D. 27¼". (Courtesy, Henry Ford Museum & Greenfield Village.) The mahogany top is a replacement.

Three other sideboards share details with the preceding ones. Each has large eagle and shield inlays on the doors, ash banding on the drawers, and various versions of icicle, paterae, and fan inlays on the frames. Because these sideboards have not been examined, they are only offered as possible products of Lombard's shop. A fourth sideboard is the most puzzling but, in many respects the most exciting example of the form (fig. 41). Pictured in a column titled "Little Known Masterpieces" in the April 1922 issue of *Antiques*, it has a beaded strip attached to the back and serpentine drawers with vertical-grained cherry veneer surrounded by chevron stringing and mahogany featherbanding, like other furniture attributed to Lombard. Although the husk and dot inlay and floral motifs on the sideboard relate to similar treatments on other case pieces, the fanciful herons on the doors are without parallel in nineteenth-century American furniture. More rococo than neoclassical, the birds are unique expressions of the chinoiserie taste in inlay. Lombard may have borrowed the design from imported British looking-glasses, many of which have carved and gilded birds attached to their crests.[20]

Although only one tall clock case can be attributed to Lombard, it serves as a veritable sampler of his decorative inlays (fig. 42). The inlaid sun on the door does not occur on other pieces from his shop, but it is a common motif on neoclassical clock cases (fig. 43). Not only did Lombard quote details found on other forms from his shop, but he combined his designs creatively. The sprigs and husks at the top of the door are arranged to form a classical shield reminiscent of the firescreen he made for Ezra Allen (figs. 43,

Figure 41 Sideboard attributed to Nathan Lombard, southern Worcester County (probably Sutton), Massachusetts, 1800–1810. Cherry, cherry veneer, mahogany banding, and light- and darkwood inlays with white pine. H. 39¹/₂", W. 76", D. 30¹/₂". (Illustrated in Homer Eaton Keyes, "Little Known Masterpieces: IV. A Heppelwhite [sic] Sideboard," *Antiques* 1, no. 4 [April 1922]: 157; photo, Winterthur Museum Library.)

54). The inlays on the clock case are also fabricated like those on other furniture by Lombard. His husks, for example, are cut from individual pieces, and the segments are articulated with shallow gouge cuts filled with a dark-colored wax or resin. The selection of woods for individual components is also consistent with his work.

Lombard's tables and stands match his case furniture in inventive details and striking decoration. Two cherry card tables with histories of ownership in central Massachusetts bear clear marks of his manufacture. The first (fig. 44) belonged to Abijah Woodward (1811–1895) of Sutton. Woodward, who married Lombard's daughter, may have inherited the table from his father-in-law or a member of his own family. The square frame with ovolo corners—often termed D-shaped today—adheres to a standard neoclassical pattern. Lombard probably bought the stylish urban inlays that edge the rails and outline the mahogany panel at the top of the legs; however, the pointed oval leaf on each leg and the light and dark stringing on the edge of the top appear to be products of his shop. Furthermore, the combination of solid cherry legs and top with mahogany veneered rails is in keeping with his use of mixed woods on chests. The presence of five legs (four fixed and one hinged) is more typical of Connecticut examples than those from Massachusetts.

The circular card table illustrated in figure 45 reportedly descended in a Brimfield family. It too has the light and dark oval leaf seen on the legs of the previous table. The decoration on the rails echoes that on Lombard's drawers; cherry veneer is framed with chevron stringing and featherbanded mahogany. The stylized motif set between each panel of the rails resembles narrower versions at the center of the columns on his most ornate chests (see fig. 17). A cherry pembroke table illustrated in *American Antiques from Israel Sack Collection* relates to other Lombard furniture in its extensive use of chevron stringing on the tapered legs, drawer front, edges of the oval top, and even as a border on the top and leaves. Like several Lombard items, icicle inlay ornaments the top of the legs.[21]

Candle stands attributed to Lombard include both simple and ornate

Figure 42 Tall clock case attributed to Nathan Lombard, southern Worcester County (probably Sutton), Massachusetts, 1800–1810. Cherry, cherry veneer, mahogany banding, and light- and darkwood inlays with white pine. H. 91", W. 21 1/4", D. 10 3/8". (Private collection; photo, Gavin Ashworth.) The feet and finials are modern replacements, and the gallery is damaged.

Figure 43 Detail of the door of the tall clock case illustrated in fig. 42. (Photo, Gavin Ashworth.)

Figure 44 Card table attributed to Nathan Lombard, Sutton, Massachusetts, 1803–1810. Cherry, mahogany veneer, and light- and darkwood inlays with white pine. H. 29 1/2", W. 36", D. (closed) 17 3/4". (Private collection; photo, Gavin Ashworth.) The table belonged to Abijah Woodward and has his name in chalk on the underside of the top.

Figure 45 Card table attributed to Nathan Lombard, southern Worcester County (probably Sutton), Massachusetts, 1800–1810. Cherry, cherry veneer, mahogany banding, and light- and darkwood inlays with white pine. H. 29 7/8", W. 29 5/16", D. (closed) 19 3/8". (Private collection; photo, Thomas Jenkins.)

Figure 46 Candle stand attributed to Nathan Lombard, southern Worcester County (possibly Sutton), Massachusetts, 1801. Cherry, mahogany banding, and light- and darkwood inlays with white pine. H. 27 7/8", W. 17 5/8", D. 17 3/8". (Courtesy, Yale University Art Gallery, Mabel Brady Garvan Collection.)

forms. Three closely related examples rank among his greatest achievements. Combining creative design, proficient carving, and imaginative inlays, they represent the best of rural craftsmanship. On the most ambitious (fig. 46), bold cabriole legs with stylized knee carving and scroll feet are joined to a turned pillar with carved leafage. The top of the pillar is tenoned into a dovetailed box fitted with a single drawer. The box in turn is pinned to cleats screwed to the underside of the top. Vibrant urn and floral inlay fills the center of the top, fan inlays grace the corners, and a band of mahogany borders the surface. Though lacking an extensive history, the stand is inscribed "E H / 1801" in the center of the inlaid urn on the top. The second example (fig. 47) differs from the first in only two noticeable details. The feet follow a more typical pattern, and the floral inlay on the top is more extensive (fig. 48). It too bears an incised date in the urn, in this case "1800." In addition, the corners of the top have inlaid quarter-fans with punchwork filled with a colored resin or wax (fig. 49). This technique closely resembles that used on many Lombard pieces (see fig. 19). The third candle stand (fig. 50) is the plainest of the three. It has a simpler leg and pillar design, and the top is decorated with a swirling paterae (fig. 51) rather than urn and floral inlay. Collectively, these stands illustrate the range of options available within the form.[22]

Lombard also made less elaborate, tilt-top stands without drawers. Two descended from his daughter Julia Ann and son-in-law Abijah Woodward. For the first (fig. 52), Lombard modified the standard New England pattern dramatically. He combined a large rectangular top, shortened pillar, and

Figure 47 Candle stand attributed to Nathan Lombard, southern Worcester County (possibly Sutton), Massachusetts, 1800. Cherry, mahogany banding, and light- and darkwood inlays with white pine. H. 27⁷⁄₈", W. 17³⁄₈", D. 17¹⁄₁₆". (Private collection; photo, Gavin Ashworth.)

Figure 48 Detail of the top of the candle stand illustrated in fig. 47. (Photo, Gavin Ashworth.)

Figure 49 Detail of the quarter-fan inlay on the top of the candle stand illustrated in fig. 47. (Photo, Gavin Ashworth.)

Figure 51 View of the candle stand illustrated in fig. 50 with the top up. (Photo, Gavin Ashworth.)

Figure 50 Candle stand attributed to Nathan Lombard, southern Worcester County (possibly Sutton), Massachusetts, 1800–1805. Cherry and light- and darkwood inlays with white pine. Dimensions not recorded. (Private collection; photo, Gavin Ashworth.)

steeply curved cabriole legs with pronounced knees and scroll feet akin to those on his most elaborate candle stand (fig. 46). Surprisingly, he fabricated these parts from mahogany, one of the few times he used the wood extensively on a surviving piece of furniture. Although the second stand (fig. 53) follows a more familiar New England design, Lombard gave the form his own individual stamp by inserting a favorite motif, the inlaid diamond, to set off the decorative oval in the top and added his preferred pattern of stringing, the everpresent light and dark border, to outline the edge. Like many of his products, the stand features a mixture of primary woods. Lombard veneered the top with a single flitch of figured mahogany and made the pillar and legs of cherry.

A striking firescreen, first published by William Short, unites the inventive base of Lombard's finest stand with a carved and inlaid, shield-shaped screen (fig. 54). The urn and floral inlay equals his most proficient work on the clock, "EH" stand, and desk-and-bookcases shown in figures 3 and 32. The leaves on the upper edge of the screen are reminiscent of the fretwork tympanum of the Winterthur desk-and-bookcase (fig. 32), but on the screen the work is carved in addition to being sawn. At the outer corners of the shield, Lombard added distinctive carved ears that echo the shape of the handles on the inlaid urn (fig. 55). At the top, he inserted a carved husk that successfully caps the masterful design. The firescreen is a remarkable achievement, a testament to the skill of New England's most adept rural artisans.[23]

The history of the firescreen links it to Ezra Allen, the owner of the chest of drawers and the sideboard illustrated in figures 15 and 37. Unfortunately,

Figure 52 Stand attributed to Nathan Lombard, Sutton, Massachusetts, 1803–1810. Mahogany with cherry. H. 27 3/4", W. 15", D. 24". (Private collection; photo, Gavin Ashworth.)

Figure 53 Stand attributed to Nathan Lombard, Sutton, Massachusetts, 1803–1810. Cherry, mahogany veneer, and light- and darkwood inlays. H. 27 3/4", W. 14", D. 19 15/16". (Private collection; photo, Gavin Ashworth.)

no record of Allen's purchase of the chest or screen survives, and the sideboard may have come to him secondhand. The incised "L" on the urn of the firescreen suggests that it too was previously owned. It seems doubtful that the letter on the screen refers to either Allen or his wife, Mary Needham. The presence of a single initial is unusual; two other objects inscribed in the same location have two initials. Perhaps Lombard made the firescreen for a member of his own family in the Brimfield area, and Allen subsequently inherited it. In 1915, Allen's granddaughter Mary Charles wrote that "uncle Bill Lumbard's old red house" was the residence nearest to the Allen family home. Could the firescreen have originally stood in this neighboring house, or, could Lombard have simply inscribed his own initial discreetly in the inlay?[24]

Although a large group of furniture can now be associated with Lombard, he remains an elusive figure. Who, for example, trained him, and what factors influenced Lombard's design? Growing up in Brimfield, he had limited access to cabinetmakers. Did his father apprentice him farther afield? In some respects, Lombard's lavish use of floral inlays compares to Providence furniture; however, exact parallels are lacking, and there is no evidence that he trained in Rhode Island. One also wonders if he had access to design books. Many of his vine and floral inlays and his paterae and fans are reminiscent of the sprightly neoclassical ornament illustrated in Hepplewhite's *Cabinet-Maker and Upholsterer's Guide*. His construction of swellfront case furniture—a very rare type in America—sparks similar questions. Was he guided by a design book? Hepplewhite illustrated a French-style "commode dressing table" that swells in much the same way as Lombard's pieces. The design book engraving, however, depicts a far more ambitious version of the form. If not relying on a pictorial source, could Lombard have been inspired by a French commode that he saw in Providence or Boston? Similarly, what influence did Lombard's swellfront forms have on Vermont fur-

Figure 54 Firescreen attributed to Nathan Lombard, southern Worcester County (possibly Sutton), Massachusetts, 1800–1805. Cherry and light- and darkwood inlays with chestnut. H. 59 1/4". (Private collection; photo, Gavin Ashworth.)

Figure 55 Detail of the shield of the firescreen illustrated in fig. 54. (Photo, Gavin Ashworth.)

niture? Members of the Lombard family moved to Vermont during the early nineteenth century, but no specific connection between Nathan and George Stedman has surfaced.[25]

Questions also persist regarding Lombard's working environment in Sutton. Did he compete with others who offered similar products? At least two cabinetmakers—Daniel Tenney (1773–1860) and Abraham Brown (fl. ca. 1803)—worked in Sutton during the first decade of the nineteenth century, but little is known about the scale of their business and nothing about the appearance of their furniture. Tenney was a neighbor of Lombard and certainly would have been familiar with his work. Their proximity also raises an important issue regarding Lombard's inlays. One assumes that he made them himself because of their unusual shapes and distinctive shading, which set them apart from other New England work. These inlays, however, vary considerably in quality. On the desk-and-bookcases shown in figures 3 and 32, they are finely rendered and skillfully arranged. On the Allen family sideboard and its eagle-inlaid cousins (see figs. 37, 38, 40), the work is coarser. Are these simply variations in one tradesman's output, as we suspect, or do the differences reflect the work of separate shops, such as Tenney's and Lombard's, on adjacent properties?[26]

Lombard continued to practice his trade well into the nineteenth century. Today, we can only raise questions about the appearance of his later products. Did he continue to use distinctive inlays, or did he abandon them as the early neoclassical style gave way to a later phase of the style? The pulpit that he and his son Alanson may have built in 1830 certainly suggests a turn to more subdued decoration that relies on figured mahogany veneer and bold architectural shapes for impact. For now, our picture of Lombard's output is limited to his earliest products—the achievements of a man in his mid-twenties.

The federal era presented numerous opportunities for rural furniture makers. Rising population and growing wealth within many communities created a sizable demand for household goods. Astute artisans with local connections and solid reputations often found considerable business. By the 1820s, their patronage began to wane as outside competition cut into their markets. Larger furniture making firms from Boston and New York usurped a portion of the luxury trade, while rural chair and table factories filled orders for inexpensive articles.

Nathan Lombard's furniture attests to his success during the early nineteenth century. Evidence suggests that he offered a range of standard forms that could be transformed through the application of pictorial inlays and, to a lesser degree, carving. Colorful, exuberant, and highly individualistic, his furniture offers a tangible sign of the confidence and ambition of a style-conscious rural clientele. No contemporary Massachusetts furniture maker better represents the aspirations of the era.

ACKNOWLEDGMENTS We thank the following individuals for their generous assistance with this article: Gavin Ashworth, David Barquist, Ronald Bourgeault, Philip and Brad Bradley, Paul Brosnihan, Wendy Cooper, Susan Doherty, Dean Failey, Paul Foley, Donald Friary, Bud Gurney, Martha Hamilton, Phillip Hayden, John Hays, Holly Izard, Robert Lionetti, Laura Luckey, Frank Levy, James Magner, Jim McCabe, Ben McLaren, Thomas Michie, Carol Ann Missant, Russell Nadeau, Helen Rettew, Donna Rossio, Albert and Harold Sack, Peter Sawyer, Nora Pat Small, Elisabeth Stillinger, and Philip Zea.

1. Advertisement by Charles Woolsey Lyon, *Antiques* 47, no. 5 (May 1945): 249. Charles F. Montgomery, *American Furniture, The Federal Period in the Henry Francis du Pont Winterthur Museum* (New York: Viking Press, 1966), p. 221, no. 177.

2. A print of the photograph is in the Decorative Arts Photographic Collection, Winterthur

Museum Library, 66.754. Robert P. Emlen and Sara Steiner, "The Short-Lived Partnership of Adrian Webb and Charles Scott," *Antiques* 127, no. 5 (May 1985): 1141–43.

3. For the recent history of the desk-and-bookcase, see Frederick Vogel III, "Milwaukee Acquires a Masterpiece: The 'ET' Desk and Bookcase," *The Scrivener, The Newsletter of the American Heritage Society, Milwaukee Art Museum* (spring 1998).

4. William H. Short, "New Additions to a Group of Federal Furniture," *Antiques* 140, no. 6 (December 1991): 960–65. Short's group also included a set of six neoclassical chairs with carving that may relate to that on the firescreen shown in figure 54. Northeast Auctions, *New Hampshire Auction*, Manchester, N.H., November 2 and 3, 1996, p. 24, lot 537. For the results of the sale, see *Maine Antique Digest* 25, no. 1 (January 1997): 2-C. Guided by a policy to collect only objects made or used in the state, the curator at the Connecticut Historical Society recommended the sale of the desk-and-bookcase. Another museum with a broader mandate—the Milwaukee Art Museum—was able to acquire the piece.

5. The chest shown in figure 5 is also inscribed "Repaired by Enoch Pond March 21th 1837." This inscription is beneath the earlier one and is in a different hand. Although both inscriptions are probably the artisans', the possibility that an owner sought to record the name of the maker and repairman cannot be discounted.

6. For information on Nathan Lombard, see *Vital Records of Brimfield, Massachusetts to the Year 1850* (Boston: New England Historic Genealogical Society, 1931), p. 90; manuscript genealogy assembled for Karl Lombard Briel, a direct descendant of Nathan Lombard. Indenture of Ariel Lombard to Abner Allen, December 5, 1785, Old Sturbridge Village Research Library, 1976.21. *Vital Records of Sturbridge, Massachusetts to the Year 1850* (Boston: New England Historic Genealogical Society, 1906), p. 228; Nathan and Delight's first child, Alanson Allen Lombard, was born in Sutton on January 25, 1803. The couple probably settled in the town at least two months earlier (*Vital Records of Sutton, Massachusetts to the end of the Year 1849* [Worcester: Franklin P. Rice, 1907], p. 110). Presumably they rented a residence in the town. Their first purchase of real estate in Sutton occurred in 1805 (Archelaus Putnam to Nathan Lombard, Worcester County Record of Deeds, vol. 158, p. 342). For information on Sutton's growth during the early nineteenth century, see Nora Pat Small, "Beauty and Convenience: The Architectural Reordering of Sutton, Massachusetts, 1790–1840" (Ph.D. diss., Boston University, 1994), pp. 60–81. Lombard owned a farm in addition to his home and cabinet shop (William A. Benedict and Hiram A. Tracy, comps., *History of the Town of Sutton, Massachusetts, from 1704 to 1876* [Worcester: Sanford & Company, 1878], pp. 212–13, 305–6). Accounts of Ezra Allen's home were written by his granddaughter, Mary L. Charles (see Martin Lovering, *History of the Town of Holland, Massachusetts* [Rutland, Vt.: Tuttle Company, 1915], pp. 383–86, and typescript essay in the accession records for the Winterthur desk-and-bookcase, 57.885). William Short's typescript history of the chairs, firescreen, and serpentine chest of drawers and sideboard shown in figures 15 and 37 is also in the accessions records for 57.885.

7. Benedict and Tracy, *History of the Town of Sutton*, p. 212. *National Aegis* (Worcester, Mass.), May 1, 1805.

8. See citation for Alanson A. Lombard in Donna Keith Baron, "Furniture Makers and Retailers in Worcester County, Massachusetts, Working to 1850," *Antiques* 143, no. 5 (May 1993): 792. See accounts mentioning Lombard in the Jonathan Dudley Account Book, 1818–1835, private collection. Benedict and Tracy, *History of the Town of Sutton*, pp. 232–33.

9. *Vital Records of Brimfield, Massachusetts to the Year 1850*, p. 305. Lombard's purchases of property are recorded in the Worcester County Record of Deeds on the following volumes and pages: 158:342; 233:320–21; 243:39; 259:53; 275:665; 300:372; 314:103; 317:13; 343:631. Lombard's pew transactions are noted in First Congregational Church Records, "Society Records," vol. 2 (1794–1822), Sutton Historical Society, pp. 62, 73, 83, 92. Nathan served as a town selectman in 1817, 1818, 1821, and 1822 (Benedict and Tracy, *History of the Town of Sutton*, p. 799). Will of Nathan Lombard, 1847, Worcester County Probate Records, vol. 89, pp. 401–2.

10. An 1837 description of featherbanding is quoted in Montgomery, *American Furniture, The Federal Period*, p. 33. Lombard also used cedrella, butternut, and what appears to be ash for banding. A characteristic Boston rococo straight bracket foot is pictured in Nancy E. Richards and Nancy Goyne Evans, *New England Furniture at Winterthur, Queen Anne and Chippendale Periods* (Hanover, N.H.: University Press of New England for the Winterthur Museum, 1997), p. 359, no. 177; for a typical New England neoclassical bracket foot with inner C scroll, see Brock Jobe, ed., *Portsmouth Furniture, Masterworks from the New Hampshire Seacoast* (Boston: Society for the Preservation of New England Antiquities, 1993), nos. 8, 28.

11. A sixth chest (at the Dallas Museum of Art) may also be a member of the group. It incor-

porates the vertical-grained cherry veneer, chevron stringing, and distinctive spur at the base of the bracket feet seen on the signed Lombard chest (fig. 5); however, the molded edge of the top and exposed dovetails binding the rear bracket feet to the rear support clearly set it apart from the others. See Charles L. Venable, *American Furniture in the Bybee Collection* (Austin: University of Texas Press, 1989), no. 37. To the authors' knowledge, the privately owned chest has never been pictured or published. Christie's, *The Collection of the Late Jeannette R. Marks*, Lexington, Kentucky, June 5–6, 1987, lot 593. John Walton purchased the chest at the Christie's sale and subsequently advertised it in *Antiques* 133, no. 5 (May 1988): 940.

12. The plainer chest originally belonged to Simeon and Susanna Clark of Hardwick, Massachusetts. It is pictured in Short, "New Additions," p. 965, pl. 8.

13. In addition to the two bowfronts illustrated here (figs. 22, 23), a third is shown in *American Antiques from Israel Sack Collections*, 10 vols. (Alexandria, Va.: Highland House Publishers, 1969–1992), 4:876, and a fourth was formerly in the collection of Bernard and S. Dean Levy of New York.

14. In addition to the chest of drawers illustrated here (fig. 24), another is shown in *American Antiques from Israel Sack Collection*, 1:276, and a third belongs to Woodbury, Connecticut, antiques dealer David Dutton. Kenneth Joel Zogry, *The Best the Country Affords, Vermont Furniture 1765–1850* (Bennington, Vt.: Bennington Museum, 1995), no. 69.

15. For a preconservation illustration of the desk-and-bookcase, see *Maine Antique Digest* 25, no. 9 (September 1997): 33-F.

16. Smaller versions of the shield and eagle motif on Rhode Island and Massachusetts card tables are shown in Alexandra W. Rollins and Clement E. Conger, *Treasures of State, Fine and Decorative Arts in the Diplomatic Reception Rooms of the U.S. Department of State* (New York: Harry N. Abrams, 1991), nos. 122, 123, 126, 127.

17. The three plainer desk-and-bookcases are illustrated in American Art Association, *Morris Berry Collection*, New York, April 25–26, 1930, lot 169; Skinner's, *Fine Americana*, Bolton, Massachusetts, May 24, 1985, lot 204; and Christie's *Important American Furniture, Silver, Folk and Decorative Arts*, New York, June 19, 1996, lot 196 (purchased by Cinnamon Hill Antiques and advertised in *Antiques* 151, no. 3 [March 1997]: 418). Michael Moses, *Master Craftsmen of Newport, The Townsends and Goddards* (Tenafly, N.J.: MMI Americana Press, 1984), p. 10. Frequently in two-part Rhode Island case furniture, the parts are anchored by a cleat. The cleat is nailed to the underside of the upper case, which fits into an opening in the top of the lower case. For more on this construction, see Brock Jobe and Myrna Kaye, *New England Furniture: The Colonial Era* (Boston: Houghton Mifflin, 1984), pp. 174–75. Lombard's method, though quite different in approach, serves the same purpose.

18. *Vital Records of Brimfield, Massachusetts to the Year 1850*, p. 211.

19. According to Jess Pavey, the antiques dealer who sold the sideboard to the Henry Ford Museum, the piece belonged to the Capron family, early settlers of Uxbridge, Massachusetts (letter from Pavey in museum accession file, 54.35.1).

20. For illustrations of the three sideboards not pictured here, see *American Antiques from Israel Sack Collection*, 1:51; Skinner's, *Fine Americana Including the Private Collection of Kenneth Hammitt of Woodbury, Connecticut*, Bolton, Massachusetts, October 30–31, 1993, lot 313A; and American Art Association, *The Philip Flayderman Collection*, New York, January 2–4, 1930, lot 431. The Skinner's sideboard reportedly descended in the family of Charles O. Childs of Stow, Massachusetts. It was purchased by Bernard and S. Dean Levy and re-sold to a private collector. The Flayderman sideboard resurfaced in the antiques trade during the early 1990s. According to one source, it had numerous repairs, including at least two new legs. We have not examined the sideboards formerly owned by Sack and Flayderman, and we are unaware of the location of the sideboard with inlaid herons. Hopefully this publication will spur its rediscovery. Carved herons and other birds also occur in American furniture and architectural carving from the last half of the eighteenth century and the early nineteenth century.

21. Benjamin A. Hewitt, Patricia E. Kane, and Gerald W. R. Ward, *The Work of Many Hands, Card Tables in Federal America 1790–1820* (New Haven, Conn.: Yale University Art Gallery, 1982), pp. 153–54. The pembroke table is illustrated in *American Antiques from Israel Sack Collection*, 1:67. It has not been examined by the authors.

22. Francis P. Garvan purchased the stand shown in figure 46 on January 18, 1929, from Charles R. Morson, a New York antiques dealer. It became part of the collection given to the Yale University Art Gallery by Garvan in honor of his wife, Mabel Brady Garvan. For more on the stand, see David L. Barquist, *American Tables and Looking Glasses in the Mabel Brady Garvan and Other Collections at Yale University* (New Haven, Conn.: Yale University Art Gallery,

1992), no. 126. A fourth stand illustrated in Montgomery, *American Furniture, The Federal Period*, no. 376, relates to the previous three in its basic design: tripod legs with a pronounced knee much like that on the Yale stand, urn-and-ring turned pillar resembling that on the plainest of the three stands, and small drawer beneath the top. In addition, the Winterthur stand features a two-headed eagle and shield inlay similar to that on the clock attributed to Lombard (see fig. 42). The stand is, however, coarser in its construction and lacks the dovetailed box housing the drawer that appears on the other three. Because of these differences, we have chosen not to attribute it to Lombard. A fifth stand illustrated in *American Antiques from Israel Sack Collection*, 3:830, relates in one key detail to others attributed to Lombard. The pattern of interlaced vines and flowers rising from an urn on its oval top resembles the treatment on the "1800" and "EH / 1801" stands; however, the shape of the inlaid urn and the design of the turned pillar are so distinctive that we have refrained from attributing it to Lombard.

23. Short, "New Additions," pl. 6.

24. A typescript of Mary Charles's account is filed in the accession records for the Winterthur desk-and-bookcase (acc. 57. 885).

25. Providence furniture with inlays reminiscent of those used by Lombard include a sideboard illustrated in *American Antiques from Israel Sack Collection*, 7:1940, 1941; another sideboard with a Killingly, Connecticut, history in Eleanore Bradford Monahon, "The Rawson Family of Cabinetmakers in Providence, Rhode Island," *Antiques* 118, no. 1 (July 1980): 138–39, pl. 4, fig. 10; and a card table in Christopher P. Monkhouse and Thomas S. Michie, *American Furniture in Pendleton House* (Providence: Museum of Art, Rhode Island School of Design, 1986), no. 79. George Hepplewhite, *The Cabinet-Maker and Upholsterer's Guide*, 3rd ed. (London: I. and J. Taylor, 1794), pl. 77.

26. Tenney made "carriages, . . . cider mill screws, all kinds of household furniture, sideboards, sofas, lounges, and chairs of every variety." He employed several journeymen and apprentices including Charles De Coster (a cabinetmaker from Charlestown), Jonathan Sibley, Zadock Woodbury, Sylvester Morse, Adams Morse, John Humphrey, Aaron Burdon, and Jonathan Howard. See Benedict and Tracy, *History of the Town of Sutton*, p. 303. Abraham Brown is identified as a cabinetmaker in Sutton in a court case of 1803; he was sued by William Darling, Jr., for failing to make "one case of Drawers & one three feet and a half maple table, exclusive of brasses" valued at $18; Worcester County Court of Common Pleas, Record Books, September 1803 term, p. 191.

Peter Follansbee

A Seventeenth-Century Carpenter's Conceit: The Waldo Family Joined Great Chair

▼ A THREE-POST, or "three-square," joined chair traditionally referred to as the Waldo chair, is the only known example of this intriguing furniture form (fig. 1). In concept, this object incorporates several recognized chairmaking designs. Like many contemporary wainscot chairs, it has a front frame with two posts connected by a seat rail and a stretcher. Decorative details include turnings on the front posts and gouge-cut carving in the crease moldings on the seat rails and back. The back is unique in the history of seventeenth-century furniture design. It consists of a single, broad post that supports an open framework of rails and stiles with diagonal, curved braces. The scroll-shaped arms tenoned into the rear stiles are elongated versions of those found on wainscot chairs.[1]

Although Wallace Nutting recorded a partial history of the Waldo chair in *Furniture of the Pilgrim Century* (1921), he stated that it was "reputed to have been brought from France, but claimed to be made of American woods" (fig. 2). In 1983, furniture historian Robert F. Trent presented new research on the history of the chair and suggested that it was made by a New England carpenter. Among several possible candidates for the maker, Trent favored John Elderkin (1616–1687), an immigrant millwright who worked in Massachusetts, Connecticut, and Rhode Island. This article will discuss the stylistic origins of the chair, examine aspects of its construction, and assess the Elderkin attribution in greater detail.[2]

Trent's assertion that the Waldo chair was made by an artisan trained in carpentry rather than furniture joinery is logical. Some aspects of its construction suggest that the maker was unfamiliar with traditional chairmaking procedures, whereas others relate to the framing of large seventeenth-century buildings. The distinctive construction of the rear facade reflects an understanding of complex structural forces that a joiner would rarely, if ever, encounter.

The Waldo chair has much in common with three-post, board-seated turned chairs, which survive in relatively large numbers and frequently appear in Dutch genre paintings of the period (fig. 3). The latter chairs are made almost entirely of turned members, but their seat construction is what distinguishes them from other forms. The seat is a riven (split) board captured in grooves in the adjacent lists (fig. 4). Because the seat lists enter the posts at the same height (to receive the feathered edges of the seat board), their tenons intersect each other. Turners often solved this problem by using a combination of rectangular tenons pierced by turned ones. Alternatively, some tradesmen combined large and small round tenons.[3]

Figure 1 Joined chair attributed to John Elderkin, eastern Connecticut, Rhode Island, or Massachusetts, 1640–1680. Oak, cherry, and ash. H. 42 1/2", W. 22 1/4", D. 19 1/4" (seat). (Chipstone Foundation; photo, Gavin Ashworth.)

Figure 2 Joined chair illustrated in fig. 1, as it appeared in Wallace Nutting's *Furniture of the Pilgrim Century,* 2 vols. (1921, reprint ed.; Framingham, Mass.: Old America Company, 1928), 2: no. 1774.

In *Academie or Store House of Armory & Blazon* (1688), Randle Holme illustrated two seating forms with board seats—a chair with a canted back and a triangular stool. His descriptions are at times misleading and vague. The chair has no arms, but he refers to it as "a Turned chaire with Armes" and notes that "these kind . . . are [also] borne without Armes"(depicted on coats of arms as a side chair). His description of the stool is more revealing:

> a Turned stoole . . . so termed because it is made by the Turner, or wheele wright all of Turned wood, wrought with Knops, and rings all over the feete, these and the chaires, are generally made with three feete, but to distinguish them from the foure feet, you may term them three footed turned stool or chair.[4]

Although over thirteen New England chairs with four feet and board seats survive, no three-footed examples are known. Two three-footed chairs

Figure 3 Turned chair, England, 1550–1600. Ash. H. 44⁷⁄₈", W. 30³⁄₈", D. 22³⁄₈". (Private collection; photo, George Fistrovitch.)

Figure 4 Detail of the underside of the turned chair illustrated in fig. 3.

have early New England histories, but both were made in England. The only New England probate reference that might designate this form is the "3 Square chaire" valued at 4s. in the 1672 inventory of Richard Jacob of Ipswich, Massachusetts. Because appraisers commonly identified chairs by their seat material, some of the numerous references to "wooden chairs" in seventeenth-century New England inventories could refer to three-footed examples with board seats.[5]

Board-seated turned chairs are made in two basic formats. In three-footed examples, the simplest version has a T-shaped back. A crest rail—either a slightly curved board or a turned rail—is mounted across the top of an extended rear post and is supported by diagonal braces. This type of chair has no layback, so the back post is perpendicular to the seat plane. When arms are employed they are turned and tenoned into the front posts and the crest rail (see fig. 5). The second type of three-footed chair has a rear facade formed

Figure 5 Turned chair, England, 1550–1650. Beech and elm. H. 34", W. 24", D. 19". (Courtesy, Plimoth Plantation; photo, Gavin Ashworth.)

by a rectangular or square frame composed of turned members mounted on top of a shortened rear post, strengthened by diagonal bracing (see fig. 3). This structure is more substantial and provides some layback for comfort.

The same basic designs also occur in four-legged chairs. Although usually quite ornamental, the straight-backed version is similar in concept to rush-seated chairs. On the Plymouth example shown in figure 6, the rear posts extend from the floor to the top of the chair's back. A more complex chair of Connecticut origin (figs. 7, 8) has a rear frame with a strong cant. The shortened back legs are tenoned up into a horizontal cross rail just above the seat, and the upper rear posts are tenoned down into the rail at an angle.

No direct antecedent for the Waldo chair is known, but two simple, shaved and planed English three-legged chairs survive. One (formerly in the Rous Lench collection) is illustrated in Victor Chinnery's *Oak Furniture: The British Tradition*; the other is illustrated in figure 9. Although both objects are made of riven and hewn timber and have rectangular mortise-and-tenon joints at the front seat rail and rear crest rails, they are not "joined

Figure 6 Turned chair, probably Plymouth, Massachusetts, 1630–1655. Red and black ash. H. 45", W. 24½", D. 18½". (Courtesy, Pilgrim Society, Plymouth, Massachusetts, gift of the heirs of William Hedge; photo, Gavin Ashworth.) The white pine seat board is a later replacement.

chairs" in the strictest sense of the term. The basic design and structure of these chairs relate more closely to turned examples. They have arms that tenon into the crest rail and diagonal braces that fit between the rear post and the crest rail. All the joinery used for the side seat rails, arms, and stretchers consists of round, shaved tenons seated in mortises bored with a brace and bit. Instead of being captured in grooves, the seat boards sit on top of the seat rails and are fastened with nails. The rear post is hewn above the seat to produce a slight layback.[6]

In design and construction, these English chairs are non-turned versions of the turned three-footed chair. The period term for these shaved and planed forms is "plain" chair. Records from the London Turner's Company

Figure 7 Turned chair, Connecticut, 1650–1700. Ash and oak. H. 41 1/8", W. 23", D. 16 1/2". (Courtesy, Connecticut Historical Society; photo, Robert Bitondi.)

Figure 8 Side view of the turned chair illustrated in fig. 7.

concerning the production of "matted" or rush-seated chairs reveal that turners made non-turned seating furniture. On February 20, 1615,

> it was directed that the makers of chairs about the City, who were strangers and foreigners, were to bring them to the Hall to be searched according to the ordinances. When they were thus brought and searched, they were to be bought by the Master and Wardens at a price fixed by them, which was 6s per dozen for plain matted chairs and 7s per dozen for turned matted chairs.

This distinction between "plain" and "turned" chairs proves that turners made shaved examples at less cost. Documentary evidence suggests that the plain chair was the most common seating form of the period, yet very few examples survive. Their construction was the most straightforward: The parts were shaved with a drawknife, then assembled by fitting round shaved tenons into bored mortises (fig. 10). The existence of plain chairs reinforces the idea that turned components were strictly ornamental in intention. Stock for a turned chair was prepared by riving and shaving the pieces prior to shaping them on the lathe. The makers of plain matted chairs simply omitted the turning stage.[7]

Although the Waldo chair's design incorporates some elements from three-footed, board-seated turned chairs, it is technically a joined chair.

Figure 9 Plain chair, England, seventeenth century. Oak. (Courtesy, Metropolitan Museum of Art.)

With the exception of the finials and pendants, it is constructed entirely with drawbored, mortise-and-tenon joints. The maker prepared his stock by riving and hewing the "stuff" from the log, then dressing it with a joiner's hatchet and planes. He selected a naturally curved, or "swept," piece of timber for the back post before hewing and planing it to refine the shape (fig. 11). This method of producing layback differs from traditional wainscot chair construction. Most joiners simply hewed and planed straight boards.[8]

The rear post of the Waldo chair is tenoned into a back frame composed of two horizontal rails, two short vertical stiles, and two diagonal braces (fig. 12). Unlike the braces in turned and plain shaved chairs, which usually fit between the post and the crest rail, those on the Waldo chair connect the rear post to short stiles. Another important distinction between this chair and turned examples is that the arms of the Waldo chair tenon into the rear stiles, not into the crest rail. This is a joiner's practice rather than a turner's. All triangular turned chairs have arms that are tenoned into crest rails.

Although the Waldo chair relates to traditional wainscot examples in certain respects, the design and construction of its back is purely architectural. The truncated rear stiles, which essentially hang from the rear rails, are sim-

Figure 10 Plain chair, Plymouth County, Massachusetts, 1650–1720. White oak and maple. H. 37", W. 20 3/4", D. 16 1/8". (Courtesy, Museum of Fine Arts, Boston; Hezekiah E. Bolles Fund.) This example came from Rochester in Plymouth County. It has a replaced bast seat. Most plain matted chairs probably had rush seats.

ilar to "jetties" or overhangs in framed house construction. Other parallels with seventeenth-century buildings are evident in the curved boards used for the upper rail and diagonal braces and the simplified lamb's tongues on the lower ends of the rear stiles. The turned finials and pendants tenoned into the rear stiles and top rail are also similar to those on jetties. Although most architectural pendants are carved from the solid, a pair from Lyme, Connecticut, are turned and tenoned into place.[9]

Only four other pieces of New England furniture have framed jetties with pendants. All are joined cupboards tentatively attributed to Newbury, Massachusetts (see fig. 13). On these examples, the middle rails extend beyond the lower stiles on the sides. The oversailing rails tenon into shortened hanging stiles with turned pendants. Many English and New England cupboards have cantilevered upper sections, but they are usually supported by turned pillars. Some English and Welsh examples also have unsupported

Figure 11   Side view of the joined chair illustrated in fig. 1. (Photo, Gavin Ashworth.)

Figure 12   Detail of the back of the joined chair illustrated in fig. 1. (Photo, Gavin Ashworth.)

jetties with turned pendants; however, none have diagonal braces like those on the Waldo chair.[10]

The complexity of the rear framing of the chair clinches the argument that the maker trained as a carpenter. As previously discussed, turned versions of these chairs have braces that join the crest rail to the rear post—a straightforward concept that triangulates the rear structure. On the Waldo chair, the diagonal braces are tenoned from the rear post into the hanging stiles. The compression forces exerted in this arrangement are more complex than those in turned chairs. The two rear rails of the back are structurally necessary. If there were only one rail, the braces would push the bottoms of the stiles apart, levering against the shoulders of the crest rail's tenons. The purpose of the upper curved rail is to resist the spreading force, effectively uniting the entire rear frame. This design involved more structural considerations than a joiner typically confronted. Because the stresses present in joined

Figure 13 Court cupboard, Newbury, Massachusetts, 1680. Oak, sycamore, maple, and walnut with tulip poplar. H. 57 3/4", W. 50", D. 21 5/8". (Courtesy, Winterthur Museum.)

furniture are usually slight, diagonal braces are not required to stabilize the framing.[11]

Other structural and stylistic features differentiate the Waldo chair from conventional joiner's work. Most wainscot chairs have back panels fitted into grooves made with a plow or "grooving" plane. Because the Waldo chair has no panels, the maker's tool kit may not have included a plow plane. Nevertheless, the open framework of the back reflects a conscious stylistic decision rather than a lack of tools, technology, or materials. Alternatives to paneled backs certainly existed during the period. The joined oak armchair illustrated in figure 14, for example, has two rows of turned spindles rather than panels.

The combination of woods used to make the Waldo chair is also distinctive. The posts, rear rails, braces, and seat boards are ash, and the seat rails, rear stiles, and arms are cherry. New England joined chairs are usually made almost entirely of oak; however, that wood only occurs on the lower stretchers of the Waldo chair. Ash appears quite frequently in turned chairs

Figure 14 Joined chair, eastern Massachusetts, 1660–1680. Oak. H. 44¼", W. 23¼", D. 15¼". (Courtesy, Museum of Fine Arts, Boston; gift of Aimée and Rosamond Lamb.)

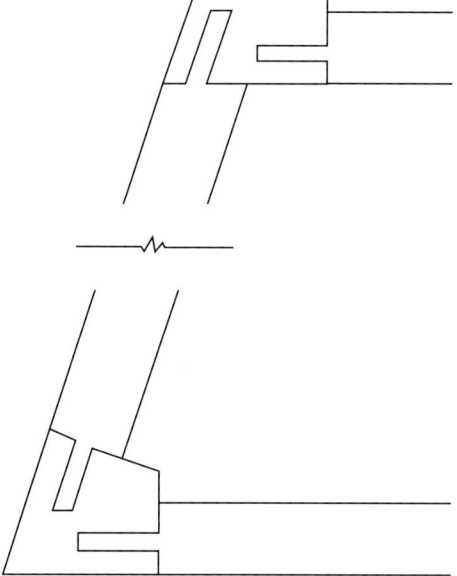

Figure 15   Diagram showing the seat and stretcher construction of a conventional New England wainscot chair.

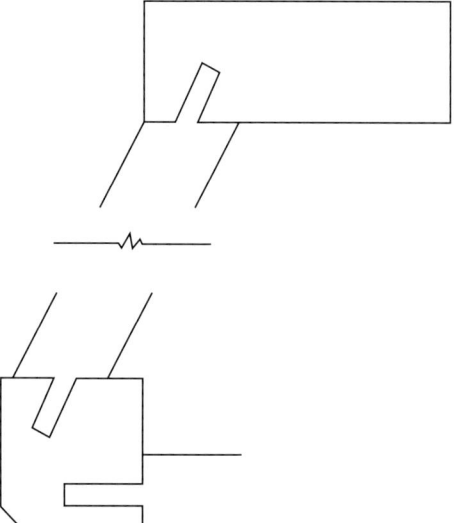

Figure 16   Diagram showing the seat and stretcher construction of the joined chair illustrated in fig. 1.

of the period, but it is only occasionally found in New England joined work. Ash is a strong, ring-porous hardwood that is easy to rive when it is straight-grained and clear of knots. It also planes and carves very well. Ash lacks the decay resistance of white oak, but for furniture (as opposed to architecture) this is not particularly critical. The cherry components of the Waldo chair represent the only occurrence of fruitwood in seventeenth-century New England furniture. Cherry rives easily in the growth ring plane, but its interwoven fibers make it very difficult to split on the radial plane. The maker of the Waldo chair clearly understood these limitations and rived his stock oversized. The finished thickness of his cherry parts averages about 1 1/2 inches, a good deal heavier than the 1-inch stock used for contemporary joined furniture.[12]

Regardless of their choice of wood, early joiners invariably worked quartered timber (the radial plane of the stock is the face of the board). The vast majority of New England joined furniture features oak riven in this orientation. There are several reasons for using quartered stock. Dimensional stability is the foremost, but ease of working is also a consideration.[13]

Like its materials, the layout and construction of the seat and stretcher system of the Waldo chair are unique in seventeenth-century New England furniture. On most wainscot chairs, the side face of the front stiles was planed to match the angle of the intersecting side rails and stretchers. This method simplified the joinery because the mortises for the side rails and stretchers could be chopped parallel to the side faces of the stiles. Because the rear face of the front stiles was planed at ninety degrees to the side face, the seat rails and stretchers have tenons with ninety-degree shoulders (fig. 15). By contrast, the front stiles of the Waldo chair are square in section. The seat rails and stretchers met the stiles at an obtuse angle, so the maker cut the shoulders of the rail and stretcher tenons to match the angle at which they joined the stile. By cutting the tenons in line with the rails and stretchers, the maker maintained the strength of the timber (fig. 16).[14]

In seventeenth-century woodworking traditions, the pins (pegs) used to secure mortise-and-tenon joints exerted a great deal of force upon the tenon. This practice was necessary to draw the joint together. The tenon had to be long enough to prevent the pin (or pins) from splitting the wood beyond the pin hole, and the corresponding mortise had to be deep enough to accommodate the tenon. Ordinarily the outer face of a mortised stile and a tenoned rail are flush. Although this is the case on the front and rear facade of the Waldo chair, the side joints deviate from the norm (fig. 16). Because of the sharply tapered seat plan, straight tenons of the side rails and stretchers, and square-sectioned front stiles, the mortises for the side rails had to be positioned further inward from the side face of the front stiles than was usual. This position minimized the chance of the mortise breaking the side of the stile while maintaining enough depth for the tenon. The pegs securing these joints are perpendicular to the tenon; they enter the same face of the stile as the mortise (fig. 17). Where the side rails meet the rear post the joinery is conventional, and the tenon shoulders are flush with the arris of the post.[15]

Although cutting the front mortises for the side rails and stretchers at an angle was necessary to create the tapering seat plan, the maker would have found it difficult to chop across the fibers of the front stiles. Pre-boring the bulk of the waste would have simplified the process and allowed him to maintain an accurate angle with his chisels. This is not a joiner's technique, for they chopped their joints exclusively with a mortise chisel. By contrast, carpenters routinely pre-bored large mortises.[16]

Although the training, tool kits, and working methods of carpenters and furniture joiners differed, the historical record suggests that woodworkers in provincial England and New England did whatever work came to hand. Scholarly discussions regarding the separation of these trades often cite the records of the London Court of Aldermen (1632), which include a lengthy court decision that demarcated the two professions and described their respective products. It is important to note, however, that this decision only applied to London and its environs.[17]

Many period documents mention carpenters making furniture. In 1653, Francis Perry of Salem and Lynn, Massachusetts, reported "that being carpenter of the [Saugus Iron] works he made many things for Gifford's house on the Company's account, including one great press, and set up two dressers." Perry's reference to a "great press" belies the notion that carpenters only made simple furniture forms such as six-board chests. The Waldo chair is another excellent case in point. Although some aspects of its framing are relatively simple, others are considerably more complicated than those of conventional wainscot chairs.[18]

Like other seventeenth-century woodworkers, carpenters frequently interacted with artisans outside their trade. The elongated scrolled arms of the Waldo chair suggest that the maker was either familiar with contemporary chairmaking practices or had access to a joiner's patterns. Regardless of this chair's design sources, the successful integration of features found on wainscot chairs, three-post, board-seated turned chairs, "plain chairs," and buildings attests to the maker's ingenuity and ability to solve complex framing problems.

The history of the chair provides clues to this artisan's identity. Nutting noted that Nathan Waldo (1740–1834) owned the chair, but he was unaware that two of Waldo's ancestors—John (1655–1700) and Daniel (1657–1737)—were woodworkers. Their father, Cornelius Waldo (1624–1700/1), emigrated from England by 1647. John married Rebecca Adams, and Daniel married her sister Susanna, whose father, Samuel (1617–1688), worked as a millwright in Braintree, Charlestown, and Chelmsford, Massachusetts. Presumably both brothers trained with their father-in-law. In 1695, Daniel received land in Chelmsford as payment for setting up and maintaining "a good and sufficient corn-mill." John owned carpenter's and cooper's tools, but his inventory does not specify his trade.[19]

Since John Waldo was Nathan's great-grandfather, it is conceivable that the chair descended through the male line; however, under New England partible inheritance laws, males typically inherited real estate, whereas females inherited "moveables," including household furniture. It is much

Figure 17 Detail of a reproduction of the joined chair illustrated in fig. 1, showing the joint angles and pins of the stretchers. (Reproduction by Peter Follansbee; photo, Gavin Ashworth.)

more likely that Nathan inherited the chair from his mother, Abigail Elderkin Waldo (b. 1715), great-granddaughter of John Elderkin.

Elderkin arrived in New England about 1637. His daughter, Abigail, was born in Dedham, Massachusetts, on September 13, 1641. Elderkin and his family moved frequently. They resided in Lynn, Massachusetts, during the mid-1640s, in New London, Connecticut, during the 1650s, and in Norwich during the early 1660s. Elderkin's career included contracts for meetinghouses, mills, and wharves. The earliest record concerning his work is an October 17, 1650, receipt for building a mill for the town of New London. Carpenters and millwrights often had to travel significant distances to ply their trade. Elderkin also worked in Providence, Rhode Island, in 1650.[20]

One of Elderkin's most important commissions involved work on the first meetinghouse in New London. On August 29, 1651, the town records noted that, "Goodman Elderkin doth undertake to build a meeting-house about the same demention of Mr Parke's . . . barne and clapboard it for the sum of eight pounds, provided the town cary the tymber to the place and find nayles. And for his pay he requires a cow and 50s. in peage." At the time, the community was holding services in Robert Parke's barn. Elderkin's proposal was rejected, and a site for the meetinghouse was not selected until December 1652, when he, joiner Samuel Lothrop, and Samuel Smith were contracted

> to buield a substantiall house Thirty foot square the wall to be Twelve foot betweene Joyntes the wall to be broake, to have six windowes convenient for the house fited for glasse with two doers eich of them to be double doers to lay one floore upon the grownd of joyce and plancke to Cover the walles with good seasoned board to be rebetted one over another to make in the roofe fowre gables with a turret in the roofe floored in the bottome to Cover the roofe with sawne board close Laide and to shingle the roofe upon the boarde with short shingles not above twenty Inches to finde all stuffe Cart all timber find all nailes and to finish this worke at or before the last of October (1653).[21]

Elderkin's services were apparently in great demand during the summer of 1651. On August 31, William Wells of Southold, Long Island, requested John Winthrop, Jr.'s, assistance in "grantinge and perswadeing your Millwright John Elderkin to come a long . . . to view the ruins of our old water mill; and build us a new." Shortly thereafter, Thomas Mayhew, a patentee of Martha's Vineyard, wrote Winthrop, "wee have greate want of a mill and there is one with you that I here is a verry Ingenuous man about such work that is goodman Elderkin, but wee here you have some Ingadement uppon him. Now these are to intreate you if possible you can disspense a while with him." Evidently, Elderkin accepted the Southold offer. In March 1652, "John Elderkin of Pequot [New London]" contracted with John Winthrop, Jr., for "one whole yeere beginning the first of April next to worke with him in any Carpentry worke that I can doe and to bueild him a Saw mill and keepe the Corn mill . . . And what time I shall be absent at South hold or upon my own occasions I shall make good."[22]

In 1659/60, the town of Moheagan (Norwich) hired Elderkin "to erect a corn-mill . . . to be completed before November 1, 1661." As part of this agreement, the mill received forty acres from the town, the land to be improved by "John Elderkin, the Miller." Thirteen years later, the town commissioned Elderkin to build a new meetinghouse. During the course of his work, he requested an increase in pay:

> Your humble petitioner pleadeth your charitie for the reasons hereafter expressed . . . it is very well known that I have been undertaker for building of the meeting hous and it being a work very difficult to understand the whole worth and value off, yet notwithstanding I have presumed to do the work for a sertain sum of money . . . 428 pound, not having any designe thereby to make myself rich, but that the town might have their meeting house dun for a reasonable consideration. But upon my experieince, I doe find by my bill of cost, I have done the said work very much to my damage, as I shall now make appear. Gentlemen I shall not say much unto you, but onley if you may be sensible of my loss in said undertaking, I pray for your generous and charitable conclusion toward me whether it be much or little, I hope will be well excepted from your poor and humble petitioner. John Elderkin.[23]

In 1677/8, the town of New London hired him to build yet another meetinghouse. The original building contract no longer survives but was summarized in Frances Manwaring Caulkins's *The History of New London, Connecticut* (1895):

> The contract for building the meeting-house was made with John Elderkin and Samuel Lothrop. It was to be forty feet square, the studs twenty feet high with a turret answerable, two galleries, fourteen windows, three doors, and to set up on all the four gables of the house, pyramids comely and fit for the work, and as many lights in each window as direction should be given: a year and a half given for its completion: £240 to be paid in provision; viz, in wheat, pease, pork and beef, in quantity proportional: the town to find nails, glass, iron-work, and ropes for the rearing. Also to boat and cart the timber to the place and provide sufficient help to rear the work.[24]

The complexity of Elderkin's architectural commissions suggests that he would have been capable of constructing the Waldo chair. An October 20, 1654, letter from John Pyncheon, Jr., to John Winthrop, Jr. (who was in Saybrook, Connecticut, at the time), alludes to Elderkin's involvement with interior finish carpentry and joinery: "Sir, I am bold to request that the room in which my wife will be in this winter may speedily be made warm. I pray let Goodman Elderkin be called on to do it out of hand in regard my wife is but tender and cold will set in quickly." Presumably, the room was to be made warm by "ceiling" it—enclosing it with frame-and-panel wainscot.[25]

Elderkin's work may also have included shipbuilding. Tradition credits him with the construction of the "New London Tryall" in 1661, the first merchant vessel built in New London. The ability to frame complex structures such as ships, mills, and meetinghouses is the essential concept differentiating the maker of the Waldo chair from joiners who produced wainscot examples. Not only was Elderkin an artisan of consummate skill, but his English background may explain the variety of turned and joined chair styles that appear to have influenced the design of the Waldo chair. These facts, coupled with his familial relationship to Nathan Waldo, strongly suggest that Elderkin made this remarkable chair.[26]

1. For the history and a proposed attribution of the Waldo chair, see Robert F. Trent, "The Waldo Chair: A Monument of Early Connecticut Joinery," *Connecticut Historical Society Bulletin* 48, no. 4 (fall 1983): 174–88. The author thanks Trent for his assistance in preparing this article and for providing photographs of various chairs.

2. Wallace Nutting, *Furniture of the Pilgrim Century* (Boston: Marshall Jones, 1921), pp. 175–76. Trent, "Waldo Chair," pp. 174–88.

3. Most of the information on board-seated turned chairs presented here is based on unpublished research by Robert F. Trent, John Alexander, and Allan Breed. For a preliminary report on that work, see Trent, "The Board-Seated Turned Chairs Project," *Regional Furniture* 4 (1990): 43–48. Other studies of turned chairs include S. Dillon Ripley, "An American Triangular Turned Chair?" in *Pilgrim Century Furniture*, edited by Robert F. Trent (New York: Main Street/Universe Books, 1976), pp. 31–33; Richard Ryder, "Three-Legged Turned Chairs," *Connoisseur* 191, no. 766 (December 1975): 243–47; Richard Ryder, "Four-Legged Turned Chairs," *Connoisseur* 191, no. 767 (January 1976): 44–49; Victor Chinnery, *Oak Furniture: The British Tradition* (Suffolk, Eng.: Antique Collector's Club, 1979), pp. 87–101; and Benno M. Forman, *American Seating Furniture 1630–1730* (New York: W.W. Norton, 1988), pp. 68–77.

4. As quoted in Chinnery, *Oak Furniture*, pp. 545–49. Also, see Forman, *American Seating Furniture*, pp. 383–84.

5. The three-legged chairs with early New England histories are the Harvard President's chair and a chair in the Smithsonian Institution. The Harvard President's chair is discussed in Jonathan Fairbanks and Robert F. Trent, eds., *New England Begins: The Seventeenth Century*, 3 vols. (Boston: Museum of Fine Arts, Boston, 1982), pp. 511–12. The Smithsonian chair (acc. 388001) is illustrated in Ripley, "An American Triangular Turned Chair?" It has a history of descent in a Topsfield, Massachusetts, family and came to the Smithsonian as part of the Greenwood Collection in 1951. The author thanks Rodris Roth for providing information on the Greenwood Collection. For Jacob's inventory, see George Francis Dow, ed., *Probate Records of Essex County, Massachusetts, 1635–1681*, 3 vols. (Salem, Mass.: Essex Institute, 1916–1920), pp. 291–96.

6. Chinnery, *Oak Furniture*, p. 92, figs. 2:75, 2:75a; this chair has a board front stretcher with rectangular tenons. The shaved front stretcher on the Metropolitan Museum of Art chair is a replacement. The original one was tenoned into round mortises in the front posts. Both chairs are made of oak, and their rear posts are raked above the seat. The author thanks Victor Chinnery and Frances Gruber Safford for providing information on these objects. For another three-legged plain chair, see Richard Ryder, "Three-Legged Turned Chairs," p. 246, fig. 6. New England joined chairs are typically made of oak, whereas turned examples from that region are usually made of ash, maple, or poplar. English turned chairs are typically made of ash, beech, or elm. Dutch turned chairs are often made of cherry.

7. A. C. Stanley-Stone, *The Worshipful Company of Turners of London—Its Origin and History* (London: Lindley-Jones & Brother, 1925), p. 121. For more on New England plain matted chairs, see Irving Phillips Lyon, "Square-Post Slat-Back Chairs," in Trent, ed., *Pilgrim Century Furniture*, pp. 40–46. John Alexander, *Make a Chair from a Tree* (Mendham, N.J.: Astragal Press, 1994), details the process involved in traditional "stick" chairmaking.

8. For more on drawboring and seventeenth-century joinery practices, see Peter Follansbee and John D. Alexander, "Seventeenth-Century Joinery from Braintree, Massachusetts: The Savell Shop Tradition," in *American Furniture*, edited by Luke Beckerdite (Hanover, N.H.: University Press of New England for the Chipstone Foundation, 1996), pp. 81–105.

9. For references to overhanging jetties see Appendix 2 in Abbott Lowell Cummings, "Massachusetts and Its First Period Houses," in *Architecture in Colonial Massachusetts*, edited by Abbott Lowell Cummings (Boston: Colonial Society of Massachusetts, 1979), pp. 193–221. Abbott Lowell Cummings, *The Framed Houses of Massachusetts Bay, 1625–1725* (Cambridge, Mass.: Harvard University Press, 1979), pp. 126, 137–38, illustrates two pendants thought to be from Newbury, Massachusetts. Norman M. Isham and Albert F. Brown, *Early Connecticut Houses: An Historical and Architectural Study* (Mineola, N.Y.: Isham and Brown, 1965), pp. 231–36, illustrate two pendants that were not applied. For two turned examples, see Christie's, *The Collection of Mr. and Mrs. Eddy Nicholson*, New York, January 27–28, 1995, p. 222, lot 1041.

10. For more on the Newbury cupboards, see Irving P. Lyon, "The Oak Furniture of Ipswich, Massachusetts," in Trent, ed., *Pilgrim Century Furniture*, pp. 66–75, figs. 26, 27, 40; and Fairbanks and Trent, eds., *New England Begins*, 3:530–32. For typical examples of English cupboards with turned pendants, see Chinnery, *Oak Furniture*, pp. 491, 494; figs. 4:178, 4:183.

11. These observations about the rear structure of the Waldo chair and the mechanics of the bracing are based on discussions with members of the Interpretive Artisans Department at Plimoth Plantation, Plymouth, Massachusetts. Their work involves reproducing seventeenth-century house frames with period tools and techniques. The author is especially grateful to Pret Woodburn, master house-carpenter at Plimoth. During the nineteenth century, English Gothic revivalist architect Augustus Welby Northmore Pugin (1812–1852) designed architectural tables with braced framing (Paul Atterbury and Clive Wainwright, eds., *Pugin: A Gothic Passion* [New Haven, Conn.: Yale University Press, 1994], pp. 134–41).

12. New England joiners used a variety of woods, including black walnut, tulip poplar, "true" poplar, sycamore, and cedar for decorative purposes or as secondary woods. The structural components of New England joined work are usually made of riven oak. Ash is common in turned chairs but only occasionally occurs in joined work. Several examples of New England joined furniture have posts made of maple, a diffuse-porous timber that rives better than cherry. Riven maple also often appears in seventeenth-century turned chairs. For examples of ash and maple in joined furniture, see Forman, *American Seating Furniture*, pp. 185–86. Philip Zea and Suzanne L. Flynt, *Hadley Chests* (Deerfield, Mass.: Pocumtuck Valley Memorial Association, 1992), p. 30, record a variety of timbers used in western Massachusetts including maple and beech. English joinery often includes a mixture of primary woods. Furniture historian Victor Chinnery reports having seen a joined press with cherry and oak as well as a number of oak pieces with ash panels.

13. For more on joiners' work habits, see Follansbee and Alexander, "Seventeenth-Century Joinery from Braintree, Massachusetts," pp. 81–104; and Robert Tarule, "The Joined Furniture of William Searle and Thomas Dennis: A Shop Based Inquiry into the Woodworking Technology of the Seventeenth-Century Joiner" (Ph.D. diss., Graduate School of the Union Institute, 1992).

14. For English chairs with square-sectioned front stiles, see the discussion of Salisbury chairs and tables in Chinnery, *Oak Furniture,* pp. 448–54. Chinnery notes that most canted table and chair frames have angled blocks that allow the use of right-angle tenon shoulders. Inexplicably, the side rails of the Salisbury folding tables shown in figs. 4:77 and 4:78 are nailed to the front stiles, whereas those on the chairs are joined. An English table with three-legged joined construction is illustrated in figures 3:182a and 3:182b. On this object the stiles are shaped to conform to the table's triangular plan. This construction allowed the rails to be flush with the stiles and have square-shouldered tenons. All three stiles have the same dimensions and cross-section. This arrangement would not have worked for the Waldo chair, because a rear stile of the same dimension as the front stiles would have resulted in an unstable, top-heavy chair. The wide rear stile of the Waldo chair makes it very stable.

15. One alternative to cutting the joints in this fashion would be to use a barefaced tenon to bring the side rails flush with the outer face of the stile. Pinning this joint would be problematic and may explain the approach used on the Waldo chair.

16. Although it is impossible to determine if the mortises of the Waldo chair were pre-bored without disassembling the frame, I tested several construction theories by making a reproduction chair with period-style tools. I attempted to chop the first angled mortise without pre-boring the waste and found it extremely difficult to maintain the proper angle and width. It became readily apparent that pre-boring would simplify the process. If the mortises for the side rails of the Waldo chair were pre-bored, they would bolster the argument that the maker was trained as a carpenter.

17. As quoted in Forman, *American Seating Furniture*, pp. 42–43; and Chinnery, *Oak Furniture,* pp. 41–48. The aldermen's decision is quoted in full in E. B. Jupp, *An Historical Account of the Worshipful Company of Carpenters* (London: Pickering & Chatto, 1887). The fact that these issues were debated in court indicates that guild restrictions were often violated.

18. For the reference to Francis Perry, see Robert Charles Anderson, *The Great Migration Begins: Immigrants to New England, 1620–1633*, 3 vols. (Boston: New England Historic Genealogical Society, 1995), 3:1438–41. In 1659, Ipswich carpenter William Averill agreed to build a table, a joined form, and a bench as part of a housebuilding contract. For more on Averill's contract and the practice of multiple trades in New England, see Cummings, *Framed Houses of Massachusetts Bay*, pp. 40–51. For an example of furniture attributed to carpenters, see Robert Blair St. George, "Style and Structure in the Joinery of Dedham and Medfield, Massachusetts, 1635–1685," in *American Furniture and Its Makers*, edited by Ian M. G. Quimby (Chicago: University of Chicago Press for the Winterthur Museum, 1979), pp. 1–47. Robert F. Trent, "The

Marblehead Pews," *New England Meeting House and Church* (Boston: Boston University, 1980), pp. 101–11, describes joined pews attributed to carpenter John Norman.

19. Trent, "The Waldo Chair," p. 179. Waldo Lincoln, *Genealogy of the Waldo Family*, 2 vols. (Worcester, Mass.: Charles Hamilton, 1902), 1:12–38.

20. Elderkin received a land grant in Lynn in 1638. Tradition maintains that he moved shortly thereafter. In a deposition later in the century, Clement Golda, "aged about 55," testified that "the grant of the old mill was in July ye 12 1633 to Edward Tomlins . . . [then sold] to Mr. Howell, second owner of the Mill . . . did sell the same mill to John Elderkin; and John Elderkin did sell it to Mr. Bennett" (Alonzo Lewis and James R. Newhall, *History of Lynn, Essex County, Massachusetts* [Boston: John L. Shorey, 1865], pp. 143, 171–74). Elderkin apparently returned to the Lynn area by 1644. In a deed dated July 16, 1643, and proven on May 15, 1644, he sold Samuel Bennett a "new built Watermill in Linn for . . . £100" (*Suffolk Deeds*, 14 vols. [Boston: Rockwell and Churchill, 1880], 1:53). On June 27, 1646, Elderkin mortgaged "unto Mary Kinsley his halfe part of the Sawe Mill in Reading in Consideration of ten pounds" (ibid., p. 78). For Abigail's birth, see *New England Historical and Genealogical Register* 4:359. Although he was primarily a carpenter and millwright, Elderkin kept a tavern in New London. For the Providence and Connecticut references, see Malcolm Freiberg, ed., *The Winthrop Papers*, 6 vols. (Boston: Massachusetts Historical Society, 1992), 6:42–43, 74, 76, 136–37.

21. Frances Manwaring Caulkins, *History of New London, Connecticut* (New London, Conn.: H. D. Utley, 1895) p. 108. "Articles of Agreement for Building a Meetinghouse in New London," in Freiberg, ed., *Winthrop Papers*, 6:236–37. The meetinghouse was completed in 1655.

22. Freiberg, ed., *Winthrop Papers*, 6:236–37, 135–36, 139, 190–91.

23. Frances Manwaring Caulkins, *History of Norwich, Connecticut* (Chester, Conn.: Pequot Press, 1976), pp. 72–73, 119–20.

24. Caulkins, *History of New London*, p. 191.

25. Trent, "The Waldo Chair," pp. 183–84. Carl Bridenbaugh, ed., *The Pyncheon Papers* (Boston: Colonial Society of Massachusetts, 1982), pp. 9–12.

26. Caulkins, *History of New London*, p. 231.

Robert F. Trent and Karin Goldstein

Notes about New "Tinkham" Chairs

▼ IN 1978 ROBERT BLAIR ST. GEORGE published an article in which he attributed a group of early turned chairs to Ephraim Tinkham II (1649–1713) of Plymouth and Middleborough in Plymouth County, Massachusetts. Not content merely to cite the relevant objects and documentation, St. George proposed a reevaluation of what might half-seriously be termed the "Wallace Nutting rules" of early American turned chair aesthetics:

1. Seventeenth-century chairs with posts of greater diameter are earlier and more valuable.
2. Seventeenth-century chairs with decorative spindles below the seat ("Brewster" chairs) are distinguished from those with spindles above the seat only ("Carver" chairs), and most Brewster chairs are more valuable than most Carver chairs.
3. Brewster and Carver chairs are earlier and more valuable than almost all seventeenth-century slat-back chairs with posts of comparable diameter.

In other words, Nutting thought of these variations as discrete "types" in a fixed temporal sequence; Brewsters preceded Carvers, and both preceded slat-back chairs. Why he valued earlier chairs more highly than later ones is unclear. Perhaps Nutting thought earlier ones were dignified by association with the founders of Plymouth Colony, like William Brewster, William Bradford, John Carver, Myles Standish, and John Churchill. All these patriarchs reputedly owned armchairs now located at Pilgrim Hall in Plymouth. The popular terms "Brewster" and "Carver" used by Nutting derive from two of the Pilgrim Hall examples, although it is not apparent when these antiquarian terms entered popular usage.[1]

St. George rightly pointed out that the Tinkham shop tradition included variants that did not conform to Nutting's notions. Chairs with essentially the same ground plan and post format could feature two tiers of spindles in the back, one tier under the arms, and one tier under the seat; only one tier of spindles in the back; or slats in the back and spindles under the arms and below the seat. The latter variant is the most unusual in this shop tradition. Nutting owned and published a slat-back example, which he termed a "semi-Brewster," but offered no explanation of how it fitted into his stylistic and dating system. St. George suggested that all these variants were available simultaneously and that Tinkham may have used prefabricated posts to assemble chairs in whatever format the customer desired. St. George also asserted that Tinkham employed the same pattern for all his posts.[2]

Over the last twenty years, several related chairs have emerged from Plymouth County families, including one example that St. George knew only from an old photograph (fig. 1). These chairs have expanded the repertoire of design and ornament as well as the probable date range of the Tinkham shop tradition. The recent discovery of Netherlandish and New England antecedents has also helped place these chairs in a broader cultural and stylistic context.

It now appears that the Tinkham shop tradition began well before Ephraim's apprenticeship, which probably commenced about 1662 or 1663. Although his master has not been identified, it seems fairly certain this anonymous tradesman introduced chairmaking styles and practices that persisted well into the eighteenth century. Ephraim Tinkham thus represents

Figure 1 Turned great chair, Plymouth County, Massachusetts, 1695–1710. Maple and ash. H. 41⁵/₈", W. 23¹/₂", D. 19¹/₄". (Chipstone Foundation; photo, Gavin Ashworth.) This chair descended in the Russell family of Plymouth, but it reputedly belonged to the Winslow family of Marshfield. It appears to have been painted red originally.

the "second generation" of this artisanal tradition. The myriad stylistic sources manifest in these chairs suggest that the tradition may have experienced temporary "aberrations" due to outside influences at several junctures. In short, the extraordinary variety encompassed by the tradition is the cumulative achievement of four or five shops over perhaps seventy years rather than the collective experience of one individual. We will, nevertheless, continue to use the generic term "Tinkham" to describe this chairmaking school and its products.

This article departs from St. George's model in several regards. Although other chairmaking traditions probably produced slat-back examples as early as 1640, all of the Tinkham ones date after 1700. The fully turned chairs influenced by Boston examples appear to be the earliest ones in the Tinkham group. It is unclear whether Tinkham chairs with two tiers of spindles in the back predate those with one tier, but careful comparison of all traits suggests that one-tier backs are either later or are not represented by earlier surviving examples. Establishing a stylistic chronology for Tinkham chairs is further complicated by the fact that some makers were regressive in their application of certain ornamental details, such as finial turnings.

Although scholars have identified the European design sources for many seventeenth-century American case pieces, they have done little to verify the antecedents of contemporary turned chairs. This is understandable given the paucity of turned chairs in European museums and the almost total lack of documented examples in England and the Netherlands. Fortunately, Dutch chairs can be analyzed by examining genre paintings. The lack of documented Continental turned chairs is unfortunate, because the historical record suggests that Dutch turned chairs were popular throughout Europe and were exported widely from the late Middle Ages until the eighteenth century. The Dutch undoubtedly established the basic three-post and four-post formulae for turned chairs and successfully competed with new styles emanating from Paris after 1670 by developing rush-seated, high-backed versions of upholstered prototypes. In many instances, it is extremely difficult to tell whether a seventeenth-century turned chair with an English history was made there or in the Netherlands. In most instances, the more stylish or well made the object, the more likely it is to be Dutch.[3]

The Dutch chair illustrated in figure 2 has no provenance, but it provides exact parallels for most of the details found on Tinkham chairs. Since Tinkham's master probably arrived in New England during the 1620s or 1630s, the Dutch chair cannot be regarded as an antecedent; nevertheless, it is likely that Tinkham's master and the maker of the Dutch chair were separated by only three or four apprenticeships from an ancestral shop in a major Netherlandish urban center. The large number of Dutch and Rhenish artisans that migrated to English ports between 1560 and 1640 render this idea rather more plausible than not.[4]

The proportions of the Dutch chair are strikingly similar to those of fully developed, second-generation Tinkham chairs, such as the Winslow example (see fig. 1). As St. George noted, many (but not all) Tinkham chairs are relatively narrow at the rear and wide at the front—in other words, they

Figure 2 Turned great chair, Netherlands, 1640–1660. Ash. H. 37 3/4", W. 22 1/2", D. 17". (Private collection; photo, John Sinkler.)

Figure 3 Detail of the finial of the great chair illustrated in fig. 2.

have a strong trapezoidal splay. The Dutch chair exhibits a peculiar approach wherein the front posts are vertical but the rear posts have a distinct backward rake, presumably for comfort. Many of the Tinkham chairs have layback, but all four of their posts are tilted to the rear (see fig. 1). These chairs sometimes have raked arms like those of the Dutch example, although none display the same labor-intensive series of five diminishing spindles under the arm.

Setting aside gross characteristics of the frame, the Dutch chair's turned ornaments provide exact parallels for the following "Tinkham" ones: the ball-reel-ball finial (fig. 3); the bilaterally symmetrical vase-ball-vase and the column-ball-column spindles (see figs. 4, 5, respectively); the ovoid pommels or grips (fig. 6); the ball turning flanked by filleted coves on the posts

Figure 4 Detail of the vase-ball-vase turning on the rear post of the great chair illustrated in fig. 2.

Figure 5 Detail of the column-ball-column turning on the rear post of the great chair illustrated in fig. 2.

Figure 6 Detail of a pommel on the great chair illustrated in fig. 2.

Figure 7 Detail of the ball-with-coves turning on the front post of the great chair illustrated in fig. 2.

Figure 8 Detail of the front seat joint of the great chair illustrated in fig. 2.

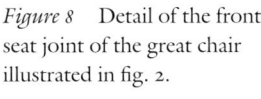

(fig. 7); and minor groupings of fine, scored accents. One feature of the Dutch chair that is absent in the Tinkham group is the board seat held in plowed seat rails. The side rails on the Dutch chair have round tenons that intersect the rectangular tenons of the front rail (fig. 8). This structure also occurs on a small number of Plymouth County turned chairs, notably the Bradford-Brewster-Standish group at Pilgrim Hall and the Reverend James Keith chair at the Museum of Fine Arts, Boston. Given the striking similarities between the Tinkham chairs and the Dutch example, it is possible that turners in the Tinkham tradition made board-seated chairs that simply have not survived.[5]

Figure 9 Turned great chair, Boston, 1640–1670. Maple and ash. H. 45¼", W. 23¼", D. 17½". (Courtesy, Wadsworth Atheneum, Wallace Nutting collection, gift of J. Pierpont Morgan.)

All of the Tinkham features that deviate from the Dutch model are either innovations influenced by other design sources or the result of simplification. In some instances, turners in the Tinkham tradition abandoned these departures and returned to earlier designs. A Boston great chair (fig. 9) and two Tinkham examples (figs. 10, 11) illustrate these points. The finials of the Boston chair are quite similar to the applied colonettes on Boston case pieces attributed to London-trained joiners Ralph Mason and Henry Messinger and London-trained turner Thomas Edsall. Several other chairs with London-inspired details and eastern Massachusetts histories survive. Not

Figure 10 Turned great chair, Plymouth County, Massachusetts, 1660–1685. Maple and ash. H. 45½", W. 24¾", D. 17¾". (Courtesy, Metropolitan Museum of Art, bequest of Mrs. J. Insley Blair.)

only do they reinforce the Boston attribution of the aforementioned example, but they help distinguish that city's chairs from those produced in Salem, Plymouth (exemplified by the Bradford-Brewster-Standish and Tinkham groups), and other towns and communities in the region.[6]

Unlike most Boston turned chairs, the one illustrated in figure 9 has two tiers of spindles in the back and one tier between the second and bottom front stretchers. It is easy to infer that a chair of this type inspired the progenitor of the Tinkham tradition to modify the traditional Anglo-Dutch back plan (see fig. 2), perhaps as early as 1650–1660. A turned great chair at the

Figure 11 Turned great chair, Plymouth County, Massachusetts, 1660–1685. Maple and ash. H. 44", W. 23¾", D. 18½". (Private collection; photo, Gavin Ashworth.) This chair descended in the Bartlett family of Plymouth.

Figure 12 Photograph of Isaac Bartlett, Plymouth, Massachusetts, 1860–1880. Tintype. 3⅝" × 2¼". (Private collection; photo, Gavin Ashworth.) The subject is seated in the great chair illustrated in fig. 11.

Metropolitan Museum of Art (fig. 10) and a related example that descended in the Bartlett family (figs. 11, 12) show this Boston influence at its strongest. Not only do they have the same distribution of spindles as the Boston chair, but their posts display the same heavy urns with flanges seen on the posts of the urban prototype (fig. 9). The finials of these Tinkham chairs also incorporate a second flange element that is an abbreviated version of the one on the finials of the Boston chair. Were it not for the finial turnings of the Tinkham chair shown in figure 10, one might attribute it to Boston on the basis of its urn spindles. On the Bartlett chair, the maker pulled back from

Figure 13 Turned great chair, Plymouth County, Massachusetts, 1695–1710. Maple and ash. H. 42⅞", W. 25¾", D. 18½". (Wadsworth Atheneum, Wallace Nutting collection, gift of J. Pierpont Morgan.)

Figure 14 Detail of a columnar spindle on the great chair illustrated in fig. 11.

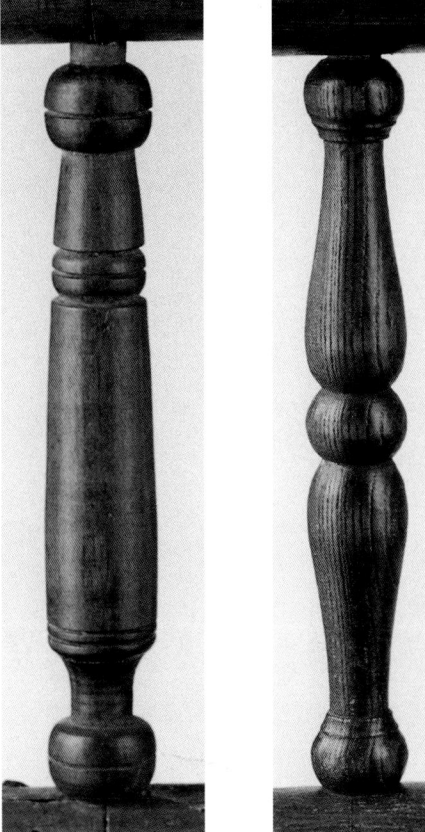

Figure 15 Detail of a vasiform spindle on the great chair illustrated in fig. 1.

such thorough-going Boston influence. He modified the urn turnings on the posts and finials but retained two variants of his standard spindle turning—the vasiform kind and the columnar kind.[7]

The Bartlett chair and the example shown in figure 13 are the only Tinkham chairs that incorporate both kinds of spindle. The Bartlett chair also suggests that spindles with relatively straight bodies may predate those with more robust vasiform shapes (see figs. 14, 15). This observation may seem routine, were it not for the fact that many scholars interpret straight-bodied turnings as "degenerate" versions of earlier ones with pronounced ogee curves.

The chair shown in figure 13 is quite close to the Bartlett chair but reverts to the base tradition in the form of the spindles and the somewhat edited

Figure 16 Turned great chair, Plymouth County, Massachusetts, 1695–1710. Maple and ash. H. 46³⁄₄", W. 25¹⁄₄", D. 17¹⁄₄". (Courtesy, Pilgrim Society, Pilgrim Hall Museum, Plymouth, Massachusetts, gift of Joseph Head; photo, Gavin Ashworth.) This chair has long been known as the Governor John Carver chair. It appears to have been painted black originally.

Figure 17 Turned great chair, Plymouth County, Massachusetts, 1695–1710. Maple and ash. H. 43¹⁄₂", W. 24", D. 15³⁄₄". (Courtesy, Museum of Fine Arts, Houston, Bayou Bend Collection; gift of Miss Ima Hogg.) This chair reputedly descended in the Ellis family of Carver, Massachusetts.

cove-ball-cove turnings on the posts. It is also the earliest example with a ball-reel-ball finial and a giant, stepped-in pillar turning on the front posts—details that became commonplace later in the tradition. Because this finial has strong affinities to those used on many Boston baroque chairs made after 1695, it represents the latest stylistic feature of the Tinkham chair and places it solidly in the 1695–1710 date range. By contrast, the stepped-in pillars on the front posts of the chair may be a conservative detail. Related pillars occur on earlier Plymouth County cupboards and tables, which suggests that Tinkham and his master may have provided ornaments for local joiners. These stepped-in pillar turnings may also represent Boston in-

Figure 18   Turned great chair, Plymouth County, Massachusetts, 1695–1715. Maple and ash. H. 42¹/₂", W. 25³/₄", D. 17³/₄". (Courtesy, Pilgrim Society, Pilgrim Hall Museum, gift of Joseph Everett Chandler; photo, Gavin Ashworth.) This chair reputedly descended in the Churchill family of Plymouth.

fluence, because the joiners and turners of Plymouth County copied many features of Boston case pieces.[8]

As the Tinkham chairs illustrated in figures 10 and 11 suggest, the design format consisting of two tiers of spindles in the back, one tier under the arms, and one tier between the second and bottom front stretcher may have been derived from a Boston prototype rather than a Dutch one. On the Dutch chair shown in figure 2, the principal spindle tiers are connected to the seat rails and are quite tall relative to the space they occupy. On the other hand, the purported Boston source has no spindles under the arms (see fig. 9). Adding to this confusion about the probable sources for the two-tiered

Figure 19 Turned great chair, Plymouth County, Massachusetts, 1705–1720. Maple and ash. H. 41⁷⁄₈", W. 24", D. 17¹⁄₂". (Private collection; photo, Gavin Ashworth.) This chair reputedly descended in the Fairbanks family of Dedham and Wrentham, Massachusetts.

spindle back in the Tinkham tradition is the existence of a one-tiered version, epitomized by the so-called John Carver chair (fig. 16). Like the William Bradford chair, the Carver example was venerated as a Pilgrim relic before the founding of the Pilgrim Society in Plymouth in 1820. Obviously this chair did not belong to John Carver (d. 1621) but is a Tinkham example of about 1690 to 1700. The great pillar motif on the front posts is typical of the group, and the three large spindles in the back are similar to the smaller columnar spindles on earlier Tinkham chairs. Missing are the pommels or hand grips, which usually have diameters that exceed those of the front posts by more than an inch. Dubbed "mushrooms" by collectors of Nutting's generation, great pommels are most often associated with slat-

Figure 20 Turned great chair, Plymouth County, Massachusetts, 1715–1730. Maple and ash. H. 45¾", W. 24", D. 17⅞". (Private collection; photo, Gavin Ashworth.)

back armchairs from Norwich, Connecticut. Such grips were wasteful of materials and labor because they were turned from the solid rather than applied. To some extent, however, they visually compensate for the otherwise plain format of chairs without many spindles. A slightly later chair that descended in the Ellis family of Carver, Massachusetts (fig. 17), indicates what the Carver chair's pommels may have looked like before they were whittled away. Despite its simplified format, the Carver chair has the same finials as the Bartlett chair (figs. 11, 16) and the example shown in figure 10, thus it must date somewhat before 1695.[9]

A group of three chairs fleshes out a progression of the two-tiered design between about 1700 and 1720. One example (fig. 1) descended in the Wins-

Figure 21 Turned great chair, Plymouth County, Massachusetts, 1715–1730. Maple and ash. H. 41³⁄₈", W. 23¹⁄₂", D. 17". (Private collection; photo, Gavin Ashworth.)

low, Hayward, Russell, and Jackson families of Plymouth and has long been known as the Isaac Winslow chair. Of all the Tinkham chairs, it has the most vigorous ogee spindle turnings. Like the design format of the chairs shown in figures 9 and 11, these spindles may represent another instance of Boston influence. The Winslow chair is quite similar to one with columnar turnings and an oral tradition of descent in the Churchill family of Plymouth (fig. 18). These chairs share many features, but the finials and the slightly softer cove-ball-cove turnings on the posts of the Churchill chair suggest that it is later than the Winslow example. The finials of the Churchill example have lost the extra flange and top button (compare figs. 3 and 18); however, they

Figure 22 Slat-back great chair, Plymouth County, Massachusetts, 1715–1730. Maple and ash. H. 45 7/8", W. 25 1/4", D. 21". (Wadsworth Atheneum, Wallace Nutting Collection, gift of J. Pierpont Morgan.)

resemble the finials of the Dutch chair (fig. 2). This elemental reduction may represent the waning of Boston influence and a return to the archetypal finial design. The Churchill chair retains the great pillar turning found on the posts of later examples in the Tinkham tradition. Another two-tiered chair that reputedly descended in the Fairbanks family of Dedham and Wrentham, Massachusetts, may date as late as 1710 (fig. 19). The spindles on the Fairbanks chair are inverted versions of the columnar ones on the Churchill chair, and its finials are simplified by the elimination of the large, lower ball. Microanalysis of pigment samples taken from the Fairbanks chair indicates that the spindles were painted black and that the rest of the

Figure 23 Slat-back great chair, Plymouth County, Massachusetts, 1715–1730. Maple and ash. H. 42 1/8", W. 25 1/8", D. 18". (Private collection; photo, Gavin Ashworth.)

Figure 24 Turned great chair, Plymouth County, Massachusetts, 1715–1730. Maple and ash. Dimensions not recorded. (Courtesy, First Congregational Church of Windham Center, Connecticut, on loan to the Windham Historical Society; photo, Gavin Ashworth.) This chair has long been known as the Governor William Bradford chair.

object was unpainted. This instance is the first in which the "tan-and-ebony" color scheme associated with seventeenth-century case furniture has been documented on a turned chair.[10]

The latest Tinkham chairs, which date between 1720 and 1730, display a number of odd innovations. Two chairs (figs. 20, 21) have two sawn, strigiform balusters in the back, highly simplified ornaments, and finials capped with baroque buttons. Other late chairs have slats, including Nutting's "semi-Brewster" (fig. 22) and an ungainly chair with two slats, a turned top rail, and eccentric finials (fig. 23). A number of these chairs (fig. 24) have slanted turned arms that hark back to the Dutch example; however, slanted

Figure 25 Detail of a misbored mortise hole in the right rear post of the great chair illustrated in fig. 1. (Photo, Gavin Ashworth.)

Figure 26 Detail of a misbored mortise hole in the right rear post of the great chair illustrated in fig. 11. (Photo, Gavin Ashworth.)

arms also appear in a number of eighteenth-century New England chair-making traditions.

The late Tinkham chair shown in figure 24 has long been associated with Governor William Bradford (1588/89–1657) of Plymouth, although his birth and death dates refute that tradition. A nineteenth-century deacon reported that one of Bradford's granddaughters brought the chair to Windham, Connecticut, from Massachusetts. Research by R. Ridgeway, however, suggests that the chair came from the governor's great granddaughter, Elizabeth Adams (1681–1766), who married the first minister of Windham, the Reverend Samuel Whiting (1670–1725). The chair became the pulpit chair of the Windham church, where it has remained until recently. As these later chairs suggest, turners trained in the Tinkham tradition may have continued working well into the eighteenth century, but after 1730 their designs are not readily distinguishable from others that also were subject to strong metropolitan influence.[11]

One working method of the Tinkham turners is distinctive and may help identify later chairs in the tradition. St. George asserted that "the scribed lines used by [Tinkham] . . . to demarcate the location of turned details . . . are in the same relative positions on all the chairs"; however, none of the pattern lines on chairs sampled for this article match. Unlike many turned chairs, which were made with a pattern stick formulated in the master's shop and copied by his apprentices, their apprentices, and so on, the Tinkham

Figure 27 Detail of a misbored mortise hole in the right rear post of the great chair illustrated in fig. 19. (Photo, Gavin Ashworth.)

chairs appear to have been laid out with a tool handle. Presumably, the turner used the length of the handle as a constant and calibrated fractional amounts by eye. This practice may explain the boring mistakes evident on at least three of the armchairs (figs. 25–27). Turners used scribed lines to locate their mortises and usually bored their joints either above or below the lines to prevent the mortises from intersecting where two horizontal members (stretchers or seat lists) enter the post at the same level. Most turners used wedges to clamp pairs of posts in a low assembly bench and aligned and bored the mortises simultaneously. Considering the rarity and complexity of large, intricately turned armchairs like the Tinkham ones and the somewhat pragmatic layout and production techniques described above, it is understandable that a turner might misbore one or more mortises, especially if he was in a hurry; nevertheless, the high incidence of boring errors seen in the Tinkham tradition is striking and demands more thorough investigation.[12]

The newly discovered Bartlett family chair and its Dutch prototype extend the stylistic chronology and probable date range of the Tinkham tradition and challenge St. George's assertion that all this furniture could have been produced during the working life of one individual. New examples may turn up that will confuse or alter the analysis and dating proposed here, but that does not negate the importance of such exercises. Much more research needs to be presented and debated before scholars can fully understand eastern Massachusetts turned seating made before 1700.

ACKNOWLEDGMENTS   The authors thank Robert Blair St. George, Peggy Baker, Caroline Kardell, Jeremy Bangs, John Sinkler, George Neumann, Robert Bartlett Freeland, Fred and Anne Vogel, Gertrude Bancroft, Dudley and Constance Godfrey, Alfred Fredette, Henry and Lorene Cone, Eddy Nicholson, and John and Marie Vander Sande for their help at various stages of researching and writing this article. We are especially grateful for the help provided by Sophie Davidson, Peter Follansbee, Gavin Ashworth, and Luke Beckerdite.

1. Robert Blair St. George, "A Plymouth Area Chairmaking Tradition of the Late Seventeenth Century," *Middleborough Antiquarian* 19, no. 2 (December 1978): 3–12. Some of the chairs and the basic argument of this article are repeated in Robert Blair St. George, *The Wrought Covenant: Source Material for the Study of Craftsmen and Community in Southeastern New England 1620–1700* (Brockton, Mass.: Brockton Art Center, 1979), pp. 26–27 and figs. 46–49. The basic source for Nutting's ideas on dating early turned chairs is the first edition of his *Furniture of the Pilgrim Century* (Boston: Marshall Jones Co., 1921), which has a discursive text. He noted that turned chairs with posts over two inches in diameter dated back "well into the first Pilgrim generation," in other words, before 1660 (pp. 182, 184, 192). On page 215, he explicitly stated that the "sizes of posts of chairs are generally above two inches if they reach back into the first pilgrim generation. The largest posts are hardly two and three quarter inches. After 1660 we begin to find posts of two inches diameter the rule. After 1680 the posts are often only an inch and three quarters." Allowing for the fact that Nutting dated the introduction of the baroque, or "William and Mary," style to the early 1680s rather than to the mid-1690s, he still presented no concrete evidence for his dating scheme. His scheme is further compromised by his reliance on the replaced posts of the Standish chair at Pilgrim Hall as a securely dated monument (the chair is thought to date from before Myles Standish's death in 1656). Modern commentators, following St. George, tend to date chairs based on a distinction between the pre-1695 mannerist style and the post-1695 baroque style, without much emphasis on a single trait like post diameter. Even this cautious approach fails to aid interpretation of mannerist-

style chairs made after 1695 by provincial turners, some of whom incorporated baroque ornaments in their old-fashioned formats.

2. In his revised *Furniture of the Pilgrim Century*, 2 vols. (Framingham, Mass.: Old America Co., 1924), Nutting drastically shortened his text and relied on captions; nevertheless, it was here that he introduced the term "semi-Brewster," which is not found in the 1921 version of his book. He used the term in reference to entry 1823 (here illustrated as fig. 10) and to entry 1826 (here illustrated as fig. 22). Nutting was clearly puzzled by the fact that these Tinkham-type chairs had only one tier of spindles under the seat, since he thought a chair required two to be a full-fledged "Brewster"; however, he referred to entry 1802 (here illustrated as fig. 9) — a Boston chair with only one tier of spindles below the seat — as a "Brewster" and noted that "The Term Brewster Is Applied to Chairs Having Spindle Work below the Seat."

3. Peter Thornton has identified Dutch chairs as a staple of the export trade and an important influence on the turned chair industry in northern Europe. See Peter Thornton, *Seventeenth-Century Interior Decoration in England France & Holland* (New Haven, Conn.: Yale University Press, 1978), pp. 206–7; and Peter Thornton, *Authentic Decor: The Domestic Interior 1620–1920* (New York: Viking, 1984), pp. 24 and 59.

4. Benno M. Forman, "Continental Furniture Craftsmen in London: 1511–1625," *Furniture History* 7 (1971): 94–120.

5. The Bradford, Brewster, and Standish chairs are by the same hand and constitute the work of a second unidentified Plymouth-area chairmaking shop. The Keith chair is illustrated in Richard H. Randall, *American Furniture in the Museum of Fine Arts, Boston* (Boston: By the museum, 1965), pp. 155–56. The Boston board-seated turned chairs consist of the Tufts family chair (Metropolitan Museum of Art), the Mather family child's high chair (American Antiquarian Society, Worcester, Massachusetts), the John Eliot chair (private institutional collection), and a chair with no history of ownership (Society for the Preservation of New England Antiquities). Board seats also occur on a small number of chairs attributed to Boston, Connecticut, New York, Virginia, and South Carolina. The Connecticut examples are the Robbins family chair (Connecticut Historical Society), a slat-back armchair with no history of ownership (Historic Deerfield), and a spindle-back armchair with no history of ownership (private collection). The only New York example reputedly descended in the Strycker family (Metropolitan Museum of Art); however, it is quite similar to the Robbins chair at the Connecticut Historical Society and may have been made in Connecticut. The only Virginia example is a child's high chair that descended in the Lee family (see Ronald L. Hurst and Jonathan Prown, *Southern Furniture, 1680–1830: The Colonial Williamsburg Collection* [New York: Harry Abrams for the Colonial Williamsburg Foundation, 1997], pp. 57–59). The only South Carolina example is also in the Colonial Williamsburg collection (see Luke Beckerdite, "Religion, Artisanry, and Cultural Identity: The Huguenot Experience in South Carolina, 1680–1730," in *American Furniture*, edited by Luke Beckerdite [Hanover, N.H.: University Press of New England for the Chipstone Foundation, 1997], p. 208, fig. 15; and Hurst and Prown, *Southern Furniture, 1680–1830*, pp. 52–54). All of these board-seated turned chairs will be the subject of articles in a future volume of *American Furniture*.

6. See Benno M. Forman, *American Seating Furniture: 1630–1730* (New York: W. W. Norton for the Winterthur Museum, 1988), pp. 76–79. The first scholar to suggest that Salem chairs could be distinguished from Boston ones was Robert Blair St. George, in "New England Turned Chairs of the Seventeenth Century: A Preliminary Survey," unpublished manuscript, 1978, in the author's possession. The most important Salem turned chair descended in the English family (Peabody-Essex Museum). A note of caution in all these attributions resides in the Dutch sources for English turned chair traditions, which, as asserted above, are not easily identified.

7. The chair from the Metropolitan Museum of Art was first identified as a Tinkham-type example in Brian Cullity, *A Cubberd, Four Joyne Stools & Other Smalle Thinges: The Material Culture of Plymouth Colony and Silver and Silversmiths of Plymouth, Cape Cod & Nantucket* (Sandwich, Mass.: Heritage Plantation of Sandwich, 1994), p. 123. The Bartlett chair traditionally resided in one of two family houses in the southern part of Plymouth called Manomet. Family tradition maintains that the chair descended in the paternal line from the patriarch Robert Bartlett until the eighth generation. The tintype illustrated in fig. 12 shows (7) Isaac Bartlett (1796–1880) seated in the chair. Tracing the chair back from Isaac's generation in both male and female lines cannot demonstrate unequivocally that the history is accurate, but it does suggest that it is plausible. Isaac's father (6) Joseph died in 1835. His room-by-room inventory lists three armchairs valued between 25 and 40 cents. The one most likely to be the chair illustrated

in fig. 11 was in the front keeping room (Plymouth County Probate Records [hereinafter cited PCPR], vol. 77, p. 180). Joseph was married to Anna Clark, but no separate inventory for her exists. The inventory of her father, James Clark (1723–1815) of Plymouth, lists two great chairs valued at $1.25 (PCPR, vol. 47, pp. 106–8). In his will, James divided his movable estate among his daughters (PCPR, vol. 47, pp. 103–5). Joseph Bartlett's father was (5) Captain Zacheus Bartlett (1725–1801), a Plymouth physician. Zacheus's inventory lists a great chair valued at $2.00 and an old great chair together with four small chairs valued at $4.00 (PCPR, vol. 37, p. 426). Zacheus married his distant cousin Margaret Barnes, daughter of Jonathan Barnes and Phoebe Finney. No inventory exists for Jonathan Barnes's estate, but his wife's father, Josiah Finney, owned three great chairs when he died in 1726 (PCPR, vol. 5, p. 220). Zacheus Bartlett's father (4) Joseph (1693–1756) married his cousin Elizabeth (Bartlett) Bartlett (ca. 1700–1773). No probate inventory exists for Joseph, and no specific listings of chairs are in the inventories of Elizabeth's father, Samuel Bartlett (PCPR, vol. 3, p. 291), or her grandfather, Benjamin Bartlett of Duxbury (PCPR, vol. 1, pp. 113–15). Joseph's parents were (3) Joseph and Lydia (Griswold) Bartlett. The elder Joseph died in 1703, and his inventory lumped all his chairs together (PCPR, vol. 3, p. 106). Lydia Griswold Bartlett was from a Connecticut family. The parents of the third-generation Joseph were (2) Joseph (ca. 1639–1711/12) and Hannah Pope (1639–1709/10). The second-generation Joseph purchased the property in Manomet. He is thought to have built the 1660 Bartlett house on the original tract, whereas his son built the 1680 house. The inventory of the second-generation Joseph is too general to identify the chair (PCPR, vol. 2, p. 52). Although it is not possible to identify the Bartlett chair in the successive inventories of the family with certainty, the patrilineal descent of the object is quite plausible, and almost all the women who married into this line came from local families. The genealogical information in this footnote is from Robert Wakefield, ed., *Mayflower Families in Progress: Robert Bartlett of the Anne* (Plymouth, Mass.: General Society of Mayflower Descendants, 1995), passim.

8. St. George, *Wrought Covenant*, p. 46. For the Boston sources of some Plymouth turned ornaments on case pieces, see Robert F. Trent, "The Lawton Cupboard: A Unique Masterpiece of Early Boston Joinery and Turning," *Maine Antique Digest* 16, no. 3 (March 1988): 1C–4C.

9. The origins of the John Carver history associated with this chair are obscure. The chair was donated to the Pilgrim Society in 1820 by Joseph Head of Boston, who also donated a pewter plate said to have belonged to Myles Standish. The entry in the minutes of the secretary to the Pilgrim Society acknowledging these donations mentions a letter from Head that accompanied the artifacts, but the letter has not been located. In 1995, Jeremy Bangs, former visiting curator of manuscripts at the Pilgrim Society, found an 1818 manuscript from a "Mr. Tufts Museum" in Plymouth that included a "Carver's Chair" (Samuel Davis Papers, Pilgrim Society). Throughout the nineteenth century, the chair was thought to have belonged to Governor John Carver, who died in 1621. It was illustrated in several publications during the 1840s and 1850s, notably Alexander Young's *Chronicles of the Pilgrim Fathers* (1841) and Calvin Wheeler Philleo, Jr., "A Pilgrimage to Plymouth," *Harper's New Monthly Magazine* 8, no. 43 (1853–1854): 49. The first attempts to determine the origin of the chair through microanalysis of the woods were either inconclusive or inaccurate (see Jonathan Fairbanks, "Four Pilgrim Chairs," *Winterthur Newsletter* 9, no. 7 [September 30, 1963]: 1–3). A sample analyzed by the Department of Forestry at the University of Massachusetts at Amherst in 1995 suggested that the chair is made partly of American ash; however, most wood anatomists dispute the validity of separating American and European ashes. The obvious inaccuracy of the Carver history has led to speculation that the chair descended from the Howland family, because John Howland came on the *Mayflower* as Governor Carver's servant. The connection between a John Carver who died in Marshfield in 1679 and the early governor has never been established, and no reason exists to think the chair belonged to this later individual. How Joseph Head obtained the Carver chair and the Standish plate is unclear. The 1790 census lists two men named Joseph Head, one in Westport (Bristol County) and the other in Boston (*Heads of Families at the First Census of the United States Taken in 1790, Massachusetts* [Washington, D.C.: U.S. Government Printing Office, 1908]). The individual in Westport had ancestors in the Plymouth area but was not alive in 1820. The Joseph Head (1761–1836) of Boston was the son of John Head (1725–1776) of Ipswich in Suffolk, England, and his wife, Jane MacKenzie (1735–1818) of Scotland (Ann Felter Sandy, "Head Family History," ms. dated July 4, 1992, Head Family Papers, Box 1, Massachusetts Historical Society). Joseph Head's first wife, Elizabeth White Frazier (1764–1798), descended from an Ipswich, Massachusetts, family. His second wife, Lydia Chandler (1770–1837), was the daughter of merchant John Chandler and Lydia Ward of Petersham,

Massachusetts. Lydia Chandler Head's ancestors were from Roxbury. Although some members of this Roxbury branch of the Chandler family (who lived in Bristol, Rhode Island, and Woodstock, Connecticut) married descendants of Plymouth County families, no leads regarding the chair donated by Head have surfaced (George Chandler, *The Descendants of William and Annis Chandler Who Settled in Roxbury, 1637* [Worcester, Mass.: Press of C. Hamilton, 1883], passim). A group of slat-back armchairs with pommels considerably greater in diameter than the posts have been associated with Lebanon and Norwich, Connecticut, since the 1890s. For more on these chairs, see Minor Myers, Jr., and Edgar D. Mayhew, *New London County Furniture 1640–1840* (New London, Conn.: Lyman Allyn Museum, 1974), p. 15. A somewhat more cogent analysis of these chairs is in Forman, *American Seating Furniture*, pp. 124–28.

10. The Russell chair, sometimes referred to as the Winslow chair or even the Winslow-Hayward-Russell chair, is illustrated in St. George, "A Plymouth Area Chairmaking Tradition," p. 6, fig. 3. This illustration was silhouetted from a photo of the interior of the Harlow house in Plymouth taken about 1900. Because of this photo, St. George associated the chair with the Harlow family. He did not realize that the chair resided a few streets away in the residence of Allen D. Russell (1897–1984). Russell recalled that the chair was always known as the Winslow chair. Genealogical research by Mr. Russell's daughter Mimi Aldrich and Robert F. Trent shows how the chair could have descended through the Winslow family to Mr. Russell: (2) Governor Josiah Winslow (1629–1680); to his son (3) Isaac (1671–1738); to his son (4) John (1703–1774); to his son (5) Pelham (1737–1784); to his daughter (6) Joanna Winslow Hayward (1773–1816), who married Dr. Nathan Hayward (1763–1848); to their daughter (7) Mary Winslow Hayward Russell (b. 1798), who married William S. Russell (1792–1863); to his nephew (8) John Jackson (1823–1897); to his son (9) John (1860–1939); to his son (10) Allen D. (1897–1984). New research suggests that both the Hayward and Winslow family lines are important in accessing the validity of tradition regarding the chair's history. No probate inventory exists for Dr. Nathan Hayward of Bridgewater, one of several physicians in the extended Hayward-Winslow-Warren family. His wife (6) Joanna Winslow is more important. She and her sister, Mary Winslow Warren, were the only children of (5) Pelham Winslow and his wife, Joanna White (1744–1829) of Marshfield (Ruth McGyre and Robert Wakefield, *Mayflower Families Through Five Generations, Edward Winslow* [Plymouth, Mass.: General Society of Mayflower Descendants, 1997], pp. 18–19). At the outbreak of the Revolution, (5) Pelham Winslow and his cousin (5) Edward Winslow fled to Boston as Loyalists, and Pelham's property was confiscated in 1779. The listing includes six mahogany chairs (PCPR, vol. 25, p. 458). Joanna and her two children remained behind in Plymouth. After Pelham's death in 1784, what little remained of his estate could not support his widow and daughters (William T. Davis, *Plymouth Memories of an Octogenarian* [Plymouth, Mass.: Bittinger Bros., 1906], p. 163). Joanna White Winslow's mother, Joanna Howland White (1716–1810), bequeathed her "the Bed Chairs and Looking Glass in the easterly back Chamber in which she usually sleeps," but her will did not mention an armchair (PCPR, vol. 43, p. 446). Joanna White Winslow's father was (5) Gideon White (1716–1779) of Plymouth. His probate inventory lists "1 armed Chair" valued at £6 in inflated Continental currency (PCPR, vol. 28, p. 16). Gideon's father, Cornelius (1682–1755), had a group of unspecified chairs listed in his inventory (PCPR, vol. 14, p. 402). Cornelius's wife, Joanna Howland, was the daughter of Thomas Howland (d. 1741), a prosperous landowner of Plymouth. His inventory included "1 Great Chair" worth 10s. (PCPR, vol. 8, p. 135). This is one possible source for the "Winslow" chair. Returning to the direct Winslow line, no inventory exists for (4) General John Winslow, who died intestate just before the Revolution; however, his father's generation provides extremely important documentation. (3) Isaac Winslow (ca. 1671–1738) and his wife, Sarah Wensley (1673–1754), owned a large Marshfield farm called "Careswell," which he inherited from his father, Governor Josiah. In 1699, Isaac built a large house that, with alterations made by his son, still stands. His probate inventory contains only a generalized listing for chairs (PCPR, vol. 8, p. 29), but his wife's inventory, taken in inflated old Tenor currency, lists one old chair at £1.6.8. Other chairs are described as cane back, flowered (presumably needlework or turkeywork rather than veneered), and easy. The "old chair" could be the one shown in fig. 1 (PCPR, vol. 13, p. 327). Isaac Winslow's father, Josiah, died in 1680, which is too early for the latter to have owned the chair. Barring a more thorough search of the evidence, it does not seem possible to corroborate the Winslow-Hayward-Russell history. The aforementioned William S. Russell (1792–1863) was the Plymouth town clerk and author of *Guide to Plymouth and Recollections of the Pilgrims* (1846). His first cousin, Nathaniel Russell II (1801–1853), owned the William Bradford turned armchair, which he inherited from his mother's LeBaron ancestors, who were Bradford descendants.

The Churchill chair survives in fragmentary condition. Only the right front post is entirely original. The right rear consists of an original maple upper half and a replaced ash lower half. The replaced left front post is oak, and the replaced right rear post is ash. Only two of the spindles in the back are original, but all those under the arms are original. The spindles under the seat, which appear to have been moved up one stretcher in the frame, are replacements. The chair was probably cut down in height due to severe insect infestation. Subsequent infestation probably prompted the wholesale replacement of many parts. The Churchill chair is illustrated and discussed in St. George, "A Plymouth Area Chairmaking Tradition," p. 5, fig. 2; Cullity, *A Cubberd, Four Joyne Stools & Other Smalle Thinges,* p. 124; and Helen Comstock, "Pilgrim Chairs," *Antiques* 68, no. 5 (November 1955): 451. Comstock suggested that the chair was originally owned by Eleazor Churchill, the son of John Churchill who arrived in Plymouth by 1643. As both St. George and Comstock noted, colonial revival architect Joseph Everett Chandler of Boston donated the chair to Pilgrim Hall. His father, Albert H. Churchill Chandler, was the son of Joseph Chandler and Eliza Churchill of Duxbury. Although St. George suggested that Eliza had inherited the chair, it may have entered the Chandler family through another route. Albert H. Churchill Chandler married Adeline F. Harlow of Plymouth, and the couple shared at least two ancestors. The most plausible line of descent for the chair through the Churchill family is similar to that proposed by St. George, except that he skipped one generation. This line is as follows: (1) John Churchill to (2) Eleazor Churchill (1652–1716), to (3) Stephen Churchill (1685–1750), to (4) Stephen Churchill (1717–1751), to (5) Stephen Churchill (b. 1743), to (6) Peleg Churchill (1769–1810), to his daughter (7) Eliza, who married Joseph Chandler.

Moving backwards through the Churchill line, several other ways in which the chair might have descended become apparent. Peleg Churchill of Plymouth married Hannah Hosea of Duxbury in 1791. He was a cooper who died in 1810 with unspecified furniture listed in his inventory (PCPR, vol. 43, p. 362). Peleg Churchill's contemporary, Joseph Chandler (1769–1795) of Kingston, was another great-grandfather of Joseph Everett Chandler, the donor. The former Joseph's inventory listed "2 great chairs, 3 crow foot chairs & 6 common Ditto" (PCPR, vol. 35, p. 190). Perhaps one of these great chairs is the example in question.

(5) Stephen Churchill of Plymouth married Lucy Burbank in 1766. No probate documents survive for either of them. His father, Stephen (1717–1751), married Hannah Barnes (1718–1793) of Plymouth in 1738. The inventory for Stephen of the fourth generation contains a generalized reference to chairs (PCPR, vol. 13, p. 106). The Barnes family of Plymouth had genealogical ties to the Bartletts, Churchills, Chandlers, Standishes, and Carvers, all of whom have some association with chairs in this article. The Barnes family descends from (1) John Barnes, who was a resident of Plymouth by 1633, and his wife, Mary Plummer. (4) Hannah Barnes Churchill's father, Jonathan Barnes (b. 1684), was a brother of (3) William Barnes (1670–1751/52), who was the great-great-great-grandfather of Adeline Harlow, mother of Joseph Everett Chandler, the donor of the Churchill chair. William Barnes married Alice Bradford (1680–1725), daughter of William Bradford and (3) Rebecca Bartlett. William and Jonathan Barnes's brother (3) John married (4) Mary Bartlett, daughter of (3) Joseph Bartlett. The Barnes brothers' sister (3) Mary (b. 1667) married John Carver of Duxbury. Their daughter, Mary Carver (b. 1695), married Thomas Standish. The aforementioned genealogical information is derived from William T. Davis, ed., *Genealogical Register of Plymouth Families* (Baltimore: Genealogical Publishing, 1975), pp. 10–12, 51–59, 124–29; Robert Wakefield, ed., *Robert Bartlett of the Anne,* pp. 54–5; Robert Wakefield, ed., *Mayflower Families Through Five Generations: Family of Myles Standish* (Plymouth, Mass.: General Society of the Mayflower Descendants, 1996), p. 13.

Stephen Churchill (1685–1750) of the third generation married Experience Ellis of Sandwich in 1708. His probate inventory has a single entry for chairs (PCPR, vol. 12, p. 426). Experience Ellis was undoubtedly related to Benjamin Ellis, the owner of the chair shown in fig. 17. Information on the second generation is sparse. Eleazor Churchill (1652–1716) married a Mary whose family is unknown. No probate documents exist for them. His daughter, Jedidah Churchill (b. 1687), married Thomas Harlow (b. 1686), a distant ancestor of Adeline Harlow. Although no exact probate references confirm the presumed line of descent of the Churchill chair cited by St. George, this one is the most plausible. The donor's mother also had ties to the Churchill family. Almost all the donor's ancestors were from Plymouth.

Of all the documented Tinkham-type chairs, the Fairbanks example was found farthest from Plymouth County. The chair was purchased by an antiques dealer from Nellie Fairbanks Beane of Phillips, Maine, in the early 1960s. Nellie was a tenth-generation descendant of Jonathan Fairbanks (d. 1668), who built the core of the extant Fairbanks house in Dedham, Massachusetts, in 1637. His descendants in Nellie's direct line remained in Dedham and Wrentham (near the Rhode Island border) until Joseph Fairbanks (1717–1794) and his wife, Frances, moved to Winthrop, Maine. Their descendants in Maine had three connections to Plymouth area families. (6) Captain Benjamin Fairbanks (1747–1828) married Keturah Luce (1749–1807) of Martha's Vineyard. Her parents were Joseph Luce (1725–1762), whose family had resided on Martha's Vineyard for three generations, and Deborah Woolen. Deborah's maternal grandparents, Stephen Presbury (ca. 1672–1730) and Deborah Skiff (1668–1743), moved to the Vineyard from Sandwich on Cape Cod. They are of the appropriate generation to have purchased the chair. Deborah Skiff's parents, Stephen Skiff (1641–1710) and Lydia Snow (1640–1711), were from Marshfield. Other members of the Fairbanks family in Maine had ties to Plymouth County, although they are not in the last family owner's direct ancestral line. They include Captain Benjamin Fairbanks's brother, (6) Colonel Nathaniel Fairbanks, whose second wife's ancestors included Chipmans and Watermans, and Benjamin's son, (7) Columbus Fairbanks (1793–1882), who married a Tinkham. The aforementioned genealogical information is derived from David Thurston, *A Brief History of Winthrop (Maine) from 1764 to October 1855* (Portland, Maine: Brown Thurston, 1855), pp. 181–83; Donald Lines Jacobus, *Descendants of Robert Waterman*, 3 vols. (New Haven, Conn.: Edgar F. Waterman, 1939), passim; Robert S. Wakefield, *Mayflower Families Through Five Generations, Peter Brown Family* (Plymouth, Mass.: General Society of Mayflower Descendants, 1992), passim; Robert S. Wakefield, *Mayflower Families in Progress, Richard Warren of the Mayflower* (Plymouth, Mass.: General Society of Mayflower Descendants, 1997), passim; Isaac Cobb, "Cobb Genealogy," unpublished manuscript, Burbank, California, 1979, passim; Philip Cobb, *A History of the Cobb Family* (Cleveland, Ohio: privately printed, 1907), passim; and Martha McCourt et al., *The American Descendants of Henry Luce of Martha's Vineyard* (Boston: New England Historic Genealogical Society, 1994), passim.

The present owner of the Fairbanks chair commissioned studies of it by the Society for the Preservation of New England Antiquities Conservation Center in 1989. David H. Mitchell examined the structure of the chair, and Joseph Godla performed pigment analysis. The Carver and Winslow chairs (figs. 1, 16) retain some of their original paint, but neither has been sampled for analysis. The Carver chair appears to have been painted entirely black, whereas the Winslow example was red.

11. These two chairs were first published in Cullity, *A Cubberd Four Joyne Stools & Other Small Thinges*, p. 125. Norwich turned chairs (see Minor Myers, Jr., and Edgar D. Mayhew, *New London County Furniture, 1640–1840* [New London, Conn.: Lyman Allyn Museum, 1974], p. 15; and Forman, *American Seating Furniture*, pp. 124–28) are a prime stylistic source for many later chairmaking traditions in Connecticut that featured slanted turned arms, and many of these traditions also featured outsized pommels or hand grips. For examples of these traditions, see Robert F. Trent, *Hearts & Crowns: Folk Chairs of the Connecticut Coast 1720–1840* (New Haven, Conn.: New Haven Colony Historical Society, 1977), pp. 56–59 and 82–86. R. Ridgeway, "Governor Bradford's Chair," *Windham Historical Society Newsletter*, July 1983, pp. 4–6.

12. St. George, "A Plymouth Area Chairmaking Tradition," p. 7. The authors recorded the scribed pattern lines of several of the principal chairs from the Tinkham tradition and plotted the measurements on a single sheet of paper using the seat rail line as a common datum point. Since the posts of many chairs have been eroded, damaged, or trimmed at the bottom, the seat rail was the most logical index. The idea that a chair design could be memorized and replicated through manipulation of a tool handle or lathe tool rest was formulated by John D. Alexander, Jr., a woodworking historian of Baltimore, Maryland.

Book Reviews

Barry R. Harwood. *The Furniture of George Hunzinger: Invention and Innovation in Nineteenth-Century America*. Brooklyn, New York: Brooklyn Museum of Art, 1997. 168 pp.; 10 color and 189 bw illus., bibliography, index. $29.95.

"The Furniture of George Hunzinger: Invention and Innovation in Nineteenth-Century America." Brooklyn Museum of Art, Brooklyn, New York, November 20, 1997, to February 15, 1998.

George Jakob Hunzinger (1835–1898) gradually has gained recognition as being among those New Yorkers of the late nineteenth century whose furniture was innovative in construction and significant in design. Marvin D. Schwartz brought him to general notice by including a Hunzinger chair in an exhibition entitled "Victoriana" held at the Brooklyn Museum of Art in 1960. Richard W. Flint advanced interest by collecting the few surviving documents and memorabilia for the Strong Museum in Rochester, New York, and by publishing three closely related articles in the early 1980s. These articles are summarized in his Victorian Society colloquium essay entitled "Prosperity through Patents: The Furniture of George Hunzinger & Son," published in *Nineteenth Century* (August 1982). The more recent exhibition at the Brooklyn Museum and the related publication by Barry R. Harwood, associate curator of decorative arts, swept the momentum of new research toward a new understanding of Hunzinger's international significance.

The exhibition is independent of the book. The book includes Arnold L. Lehman's "Director's Foreword," which addresses institutional concern with the subject, and Harwood's preface, which provides a perspective on the research. Harwood adds a chronological exposition of Hunzinger's career, a brief "Appendix: Original Upholstery," "Notes" that securely document the text, a succinct "Bibliography," and a practical index. Ten illustrations are in accurate color, and 179 others appear in clear black and white. The prose is clear, and the design is appealing.

Figure 1 Overall view of "The Furniture of George Hunzinger: Invention and Innovation in Nineteenth-Century America." Blum Gallery, Brooklyn Museum of Art, November 20, 1997 to February 15, 1998. (Courtesy, Brooklyn Museum of Art.)

Figure 2 Detail of the installation of "The Furniture of George Hunzinger."

Harwood's investigation faced unusual challenges. Workshop records or business accounts have not been located; wear usually led to replacing upholstery or even discarding furniture; the whereabouts of extant furniture is unknown for some documented designs; and personal information is limited for Hunzinger and his eight unmarried children, several of whom worked in the firm (George, Jr., became a principal in 1888).

Harwood traces Hunzinger's fortunes from a poor cabinetmaker emigrating to the United States in 1855 from Württemberg to a prosperous manufacturer after moving his shop from Brooklyn to Manhattan in 1861. Credit ratings reveal that by 1872 he achieved a successful business of fifty employees; the firm evidently remained about this medium size for local firms until his sudden death at age sixty-three in 1898. Various sources—including an illustration on business stationery—document his move to a new and final brick workshop and showrooms of six stories and six bays, still standing as no. 325 on West 16th Street. Harwood offers information about furniture construction, finishing, and upholstery there and in other locations by analyzing surviving furniture, furniture identified by photographs, furniture illustrated in advertisements, and Hunzinger's twenty-one patents. Success rested on "fancy" chairs, folding chairs, platform rockers, and lounge chairs as accents to other domestic furniture. To an unknown degree, Hunzinger offered tables and suites of chairs in different sizes, settees, and daybeds. No furniture can be identified with patents for extension dining tables, folding beds, and chair-tables, although a table combined with chairs and a game table with a revolving top are rare survivals from other patents. Analysis of all of these sources leads to Harwood's conclusion that Hunzinger ingeniously manipulated elements of form, decoration, finish, and upholstery for a wide range of variations and budgets. Some are

Figure 3   George J. Hunzinger, armchair, New York, designed 1869. Wood; original upholstery. H. 35⅝"; W. 27¼"; D. 25½". (Brooklyn Museum of Art; H. Randolph Lever Fund.)

known only through documentary evidence. One strength of the text is that such inevitable information lapses are not obscured but are clearly stated.

Harwood ingeniously documents through period photographs the use of Hunzinger's furniture throughout the United States. These illustrations include not only the expected furniture showrooms but also photography studios where chairs were used as props. The domestic interiors depicted range from modest and substantial to occasionally luxurious. The search nationally for the photographs in university libraries and historical societies, as well as familiar archives, well fulfilled the purpose of demonstrating the middle-class context and widespread appreciation of the furniture. Hunzinger achieved these sales, Harwood reveals, through his showroom in Manhattan, through agents, and through distributors (wholesale and retail).

Hunzinger's obituary emphasized that he was the sole designer for the firm. Furniture specialists will support Harwood's contention that general similarity of some of Hunzinger's forms to those by his contemporaries is a very minor theme compared to the major ones of reinterpretation and originality. Examples include the vague relationship of curved members to the bentwood furniture of Michael Thonet (1796–1871) or the loose similarity of obvious structure to furniture by Augustus Welby Northmore Pugin (1812–1852). For decorative details, text and illustrations emphasize Hunzinger's swift recognition of fashions by adapting or discarding motifs, turning shapes, surface decorations, and finishes. Harwood reveals Hunzinger's personal taste in 1869 with a patent application in that year stating his preference for legs and braces with "ornamented" turnings over carved or plain ones.

Hunzinger's simple furniture offers similarities in design to midtwentieth-century modernism. But Harwood cautions that furniture that seems proto-modern may derive from historical sources. An outstanding example is a suite of settee, daybed, center table, armchairs, and side chairs incorporating spheres, cones, and other geometric elements. Harwood credibly traces these items to their probable inspiration in designs described as "Assyrian" and "Medieval" in Jacob von Falke's *Art in the House*, published in Boston in 1878.

Harwood's scholarly book would be improved only by additional technical information. In furniture captions, the identification of woods, complete measurements, and identification of upholstery fibers, weave, and origin would be pertinent. For the text, authoritative but rare comment about construction of elements within the patented engineering (pp. 110–11) reveals Harwood's potential for more thorough discussion.

One gallery (fig. 1) and a small anteroom served the accompanying exhibition of thirty-nine pieces of furniture that accurately exemplify Hunzinger's career. The spare approach of beige walls and low, even, lighting to prevent fading in fabrics and woods forced attention on the platforms of furniture against all walls and the one row of two diagonal platforms down the center. The generally chronological sequence from the right of the entrance included juxtapositions for comparing variations on basic chair forms. One chair was exhibited without upholstery for frame study. Upholstery received emphasis through a significant number of chairs with original fabrics, trim, and muslin foundation upholstery documenting shapes. Wall placards offered information about Hunzinger's career, patents, and clients. Furniture labels, pictures of related objects, and pertinent comments were mounted on posts, where they were conveniently at eye level (fig. 2). Memorabilia included Hunzinger's bust-length portrait in oils that dates about 1880. Highlights and shadows indicate that the unidentified artist developed it from a photograph. The portrait significantly reveals that the inventor concerned with upper-middle-class taste was not equally sensitive to new directions and quality in contemporary painting. He was satisfied with an artist's shortcut and listless result. If furniture historians could not visit the exhibition, the labels and book captions reveal that they can study Hunzinger's furniture on a limited basis at the Brooklyn Museum, the major repository of his furniture in quality, variety, condition, and number of examples (fig. 3).

Hunzinger's furniture deserves the efforts by the Brooklyn Museum. His most successful designs, whether elaborate and informed by historical sources or simple and relying on a sensitive organization of structural members, aggressively pierce space in a linear manner distinctive among his American contemporaries. For the engineering of furniture, Hunzinger merits recognition for two concepts. By 1869 he had perfected the structure of a crest rail and cantilevered seat supported by diagonal braces continuing as legs and interlocking with a stretcher distributing weight from two uprights between it and the seat. Equally revolutionary is the invention by 1888 of vertical elements in chair backs and under arms secured by threading continuous wires through holes at the top and bottom with tension adjusted by a nut at each threaded end. The construction eliminated the common problem of traditional joints becoming loose because of shrinking wood or drying glue. This development in 1888 and that of the diagonal brace in 1869 received patents preventing use by other manufacturers. Both constructions still are relatively unknown abroad, because Hunzinger could not profitably arrange distribution. Harwood's research proves, however, that Hunzinger's designs and constructions, considered eccentric and rare by connoisseurs and historians since the 1960s, were widely accepted by American consumers in their own day.

Harwood's book is a significant record of Hunzinger's unique engineering and original designs. His taste, as the exhibition demonstrated and the book reveals through selected examples, influenced his contemporaries. Harwood's new perspective on Hunzinger will not soon be dated. His research is thorough, and his analysis of it is perceptive.

Milo M. Naeve, Field-McCormick
Curator Emeritus of American Arts,
Art Institute of Chicago

Peter M. Kenny, Frances F. Bretter, and Ulrich Leben. *Honoré Lannuier, Cabinetmaker from Paris: The Life and Work of a French Ébéniste in Federal New York*. New York: The Metropolitan Museum of Art, 1998. xviii + 253 pp.; 101 color and 137 bw illustrations, appendixes, bibliography, index. Distributed by Harry N. Abrams, Inc., New York. $75.00.

In the arena of American furniture scholarship, rarely is a single publication (and exhibition) devoted solely to the "life and work" of a pre-1820 cabinetmaker. Whereas European and American artists, printmakers, and sculptors often receive "one-man" status, few American or emigré American craftsmen achieve similar recognition. The dearth of focused work on individual American cabinetmakers is understandable, since usually only a small amount of their production is marked and often a significant body of supporting, written documentary material does not survive. For Honoré Lannuier, one might at first wonder whether enough material, both surviving production as well as contemporary documentation, exists to make a significant presentation both as an exhibition or a major publication. Peter Kenny and company (Frances Bretter and Ulrich Leben), however, have risen to the challenge, unearthing new labeled examples of his work, and leaving practically no primary or secondary source unexplored. The result is an amazingly complete representation of his work interwoven not only with an account of the youth, training, and subsequent success of this skillful and savy Frenchman but also with the story of the community of related craftsmen and patrons in which he was a principal player. As an institution seemingly devoted primarily to the advancement of the fine arts, the Metropolitan Museum of Art is to be applauded (along with Kenny's immediate colleagues at the museum) for its support and encouragement of this stunningly significant contribution to the understanding of cabinetmaking in early nineteenth-century New York.

At the outset the modest Kenny acknowledges in the preface his debt to the "scholarship laid down by several preceding generations"; as he aptly states, "this entire project stands on their broad shoulders." Beginning with emigré German cabinetmaker Ernest Hagen's interest in early New York cabinetmakers in the late nineteenth century, Kenny cites the work and contributions of many scholars, curators, and collectors ranging from Metropolitan Museum curators Charles Over Cornelius and Joseph Downs to scholar Thomas Hamilton Ormsbee and noted collector Louis Guerineau Myers. By the second half of the twentieth century, the center of Lannuier interest and scholarship shifted from New York southward to Winterthur Museum with the research of Lorraine Waxman and her 1958 Winterthur master's degree thesis on Lannuier and the French influence on American decorative arts. Waxman's work continued when she joined the White House staff as its first curator, working with Francophile First Lady Jacqueline Bouvier Kennedy and adding two important pieces of Lannuier's documented work to the White House collection. Kenny's final debt is to the research of Metropolitan curator Berry B. Tracy, whose work on New York cabinetmakers of the early nineteenth century greatly assisted him in placing Lannuier in the context of his contemporaries. It is not surprising that all of the avid furniture scholars of the twentieth century cared about the very same concerns that Kenny and company have built their comprehensive study upon: documented knowledge of Lannuier's past, the capture and connoisseurship of marked examples of his work, and Lannuier's relationship to contemporary cabinetmakers and patrons in early federal New York.

The remarkably comprehensive portrayal of Lannuier's life and work that this publication presents is developed systematically and logically through four chapters focused on his family background, youth, and training as an ébéniste in Paris; his career in New York within the context of his contemporaries; his production for specific patrons; and the connoisseurship of his work compared with that of contemporaries following his style. Although each chapter might stand alone, each one builds on the information in the former, resulting in the whole resonating like a symphony in four movements.

Critical to the understanding of any craftsman is knowledge of the influences that surrounded him in his youth and throughout his initial training. Kenny identified precisely the perfect European scholar, Ulrich Leben, to explore and interpret this aspect of Lannuier's life. As deputy keeper of Waddesdon Manor in Buckinghamshire, England, Leben is the preeminent authority on the work of Bernard Molitor, a Luxemburg-born cabinetmaker who came to Paris in his early years and became one of the most renowned Parisian ébénistes. Familiar with French archives and sources, Leben expertly documents Lannuier's family background, beginning with the information that he came from a family of craftsmen involved in the building trades. Born in Chantilly in 1779, Lannuier's early years were doubtless affected by the death of his mother when he was just under two years old and the subsequent bankruptcy of his innkeeper father when he was about ten. Shortly thereafter his father moved the family to Paris, where Honoré's elder brother, Nicolas, was already an established ébéniste. Presumably, shortly afterward Honoré, at about age twelve, was apprenticed to his brother. Leben systematically details all the existing information on Honoré's siblings, including Nicolas, and extensively discusses the contemporary Parisian craftsmen Nicolas interacted with, providing enormous insights into the methods and manner in which Parisian ébénistes of the period operated. Collaboration among craftsmen, as well as the merchandising of other ébéniste's furniture, was not uncommon. Illustrations of contemporary design sources and of the exact styles and forms of furniture made by this array of craftsmen demonstrate the precise models that informed Honoré in the years prior to his departure for America. Leben's discussion of the techniques and materials employed by Parisian ébénistes further expands our understanding of the standards and practices that Honoré was imbued with as a young apprentice and of how he continued to employ these through his years of work in New York. For instance, his use of high-quality hardwoods and exquisitely patterned veneers, white Carrara marble tops, and superior gilt-bronze ornaments and mounts was a practice he brought with him to New York from his Parisian training. Leben specifically recognizes, however, that Honoré's move to New York did not simply transplant a French cabinetmaker to another continent. As a creative artist, Lannuier not only retained "the basic precepts of his training," but in New York he matured and adapted his work to changing tastes and fashions as he created strikingly original expressions prized by his contemporary patrons as well as late twentieth-century connoisseurs.

In Kenny's primary chapter on "Lannuier's Life and Work in New York, 1803–1819," he proves himself to be a paramount detective and analytical observer. Admitting in advance the paucity of written documents surrounding Lannuier's career (in contrast to the relative abundance of his stamped and labeled furniture), Kenny proceeds to paint an amazingly vivid and complete picture of this emigré cabinetmaker's enterprising career in New York. Interweaving into an intricate network what might individually seem like irrelevant bits of data, Kenny unfolds a richly embroidered cloak that surrounds one of the most dedicated and individualistic craftsmen of his day. Beginning with a query into the reasons for Lannuier leaving Paris in 1802–1803, about which Kenny confesses that "too many unanswered questions remain," he cites the provocative first recorded mention of Lannuier in New York on June 3, 1803, when turner James Ruthven recorded the sale of sixteen table legs to him. Characteristic of Kenny's cautious yet analytical approach to his subject, he uses each shred of evidence to illuminate Lannuier's situation, or that of the contemporary scene, stating, "Buying furniture parts from a turner may have been a fairly standard New York practice in trade, but it is just as likely that Lannuier's purchase may have been necessitated by the lack of a proper shop and a full complement of machinery at this early date." As this chapter continues, it is difficult to believe that there is any lack of documentation, given the recently discovered sources (found in France), such as the "acte de marriage" between Honoré and Therese Baptiste, the sister of his brother Auguste's wife. This abundance of new information is assimilated and amplified throughout the text and punctuated with a lavish number of color and black and white illustrations of Lannuier's documented work, occasionally contrasted with the work of his contemporaries.

Kenny is dauntless in tackling the toughest topics, such as Lannuier's shop organization and scale of production, even in the absence of any of his account books and other business records. He successfully accomplishes this task by making careful comparisons between the production of Lannuier and other cabinetmakers, especially his principal competitor, Duncan Phyfe (1768–1854). This methodology continues to enhance the rich contextual nature of this study, so that the reader rarely confronts only Lannuier; more often he is viewed within the very community he so aptly served. Given Lannuier's strong French ties, it is not surprising that four French cabinetmakers can be documented as working in his shop or at least as having had direct ties to his shop. His close relationships with others in the New York cabinet trade can be gleaned from his detailed inventory of property and will of 1819. These associations included five cabinetmakers, four merchants, and two mahogany dealers, once again indicating the intricate relationships in making and marketing furniture in early nineteenth-century New York. Another aspect of craft structure cited in this section is the close relationship between upholsterers and cabinetmakers in the early nineteenth century. Indeed, Honoré's brother Nicolas referred to himself as a cabinetmaker and upholsterer on his French label, and though Lannuier appears not to have carried on in this same dual role, his associations with the upholstery trade were close.

Perhaps the most original and analytical aspect of this chapter is a discussion of the forms and styles of furniture Lannuier produced. Which examples closely paralleled French Directoire and Consulate periods? What was *le goût moderne* and *le goût antique,* and how did Lannuier's work manifest these expressions? Finally, how did Lannuier merge these French styles with the preferences of his New York clients? This closer look at French design sources, the objects Lannuier made, and the parallels with specifications in the New York price books of the early nineteenth century further illuminates the individualistic and creative side of Lannuier's workmanship. The dating of Lannuier's furniture based on its style as well as on the type of stamp or label used on it is also analyzed. The body of material in this chapter is not only about Lannuier but about the entire cabinetmaking community in New York between 1803 and 1819. Lannuier's premature death at age forty deprived his New York patrons of one of their most inspired artists; however, Lannuier has left his twentieth-century patrons an inheritance far greater than the mere $174.62 cash he had in the bank when he died in 1819.

Frances Bretter, Kenny's principal colleague and research associate in this project, has written an intriguing and extremely well-documented chapter on twenty of Lannuier's patrons. By locating and carefully combing through volumes of family papers, newspaper advertisements, and New York City archives, she has been able to describe, and often illustrate, the types of pieces they purchased, the prices they paid, who else they were patronizing, and sometimes even what the furniture interiors looked like. In several instances, such as the Van Rensselaer and Campbell furniture, her indefatigable research has corrected attributions of ownership. Lannuier was clearly the cabinetmaker of choice for French-style goods, but it is interesting that a number of consumers who patronized Lannuier also bought from Phyfe. Principal among his clients were merchants William Bayard and James Brinkerhoff. Bayard began patronizing Lannuier as early as February 1805 and ultimately wound up purchasing suites of furniture for his daughters Maria and Harriet when they married, respectively, Duncan Campbell and Stephen Van Rensselaer IV in 1817. The Bayard-Campbell-Pearsall Papers at the New York Public Library are just one of the many sources that have yielded a wealth of data for Bretter. She has ably used this new information to detail the taste and preferences over time of the family of one of Lannuier's biggest fans. Heretofore, the name of William Bayard was probably most frequently invoked by furniture scholars when they thought of Duncan Phyfe and the parlor furniture (some now at Winterthur) ordered from him by Bayard. Although both Bayard and Brinkerhoff bought large orders from Phyfe, they also turned to Lannuier for their showiest furniture—elaborated, winged caryatid furniture in the late Empire style.

Bretter's discussions of Lannuier's French clients in America and his southern patronage are equally rich in new material and astute observations.

The existence of Lannuier furniture in the most northern reaches of New York State, purchased in 1816 by emigré James Leray de Chaumont, or his son Vincent, is an eye opener for most Lannuier aficionados. Also, although the only known suite of Lannuier furniture that includes seating forms for a domestic residence was owned by James Bosley, a Baltimore merchant, Bretter speculates in a footnote that Bosley's furniture, presumably purchased for a new house in 1822, might have been that originally bought from Lannuier by A. S. Bulloch of Savannah. It is just this type of continuing critical analysis that demonstrates the total understanding by this remarkable team of the man, his times, and his work.

Kenny's concluding chapter, "The Essence of Lannuier: Connoisseurship of His Known Work," most profoundly demonstrates the heights to which he has taken this study of craftsmanship. As he aptly remarks, Lannuier is a "connoisseur's dream" due to his "near-obsessive labeling and stamping of his furniture." In this chapter it is evident how closely he and his curatorial and conservation colleagues have studied these documented works. They have merged both exhaustive visual examination with a variety of analytical techniques to understand his skill and technique. Why did Lannuier so often stamp (as was the Parisian practice) or label (having three different labels over time) his furniture? Could the tight competition from Phyfe and others have been one of the reasons for this type of presence in print he maintained? Because there are more than 125 documented or firmly attributed works by Lannuier, there is ample opportunity to take full note of his talent and dogged dedication to quality production, which emphasized extraordinary woods, particularly select book-matched veneers, and the finest quality gilded cast-brass ornaments, applied brass moldings, and inlaid brass. Kenny's inquiries shed new light on the inlaid brass and wood bands used by Lannuier, for his research establishes a link between Lannuier and Parisian Denis-Michel Frichot whose talents in the manufacture of these "inlayings" were renowned. Kenny continues in his role as detective as he carefully examines the furniture—combining his ever-increasing understanding of Lannuier and his context with a studied analysis of these pieces. Working closely with conservators and employing modern analytical techniques when appropriate, he reaches new understandings of construction as well as of the various finished surfaces employed by Lannuier. This chapter sets a new standard for the examination of any body of material, large or small, from both a visual and analytical perspective.

Since this publication also served as the catalogue for the exhibition, a complete catalogue of all documented (103) and firmly attributed (22) pieces follows the final chapter. These entries contain valuable notes providing information on condition/alterations, provenance, and references. For those objects not illustrated within the text, a black and white illustration appears beneath the entry. When the object is illustrated within the text, this is referenced at the top of the entry. Unfortunately, the objects that were shown in the exhibition are only identified in the list of lenders at the front of the book. Equally frustrating is the fact that the captions for Lannuier objects in the text only reference the catalogue entry but do not state ownership, or if they were in the exhibition, under the illustration. These are minor points of inconvenience, which are eclipsed by the high quality of Bruce White's photographic images and the simple elegance of Malcolm Grear's overall design of the publication. Like the work of the master craftsman Lannuier, this volume is a model of well-crafted and seamlessly executed workmanship. There is no doubt that for generations to come it will serve classical connoisseurs as the penultimate source on Lannuier and his contemporary New York scene.

Wendy A. Cooper
Winterthur Museum

Nancy Richards and Nancy Goyne Evans, with Wendy A. Cooper and Michael S. Podmaniczky. *New England Furniture at Winterthur: Queen Anne and Chippendale Periods.* Winterthur, Del.: Winterthur Museum, 1997. 534 pp.; 482 bw illus., bibliography, index. Distributed by University Press of New England, Hanover and London. $75.00.

Collectors and scholars of American furniture have been anticipating publication of this Winterthur Museum collection catalogue for many years. Because it updates the scholarship presented by Joseph Downs in his *American Furniture, Queen Anne and Chippendale Periods,* published in 1952, and because it includes the additions to the collection made since Downs appeared, the catalogue is a highly important contribution to the field of American furniture. Indeed, the book "will be an invaluable resource for those who have relied on Downs' ambitious, but dated volume," as Winterthur Deputy Director Brock Jobe states in his introduction. Jobe also points out that intense scholarship in the intervening years permits a much more detailed and accurate assessment of furniture production in New England. In most respects, the book achieves these goals and makes some new steps forward.

The inclusion of technical descriptions of the conservation work performed on each object, as well as the discussion of the scientific analysis of finish, greatly advances the teamwork approach, which combines the various developing specialties in the study of decorative arts. It is hoped that other institutions and curators will follow this general approach. The thoroughness and honesty in discussing repairs, condition, enhancements, and forgery in the catalogue entries follow recent trends in scholarship aimed at providing a more accurate view of material culture.

The index, an important component of a reference book, is excellent. It covers the usual areas of proper names and also indexes woods and construction. A spot check of numerous entries resulted in 100 percent accuracy, but the index suffers from one major omission. Regarding the discussion of styles, the index totally omits the numerous references to "Queen Anne" (although it includes "William and Mary style") and covers references to "Thomas Chippendale" but not to "Chippendale style," a term used often in the book.

In the area of object analysis, this catalogue meets the high standards one expects from the Winterthur Museum. In the context of general decorative arts scholarship, however, the work is lacking in important aspects and does not take a leadership role in the field. An overshadowing heritage of the 1950s and 1960s appears to dominate the book, thus forming a barrier to current scholarship and presentation.

The use in the subtitle of the terms "Queen Anne" and "Chippendale" is especially unfortunate. These terms are misnomers and should be abandoned as incorrect and misleading. More than twenty years have passed since scholars identified the problems with these terms and began to choose more accurate art historical designations, specifically, *late baroque* and *rococo*.

Although the old trade term "Queen Anne" may have appeal in the commercial market, its continued use establishes an educational barrier. Neither is the exploration of the Eastern (Chinese and Indian) impetus for this style undertaken nor does the work discuss the probability that the style postdates Queen Anne herself (see the article by Joan Barzilay Freund and Leigh Keno in this volume, pp. 1–40). The omission of a discussion of the burgeoning Western taste for Asian design misses an opportunity to put New England furniture within a stylistic and cultural movement in which Boston japanning and cabriole furniture make a strong statement. By contrast, Charles F. Montgomery, in his Winterthur collection catalogue published in 1966, rejected the terms *Hepplewhite* and *Sheraton* and titled his book *American Furniture, the Federal Period,* in an attempt to accurately label the style. A decade ago, Benno M. Forman in his Winterthur book, *American Seating Furniture, 1630–1730* (1988), examined the term "Queen Anne" and stated that "perhaps our European colleagues have tended to date their examples somewhat too early" (p. 302) because of their use of this term. This certainly appears to have been the case with many English furniture books published between 1900 and 1950—a trend that appears to have been followed in studies of American work. Forman, however, did not propose changing the stylistic designation. In 1982, the Museum of Early Southern Decorative Arts began to phase out the term "Queen Anne" after John Bivins proposed in the museum newsletter using the term "baroque" (see *The Luminary,* vol. 3, no. 1). The Colonial Williamsburg Foundation, when it opened the Dewitt Wallace Decorative Arts Gallery in 1985, officially abandoned the terms "Queen Anne" and "Chippendale." The Metropolitan Museum of Art, in their 1992 exhibition and catalogue entitled "American Rococo, 1750–1775," signaled a change in their dealing with the issue. Clearly, when confronted with a larger cross-section of cultural material, the art history terms are the most logical choice.

Like Forman's essays in *American Seating Furniture,* Evans's entries for the earliest chairs in *New England Furniture* discuss the introduction of the "new style" by citing Boston upholsterer Samuel Grant's November 21, 1730, account book entry for a chair with "horsebone feet." Although Forman dated the Boston side chair illustrated as catalogue no. 1 in *New England Furniture* as 1730–1732, Evans expands the range to 1728–1735. However, Evans herself is perhaps being a little narrow and conservative in regard to the possibility of the chair being made in the 1720s. A 1725 to 1735 date range would seem appropriate given the information presently available. If the "horsebone" reference means squared cabriole legs (a logical hypothesis but at present not a proven fact), the introduction of the late baroque "Indian" chair in the 1720s seems likely.

"Queen Anne" is the term for this style used throughout the catalogue, but in her introductory section on "Chests of Drawers, Bureau Tables and Chests-on-Chests," Evans cites the "Georgian style, called the Queen Anne style in America" (p. 354). If we must use a monarchial designation (and I am not suggesting that we do), Georgian is more correct and would be in harmony with most architectural studies. Because the Winterthur Program in Early American Culture at the University of Delaware is a principal training ground for future curators and other museum professionals, it is important that the Winterthur Museum take a close look at this issue of stylistic terminology.

A larger and more complete cultural overview would have added to the effectiveness of this book. Jobe's overall introduction and Richards's and Evans's introductions to specific forms have considerable information on the types of furniture, cabinetmakers' styles, furniture usage, and the trade; nevertheless, an introduction that set the stage more fully by examining patronage, the timber industry, shipping, architecture, the overall economy, and the woodworking communities would have provided a stronger context for understanding furniture production. Given the quality and quantity of research available on colonial New England, the authors could have positioned the cabinetmaking industry within each society. New England's many urban and rural cultures account for the region's diverse and extraordinary furniture production.

Many inconsistencies—perhaps symptoms of the catalogue being the production of several people over a long time—are disruptive. Most notable is the introduction to the seating furniture section (pp. 1–6), which has only one footnote where it should have many. In this section, the date for the third edition of Chippendale's *Director* is given in a list of influential English pattern books (p. 2)—normally, in such a list, the date of the first edition should be given (as it is elsewhere in the volume). In other introductory sections (in "Chests . . . ," for example, pp. 353–55), the same writer footnotes extensively. Likewise, the lack of any sort of explanatory introduction to the section of the catalogue entitled "Case Studies" (pp. 473–94) is puzzling. This section sorely needs a statement indicating the reasons for including (and segregating) these objects and defining the type of study object involved, be it a fake, a heavily restored piece, an enhanced object, or whatever.

The illustrations are not up to current standards, and there are no color photographs except for the dust jacket. The book's design and photo layout creates many partially filled pages with large areas of white space—areas that could have been used to make the overall photographs and details larger. Although this layout may be defended as reflecting the style of the designer, decorative arts students want to get close to the furniture. Many of the photographs are small, leaving the viewer too far from the object, and the choice of a dark sepia tone printing adds to this problem. The decision to silhouette the overall objects is puzzling, since the process is usually associated with field photography where backgrounds and shadows are disruptive. Using studio shots (which these are) usually eliminates such problems. Silhouetting is a process that can cause losses and inaccuracies in profiling; studio shots eliminate this potential problem and show some shadows, forming a base for the furniture and, avoiding that "floating object" look created by masking. The omission of an interior drawer in the overall view of the highly important desk-and-bookcase (cat. no. 206), the lack of a photograph of its bookcase section, and a chair splat pictured upside down (fig. 1, p. 63) are unfortunate editorial lapses.

This book is an important element in New England furniture studies, and everyone with an interest in American furniture and decorative arts should have it. The work does not meet the earlier standards of Winterthur publications on furniture, however, and it falls well below current expectations of such an important institution and collection.

Wallace B. Gusler
Colonial Williamsburg Foundation

John T. Kirk. *The Shaker World: Art, Life, Belief.* New York: Harry N. Abrams, 1997. 288 pp.; 82 color and 195 bw illus., map, appendix, bibliography, chronology, index. $60.00.

John T. Kirk's *The Shaker World: Art, Life, Belief* is one of the most important books on the Shakers to be published in the past decade. The book makes a significant contribution to American decorative arts scholarship by placing the Shaker aesthetic within the larger history of design and by advancing the study of Shaker furniture.

The Shaker World is an audacious title for a big, bold, and brash book, which will serve for many years to come as an art historical complement to Stephen J. Stein's *The Shaker Experience in America: A History of the United Society of Believers* (1992). In many respects, Kirk surveys the material history of the Shakers, just as Stein surveyed their intellectual, religious, and organizational history. The two books are essential reference works on the Shakers and are complementary, even though they are dissimilar in tone and organization. Although both are necessary foundation blocks for understanding the Shakers, both struggle with the same difficulty—how to fit all Shakers into "The Experience" or "The World."

The book is also a landmark in the evolution of John Kirk's distinguished career as a design historian. The Shakers, as Kirk now freely admits, were not always on his design horizon. In *The Impecunious Collector's Guide to American Antiques* (1975), Kirk wrote: "The myth persists that anything Shaker is great, and that anything simple is Shaker. . . . [D]espite what is generally believed the Shakers did not—as a result of their retirement from the world and their focus on spiritual things—create a radically new concept of design contrary to their surrounding world" (pp. 19, 35).

In short, the Shakers were hardly worth the attention of decorative arts and design historians in 1975, according to John Kirk. Edward and Faith Andrews had created a particularistic myth of the Shakers, and their tunnel vision could be dismissed either as a lack of interest in a broader historical context or, more cynically, as a point of view serving their collector/dealer interests. In 1975 Kirk was more interested in exposing and debunking the myth than in trying to explain what the Shakers were doing.

Fast forward to 1997. *The Shaker World* is a major book on the Shakers by the same John Kirk, who has spent the past several years looking at Shaker-made objects, visiting Shaker museums, creating Shaker exhibitions, and consulting with curators, collectors, and dealers who specialize in Shaker materials. In addition, he has sought insight from the remaining Shakers at the last community at Sabbathday Lake, Maine.

What is the result of this twenty-two-year odyssey? Kirk's thesis in *The Shaker World* is that Shaker design is an intentional refinement of the prevailing rural vernacular expression of American neoclassicism. The Shakers took the design aesthetic of their region and time and adjusted it to fit their particular theological injunctions (p. 7). In this study, Kirk wants to forever bury the myth of celebratory particularism that has had a persistent hold on Shaker decorative arts studies, in spite of numerous challenges to the work of the Andrews. His goal is to link Shaker and non-Shaker design history, to contextualize the Shakers, and to bring them into the general history of design.

Kirk's new-found respect for Shaker design allows him to credit the Shakers with a positive, selective reduction of vernacular neoclassicism to its essential components of form, geometry, and color, and with a refinement of that style over a longer time than that of the rural New England vernacular tradition from which the Shakers drew their original inspiration. In Kirk's view, the Shakers developed a well-defined aesthetic sense in the early years of the nineteenth century, borrowing freely from the world in executing their design concepts and expressing gospel order. Freely accepting change and, at the same time, managing the marketing of their public image of simplicity, the Shakers maintained design flexibility over time.

The Shaker World is organized in a general chronological sequence, with the first two chapters devoted to the theological and historical contexts of Shakerism in the late eighteenth and early nineteenth centuries. The subsequent eight chapters develop the following themes and topics: "Shaker Design: Sources, Central Control, and Regional Differences"; "The Shakers and Beauty"; "Visual Affirmation of Order—A Gift Drawing, a Case of Drawers, a Meetinghouse, a Barn, and Dances"; "The 'Classic' Objects"; "Color and Varnish: History and Worldly Practices, and Shaker Use"; "Era of Manifestations, 1837–1850"; "After 1860"; and "The Twentieth Century."

John Kirk's writing is creative and engaging, but *The Shaker World* is a dense, rambling work, difficult to penetrate. My first reading was sequential within a short period of two weeks. I was filled with the anticipation of discovery, and I was richly rewarded. But one of the discoveries was that *The Shaker World* is a book to be mined over time. Kirk has given us a series of essays on the history of design that are loosely connected but, for the most part, can be profitably read on their own. Although Kirk uses Shaker furniture as an organizing theme for the book, it is not a catalogue of furniture or of any other body of Shaker artifacts.

The first two chapters of history are competently done and provide critical background information on the history and beliefs of the Shakers. There is little new information here, but this introduction is not where Kirk has chosen to develop his thesis. Instead, he is intent on laying out the theological and social framework within which the Shakers work out their aesthetic preferences.

In chapter 3, "Shaker Design: Sources, Central Control, and Regional Differences," Kirk develops his thesis that "Shaker design, as it emerged around 1800 to 1810, mixed two parallel and complementary themes: the elimination of unnecessary features and the expression of the neoclassical aesthetic. The congruence of these two impulses produced what is now called the 'Shaker look,' or 'Classic Shaker'" (p. 39). To illustrate his thesis, Kirk discusses four drop-leaf tables and three two-drawer blanket chests, all of which seem to confirm his contention that the Shakers selectively borrowed from the rural, vernacular expressions of neoclassicism and made them their own. No matter how one reads Kirk, there is no escaping the fact that his approach is traditionally art historical in spite of the subject matter and his inclusion of topics from barns to naked dancing. Kirk endorses a cardinal principle of traditional design history—namely, that sources can be specifically identified, that such sources are linked to known designers and styles, and that the diffusion of these sources flows from urban centers to the countryside and down through the class structure of society.

On this central point of source and diffusion, Kirk's book ultimately fails to offer a new way of thinking about the Shakers, their world, and their products. For example, drop-leaf tables and blanket chests are not the most common furniture forms among the Shakers, and not the signature bearers of Shaker cultural tradition. Kirk has developed a thesis and looked for examples to prove it rather than building his thesis from the full archaeology of Shaker material culture. Surely ladder-back chairs, work counters, and storage cupboards are more expressive of Shaker culture, and these forms are not the signature bearers of neoclassical style. In short, to label the Shaker look vernacular neoclassicism tells us little that is new or significant.

The section on sources offers useful insights on the transmission of design and production ideas among the Shaker communities. The part on central control (or lack of it) is an excellent brief summary (pp. 44–48). Kirk also adds to the thinking on regional variations among the Shakers, which was a major contribution of Tim Rieman and Jean Burks's *The Complete Book of Shaker Furniture* (1993). In addition, the depth of his knowledge about the various influences on general furniture design pervades the chapter, as when he delineates the role of choice—in woods, in design, in timing, in ornamentation—as it intersects with the training and habits of the woodworkers.

"The Shakers and Beauty," chapter 4, is a tantalizing essay but ultimately disappointing. The central point here is Kirk's assertion that the Shakers made aesthetic choices in everything they produced. "The Shakers were, and are, not against beauty, but against ostentation" (p. 54). The Shaker aesthetic, according to Kirk, was dominated by order, harmony, utility, regularity, and appropriateness.

This approach is so obvious that one must ask why John Kirk strains to kill the gnat of ostentation. Most likely, Kirk is still jousting with Edward Deming Andrews here, in a debate that Shaker enthusiasts may appreciate but may well leave the general reader in a fog. It is helpful, nevertheless to be reminded that the 1845 Millennial Laws are an extreme expression of Shaker order and to have the 1821 Millennial Laws included as an appendix. After warning the reader not to accept the 1845 version of the laws as Shaker truth, however, Kirk seems to accept the 1821 laws as operative gospel truth. In fact, the Millennial Laws for the Shakers were primarily codifications of ministerial intent. In practice they were regulators of gospel order, especially for novitiates, but they were less theological dogma and more practical guidelines to grease the skids of group living.

One of the most provocative ideas in the chapter on beauty is Kirk's suggestion that, for ministerial objects, "their intention to be finer is observable" (p. 59). This point could be key to understanding Shaker design, but Kirk drops the idea without teasing out its implications. Why was he not intrigued enough to explore the influence of the ministry as it affected particular material forms of expression?

Another prescient moment occurs when the author discusses the choices of the Shakers that led to a "plain" aesthetic. "What the Shakers made flowed naturally from both experiences and intentions, which are finally inseparable" (p. 54). Kirk notes that in their avoidance of ostentation the Shakers did not choose to land at the penultimate extremity of plainness but chose a middle ground for the early nineteenth century, especially in their extensive use of color to finish furniture, many woodenwares, and even architectural woodwork. "Color was everywhere in Shaker life" (p. 60).

John Kirk is superbly qualified to juxtapose the Shaker aesthetic with the "fancy" aesthetic of urban America in the 1815–1845 era. He chooses, however, to avoid the comparison except in passing references to the importance of gold in neoclassical decoration and the corresponding prevalence of yellow on and in middle-class American homes, including those of the Shakers.

As he warms to his topic, Kirk engages in some freewheeling speculation in chapter 5, "Visual Affirmation of Order: A Gift Drawing, a Case of Drawers, a Meetinghouse, a Barn, and Dances." This chapter is fascinating reading, and only a scholar of Kirk's stature could get away with being so speculative. This reviewer, for one, accepts the chapter as a bold, honest attempt to throw a hand grenade into the treasurehouse of Shaker studies, but most readers will have difficulty following the logic or accepting many of the conclusions in this chapter.

Kirk's thesis in chapter 5 is that Shaker adherence to gospel order had its roots in Enlightenment rationality, as expressed in a passion for geometry and other patterns of regularity for achieving harmonious relations in design and life (p. 66). To illustrate his point, Kirk discusses the 1832 gift drawing entitled "Holy City," a square city plan with detailed geometric patterns; an 1806 tall case of drawers with drawers decreasing in size in descending order;

the 1824 New Lebanon Meetinghouse with its curved ceiling; the 1826 Round Barn at Hancock; and Shaker laboring exercises, or dances, especially those dances using squares and circles to regulate performance.

With several examples—the gift drawing, the meetinghouse, and the Round Barn—Kirk chooses three of the most exceptional Shaker creations on which to build his case for neoclassical influence upon Shaker design. Granted that all three are evocative Shaker objects, why should these three be taken so seriously as templates of Shaker design? For example, the gift drawing of the "Holy City" is a finely executed expression of idealistic community design, but it has no direct relationship to the actual planning and layout of Shaker communities, and there is no evidence that many Shakers ever saw it. The New Lebanon Meetinghouse certainly was revered among the Shakers and, in basic form, was the template for second-generation Shaker meetinghouses; however, the feature that Kirk touts as its most significant design feature, and its most neoclassical element, was the barrel roof, with the curved ceiling in the main worship space. What he does not mention is that no other Shaker community emulated the curved ceiling. As with the "Holy City" drawing, we are left with a template that other Shakers did not choose to follow.

The Round Barn at Hancock is another example of a spectacular Shaker creation that is more anomaly than template. The 1826 barn may testify to Shaker innovation as "the first truly round barn built in America" (p.76), and it may indeed have been inspired by neoclassical forms, but the Hancock community had to hire outside masons to construct the Round Barn, and no other Shaker communities followed Hancock's example. The typical Shaker barn was a long, rectangular structure of multiple levels, laid out on the northern boundary of the physical complex where it helped serve as a windbreak from northern winds for the livestock paddocks on the southern sides of the barn.

Kirk most certainly does hit the mark in chapter 5 when discussing the geometry of Shaker dance formations and the remarkable visual floor cues that have been documented to at least three of the Shaker meetinghouses—those at Watervliet, Harvard, and Canterbury. In his relentless and thorough search for design sources, Kirk also offers here an interesting hypothesis about the origin of the idea for a curved ceiling in the 1824 New Lebanon Meetinghouse. After noting that the design has similarities to the work of Benjamin Latrobe and is clearly in the vocabulary of neoclassical design, Kirk looks to a nearby Masonic hall as the specific source for the curved ceiling. In this reference, and later in the book when he seeks design sources of spirit or gift drawings, Kirk suggests that Masonic symbols and ideas worked their way into Shaker thinking, most likely from converts who were formerly Masons. Masonic symbolism is an important and generally overlooked topic. The importance of their art and architecture in England and America, particularly in the century between 1750 and 1850, and the remarkable spread of Masonic influence have been highlighted recently in James Stevens Curl's well-illustrated *The Art and Architecture of Free Masonry* (1993).

Once again, the potential Masonic source is a tantalizing idea that needs further investigation, but ultimately it may not yield much of significance for understanding the nature of Shakerism or Shaker design. The Masonic order and its rituals were for men only and were designed to mystify and obfuscate understanding for the uninitiated. The Shakers were, in spirit at least, fundamentally anti-Masonic, since they sought to bring gospel order to the world in fulfillment of the millennium.

The heart and soul of *The Shaker World* lies in chapter 6, "The Classic Objects," and in chapter 7 "Color and Varnish: History and Worldly Practices, and Shaker Use." It is in these chapters that Kirk makes his most original contributions to American art history generally and to furniture study in particular. After noting that the Shakers made objects that look like those made in the world, and had objects made for them by non-Shakers, he settles down to treat those Shaker-made objects with what he calls "the look" of Shaker. These "classic" objects "are imbued with the unique qualities of the sect's design attitude. They exhibit an ethos so powerful that they stand out as new: original in intention and appearance" (p. 82).

For Kirk, these classic objects convey a "variety of expressions" responding to variations in the Shaker experience. It is here that Kirk departs most markedly from Edward Deming Andrews's concept of Shaker perfection in furniture. Kirk accepts the basic premise that the Shaker look is the result of a living, changing process rather than a static definition of perfection. The classic objects in Kirk's eye, nevertheless, exhibit five characteristics consistently: They are "ordered," "stretched," "fragile," "rugged," and "improvised" (p. 83). We must give John Kirk credit for trying to break molds and stereotypes, but is this appropriate language for academic art history? To push the reader even farther, Kirk throws all types of Shaker products into the pool for consideration—furniture, textiles, stoves, ladders, brooms, and buildings.

The key to understanding this section of *The Shaker World* is the word "look." John Kirk's forte is his skill at looking at things. To his credit, in this book he has also made a major intellectual effort to understand the Shakers on their own terms. The footnotes are often entertaining (at least for those with a penchant for the obscure and arcane), helpful, and extensive in range and volume. As impressive as the research may be, however, the central fact is that John Kirk sees details that others miss. The danger, of course, is that he may also be reading his fertile imagination into the analysis of the material. Caveat emptor!

Based on the Shaker love of order, as expressed in grids, numbers, and the power of rhythm and repetition, Kirk establishes the characteristic of "ordered" in Shaker life (pp. 83–100). The second characteristic is "stretched"—an exaggerated elongation of buildings, corridors, walkways, peg rails, dining tables, and so on—which underscores the special significance of the "long line" for Shakers. Kirk links this linear proclivity to the linear progression of the Shaker spiritual journey, but the link is asserted rather than documented (pp. 100–108).

The third characteristic of the classic Shaker look lies in the "fragile" nature of products, which are "consciously precious" (p. 115). Kirk is quite original here (but I think ultimately misleading) in describing one of the features that has been most appealing to collectors of Shaker things—a lightness of design that is revealed in the thinness of lapboards, small tabletops, woodenwares, and ladder-back chairs. Kirk attributes this fragility largely to the fact that the objects were made primarily for Shaker use, and that the Shakers operated under injunctions to exercise care of all things so as to preserve them throughout the millennium (pp. 108–14). In fact, the lightness in weight and thinness of materials—in oval boxes, for example— is due to the use of high-quality, quartersawn, hardwood. The Shakers sought durability, not fragility.

The fourth characteristic—"rugged"—appears at first to be contradictory to fragile, but it is the same principle, namely, preservation for long-term use of objects of everyday use or hard labor such as tools, agricultural implements, and walkways. Granite walks were more expensive to lay than boardwalks, but the granite walks had no foreseeable replacement time. Wooden shovels were by definition consumable, but adding a metal edge to the blade greatly extended their lifetimes (pp. 115–19).

The fifth and final characteristic of the Shaker look is what Kirk calls "improvised." This feature involves the ability to design to fulfill a specific need and to convert from one use to another (pp. 119–23). This practical "make do" attitude leads to some ingenious devices that served Shaker community enterprises and improved the efficiency of daily living. For some reason, this characteristic fails to engage Kirk's full attention. He sees these products as proof of Shaker practicality, efficiency, and ingenuity, but he regards the products as exceptional answers to specific needs. This characteristic of customizing is, I think, more central to the Shaker ethic, if not to their aesthetic, than Kirk acknowledges. The principle is certainly applicable to Shaker buildings and their adaptation over time, but buildings are not featured in this book.

After describing what he feels are the five characteristics of the classic Shaker look, Kirk summarizes recent discoveries about the Shaker use of paint and varnish. Once again, he butts heads with the Andrews myth. Andrews's books are filled with the austere black and white photographs of William Winter. In words and pictures, Andrews emphasized Shaker form, detail, and construction in an effort to depict his "religion in wood." Many of the objects that Andrews collected and sold had already been stripped of color by the Shakers to make them more appealing to buyers from the world, who seemed to want glossy finishes highlighting the natural wood. In chapter 7 on "Color and Varnish," Kirk deals a knockout blow to the Andrews/Winter team, with considerable help from conservator Susan L. Buck, who provided much of the testing and technical information for this chapter.

Kirk's essay on color is the single best summary of this topic, and it is bound to stimulate new research. As Kirk notes, "it is now hard to visualize how colorful the Shakers' world was throughout most of the nineteenth century" (p. 129). Kirk naturally sees a strong connection between the use of color in neoclassical architecture and furniture and among the Shakers. To this connection he overlays information about the Masonic use of color, once again assuming that the Shakers borrowed ideas about color from both the Masons and the rural vernacular neoclassical usage around them.

The bulk of chapter 7 is devoted to Shaker use of color, introduced by the Shakers own explanation for the meaning of colors in a document accompanying the 1843 gift drawing of the "Holy City," in a very specific quotation by Calvin Green of New Lebanon, and in other Shaker manuscripts. Kirk wants to find meaning in the Shaker use of color, but the quotations themselves do not help answer the question about whether or not the Shakers assigned meaning to specific colors. For example, in the three separate Shaker sources quoted in Kirk's book, blue signifies water in one, heaven in another, and "the color the devil hates" in the third.

Whatever the meaning, there is consistency in the Shaker use of color, and scholars are beginning to understand the particular Shaker color code of the 1815–1860 era. Although serious research on Shaker color is still in its early stages, Kirk has done justice to the subject, and the information he presents is generally unknown in the wider world of American decorative arts scholarship.

The bulk of the chapter on color is devoted to sections on the Shaker use of the following colors: blue and white; blue; yellow; yellow, red, and orange; red; black; and patterned surfaces. In each section he includes information on furniture, woodenwares, clothing, and textiles, with all too few references to building exteriors and interiors.

Kirk and Susan Buck greatly advance knowledge about the Shaker use of color. They show that the Shakers rarely used casein-based paint, that they used the best pigments available commercially, that they generally mixed their pigments as did people in the world (with lead), and that they used varnishes sparingly and for specific purposes. Kirk is not willing to speculate on whether Shaker furniture was painted to match interior woodwork in order to create an en suite effect.

Chapter 8 on the "Era of Manifestations, 1837–1850: Angels, Purges, Gift Drawings, the Narrow Path, and Sexuality" is the book's weakest link. Once again, Kirk deserves credit for trying to strike down stereotypes and offer fresh interpretation. Unfortunately, this chapter interrupts the flow of the book and seems to be a collection of miscellany that does not easily fit anywhere else. Clearly the "Era of Manifestations" is an important episode in Shaker history and may have been difficult to leave out of a book on *The Shaker World*, but Kirk's primary contribution to this complex spiritual era among the Shakers is to suggest that Masonic design motifs appear frequently in the two hundred known spirit drawings of the era (pp. 166–68). The similarities here are too striking to dismiss as coincidental, but Kirk does not really answer the obvious question of how the artists of the spirit drawings (principally young women of the Shaker communities) would have known these symbols and motifs.

Chapter 9, "After 1860: 'Very Much Like the Inhabitants of the Section of the Country Where They Reside,'" is another collection of miscellaneous topics gathered under a general umbrella of chronology. Kirk, like most observers, sees an inevitable movement of the Shakers toward accommodation with the world in terms of practice, such as the introduction of musical instruments, and in terms of design, such as the Victorianizing of Shaker furniture and interiors. He follows in the footsteps of Jean Burks's pioneering work on Victorian Shakers, and like Burks he avoids a pejorative tone. He advances her work in some specific areas, for example in the fact that the Shakers made chair cushions for sale to the world as early as 1834 (p. 200), and provides additional visual and documentary records of Shaker practice after 1860 (pp. 220–23).

The most original subsection of this chapter is Kirk's very informative treatise on the ingenious ways the Shakers marketed their past to benefit their communities. They were, on the one hand, remarkably open to change, yet creative in perpetuating their past. Unlike Colonial Williamsburg and other twentieth-century creations that made up a past that never really quite existed, the Shakers kept alive and exploited an image of a real past while living differently in the present. By "living in complexity, yet showing visitors simplicity" (p. 223), the Shakers doctored their past for public consumption, generated pride among the remaining Shakers, and to some degree provided justification for what the Shakers were doing in the twentieth century.

This topic of self-generated marketing deserves an entire book. All one can say here is that Kirk has struck a rich vein of truth in opening up this topic, which will hopefully encourage other scholars. The role of the Shakers in contemporary life needs to be placed in the context of wider cultural studies such as Michael Kammen's *The Mystic Chords of Memory: The Transformation of Tradition in American Culture* (1993) and Dona Brown's *Inventing New England: Regional Tourism in the Nineteenth Century* (1995).

The last chapter of *The Shaker World* is an essay on "The Twentieth Century: Myth Makers, Revisionists, and a Comparative Awareness of Perfection." Here Kirk returns to the seminal role of the Andrewses in creating a myth of Shaker perfection and to important early collectors such as Charles Sheeler, who freely used Shaker objects and buildings as sources of inspiration. He traces revisionist scholarship of the last twenty-five years, starting with the Winterthur thesis of Mary Lynn Ray (and her subsequent article in *Winterthur Portfolio* 8 [1973]), the book *Seven American Utopias: The Architecture of Communitarian Socialism, 1790–1975* (1976) by Dolores Hayden, and recent work by Jean Burks and Tim Rieman.

The book closes with a mini-essay comparing the Shaker aesthetic with certain contemporary artists, such as Donald Judd, who share a common impulse to "communicate by essentials" by reducing design to minimalist form and treatment (p. 248). In Kirk's view, the ultimate Shaker masterpiece is a minimalist, pinkish-red chest of drawers with sixteen drawers (p. 250, fig. 261; see also fig. 80).

How can we take measure of John Kirk's achievement in *The Shaker World*? Certainly it is the most ambitious and comprehensive revisionist work to date, so Kirk's impact on Shaker studies will be monumental. Where does *The Shaker World* fit into the larger field of scholarship? Its impact on religious studies, communitarian studies, social history, women's studies, and architectural studies will be minimal, but these were not the fields Kirk was trying to plough. His goal was to bring the Shakers into the canon of American decorative arts scholarship and to write the definitive design history of the Shakers. This reviewer believes he may well have accomplished the first goal, but certainly not the second; nevertheless, no serious student of the Shakers, or American decorative arts, can afford to ignore John Kirk's *The Shaker World*.

Scott T. Swank
Canterbury Shaker Village

Geoffrey Beard. *Upholsterers and Interior Furnishing in England, 1530–1840*. New Haven and London: Yale University Press for the Bard Graduate Center for Studies in the Decorative Arts, 1997. xiv + 346 pp.; 212 color and 164 bw illus., appendices, glossary, bibliography, index. $75.00.

Given Geoffrey Beard's many distinguished publications on English furniture and interior decoration, it does not come as a surprise that he has produced a remarkable and extremely valuable study of English upholstery from the period 1530 to 1840. Beard's *Craftsmen and Interior Decoration in England, 1660–1820* (1981) and the *Dictionary of English Furniture Makers, 1660–1840*, which he co-edited with Christopher Gilbert in 1986, are now standard reference works for historians of English furniture. One can assume that *Upholsterers* will achieve the same status, for it adds enormously to our understanding of upholstery and upholstery practices. *Upholsterers* is the first title in a series of books to be produced by the Bard Graduate Center for Studies in the Decorative Arts, which can take much pride in this initial effort.

At the end of the preface, Beard asks the reader to remember the words of Dr. Johnson when evaluating his book: "In this work, when it shall be found that much is omitted, let it not be forgotten that much likewise is performed." And, indeed, a vast amount is performed. Beard examines with great thoroughness the history of upholstery during the period under consideration, focusing on the important role accorded to upholstered furniture, the status of furnishing fabrics, the cost and types of fabrics used, and the upholstery trade itself. As Beard notes in the preface, he has ordered the book chronologically, taking the unfashionable route of following (1530 and 1840 apart) the dates of the reigning monarchs. As the book demonstrates, this approach is valid because upholstery was so profoundly dependent upon the patronage of the crown, of the court, and often of those elevated by the ruling monarch. Beard makes a point of trying to set upholstery in the larger context of English history, and he successfully demonstrates how closely the two are intertwined. Coronations, royal funerals, and elevations to the peerage with the attendant material rewards are major occasions for lavish upholstery projects. The book focuses almost entirely upon upholstery that was undertaken for the court and upper classes; those readers looking for information regarding more humble upholstery activities will have to look elsewhere. This focus can be justified for a variety of reasons, the most important of which may be the availability of detailed documentary evidence regarding royal and court-level upholstery and interior furnishing projects.

Beard has done a prodigious amount of archival research while preparing this book, and the documents that are cited continuously throughout the text add very significantly to our understanding of upholstery, furniture, and the upholstery trade during this period. The author has mined the Calendar of State Papers, the Public Records Office, the Exchequer and Audit Accounts, the Lord Chamberlain's Department, insurance company records, and innumerable house inventories—to cite a few examples—and the results of this primary research provide us with a much richer and fuller picture of upholstery and its importance. It could be argued that the chapters of Beard's book that span the period 1530–1760 make the most significant contribution, in large part because post-1760 furniture has been studied in greater depth. Beard begins by tracing what is known about upholstery as a trade in the sixteenth and seventeenth centuries, and his exhaustive survey of inventories, insurance records, and trade cards serves as the basis for detailed discussions of an upholsterer's workshop in those years. To my knowledge, Beard is the first author to do primary archival work for pre-1660 English upholstery, and his research into late seventeenth-century and early eighteenth-century upholstery also uncovers a great deal of new information. We gain increased knowledge of important English upholsterers such as Richard Bealing, Thomas How, and Thomas Phill, and new archival evidence emerges about the French emigré Francis Lapiere, that corrects earlier, frequently published misinformation (to which Beard admits his own contribution). We learn of the significant role played by Lapiere and his fellow emigré Jean Poictevin in England in the late seventeenth and early eighteenth century and thus better understand the strong influence of French taste on English court circles.

In his chapters covering the sixteenth and seventeenth centuries, Beard underscores repeatedly the enormous importance and high status of upholstered furnishings, as well as their substantial cost. Of the many examples cited, the contrast between the cost of the frames of Queen Anne's elaborate gilded throne and stool (£20) and that of their upholstery in a blue and gold brocade (£72) is a particularly telling one. Beard also reinforces the primacy of the state bed in seventeenth- and early eighteenth-century upholstery, and the numerous examples cited in inventories make this point clearly, as do the surprisingly numerous photographs of existing English state beds. In the chapter covering 1760–1790, Beard summarizes what is known about the upholstery activities of the more familiar names in English furniture making, such as Mayhew and Ince, the Linnells, and, of course, Thomas Chippendale and also informs us about the less well-known upholsterers and the various firms that executed upholstery on a significant scale. The last chapter, which concludes with the year 1840, examines the patronage of George IV, the important upholstery firms of the early nineteenth century, and the proliferation of revival styles. Beard deliberately decides to avoid the subject of factory-produced upholstery, thus choosing the middle of the nineteenth century as the end point for his book.

All of this material is strongly supported by a wealth of illustrations, and the photography is notable for its quality, quantity, and distribution throughout the book. Upholstery is a subject for which color photography is obviously of particular importance, and Beard has managed to include an unusually generous number of color illustrations. Conveniently for the reader, both the color and the black and white illustrations are grouped appropriately at the conclusion of each chapter; it is a pleasure not to find all the color bound together at just one point in the book. Almost all the illustrations are provided with informative captions, and although some of these repeat information found in the body of the text, a number of captions make important points not found elsewhere (for example, pls. 196–97 in which webbing is discussed). Beard has clearly gone to great lengths to include numerous detailed photographs, many of which I suspect he took himself (not because of their quality but rather because no one else would know enough or care enough to photograph those specific details). We are able to see many details of bed upholstery, the undersides of chairs, decorative nailing patterns, the fastenings of seat covers, and other technical aspects that are extremely valuable and not readily found in other publications.

Beard is also to be commended for the extensive and useful glossary, bibliography, and, perhaps most importantly, appendices that provide a wealth of documentary evidence concerning upholstery. The many inventories and accounts that comprise appendix A are the proverbial gold mine of information regarding the types of furniture ordered, the types of furnishing fabrics employed, the more humble under-upholstery materials such as feathers, thread, and tacks, and the various costs of materials and labor. *Upholsterers* is first and foremost an archival work; the documents unearthed, combed, and interpreted by Beard form the foundation of the book, and a perusal of the documents listed in the first appendix help one appreciate the magnitude of Beard's accomplishment.

Beard's enormous knowledge of furniture and upholstery is evident throughout the book, but he wears his knowledge lightly and allows humor to appear in unexpected places ("the inventory is eleven yards long, so, obviously, I must be very selective"). There is much to like about this book aside from its obvious important contributions, such as the citing of recent conservation treatments and those specifically responsible for them to the location of the footnotes at the end of each page (much appreciated by at least this reader). The only appropriate criticism might be directed to the editing, which is not up to the quality of the rest of the book. The editorial oversights are minor ones and are confined to small inaccuracies (for example, 1976 instead of 1764 in appendix A, no. #36; pl. 348 referred to as pl. 347 in the text; the repetition of information in the captions to pls. 185–87), but they nevertheless are distracting and need not have occurred. One hesitates to mention them, however, given the achievement that *Upholsterers* represents. It greatly expands our understanding of the history of English upholstery and furniture and should be regarded as a major contribution to the literature for furniture historians. Although students of American furniture might question the relevance of this book because of its high-style focus, Beard's tracing of the history of English upholstery from the sixteenth to the eighteenth centuries establishes the context from which American furniture developed.

Jeffrey H. Munger
Museum of Fine Arts, Boston

Ronald L. Hurst and Jonathan Prown. *Southern Furniture, 1680–1830: The Colonial Williamsburg Collection*. Williamsburg, Va.: Colonial Williamsburg Foundation, in association with Harry N. Abrams, 1997. 639 pp.; numerous color and bw illus., line drawings, maps, glossaries, bibliography, index. $75.00.

"Furniture of the American South: The Colonial Williamsburg Collection." DeWitt Wallace Gallery, Colonial Williamsburg Foundation, Williamsburg, Virginia, November 21, 1997, to December 1998.

To those familiar with the study of southern furniture over the past five decades, the story of Joseph Downs's lecture at the first Williamsburg Antiques Forum in 1949 has become legendary. Then curator of the American Wing at the Metropolitan Museum of Art, Downs announced that "little furniture of artistic merit was ever produced south of Baltimore." During the question and answer period that followed, one southern matron rose from her chair with quiet indignation to ask politely, "Mr. Downs, did you make that remark out of prejudice or ignorance?" Downs's comment had the perhaps fortunate effect of sparking a new civil war in American decorative arts, spawning the landmark 1952 exhibition "Furniture of the Old South, 1640–1820" at the Virginia Museum and a special issue of *The Magazine Antiques* dedicated to southern furniture. In 1965, at least partly in response to Downs's remark, Frank L. Horton established the Museum of Early Southern Decorative Arts (MESDA) in Winston-Salem, North Carolina, which has been the major research engine for the study of southern material culture, setting out to prove the existence of meritorious fur-

Figure 1 Introductory panel to the exhibition, "Furniture of the American South." (Courtesy, Colonial Williamsburg Foundation.)

Figure 2 Sideboard table attributed to William Buckland and William Bernard Sears, Richmond County, Virginia, 1761–1771. Cherry with beech. H. 32", W. 45 3/8", D. 31 1/4". (Courtesy, Colonial Williamsburg Foundation.)

niture produced in the antebellum South. Now, almost fifty years after the infamous Downs lecture, Ronald L. Hurst and Jonathan Prown, curator and assistant curator of furniture at Colonial Williamsburg Foundation, have produced a scholarly book, *Southern Furniture, 1680–1830: The Colonial Williamsburg Collection,* with a special exhibition of southern furniture in Colonial Williamsburg (fig. 1), which definitively ends this civil war. With 639 pages of careful, documented analysis, Hurst and Prown have produced a milestone in the study of not just southern but American furniture. To play on Downs's own words, few books of equal merit have ever been published north of Baltimore.

Serious scholarship in southern furniture developed more slowly than furniture scholarship in the North. Since 1920, for example, more than two hundred books have been written on furniture production in the New England and Middle Atlantic colonies, whereas fewer than a dozen have been published on the South. The earliest book on southern furniture, Paul H. Burroughs's *Southern Antiques* (1931), was essentially a photographic essay with lengthy captions on provenance. This work was followed by several more scholarly monographs analyzing the furniture of particular southern subregions, most importantly, E. Milby Burton's *Charleston Furniture, 1700–1825* (1955), Wallace Gusler's *Furniture of Williamsburg and Eastern Virginia, 1710–1790* (1979), and John Bivins's *The Furniture of Coastal North Carolina, 1700–1820* (1988). In 1975, MESDA initiated an aggressive publication schedule, launching the *Journal of Early Southern Decorative Arts* followed by the Frank L. Horton book series. Numerous articles over recent years in the MESDA journal and in other scholarly venues by Hurst, Prown, Gusler, Bivins, and others—most notably, Luke Beckerdite, Sumpter Priddy, Bradford Rauschenberg, and Thomas Savage—have promoted our understanding of specific aspects of southern furniture. As the first comprehensive study of furniture produced in the South, Hurst and Prown's

Figure 3 Tall clock attributed to Peter Rife and Peter Whipple, Southern Valley of Virginia, probably Montgomery (now Pulaski) County, ca. 1810. Mahogany, mahogany veneer and cherry with tulip poplar, oak, black walnut, holly, cherry, maple, horn, bone, silver, and brass; iron, brass, and steel movement. H. 108 1/2", W. 25", D. 15". (Courtesy, Colonial Williamsburg Foundation.)

book stands at the apex of this mountain of research and promises to remain the standard work in the field for the next generation.

The authors have achieved one of the most reader-friendly books on American furniture yet written. As a catalogue of the Colonial Williamsburg collection, it presents 183 of the nearly 700 southern furniture objects in the foundation's collection. The book is brilliantly organized by furniture group, enabling the reader to move quickly through sections on seating furniture, tables, case furniture, and other, more highly specialized forms to find the objects and categories that might be of particular interest. The book incorporates extensive use of maps, illustrations, photographs, line drawings of construction details, glossaries of furniture terminology, and a comprehensive bibliography of titles previously published on southern furniture. An abundance of information useful to both curators and collectors on the materials and construction techniques used throughout the region is also provided.

Ironically, Hurst and Prown have extended the cataloging methodology first devised by Joseph Downs more than forty years ago in his groundbreaking book *American Furniture, Queen Anne and Chippendale Periods* (1952) to its fullest potential with complete descriptions of construction, condition, materials, dimensions, marks, and provenance. Each catalogue entry begins with a thorough discussion of the object, its known history, regional context, development of the furniture form, and specific information on the maker and patron, drawing from extensive documentary research through period newspapers and probate inventories of the region. Each entry is fully referenced and endnoted. Extensive color photography, funded by a grant from the Chipstone Foundation, combines with numerous black and white photographs of construction details and of similar, related objects to make the book visually as well as intellectually stimulating.

In the opinion of this reviewer, the authors' most important contribution has been to slay many of the subtle prejudices that have tagged the South since General Robert E. Lee surrendered to Grant at Appomatox in 1865. Jonathan Prown explained in his recent article in the 1997 issue of *American Furniture* that, since that moment in our nation's history, American historians have traditionally viewed the South as a "culturally impaired place." "In the American furniture story," Prown continued, "southern furniture exists less as an accepted regional craft tradition than as a chronic interpretive problem." The authors quickly move beyond such models of traditional, "good-better-best" furniture connoisseurship to illustrate the need to examine southern furniture within the broader context of regional material culture for a better understanding of American culture generally. E. Milby Burton stated as early as 1955 in his monograph on Charleston furniture, "The culture of any society, whether it be primitive or highly civilized, is unerringly revealed by the material things which the society needs and the degree of skill which it displays in producing or acquiring them." The material culture studies approach has characterized the southern furniture school for the past several decades, greatly advanced by the establishment of MESDA and the publication of Wallace Gusler and John Bivins's books on

Figure 4 Interior view of the southern furniture exhibition showing four important masterpieces, a mahogany easy chair, 1765–1775, and mahogany double chest with open carved pediment, 1765–1780, made in Charleston, South Carolina, on display in the Carolina Low Country gallery, juxtaposed against a painted chest, 1795–1807, and tall clock, 1800, by Johannes Spitler of Shenandoah (now Page) County, Virginia, in the gallery on furniture of the southern Backcountry. (Courtesy, Colonial Williamsburg Foundation.)

eastern Virginia and North Carolina furniture. Slowly, the material culture approach has been incorporated into more recent publications on northern regional furniture such as Brock Jobe's *Portsmouth Furniture: Masterworks from the New Hampshire Seacoast* (1993) and Kenneth Zogry's *"The Best the Country Affords": Vermont Furniture, 1765–1850*, but Hurst and Prown have raised this model of furniture analysis to a new level.[1]

In the preface, Hurst points to the national importance of the argument, noting that on the eve of the American Revolution the Old South, comprised of Maryland, Virginia, North Carolina, South Carolina, and Georgia, constituted almost half the United States' land mass with more than 46 percent of its population. "Until students of material culture have greater access to information about the furniture made and used by the people in this vast territory," argues Hurst, "our understanding of the early American furniture trade will be fragmentary at best."

The opening essays written by Hurst on the Chesapeake, Prown on the Backcountry, and Thomas Savage of Historic Charleston Foundation on the Carolina Low Country, explore the cultural, social, and economic factors that define the three principal subregions of the South. These essays present the important themes that are woven throughout the book, most significantly the region's generally misunderstood and under-appreciated ethnic diversity. As a geographic and socioeconomic entity, the South can be defined by at least six major, unifying characteristics: a warm climate and topography conducive to agriculture, relatively inexpensive and readily available land, an alluvial transportation system, an agrarian economy, a labor system based partially (but not exclusively) on race-based chattel slavery, and settlement patterns that by the late eighteenth century were generally stable. Within this dynamic region, however, numerous subregions existed (far more than just the Chesapeake, the Low Country, and the Backcountry), each with its own unique character manifested through furniture production. The first key to understanding "southern" furniture is the realization that there was never a monolithic "South."

Although the South clearly began as an English settlement with the arrival of colonists at Jamestown in 1608, the influence of Continental Europeans from the Netherlands, Germany, and France was significant enough by the late seventeenth century to broadly impact the region's material culture. The Dutch enjoyed an extensive trade in Chesapeake tobacco throughout the seventeenth century and established half a dozen permanent trading stations. In his introductory essay to the Carolina Low Country, Thomas Savage points out that from its inception in 1670 the South Carolina colony was a multiethnic polyglot of settlers who were not only English, Irish, Scottish, and Welsh but also French Huguenots, Dutch, Germans, and Swiss, combined with Sephardic Jews from Spain and Portugal. Fewer than two dozen examples of the South's earliest furniture from the seventeenth century have survived, although the specimens that remain clearly show enough Continental European influence to differentiate them from the more English furniture of the New England colonies. These pieces are discussed thoroughly in Hurst and Prown's book.

In his lecture at the 1997 symposium co-sponsored by the Colonial Williamsburg Foundation and the Chipstone Foundation, James P. Whittenburg, professor of history at the College of William and Mary, suggests a new reason for the narrow survival rate of seventeenth-century southern furniture, aside from the widely accepted notions regarding the effects of climate, war, post–Civil War poverty, and destruction. In his comparative analysis of the southern and New England colonies, Whittenburg discerns development versus declension models for the two regions. In the South seventeenth-century furniture objects would have been relatively quickly discarded and exchanged for objects in the latest style (like the unused toys of overgrown children). Seventeenth-century New England furniture, on the other hand, became like holy relics to a bygone era, essential to connecting the descendants of the founding settlers to the symbolic, religious beginnings of their colony. The economic development model advanced by Whittenburg is another important key to understanding southern furniture and the development of the southern cabinetmaking industry.[2]

As Hurst and Savage discuss in their introductory essays, by the mid-eighteenth century, economic progress in the South was such that plantation owners in the Chesapeake and Low Country enjoyed the highest per capita incomes in British North America. The major coastal towns—Charleston, Williamsburg, and Annapolis—received constantly replenished waves of emigrating British cabinetmakers. Unlike their northern counterparts who frequently represented multigenerational craft traditions within particular families and communities, these tradesmen sought to fill the needs of the expanding local market and eventually hoped to retire from trade by purchasing land and slaves to secure for their children the lifestyle of the planter gentry. These emigrants brought training and a reliance on British pattern books to produce furniture deeply rooted in British cabinetmaking traditions. Their case furniture typically featured urban British construction practices with full dustboards, panel-and-frame backs, stacked foot blocking, and drawer bottoms with glue blocks. These traits became hallmarks of the "neat and plain" style typical of coastal southern furniture. Although less adorned than exuberantly carved, rococo Philadelphia high chests or bombé Boston case pieces, their furniture was structurally superior to that of most northern cabinetmakers. Importantly, the preference for such "neat and plain" furniture, as it was called, embodied a social ideology as well as a design choice. In 1772, Peter Manigault, a wealthy Low Country planter and Speaker of the South Carolina Commons House of Assembly, wrote to his London factor ordering furniture "the plainer the better so that it is fashionable." A contemporary description of the style defined it as "free from what is unbecoming, inappropriate, or tawdry; simple elegance; tasteful and refined." In many ways, the "neat and plain" style represents a solid cultural expression of the coastal planter class who sought to emulate the British country gentry through the creation of landed estates with primogeniture, republican government, and an established Anglican church.[3]

Hurst's catalogue entry for a marble-top sideboard table (fig. 2) attributed to William Buckland (1734–1774) and William Bernard Sears (d. 1818) highlights many of the important themes presented in his essay. The table was designed by Buckland and carved by Sears for the Tayloe family of Mount Airy plantation in Richmond County, Virginia. Born in Oxfordshire, England, Buckland epitomized the successful southern tradesman. Migrating to Virginia after completing his apprenticeship in house joinery in London in 1755, he quickly enjoyed the patronage of many of northern Virginia and Maryland's most prominent planters. Buckland's most important commissions include Mount Airy and Gunston Hall in Virginia and the Chase-Lloyd and Hammond-Harwood houses in the town of Annapolis. The legs on his Mount Airy sideboard table point to his architectural training and reliance on British pattern books for design by resembling the consoles for a chimneypiece in Abraham Swan's, *The British Architect; or, The Builder's Treasury of Staircases* (London, 1745). The table as well as another marble-top sideboard table designed by Buckland for Mount Airy in the MESDA collection reflect his most "aspiring" designs and speak to the ambitiousness of both artisan and patron in eighteenth-century Virginia. William Bernard Sears's work as both a house and furniture carver further illustrates the flexible role required of woodworkers in the agrarian, mostly rural, southern economy.

In his essay on the Backcountry, Jonathan Prown speaks brilliantly to the rich furniture traditions that developed in this unique, but misunderstood,

American region. The Backcountry was settled by migrants from the coastal South who fanned out in search of additional land. They mingled with Germans, Swiss, and Scots-Irish, many newly arrived to America, who had traveled down the Great Wagon Road from Pennsylvania into the Shenandoah Valley of Virginia and the Piedmont region of the Carolinas and Georgia. Important religious communities in the Backcountry included Moravians from central Germany and Mennonites from the Palatine. Small pockets of Quakers and Baptists transplanted from New England added to the region's diverse ethnic mix. Each group contributed to the region's distinctive furniture making traditions. The high chest form, for example, which was eschewed throughout the coastal South in favor of the more quintessentially British double chest form, developed in the Shenandoah Valley of Virginia due to Pennsylvania migration. Similarly, the chests-on-frame commonly found in Randolph County, North Carolina, suggest the influence of New Light Baptists who migrated to the Piedmont from the Connecticut River Valley of New England. The decorative painting on many western Virginia case pieces strongly reflects a Germanic contribution. Although a desk-and-bookcase by the highly eccentric Martinsburg, Virginia, cabinetmaker John Shearer might not accord easily with modern, twentieth-century, decorator-inspired concepts for a Manhattan brownstone or neo-Georgian mansion on the Philadelphia mainline, Prown explains that Backcountry furniture should be seen within the context of its place and time as an expression of our American culture.

Prown's catalogue entry for a tall clock (fig. 3) made in the southern valley of western Virginia by Peter Whipple and Peter Rife, for example, suggests the highly complex character of Backcountry furniture. It was made for Sebastian Wygal (1762–1835), the son of a Swiss emigrant who migrated to southwestern Virginia from Pennsylvania in the 1750s. Similarly, Peter Rife was born in Rockland Township, Pennsylvania, and resided in Montgomery County by the 1770s. Rife's patron, Sebastian Wygal, was a prosperous man who owned slaves and more than two thousand acres in Montgomery County, Virginia. Rife's tall clock speaks to his ambition as a Backcountry artisan. The clock case combines nearly every variety of wood and other materials available to a cabinetmaker working in southwestern Virginia in the early nineteenth century. Symbolically, its inlay combines neoclassical design with Germanic folk traditions, surmounted in the tympanum by an American eagle.

Throughout their book, Hurst and Prown introduce important, new characters into the lexicon of American cabinetmaking: important southern craftsmen working in the Backcountry such as Johannes Spitler of Shenandoah (now Page) County, Virginia, and artisans who practiced their craft in the major southern towns and cities such as Chester Sully of Norfolk, William King of the District of Columbia, and Thomas Lee of Charleston. American furniture scholars have been familiar for some time with only a handful of the best-known, best-documented southern furniture makers, such as Anthony Hay and Peter Scott of Williamsburg, John Shaw of Annapolis, and Thomas Elfe of Charleston, but by their use of the signed, labeled, and documented examples of southern furniture in the Colonial Williamsburg collection, Hurst and Prown have expanded our knowledge of American, not just southern, cabinetmaking. Combined with their exhibition, the publication of Hurst and Prown's book guarantees that henceforth serious American furniture scholars will be required to know the names of Spitler, Sully, King, and Lee as well as Goddard, Townsend, Dunlap, and Dominy.[4]

On long-term display at the DeWitt Wallace Gallery, the southern furniture exhibition (fig. 4) follows the book's lead as a well-organized, user-friendly presentation of its topic. Designed by Rick Hadley with impressive curatorial supervision by Hurst and Prown, it effectively outlines the important topics essential to explaining southern furniture. It elucidates the region's major settlement and migration patterns, the impact of emigré craftsmen on southern furniture, the region's multiethnic influences, the importance of European pattern books on its designs, the role of the woodworker in the agrarian southern economy, the impact of changing technologies on southern cabinetmaking, and furniture making's eventual decline as mechanized factories in the North began to export cheap, mass-produced goods to the southern market. The exhibition moves visitors geographically through the South with galleries dedicated to furniture of the Chesapeake, the Low Country, and the Backcountry. As one of the most dynamic and interesting urban centers in the South, Baltimore receives its own gallery. Interesting education tools incorporated into the display include an exhibition for schoolchildren on joinery and three videos, totaling twenty-seven minutes, on the three principal subregions of the South, the steps of timber production from felled tree to finished lumber, and the making of an eighteenth-century-style tea table by artisans in the Anthony Hay cabinet shop in Williamsburg.

In this reviewer's opinion, the book's single shortcoming is its failure to include an introductory essay by the two authors on the principal themes that are carefully and thoughtfully presented in the exhibition. A succinct discussion by Hurst and Prown on the major developments of southern cabinetmaking, its defining characteristics, and its general trends would have been an important and welcome addition to the book. These topics are discussed intermittently in the three introductory essays and woven throughout the catalogue entries but are systematically explained only in the exhibition, making a visit to the Wallace Gallery an important addition to reading the book.

The initial image upon entering the exhibition (fig. 1), for example, is a thought-provoking presentation. It explains the tremendous diversity of southern furniture by contrasting an elaborately carved mahogany armchair of 1745–1765 produced in Edenton, North Carolina, with an unusual armchair made between 1770 and 1800 found in Anne Arundel County, Maryland, earlier this century. Although both chairs feature similarly designed splats and served the same obvious seating function, the Edenton chair relates closely to known British prototypes for drawing room and dining room chairs and speaks to the increasing collectability of high-style southern furniture. The design of the Maryland chair, on the other hand, is deeply rooted in vernacular Welsh tradition, resembling similar, three-legged, low-lying chairs found in western Great Britain used for hearthside cooking that suggest its original use by a white indentured servant working in an eighteenth-century Maryland, plantation kitchen. Hurst and Prown have united both these examples for a better understanding of the complexity of southern furniture.

The dean of southern furniture studies, Frank L. Horton, has pronounced Hurst and Prown's book the finest cultural study of American furniture yet published. Hopefully, it will inspire future publications on the various, unique subregions of the South, especially those areas not discussed in the book such as Kentucky and Tennessee. Hurst and Prown's book should lay to rest many of the antagonisms that have divided northern and southern furniture historians since the famous Joseph Downs lecture. Southern furniture historians have earned their place at the proverbial American gate-leg table and should remove any leftover chips from shoulders. Like the famous Civil War veterans' reunions that occurred at the beginning of the twentieth century, it is time for scholars of northern and southern furniture to meet in the center of the field and recognize the important contributions that both sides have made to our national understanding.

Robert A. Leath
Historic Charleston Foundation

1. Jonathan Prown, "A 'Preponderance of Pineapples': The Problem of Southern Furniture," in *American Furniture*, edited by Luke Beckerdite (Hanover, N.H.: University Press of New England for the Chipstone Foundation, 1997), p. 4. E. Milby Burton, *Charleston Furniture, 1700–1825* (Charleston: Charleston Museum, 1955; reprint, Columbia, S.C.: University of South Carolina Press, 1970), p. 3.

2. James P. Whittenburg, "Myths and Realities Revisited: More Societies of the Colonial South," unpublished lecture delivered on November 14, 1997, at the symposium, *A Region of Regions: Cultural Diversity and the Furniture Trade in the Early South*, co-sponsored by the Colonial Williamsburg Foundation and the Chipstone Foundation.

3. Peter Manigault to Benjamin Stead, April 2, 1771, as quoted in "The Letterbook of Peter Manigault, 1763–1773," edited by Maurice A. Crouse, *South Carolina Historical and Genealogical Magazine* 70 (July 1969): 188–89.

4. Prown, "A 'Preponderance of Pineapples,'" p. 4.

*Compiled by
Gerald W. R. Ward*

Recent Writing on
American Furniture:
A Bibliography

▼ THIS YEAR'S list includes primarily works published in 1997 and through June of 1998; as always, a few earlier publications that had previously escaped notice are also cited. The short title *American Furniture 1997* is used in citations for articles and reviews published in last year's issue of this journal, which is also cited in full under Luke Beckerdite's name.

For the first time, this section includes reviews of exhibitions (and their attendant publications) as well as the traditional book and catalogue reviews.

Several works on furniture published in 1996 received awards from the Decorative Arts Society and deserve recognition here. The Charles F. Montgomery Prize, awarded annually for the most significant contribution to the study of American decorative arts, was shared by Nancy Goyne Evans, author of *American Windsor Chairs*, and Edward S. Cooke, Jr., author of *Making Furniture in Preindustrial America: The Social Economy of Newtown and Woodbury, Connecticut*. The Robert C. Smith Award, presented annually by the society for the best article on decorative arts, went to Milo Naeve for his article in *American Furniture 1996* on "Louis Comfort Tiffany and the Reform Movement in Furniture Design."

For their assistance in various ways, I am grateful to Jonathan Fairbanks, Steve Stenstrom, Ned Cooke, Phil Zea, Anne Rogers Haley, Cynthia Van Allen Schaffner, and especially Neville Thompson of Winterthur. Staff members of the library of the Museum of Fine Arts, Boston; the Portsmouth Athenaeum; and the Winterthur Museum Library have also been helpful.

I would be delighted to receive suggestions for material that should be included in these annual lists. Review copies of significant works would also be much appreciated. Copies and citations may be sent to:

Gerald W.R. Ward
Carolyn and Peter Lynch Associate Curator of
American Decorative Arts and Sculpture
Museum of Fine Arts, Boston
465 Huntington Avenue
Boston, Massachusetts 02115

Adams, Peter Michael, et al. *Earth Links*. [Tasmania, Australia], 1997. Unpaged; color illus., line drawings. (Re contemporary seating furniture.)

Adamson, Glenn, and Sarah Rich. Review of Pat Kirkham, *Charles and Ray Eames: Designers of the Twentieth Century*. In *American Furniture 1997*, pp. 367–72.

Albertson, Karla Klein. "Furniture of the American South" (exhibition review). *Antiques and the Arts Weekly* (December 5, 1997): 1, 68–72. 19 bw illus.

Albrecht, Donald, et al. *The Work of Charles and Ray Eames: A Legacy of Invention*. New York: Harry N. Abrams in association with the Library of Congress and the Vitra Design Museum, 1997. 205 pp.; numerous color and bw illus., filmography, bibliography, index.

[American Association of Woodturners]. *Turned for Use: The First Juried Show of the American Association of Woodturners*. Edited by Rick Mastelli. Shoreview, Minn.: American Association of Woodturners, 1997. Unpaged; bw illus. (Re exhibition at San Antonio Museum of Art, July 17–September 21, 1997.)

American Expressions of Liberty: Art of the People, By the People, For the People. San Diego, Calif.: Mingei International Museum in association with Harry N. Abrams, 1996. 168 pp.; color illus., bibliography. (Includes some furniture.)

Andrews, John. *Antique Furniture*. Starting to Collect Series. Woodbridge, England: Antique Collectors' Club, 1998. 180 pp.; 200 illus.

Arnoldsche Art Publications Staff. *Plastics and Design*. Woodbridge, England: Antique Collectors' Club, 1998. 162 pp.; illus.

"Arts and Crafts Design: The New York State Museum." *Antiques and the Arts Weekly* (February 6, 1998): 1, 68–69. 8 bw illus.

Baker, Malcolm, and Brenda Richardson, eds. *A Grand Design: The Art of the Victoria and Albert Museum*. New York: Harry N. Abrams with the Baltimore Museum of Art, 1997. 431 pp.; numerous color and bw illus. (Of interest re the history of collecting decorative arts.)

Bamberger, Bill (photographs), and Cathy N. Davidson (text). *Closing: The Life and Death of an American Factory*. New York: Norton/Double Take, 1998. 224 pp.; 31 color and 61 bw illus. (Re White Furniture Company of Mebane, North Carolina.)

Banham, Joanna, ed., and Leanda Shrimpton, picture ed. *Encyclopedia of Interior Design*. 2 vols. London and Chicago: Fitzroy Dearborn, 1997. xvii + 1,450 pp.; numerous bw illus., index.

Bayer, Patricia. *Art Deco Interiors: Decoration and Design Classics of the 1920s and 1930s*. 1990. Reprint. New York: Thames and Hudson, 1998. 224 pp.; 300+ color and bw illus.

Beach, Laura. "American Painted Furniture: Folk Art Scholars Schaffner and Klein Update a Classic" (book review). *Antiques and the Arts Weekly* (April 10, 1998): 1, 68–71. 21 bw illus.

Beach, Laura. "The Furniture of George Hunzinger" (exhibition and catalogue review). *Antiques and the Arts Weekly* (January 9, 1998): 1, 68–71. 13 bw illus.

Beach, Laura. "Learning from Lannuier: Honoré Lannuier, Cabinetmaker from Paris" (exhibition and catalogue review). *Antiques and the Arts Weekly* (May 29, 1998): 1, 68–72. 23 illus.

Beard, Geoffrey. *Upholsterers and Interior Furnishings in England, 1530–1840*. New Haven and London: Yale University Press for the Bard Graduate Center for Studies in the Decorative Arts, 1997. xiv + 346 pp.; 376 color and bw illus., appendices, glossary, bibliography, index.

Bebb, Richard. Review of Edward S. Cooke, Jr., *Making Furniture in Preindustrial America: The Social Economy of Newtown and Woodbury, Connecticut*. In *Regional Furniture Society Newsletter*, no. 27 (winter 1997/1998): 5–6.

Beckerdite, Luke. "Introduction." In *American Furniture 1997*, pp. xi–xiv.

Beckerdite, Luke. "Religion, Artistry, and Cultural Identity: The Huguenot Experience in South Carolina, 1680–1725." *American Furniture 1997*, pp. 196–227. 45 color and bw illus., appendix.

Beckerdite, Luke, ed. *American Furniture 1997*. Milwaukee, Wis.: The Chipstone Foundation, 1997. xiv + 407 pp.; numerous color and bw illus., bibliography, index. Distributed by University Press of New England, Hanover and London.

Berns, Marla C., ed., with David Gebhard and Patricia Gebhard. *The Furniture of R. M. Schindler*. Seattle: University of Washington Press, 1997. 176 pp.; illus.

Binzen, Jonathan. "Assessing an Icon: Sam Maloof." *Home Furniture*, no. 13 (October–November 1997): 66–71. 19 color illus.

Bivins, John. "The Convergence and Divergence of Three Stylistic Traditions in Charleston Neoclassical Case Furniture, 1785–1800." *American Furniture 1997*, pp. 47–105. 40 color and bw illus.

Blackburn, Roderic H. "The Fred J. Johnston Museum." *Antiques* 152, no. 2 (August 1997): 168–77. 13 color illus.

Blotner, Pamela. "The Wizardry of John Cedarquist." *Woodwork*, no. 50 (April 1998): 20–29. 20 color illus.

Brewer, John. *The Pleasures of the Imagination: English Culture in the Eighteenth Century*. New York: Farrar Straus Giroux, 1997. xxx + 721 pp.; 12 color and 241 bw illus., bibliography, index. (Although furniture is not discussed here, this work will be of great interest to furniture historians; see also the three-volume work edited by Brewer, Roy Porter, Susan Staves, and Ann Bermingham, entitled *Consumption and the World of Goods* [1993], *Early Modern Conceptions of Property* [1995], and *The Consumption of Culture, 1600–1800: Image, Object, Text* [1995].)

Brown, Peter B., and Ivan Day. *Pleasures of the Table: Ritual and Display in the European Dining Room, 1600–1900*. York, England: Fairfax House, 1997. 96 pp.; 97 color and bw illus., index.

Burgess, Arene. *19th Century Wooden Boxes*. Atglen, Pa.: Schiffer Publishing, 1997. 160 pp.; illus., bibliography.

Burks, Jean M. "The Origins of Shaker Furniture." *Home Furniture*, no. 12 (August–September 1997): 22–27. 8 color and 5 bw illus.

Burt, Owen H. "Seth Thomas 9" Cottage Clocks: Stage I (1852–1864)." *NAWCC Bulletin* 40, no. 1 (February

1998): 5–19. 38 bw illus., tables. "Stage II (1865–1871)." *NAWCC Bulletin* 40, no. 2 (April 1998): 133–49. 50 bw illus., tables. "Stage III (1872–1898)." *NAWCC Bulletin* 40, no. 3 (June 1998): 261–87. 73 bw illus., tables.

"Butterfield to Auction Dorr Family Queen Anne Japanned Flat-top Highboy." *Antiques and the Arts Weekly* (October 10, 1997): 42. 2 bw illus.

Byars, Mel. *50 Chairs: Innovations in Design and Materials*. Crans-Prés-Celigny, Switzerland: RotoVision, 1997. 159 pp.; numerous color and bw illus., line drawings, index. Distributed by Watson-Guptill, New York.

Byars, Mel. *50 Tables: Innovations in Design and Materials*. Crans-Prés-Celigny, Switzerland: RotoVision, 1997. 159 pp.; numerous color and bw illus., line drawings, index. Distributed by Watson-Guptill, New York.

[Calyer, Sean]. "Portfolio: Sean Calyer." *American Craft* 57, no. 6 (December 1997/January 1998): 55. 1 color illus. (Re contemporary furniture maker.)

Cantor, Jay E. *Winterthur: The Foremost Museum of American Furniture and Decorative Arts*. 1985. Rev. ed. New York: Harry N. Abrams for Winterthur Museum, 1997. 272 pp.; 112 color and 117 bw illus., index.

[Castle, Wendell]. "Gold Medal: Wendell Castle." *American Craft* 57, no. 5 (October/November 1997): 86. 1 color and 1 bw illus.

"A Central Park for the World." *Antiques and the Arts Weekly* (January 16, 1998): 1, 68–70. 8 bw illus. (Re exhibition in New York of objects, including some rustic furniture, from the collection of the Adirondack Museum.)

[Chapman, David]. "Portfolio." *American Craft* 57, no. 4 (August/September 1997): 60. 1 color illus. (Contemporary furniture.)

"Chinoiserie: The Lure of the East." *Antiques and the Arts Weekly* (October 10, 1997): 1, 68–69. 10 bw illus. (Re exhibition at Museum of Fine Arts, Boston, that included some American furniture.)

[Christie's, London]. *The Chair* (auction catalogue). London: Christie's, October 29, 1997. Sale 5868. 120+ pp.; numerous color and bw illus., index. (Contains introduction by Peter Fiell, and includes some American chairs.)

[Christie's, New York]. *American Furniture and Decorative Arts: The Thomas Mellon Evans Collection*. New York: Christie's, June 18, 1998. Sale 8938. 129 pp.; numerous color and bw illus.

[Christie's, New York]. *The Collection of Mr. and Mrs. Bertram D. Coleman*. New York: Christie's, January 16, 1998. Sale 8842. 152 pp.; numerous color and bw illus.

[Christie's, New York]. *Important Philadelphia Chippendale Furniture from the Hollingsworth Family*. New York: Christie's, January 16, 1998. Sale 8882. 32 pp.; color illus. (Re high chest, dressing table, and side chair by Thomas Affleck, sold by the Chipstone Foundation.)

[Christie's, New York]. *The Sarah Slocum Chippendale Mahogany Block-and-Shell Carved Chest-of-Drawers Labelled by John Townsend: A Comparative Analysis and Documentary Material*. New York: Christie's, June 18, 1998. 23 pp.; tables, bibliography.

Churchill, Edwin A. *Simple Forms and Vivid Colors: Maine Painted Furniture, 1800–1850*. Augusta: Friends of the Maine State Museum, 1997. 117 pp.; color and bw illus. (Reprint of 1983 work, reissued to accompany exhibition at Maine State Museum entitled "Out of the Woods: Two Hundred Years of Maine Furniture.")

Cirillo, Dexter. *Across Frontiers: Hispanic Crafts of New Mexico*. San Francisco: Chronicle Books, 1998. 160 pp.; numerous color and bw illus., glossary, bibliography, index. (See chapter 2, "Woodworking and Furniture Making.")

Clarkson, Ron. *Making Classic Chairs: A Craftsman's Chippendale Reference*. Lancaster, Pa.: Fox Chapel Publishing Co., 1997. 158 pp.; 400+ color and bw illus., line drawings, glossary, bibliography, index. (Includes "Chippendale Furniture and the Philadelphia Style" by Leigh Keno, pp. 2–11.)

Clemens, Paul G. E. "Crafting an Alternative to Capitalism." *Reviews in American History* 25, no. 2 (June 1997): 200–206. (Review of Edward S. Cooke, Jr., *Making Furniture in Preindustrial America: The Social Economy of Newtown and Woodbury, Connecticut*.)

Clunas, Craig. *Chinese Furniture*. London: Christie's and Victoria and Albert Museum, 1997. 120 pp.; 36 color and 54 bw illus.

Collins, Philip. *The Golden Age of Televisions*. Santa Monica, Calif.: General Publishing Group, 1997. 132 pp.; illus.

Collins, Philip. *Radios: Furniture That Talks*. Santa Monica, Calif.: General Publishing Group, 1997. 132 pp.; illus.

[Concord (Massachusetts) Museum]. "Distinguished Gift Comes to the Museum." *Concord Museum Newsletter* (winter 1998): 3. 1 bw illus. (Re Concord high chest of drawers, 1770–1780, cherry and white pine, that descended in the Wheeler family.)

[Concord (Massachusetts) Museum]. "A Recent Accession." *Concord Museum Newsletter* (spring 1998): 1, 7. 1 bw illus. (Re wall clock by Daniel Munroe of Concord and Boston, ca. 1815.)

[Concord (Massachusetts) Museum]. "Reverend William Emerson's Other Case of Drawers: A New Acquisition." *Concord Museum Newsletter* (summer 1998): 1, 7. 2 bw illus. (Re Concord high chest of ca. 1770–1780.)

Cook, Cindy. "Interview: Donald Albrecht, Director and Catalogue Editor, *The Work of Charles and Ray Eames: A Legacy of Invention*. . . ." *Newsletter of the Decorative Arts Society* 5, no. 2 (fall 1997): 16–18.

Cooke, Edward S., Jr. "Turning Wood in America: New Perspectives on the Lathe." *Turning Points* 10, no. 2 (summer 1997): 8–11. 4 bw illus.

Cooper, Jeremy. *Victorian and Edwardian Furniture and Interiors: From the Gothic Revival to Art Nouveau*. 1987. Reprint. New York: Thames and Hudson, 1998. 256 pp.; 74 color and 609 bw illus.

Cotton, Bernard D. Review of Nancy Goyne Evans, *American Windsor Chairs*. In *Studies in the Decorative Arts* 5, no. 1 (fall/winter 1997–1998): 137–39.

"Craftswomen of the Southern Appalachians: A Self-Portrait." *Woodwork*, no. 51 (June 1998): 70–76. 14 color illus.

Crombie, David. *Piano: A Photographic*

History of the World's Most Celebrated Instruments. San Francisco: Miller Freeman Books, 1995. 112 pp.; 200 color illus., appendix, glossary, bibliography, index.

Crosby, Alfred W. *The Measure of Reality: Quantification and Western Society, 1250–1600*. Cambridge: Cambridge University Press, 1997. xii + 245 pp.; 19 bw illus., index. (Re development of double-entry bookkeeping and the evolution of timekeeping.)

Cummings, Abbott Lowell. "Three Hearths: A Socioarchitectural Study of Seventeenth-Century Massachusetts Bay Probate Inventories." *Old-Time New England* 75, no. 263 (1997): 5–49. 15 bw illus.

Curry, David Park, with Elizabeth L. O'Leary and Susan Jensen Rawles. *American Dreams: Paintings and Decorative Arts from the Warren Collection*. Richmond: Virginia Museum of Fine Arts, 1997. vii + 79 pp.; numerous color and bw illus., index. (Includes a few pieces of nineteenth-century furniture.)

Curta, Lucia. "Constructing an 'Imagined Community': The Romanian Classroom at the University of Pittsburgh, 1927–1943." *Studies in the Decorative Arts* 5, no. 2 (spring/summer 1998): 40–68. 10 bw illus. (Includes some furniture.)

[Dallas Museum of Art]. "Ten Years of Acquisitions by Friends of the Decorative Arts." *Friends of the Decorative Arts Newsletter* 8, no. 1 (winter 1998): 4–5. 8 bw illus. (Includes some furniture.)

Danto, Arthur C., and Nancy Princenthal, with an introduction by Kenneth R. Trapp. *The Art of John Cederquist: Reality of Illusion*. Oakland: Oakland Museum of California, 1997. 132 pp.; numerous color and bw illus., biography.

"Deceit, Deception, and Discovery: Fakes, Forgeries, and Fascinating Findings at Winterthur" (exhibition notice). *Antiques and the Arts Weekly* (October 3, 1997): 1, 68. 5 bw illus.

"Designed for Delight: Alternative Aspects of Twentieth Century Decorative Art" (exhibition review). *Antiques and the Arts Weekly* (August 15, 1997): 1, 68–69. 7 bw illus.

Diehl, Daniel. *Constructing Medieval Furniture: Plans and Instructions with Historical Notes*. Mechanicsburg, Pa.: Stackpole Books, 1997. 192 pp.; illus.

Don, Dick. "What Is a Kitchen Clock?" *NAWCC Bulletin* 39, no. 4 (August 1997): 403–21. 40 bw illus.

"Dorr Family Japanned Chest Sells for $772,500." *Maine Antique Digest* 25, no. 12 (December 1997): 9A. 1 bw illus.

Druesedow, Jean L., ed. *Authentic Art Deco Interiors and Furniture in Full Color*. New York: Dover Publications, 1997. 80 pp.; 108 color illus.

Dubrow, Eileen, and Richard Dubrow. *Styles of American Furniture, 1860–1960*. Atglen, Pa.: Schiffer Publishing, 1997. 208 pp.; color and bw illus., bibliography, index.

Duce, William R. "An Interview with Curator Donald Webster." *Maine Antique Digest* 26, no. 3 (March 1998): 22B. 1 bw illus. (Review of Webster, *Canfake: An Expert's Guide to the Tricks of the Canadian Antiques Trade*.)

Duncan, Alastair. *Modernism: Modernist Design, 1880–1940*. Woodbridge, England: Antique Collectors' Club, 1998. 256 pp.; 250 color and 80 bw illus.

"A Dunlap Chest Re-Surfaces." *Maine Antique Digest* 25, no. 12 (December 1997): 11A. 2 bw illus.

Edwards, Clive. *Eighteenth-Century Furniture*. Manchester, England, and New York: Manchester University Press, 1997. 227 pp.; 38 bw illus., bibliography, index.

Evans, Nancy Goyne. *American Windsor Furniture: Specialized Forms*. New York: Hudson Hills Press in association with the Henry Francis du Pont Winterthur Museum, 1997. 256 pp.; 31 color and 249 bw illus., bibliography, index.

Evans, Nancy Goyne. "American Windsors." *America in Britain* 35 (1997): 22–23. 3 color illus.

Eversmann, Pauline. *Discover the Winterthur Period Rooms*. Winterthur, Del.: Winterthur Museum, 1998. 48 pp.; 40 illus. Distributed by University Press of New England, Hanover and London.

Fodera, Peter L., Kenneth N. Needleman, and John L. Vitagliano. "The Conservation of a Painted Baltimore Side Chair (c. 1815) Attributed to John and Hugh Finlay." *Journal of the American Institute for Conservation* 36, no. 3 (fall/winter 1997): 183–92. 15 color and bw illus., bibliography. (Re chair in collection of the Kaufman Americana Foundation.)

Ferencsik, Robert, with Will Neptune. *The Fundamentals of Fine Woodworking*. New York: Sterling Publishing Co., 1996. 192 pp.; numerous bw illus., line drawings, index. (Geared to modern woodworker, but also of interest to furniture historians.)

Fiell, Charlotte, and Peter Fiell. *1000 Chairs*. Köln: Benedickt Taschen, 1997. 768 pp.; 1,500+ color and bw illus., biographies, bibliography, index.

Fleming, Elizabeth A. "Staples for Genteel Living: The Importation of London Household Furnishings into Charleston During the 1780s." *American Furniture 1997*, pp. 335–58. 10 bw illus., 3 tables.

Flinchum, Russell. *Henry Dreyfuss, Industrial Designer: The Man in the Brown Suit*. New York: Cooper-Hewitt, National Design Museum, Smithsonian Institution, and Rizzoli, 1997. 222 pp.; color and bw illus., bibliography, index.

Forster, Kurt W. Exhibition review of "The Work of Charles and Ray Eames," The Vitra Design Museum, Weil-am-Rhein, Germany, September 19, 1997–March 22, 1998. In *Journal of the Society of Architectural Historians* 57, no. 2 (June 1998): 201–4. 2 bw illus.

Frank Lloyd Wright: The Seat of Genius, Chairs, 1895–1955. Seattle: University of Washington Press, 1997. 76 pp.; 21 color and 37 bw illus. (Includes essays by Penn Fowler and Mary Anna Eaton.)

Franklin, Wayne. Review of Edward S. Cooke, Jr., *Making Furniture in Preindustrial America: The Social Economy of Newtown and Woodbury, Connecticut*. In *Journal of American History* (June 1997): 207–8.

Friedman, Michael L. "From Federal to Empire: Investigating the Success of Aaron Willard, Jr." *NAWCC Bulletin* 40, no. 2 (April 1998): 193–95. 5 bw illus.

"Furniture Forward." *American Craft* 57,

no. 6 (December 1997/January 1998): 32–35. 11 color illus. (Re exhibition by new Furniture Society of contemporary objects.)

Furniture History 33 (1997): 1–324. Numerous bw illus., bibliography.

"Furniture of George Hunzinger." *Maine Antique Digest* 25, no. 12 (December 1997): 5A. 3 bw illus. (Re exhibition at Brooklyn Museum.)

[Furniture Society, The]. *Furniture '97 Conference Program [and] Resource Directory '97*. Free Union, Va.: The Furniture Society, 1997. 112 pp.; bw illus. (Re contemporary furniture.)

Gallini, Mark. "The Two Faces of an American Masterpiece." *Home Furniture*, no. 13 (October–November 1997): 22–27. 13 color illus.

Garrett, Elisabeth D. "Living with Antiques: A House in the North Carolina Piedmont." *Antiques* 152, no. 6 (December 1997): 846–53. Several color illus.

Garrett, Wendell. "The True Style: Neoclassicism and the American Arts." In [Catalogue of the] *38th Annual Ellis Memorial Antiques Show* (Boston, 1997), pp. 78–85. 9 color and bw illus.

Gavin, Robin Farwell. "From the Collections: Cosas Pintadas." *El Palacio: The Museum of New Mexico Magazine* 102, no. 2 (winter/spring 1997/1998): 16–18. 8 color illus. (Re painted furniture in Spanish tradition.)

Geissler, Marie. "Objects of Contemplation: Peter Adams." *Craft Arts International*, no. 42 (1998): 36–43. 21 color illus.

Gordon, Glenn. "Misugi Designs: Fine Works in Wood." *Woodwork*, no. 48 (December 1997): 58–64. 16 color illus.

Gordon, Glenn. "The Patient Work of Peter Benenson." *Woodwork*, no. 47 (October 1997): 54–59. 15 color illus.

Goss, Peter L., and Kenneth R. Trapp. *The Bungalow Lifestyle and the Arts and Crafts Movement in the Intermountain West*. Salt Lake: Utah Museum of Fine Arts, University of Utah, 1995. 48 pp.; color and bw illus.

Graves, Leroy, and F. Carey Howlett. "Leather Bottoms, Satin Haircloth, and Spanish Beard: Conserving Virginia Upholstered Seating Furniture." *American Furniture 1997*, pp. 266–97. 50 color and bw illus.

Gray, Virginia. "Paint in Pennsylvania: New Exhibition Looks at the Craftsmanship and Artistry of Pennsylvania German Painted Furniture." *Winterthur Magazine* 43, no. 4 (winter 1997–1998): 15. 3 color illus. (Re small exhibition at Winterthur Museum.)

Gusler, Wallace. "The Furniture of Winchester, Virginia." *American Furniture 1997*, pp. 228–65. 56 color and bw illus.

Gustafson, Eleanor. "Museum Accessions." *Antiques* 152, no. 2 (August 1997): 150. 1 color illus. (Re English eighteenth-century bedhangings acquired by Warner House Association, Portsmouth, New Hampshire, owned by the Barnard family.)

Gustafson, Eleanor. "Museum Accessions." *Antiques* 153, no. 5 (May 1998): 652. 3 color illus. (Re New Jersey desk and bookcase, ca. 1750–1770, acquired by Monmouth County Historical Association, Freehold, New Jersey; wooden garden seat, ca. 1780, from Maryland, acquired by MESDA; and Herter Brothers firescreen of ca. 1880 purchased by the Cleveland Museum of Art.)

Haley, Anne Rogers. "New Study Center for British Furniture Opens in High Wycombe." *Antiques and the Arts Weekly* (September 5, 1997): 76–77. 6 bw illus.

Haley, Anne Rogers. "Seymour Furniture Discoveries." *America in Britain* 35 (1997): 10–14. 2 color and 5 bw illus.

Hammett, Kingsley H. *Classic New Mexican Furniture: A Handbook of Plans and Building Techniques*. Sante Fe, N.M.: Fleetwood Press, 1996. 96 pp.; bw illus., line drawings, bibliography, index.

Hardyment, Christina. *Behind the Scenes: Domestic Arrangements in Historic Houses*. London: National Trust, 1997. 256 pp.; 150 color and 50 bw illus., gazetteer. bibliography, index. (Re service functions of English houses.)

Harrison, Renée du Pont. "The Stanley Paul Sax Collection." *Sotheby's Preview* (Janaury 1998): 20–22. 8 color illus.

Harwood, Barry R. *The Furniture of George Hunzinger: Invention and Innovation in Nineteenth-Century America*. Brooklyn, N.Y.: Brooklyn Museum, 1997. 168 pp.; 10 color and 189 bw illus., bibliography, index.

Harwood, Barry R. "The Furniture of George Jacob Hunzinger." *Antiques* 152, no. 6 (December 1997): 832–41. 17 color and 3 bw illus.

Harwood, Barry. "George Jacob Hunzinger Exhibition at BMA." *Newsletter of the Decorative Arts Society* 5, no. 2 (fall 1997): 5–7. 2 bw illus.

Heckscher, Morrison H. "American Furniture and the Art of Connoisseurship." *Antiques* 153, no. 5 (May 1998): 722–29. 16 color illus.

Hennessey, William J., with a new introduction by Stanley Abercrombie. *Modern Furnishings for the Home*. The 20th Century: Landmarks in Design, vol. 7. 1952. Reprint. New York: Acanthus Press, 1997. 320 pp.; numerous illus.

Herrmann, Georgina, ed. *The Furniture of Western Asia, Ancient and Traditional: Papers at the Conference Held at the Institute of Archaeology, University College, London, June 28 to 30, 1993*. Mainz: Verlag Philipp von Zabern, 1997. 301 pp.; 1 color and 92 bw illus., line drawings, bibliography.

Hiesinger, Kathryn B., and George R. Marcus. *Antique Speak: A Guide to the Styles, Techniques, and Materials of the Decorative Arts, from the Renaissance to Art Deco*. New York: Abbeville Press, 1997. 216 pp.; numerous color and bw illus., line drawings, bibliography, index.

Hillier, Bevis, and Stephen Escritt. *Art Deco Style*. San Francisco: Chronicle Books, 1997. 240 pp.; 140 color and 50 bw illus.

Hollingsworth, Charles, and Bradley Keyser. "The Influence of the Classical Aesthetic of Architecture on American Furniture." *Antiques and the Arts Weekly* (April 17, 1998): S29. 1 bw illus.

Home Furniture, no. 12 (August–September 1997) through no. 13 (October–November 1997). (This journal has ceased publication.)

Hunting, Mary Anne. "Living with Antiques: The Johannes Decker Farm in Ulster County, New York." *Antiques* 153, no. 4 (April 1998): 572–81. 16 color, 2 bw illus., 1 line drawing.

Hurst, Ronald L. "Irish Influences on Cabinetmaking in Virginia's Rappahannock River Basin." *American Furniture 1997*, pp. 170–95. 39 color and bw illus.

Hurst, Ronald L., and Jonathan Prown. *Southern Furniture, 1680–1830: The Colonial Williamsburg Collection*. New York: Harry N. Abrams, 1997. 640 pp.; 220 color and 616 bw illus., appendix, bibliography, glossaries, index.

Indiana Cabinets, including Hoosier, Sellers, McDougall, Napanee, etc. Gas City, Ind.: L-W Book Sales, 1997. 104 pp.; color and bw illus.

"Ingenious and Practical." *SPNEA* [Newsletter], series 71 (summer 1998): 4. 1 color illus. (Re George Hunzinger furniture.)

[Israel Sack, Inc.]. *Opportunities in American Antiques*. New York: Israel Sack, Inc., [1998]. 43 pp.; color and bw illus.

Izard, Holly V. "Random or Systematic?: An Evaluation of the Probate Process." *Winterthur Portfolio* 32, no. 2–3 (summer–autumn 1997): 147–67. 5 bw illus., 4 tables.

Jardine, Lisa. *Worldly Goods: A New History of the Renaissance*. New York: Doubleday, 1996. xxvi + 470 pp.; 33 color and 161 bw illus., bibliography, index. (Of interest to students of furniture as material culture, broadly conceived, and as evidence of the consumer revolution.)

Jenkins, Emyl. "A Walk Through Southern Furniture History." *Home Furniture*, no. 12 (August–September 1997): 10, 12. 2 color illus. (Re Museum of Early Southern Decorative Arts, Winston-Salem, North Carolina.)

[Jones, Ray]. "Portfolio: Ray Jones." *American Craft* 58, no. 2 (April/May 1998): 70. 1 color illus. (Re contemporary woodworker.)

Katz-Stone, Adam. "John Alexander: The Science of Simplicity." *Woodwork*, no. 47 (October 1997): 22–29. Color illus., line drawings.

Kaye, Myrna. Review of Jeffrey P. Greene, *American Furniture of the 18th Century: History, Technique, Structure*. In *American Furniture 1997*, pp. 362–67.

Kenny, Peter. "Honoré Lannuier's Furniture and Patrons: Recent Discoveries." *Antiques* 153, no. 3 (May 1998): 712–21. 20 color and 4 bw illus.

Kenny, Peter, Frances F. Bretter, and Ulrich Leben. *Honoré Lannuier, Cabinetmaker from Paris: The Life and Work of a French Ébéniste in Federal New York*. New York: Metropolitan Museum of Art, 1998. xviii + 253 pp.; 101 color and 137 bw illus., appendices, bibliography, index. Distributed by Harry N. Abrams, New York.

[Keyser, William]. "William Keyser: Fellow." *American Craft* 57, no. 5 (October–November 1997): 87. 1 color and 1 bw illus.

Killen, Geoffrey. "The Style and Development of Ancient Egyptian Furniture: Part II, Decoration and Embellishment." *Antiques* 152, no. 3 (September 1997): 354–61. 13 color illus.

Kirk, John T. *The Shaker World: Art, Life, Belief*. New York: Harry N. Abrams, 1997. 288 pp.; 82 color and 195 bw illus., map, appendix, bibliography, chronology, index.

Kirkham, Pat. Review of eight books on the arts and crafts movement. In *Studies in the Decorative Arts* 5, no. 2 (spring–summer 1998): 98–102.

Kleckner, Susan. "Flowering Independence." *Christie's Magazine* 15, no. 5 (June 1998): 60–61. 2 color illus. (Re collection of Thomas Mellon Evans to be offered at auction.)

[Knoblauch, Paul]. "Portfolio: Paul Knoblauch." *American Craft* 58, no. 1 (February–March 1998): 79. 1 color illus.

Knowles, Eric. *Miller's 100 Years of the Decorative Arts: Victoriana, Arts and Crafts, Art Nouveau*. London: Miller's Publishers, 1998. 254 pp.; 1,000 color illus., bibliography, index. (First published in 1993 as *Miller's Victoriana to Art Deco*.)

Koster, Michael. "The Nicolai Fechin House in Taos, New Mexico." *Antiques* 153, no. 5 (May 1998): 730–39. 19 color illus.

Kramer, Fran. "Making His Mark: The Work of Shaker Craftsman Orren Haskins: Shaker Museum and Library." *Antiques and the Arts Weekly* (July 18, 1997): 1, 68–69. 13 bw illus.

[Kuehne, Richard]. "Silent Auction for Kuehne Tables." *Cape Ann Historical Association* [Newsletter] 17, no. 3 (July–September 1997): 1. 2 bw illus. (Re contemporary furniture by Rockport artist.)

Leath, Robert A. "Dutch Trade and Its Influence on Seventeenth-Century Chesapeake Furniture." *American Furniture 1997*, pp. 21–46. 20 color and bw illus., appendices.

Ledes, Allison Eckhardt. "Current and Coming: American Case Furniture." *Antiques* 152, no. 2 (August 1997): 144. 2 color illus. (Re exhibition at DAR Museum, Washington, D.C.)

Ledes, Allison Eckhardt. "Current and Coming: American Painted Furniture." *Antiques* 153, no. 4 (April 1998): 498, 500. 2 color illus. (Re exhibition at Philadelphia Antiques Show.)

Ledes, Allison Eckhardt. "Current and Coming: A California Collection." *Antiques* 152, no. 3 (September 1997): 240. 2 color illus. (Re Gail Oxford Collection exhibition at Long Beach Museum of Art, Long Beach, California.)

Ledes, Allison Eckhardt. "Current and Coming: New England in New York." *Antiques* 153, no. 1 (January 1998): 28. 2 color illus. (Re exhibition at Winter Antiques Show of objects from the collection of the Historic Deerfield Foundation.)

Ledes, Allison Eckhardt. "Current and Coming: A Renovated Museum in Louisville." *Antiques* 153, no. 1 (January 1998): 30, 32. 1 color illus. (Re Speed Art Museum.)

Ledes, Allison Eckhardt. "Current and Coming: Southern Case Furniture." *Antiques* 152, no. 3 (September 1997): 236, 238. 3 color illus. (Re exhibition at Colonial Williamsburg.)

Ledes, Allison Eckhardt. "Current and Coming: Thomas Day, Cabinetmaker." *Antiques* 152, no. 2 (August 1997): 146, 148. 2 color illus. (Re exhibition at North Carolina Museum of History, Raleigh, North Carolina.)

Ledes, Allison Eckhardt. "Current and Coming: Transplanted American Decorative Arts." *Antiques* 152, no. 6 (December 1997): 772. 3 color illus. (Re exhibition at Minneapolis Institute of Arts entitled "Inherited and Collected: The Arts of New England in Minnesota.")

Levy, Bernard, and S. Dean, Inc. *Gallery Catalogue IX: Fall 1997*. New York: By the gallery, 1997. 24 pp.; 24 color illus.

Levy, Bernard, and S. Dean, Inc. *Gallery Catalogue X: Winter 1998*. New York: By the gallery, 1997. 24 pp.; 25 color illus.

Linzee, Jill, and Michael P. Chaney. *Deeply Rooted: New Hampshire Traditions in Wood*. Durham: The Art Gallery and The Center for the Humanities, University of New Hampshire, 1997. 54 pp.; numerous color and bw illus. Distributed by University Press of New England, Hanover and London. (Exhibition catalogue dealing with traditions of basketmaking, boatbuilding, decoy carving, dogsled making, and fiddle making.)

Locklair, Paula. "New in the Collection." *The Luminary* (Newsletter of the Museum of Early Southern Decorative Arts) 19, no. 1 (spring 1998): 6–9. 9 bw illus. (Includes a pembroke table labeled by John Shaw, Annapolis, ca. 1780, and a chest of drawers of ca. 1780 from Winchester, Virginia.)

Longworth, Joyce. "Journeys to Cathay: Asian Influences in the American Decorative Arts." *Winterthur Magazine* 43, no. 4 (winter 1997–1998): 24–27. 8 color illus.

Loomes, Brian. *Brass Dial Clocks*. Woodbridge, England: Antique Collectors' Club, 1998. 464 pp.; 48 color and 700 bw illus.

Lowenthal, David. *Possessed by the Past: The Heritage Crusade and the Spoils of History*. New York: The Free Press, 1996. xiii + 338 pp.; bibliography, index. (A thoughtful analysis with implications for the collector of furniture and other objects.)

Ly, Tran Duy. *New Haven Clocks and Watches with a Special Section on New Haven Movements*. Fairfax, Va.: Arlington Book Co., 1997. 520 pp.; numerous illus. (Includes history of New Haven Clock Company by Chris Bailey.)

Ly, Tran Duy. *Seth Thomas Clocks and Movements*. 2d ed. Fairfax, Va.: Arlington Book Co., 1996. 496 pp.; 2,100+ bw illus.

[McArthur, Warren]. *Catalog of Warren McArthur Twentieth-Century Furniture: An Auction to Benefit the Collections of the Library of Virginia*. Richmond: Library of Virginia, 1997. Unpaged; several color illus.

McDermott, Catherine. *Design Museum Book of Twentieth Century Design*. Woodstock, N.Y.: Overlook Press, 1998. 400 pp.; 390 color illus.

McDonald, Janet Strain. "Furniture Making in Albemarle County, Virginia, 1750–1850." *Antiques* 153, no. 5 (May 1998): 746–51. 7 color illus., checklist of cabinetmakers and related craftsmen.

McFadden, Tom. "Paul Reiber: The Art and Spirit of a Chairmaker." *Woodwork*, no. 50 (April 1998): 68–76. 14 color illus.

McKinstry, E. Richard, comp. *Personal Accounts of Events, Travels, and Everyday Life in America: An Annotated Bibliography*. Winterthur, Del.: Winterthur Museum, 1997. 236 pp.; bw illus., bibliography, indexes. Distributed by University Press of New England, Hanover and London. (Guide to primary sources at Winterthur, many of use to the furniture historian.)

McPherson, Anne S. "Adaptation and Reinterpretation: The Transfer of Furniture Styles from Philadelphia to Winchester to Tennessee." *American Furniture 1997*, pp. 298–334. 36 color and bw illus.

McPherson, Anne S. "'That Article of Household Furniture Peculiar to Earlier Days in the South': Sugar Chests in Middle Tennessee and Central Kentucky, 1800–1835." *Journal of Early Southern Decorative Arts* 23, no. 2 (winter 1997): 1–65. 32 bw illus.

"*M.A.D.*'s Cabinetmakers Database Nears Initial Completion; Winterthur Signs On." *Maine Antique Digest* 25, no. 8 (August 1997): 9A. 1 bw illus.

Maher, Virginia Jones. "George M. Niedecken: Search for an American Design Style." *Wisconsin Academy Review: A Journal of Wisconsin Culture* 43, no. 3 (summer 1997): 4–9. 10 bw illus.

Maine Antique Digest staff. "Books Received." *Maine Antique Digest* 25, no. 11 (November 1997): 36E. (Includes review of John T. Kirk, *The Shaker World: Art, Life, Belief*.)

Martin, Ann Smart, and J. Ritchie Garrison, eds. *American Material Culture: The Shape of the Field*. Winterthur, Del.: Winterthur Museum, 1997. 428 pp.; bw illus. Distributed by University of Tennessee Press, Knoxville.

Martinez, Katharine, and Kenneth Ames, eds. *The Material Culture of Gender/The Gender of Material Culture*. Winterthur, Del.: Winterthur Museum, 1997. 465 pp.; bw illus. Distributed by University Press of New England, Hanover and London.

Mascolo, Frances. "Order and Elegance: Masterpieces of Federal Furniture from Coastal Massachusetts." *Antiques and the Arts Weekly* (July 25, 1997): 1, 68. 5 bw illus., 1 line drawing. (Re exhibition at Peabody Essex Museum, Salem, Massachusetts.)

Massey, James, and Shirley Maxwell. *Arts and Crafts Design in America: A State-by-State Guide*. San Francisco: Chronicle Books, 1998. 272 pp.; numerous color and bw illus., index.

Mayor, Alfred. Review of Donald Webster, *Canfake: An Expert's Guide to the Tricks of the Canadian Antiques Trade*. In *Antiques* 154, no. 1 (July 1998): 38. 1 color illus.

Mayor, Alfred. Review of Geoffrey Beard, *Upholsterers and Interior Furnishing in England, 1530–1840*. In *Antiques* 152, no. 4 (October 1997): 434. 1 color illus.

Mayor, Alfred. Review of Georg Himmelheber, *Cast-iron Furniture and All Other Forms of Iron Furniture*. In *Antiques* 152, no. 4 (October 1997): 434. 1 color illus.

Mayor, Alfred. Review of *Inspiring Reform: Boston's Arts and Crafts Movement*. In *Antiques* 152, no. 2 (August 1997): 154. 1 color illus.

Mayor, Alfred. Review of John Kassay, *The Book of American Windsor Furniture: Styles and Technologies*. In *Antiques* 153, no. 5 (May 1998): 660. 1 color illus.

Mayor, Alfred. Review of R. A. Salaman, *Dictionary of Woodworking Tools c. 1700–1900 and Tools of Allied Trades*. In *An-

tiques 153, no. 5 (May 1998): 660. 1 color illus.

Meadmore, Clement. *The Modern Chair: Classic Designs by Thonet, Breuer, Le Corbusier, Eames, and Others*. 1974. Reprint. New York: Dover Publications, 1997. 192 pp.; illus.

Meiland, David. "Fabiane Garcia: The Art of the Absurd." *Woodwork*, no. 51 (June 1998): 48–53. 18 color illus.

Microulis, Laura. "Charles Hindley & Sons, London House Furnishers of the Nineteenth Century: A Paradigm of the Middle-Range Market." *Studies in the Decorative Arts* 5, no. 2 (spring–summer 1998): 69–96. 15 bw illus.

Monkman, Betty C. "The White House Collection: James Buchanan's White House." *White House History* 2, no. 1 (June 1997): 60–63. 5 bw illus.

Montgomery, Liza. "An Elusive Shade of Red." *Antiques and the Arts Weekly* (November 14, 1997): 121. 2 bw illus. (Re Dunlap chest of drawers sold at auction.)

Moore, C. Eugene. *Inspiring Interiors: 1950s*. Atglen, Pa.: Schiffer Publishing, 1998. 160 pp.; 253 color illus. (Based on advertising by the Armstrong Company.)

Morgan, Marie. Review of Edward S. Cooke, Jr., *Making Furniture in Preindustrial America: The Social Economy of Newtown and Woodbury, Connecticut*. In *New England Quarterly* 70, no. 3 (September 1997): 483–86.

[Museum of the City of New York]. *Our Town: Images and Stories from the Museum of the City of New York*. New York: Harry N. Abrams, 1997. 222 pp.; numerous color and bw illus., index. (Illustrates some furniture in the MCNY collection.)

Museum School Traveling Scholars 1997. Boston, Mass.: School of the Museum of Fine Arts, Boston, 1997. Unpaged; color illus. (Includes chair by Michael Joseph.)

Naeve, Milo. *Identifying American Furniture: A Pictorial Guide to Styles and Terms, Colonial to Contemporary*. 3d rev. ed. Walnut Creek, Calif.: Altamira Press in cooperation with the American Association for State and Local History, 1998. 108 pp.; 200+ bw illus., bibliography, index.

Nelson, Harold B. *Bountiful Harvest: American Decorative Arts from the Gail Oxford Collection*. Long Beach, Calif.: Long Beach Museum of Art, 1997. Brochure; color illus.

Noll, Terrie. "Return of the Native: Kristina Madsen Revisited." *Woodwork*, no. 51 (June 1998): 20–27. 14 color illus.

"Not Your Grandma's Chair: Furniture Society Show Opening July 13." *Antiques and the Arts Weekly* (July 4, 1997): 19. 1 bw illus.

Oettinger, Marion, ed. *Folk Art of Spain and the Americas: El Alma del Pueblo*. New York: Abbeville Press and San Antonio Museum of Art, 1997. 200 pp.; 123 color and bw illus., index. (See especially Carlos Piçel, "Popular Furniture," pp. 80–93.)

Palladio, Andrea. *The Fours Books on Architecture*. Trans. Robert Tavernor and Richard Schofield. Cambridge: The MIT Press, 1997. xxxv + 436 pp.; line drawings, glossary, bibliography, index. (Modern, accurate translation of 1570 edition, supplanting the commonly used Dover 1964 reprint of Isaac Ware's 1738 edition and including reproductions in facsimile of the original woodcuts and scholarly apparatus.)

Palmer, Arlene. *A Guide to Victoria Mansion*. Portland, Maine: Victoria [Morse-Libby] Mansion, 1997. 32 pp.; 39 color and bw illus.

Parker, George. "Early American Furniture in Wisconsin Collections." *Wisconsin Academy Review: A Journal of Wisconsin Culture* 43, no. 2 (spring 1997): 4–16. bw illus.

Penny, Nicholas. *Frames: National Gallery Pocket Guide*. London: National Gallery, 1997. 64 pp.; 52 color and 5 bw illus.

Phoenix Chair Company. *American Wooden Chairs, 1895–1908*. Atglen, Pa.: Schiffer Publishing Co., 1997. 367 pp.; illus. (Reprint of 1908 trade catalogue of firm in Sheybogan, Wisconsin.)

Pierce, Kerry. "Brian Boggs: Commitment to Excellence." *Woodwork*, no. 49 (February 1998): 22–32. 21 color illus.

Pierce, Kerry. "Rob Gartzka and Kathie Johnson: Art or Furniture?" *Woodwork*, no. 47 (October 1997): 66–72. 18 color illus.

Piña, Leslie. *Classic Herman Miller*. Atglen, Pa.: Schiffer Publishing, 1998. 216 pp.; 260+ color illus., index.

Piña, Leslie, ed. *The Herman Miller Collection: The 1955/1956 Catalog*. Atglen, Pa.: Schiffer Publishing, 1998. 168 pp.; illus.

Pointon, Marcia. "Quakerism and Visual Culture, 1650–1800." *Art History* 20, no. 3 (September 1997): 397–431. bw illus.

Pons, Bruno. *French Period Rooms, 1650–1800, Rebuilt in England, France, and the Americas*. Dijons, France: Éditions Faton, 1995. 439 pp.; numerous color illus., index.

Popular Furniture of the 1920s and 1930s. Atglen, Pa.: Schiffer Publishing, 1998. 226 pp.; 863 bw illus. (Reprint of trade catalogue issued by the Elgin A. Simonds Company.)

[Prickett, C.L., Antiques]. *Fine Authenticated American Antiques*. Yardley, Pa.: By the firm, 1998. 32 pp.; color illus. (A sales pamphlet.)

Priddy, Sumpter, III, and Joan K. Quinn. "Crossroads of Culture: Eighteenth-Century Furniture from Western Maryland." *American Furniture 1997*, pp. 127–69. 60 color and bw illus.

Prown, Jonathan. "A 'Preponderance of Pineapples': The Problem of Southern Furniture." *American Furniture 1997*, pp. 1–20. 23 color and bw illus.

Prown, Jonathan. Review of Nancy Goyne Evans, *American Windsor Chairs*. In *American Furniture 1997*, pp. 359–62.

Rand, Richard. "The Intimate Interior in Eighteenth-Century French Genre Painting." *Antiques* 152, no. 3 (September 1997): 324–33. 15 color and 2 bw illus.

[Radtke, Charles]. "Portfolio: Charles Radtke." *American Craft* 58, no. 3 (June–July 1998): 64. 1 color illus. (Re contemporary woodworker.)

Rees, Jane, and Mark Rees. *Christopher Gabriel and the Tool Trade in 18th Century London*. Mendham, N.J.: Astragal Press, 1997. 92 pp.; bw illus.

Regional Furniture: The Journal of the

Regional Furniture Society 11 (1997): 1–102. 2 color and numerous bw illus. (Eleven articles on English vernacular furniture.)

Regional Furniture Society Newsletter, no. 26 (summer 1997), no. 27 (winter 1997/98). 17 pp.; bw illus. (News, notes, reviews, pictures, and other useful information, primarily about English vernacular furniture.)

[Renwick Gallery]. "Recent Acquisition of Furniture at Renwick Gallery." *Antiques and the Arts Weekly* (May 1, 1998): 10. (Re exhibition of contemporary studio furniture by Wendell Castle, Alphonse Mattia, Albert Paley, Bob Trotman, Timothy Philbrick, and Peter Danko.)

[Renwick Gallery]. "Renwick Gallery Kicks Off 25th Anniversary with Special Exhibition." *Antiques and the Arts Weekly* (July 4, 1997): 89A–90A. 6 bw illus. (Includes some contemporary furniture.)

"Report from Europe: American Culture in London." *Antiques* 153, no. 1 (January 1998): 60, 62. 2 color illus. (Re exhibitions, including one of Shaker furniture, at Barbican Art Gallery.)

Richards, Nancy, and Nancy Goyne Evans, with Wendy A. Cooper and Michael S. Podmaniczky. *New England Furniture at Winterthur: Queen Anne and Chippendale Periods*. Winterthur, Del.: Winterthur Museum, 1997. 534 pp.; 482 bw illus., bibliography, index. Distributed by University Press of New England, Hanover and London.

[Riley, Cheryl]. "Evolution of a Design: An Interview with Cheryl Riley." *Woodwork*, no. 51 (June 1998): 32–38. 12 color illus.

Rothenberg, Winifred B. Review of Edward S. Cooke, Jr., *Making Furniture in Preindustrial America: The Social Economy of Newtown and Woodbury, Connecticut*. In *Journal of Economic History* 57, no. 3 (September 1997): 760–61.

Rothrock, Kate. "John Cedarquist: The Reality of Illusion." *The Museum of California* 21, no. 3 (summer 1997): 6–7, 24–27. 5 color illus.

Royka, Paul A. *Mission Furniture: Furniture of the American Arts and Crafts Movement*. Atglen, Pa.: Schiffer Publishing, 1997. 208 pp.; color illus., bibliography.

Ruddy, Robin. *French Provincial Furniture*. Atglen, Pa.: Schiffer Publishing, 1998. 128 pp.; 138 color and 79 bw illus.

"Rustic Furnishings." *Maine Antique Digest* 25, no. 11 (November 1997): 6A. 2 bw illus. (Re exhibition at The Montreal Botanical Gardens from collection of Ralph Kylloe.)

"Rustic Furnishings Come Out of the Woods and Into Montreal: Antique Pieces from Ralph Kylloe's Collection on View to December 1." *Antiques and the Arts Weekly* (November 7, 1997): 102. 5 bw illus.

Salaman, R. A. *Dictionary of Woodworking Tools, c. 1700–1900, and Tools of Allied Trades*. 1975. Rev. ed. Mendham, N.J.: Astragal Press, 1998. 546 pp.; illus., line drawings.

Savage, J. Thomas. "The Holmes-Edwards Library Bookcase and the Origins of the German School in Pre-Revolutionary Charleston." *American Furniture 1997*, pp. 106–26. 29 color and bw illus., appendix.

Schaffner, Cynthia V. A., and Susan Klein. *American Painted Furniture, 1790–1880*. New York: Clarkson Potter, 1997. xv + 223 pp.; numerous color and bw illus., appendices, glossary, bibliography, index.

Schaffner, Cynthia V. A., and Susan Klein. "America's Painted and Gilded Legacy: 19th Century Painted Furniture." In *The 1998 Philadelphia Antiques Show* [Catalogue], pp. 37–67. Philadelphia, 1998. 28 color and 1 bw illus.

Schaffner, Cynthia V. A., and Susan Klein. "Two-Toned Finishes: American Grain-Painted Furniture, 1790–1880." *Folk Art* 23, no. 1 (spring 1998): 36–43. 14 color illus.

Schinto, Jeanne. "Murder on Tick Tock Lane." *Yankee Magazine* (September 1997): 56–60, 116, 188, 120. 6 color illus. (Re Elmer O. Stennes [1911–1975], maker of reproduction clock cases.)

Schreiner, Timothy. "A Democracy of Furniture." *Home Furniture*, no. 13 (October–November 1997): 54–59. 15 color illus. (Re installation at Museum of Fine Arts, Boston.)

Sembach, Klaus-Jurgen, ed. *Modern Furniture Designs, 1950–1980s*. Atglen, Pa.: Schiffer Publishing, 1997. 320 pp.; 500+ illus.

Sheary, Patrick. "American Case Furniture at the DAR Museum." *Antiques and the Arts Weekly* (September 12, 1997): W32–W37. 15 bw illus.

[Simpson, Tommy]. "Tommy Simpson: Fellow." *American Craft* 57, no. 5 (October–November 1997): 90. 2 color illus.

[Slifer House]. "Slifer House Receives Victorian Furniture." *Antiques and the Arts Weekly* (September 26, 1997): 69C. (Re acquisitions by museum in Lewisburg, Pennsylvania.)

Smith, Laurence. "New Mexican Furniture: Sotheby's Profits from Primitives with Al Luckett, Jr., Collection." *Antiques and the Arts Weekly* (February 6, 1998): 79A–80A. 10 bw illus.

[Society for the Preservation of New England Antiquities]. "Offin Boardman's Table." *SPNEA* [Newsletter], series 70 (spring 1998): 8. 1 color illus. (Re drop-leaf table, Newburyport, Massachusetts, area, 1755–1760, owned originally by Boardman [1748–1811] and recently acquired by the society.)

Solis-Cohen, Lita. "Chipstone Furniture Journal Rewrites Furniture History" (book review). *Maine Antique Digest* 25, no. 8 (August 1997): 10A. 1 bw illus.

Solis-Cohen, Lita. "Chipstone Journal Explores Furniture Trade in the Early South" (book review). *Maine Antique Digest* 26, no. 2 (February 1998): 36A–37A. 1 bw illus.

Solis-Cohen, Lita. "Deceit, Deception, and Discovery"(exhibition review). *Maine Antique Digest* 25, no. 12 (December 1997): 12B–14B. 14 bw illus. (Re exhibition at Winterthur Museum.)

Solis-Cohen, Lita. "Heritage Center Raises $52,000." *Maine Antique Digest* 25, no. 11 (November 1997): 8A. 3 bw illus. (Re deaccessioning by Heritage Center, Lancaster, Pennsylvania, of three examples of eighteenth-century furniture.)

Solis-Cohen, Lita. "John Townsend Chest of Drawers." *Maine Antique Digest* 26, no. 7 (July 1998): 10A. 2 bw illus.

Solis-Cohen, Lita. "A Shaker Signed His

Work: Shaker Museum and Library, Old Chatham, New York" (exhibition review). *Maine Antique Digest* 25, no. 9 (September 1997): 46E–47E. 14 bw illus. (Re exhibition of work by Orren Haskins.)

Solny, Susan. "Some Unusual Stylistic Preferences in New York Cellaret Design, 1810–1834." *Studies in the Decorative Arts* 5, no. 1 (fall–winter 1997–1998): 83–128. 19 bw illus., table, appendices. (See also this author's note and illustration on p. 159, Research Inquiries.)

[Sotheby's]. *American Furniture and Decorative Arts from Spain's Northern Colonial Frontier, 1700–1900: The Collection of Mr. and Mrs. Al Luckett, Jr.* New York: Sotheby's, January 15, 1998. Sale 7086. Unpaged; numerous color and bw illus. (Includes text by Wendell Garrett, Betsy Fleming, John W. Grassham, Ward A. Minge, Larry Frank, and Thomas J. Steele, and a reprint of Lonn Taylor and Dessa Bokides, *Carpinteros and Cabinetmakers: Furniture Making in New Mexico, 1600–1900* [1983].)

[Sotheby's]. "The Collection of Stanley Paul Sax." *At Sotheby's* 3, no. 1 (January 1998): 4. 3 bw illus.

[Sotheby's]. "Furniture and Decorative Arts from the American Southwest." *At Sotheby's* 3, no. 1 (January 1998): 5. 1 color illus. (Re auction of collection of Mr. and Mrs. Al Luckett, Jr., in January 1998.)

[Sotheby's]. *Highly Important Americana from the Collection of Stanley Paul Sax.* New York: Sotheby's, January 16–17, 1998. Sale 7087. Unpaged; numerous color and bw illus.

[Sotheby's]. *Important American Furniture from the Collection of the late Thomas Mellon and Betty Evans.* New York: Sotheby's, June 19, 1998. Sale 7164. Unpaged; numerous color and bw illus.

[Sotheby's]. *Property from the Estate of the Late Richard C. von Hess.* New York: Sotheby's, June 16, 1998. Sale 7163. Unpaged; numerous color and bw illus.

Southern Highland Craft Guild. *The Chair Show 2.* Asheville, N.C.: Folk Art Center, 1997. 6 pp.; illus. (Brochure containing text by Charlotte Vestal Brown and others.)

Sparke, Penny, et al. *The New Design Sourcebook.* New York: Knickerbocker Press, 1997. 224 pp.; numerous color and bw illus., index, bibliography.

Spivey, Samuel O. J. *The Craftsman on CD-ROM.* New York: Interactive Bureau, 1997. 2 CD-ROMs plus manual. (Text and images from 183 issues of Gustav Stickley's *The Craftsman*, plus an index and articles by Beverly K. Brandt, David M. Cathers, Stephen Gray, and Shax Riegler.)

Steblecki, Edith. "Descendant Donates Dresser Owned by Mary Revere Lincoln." *Revere House Gazette*, no. 48 (autumn 1997): 4. 2 bw illus. (Re mahogany chest of drawers, ca. 1830, owned by Paul Revere's daughter and recently acquired by the Revere House, Boston.)

Sweeney, Kevin M. Review of Edward S. Cooke, Jr., *Making Furniture in Preindustrial America: The Social Economy of Newtown and Woodbury, Connecticut.* In *American Furniture 1997*, pp. 380–86.

Three Centuries of New Hampshire Furniture Making: New Hampshire Furniture Masters Association Second Annual Exhibition and Catalogue. Concord: New Hampshire Historical Society, 1997. Unpaged; 35 color illus.

Townes, Brooks. "Grif Okie Loves Wood." *Woodwork*, no. 48 (December 1997): 22–30. Color illus. and line drawings.

Trapp, Kenneth R., and Howard Risatti. *Skilled Work: American Craft in the Renwick Gallery.* Washington, D.C.: Smithsonian Institution Press, 1998. 192 pp.; 104 color and 20 bw illus., chronologies, biographies.

Trent, Robert F. "Philadelphia Gothic Niche Pilasters and a French Secretary by Crawford Riddell." *Furniture History* 33 (1997): 253–58. 4 bw illus.

Trent, Robert F. Review of Cary Carson, Ronald Hoffman, and Peter J. Albert, eds., *Of Consuming Interests: The Style of Life in the Eighteenth Century.* In *American Furniture 1997*, pp. 376–78.

Turner, Tran. "Perfection in Form: Works by Sam Maloof, Kay Sekimachi, and Bob Stocksdale." *Craft Arts International*, no. 42 (1998): 92–95. 19 color illus.

Van Dine, Lynn. "Who Was Peter Hunt?" *Yankee Magazine* (February 1998): 58–63, 105–7. 10 color and 1 bw illus. (Hunt [1896–1967] was a "folk art furniture decorator of the 1930s and 1940s.")

Vermette, Luce. Review of Edward S. Cooke, Jr., *Making Furniture in Preindustrial America: The Social Economy of Newtown and Woodbury, Connecticut.* In *Material History Review* 46 (fall 1997): 100–101.

[Virginia Museum of Fine Arts]. "Virginia Museum Acquires 'Iris' Paintings." *Antiques and the Arts Weekly* (December 26, 1997): 54. 4 bw illus. (Includes reference to pair of side chairs by Greene and Greene, ca. 1907–1909, also recently acquired by the museum.)

[Virginia Museum of Fine Arts]. "Virginia Museum's New Acquisitions Come from Colonial America, Asia, and Africa." *Antiques and the Arts Weekly* (September 12, 1997): 73. 2 bw illus. (Re Philadelphia side chair, ca. 1765–1770, recently acquired by the museum.)

von Vegesack, Alexander. *Thonet: Classic Furniture in Bent Wood and Tubular Steel.* New York: Rizzoli, 1997. 160 pp.; numerous color and bw illus., index.

"Wallace Gallery Mounts Southern Furniture Show." *Colonial Williamsburg* 20, no. 1 (autumn 1997): 76. 2 color illus.

Ward, Gerald W. R. Review of Patrick Sheary, *American Case Furniture, 1680–1840: Selections from the DAR Museum Collection.* In *American Furniture 1997*, pp. 378–80.

Ward, Gerald W. R., comp. "Recent Writing on American Furniture: A Bibliography." In *American Furniture 1997*, pp. 387–96.

Wardwell, Alan. *Tangible Visions: Northwest Coast Indian Shamanism and Its Art.* New York: The Monacelli Press with The Corvus Press, 1996. vii + 336 pp.; 499 color and 50 bw illus., bibliography, synonymy.

Warren, Winthrop D. "Which Willard Made This Clock?" *NAWCC Bulletin* 40, no. 1 (February 1998): 31–38. 18 bw illus., bibliography.

Webster, Donald. *Canfake: An Expert's Guide to the Tricks of the Canadian Antiques Trade*. Toronto: McClelland and Stewart, 1997. xiv + 226 pp.; illus., bibliography, index.

Wells-Cole, Anthony. *Art and Decoration in Elizabethan and Jacobean England: The Influence of Continental Prints, 1558–1625*. London and New Haven: Yale University Press for the Paul Mellon Centre for Studies in British Art, 1997. xii + 344 pp.; 125 color and 375 bw illus., bibliography, indexes.

Wheaton, Sarah. "In the Finishing 'Test Kitchen' with Kim Kelzer." *Woodwork*, no. 51 (June 1998): 59–61. 4 color illus.

Whisker, James Biser, Daniel David Hartzler, and Steven P. Petrucelli. *Clockmakers and Watchmakers of Maryland, 1660–1900*. Cranbury, N.J.: Adams Brown Co., 1997. 256 pp.; 282 bw illus.

[White House, The.] *The White House: The George Bush Administration, 1989–1993*. Washington, D.C.: Office of the Chief Usher, The White House, Washington, D.C., in cooperation with the White House Historical Association and the National Park Service, 1997. 72 pp.; color and bw illus., bibliography, appendix. (Includes references to furniture acquisitions.)

Willoughby, Martha H. "Patriot Games." *Christie's International Magazine* 14, no. 8 (October 1997): 80–81. 1 color illus. (Re Connecticut cherry high chest, ca. 1770, owned by Hawley-Clarke-Lyman family of Northampton, Massachusetts.)

Wood, David F. Review of Donald L. Fennimore, *Metalwork in Early America: Copper and Its Alloys from the Winterthur Museum*. In *American Furniture 1997*, pp. 372–76.

[Wooden Artifacts Group, American Institute for Conservation]. *Postprints of the Wooden Artifacts Group Presented at the 24th Annual Meeting of the American Institute for Conservation, Norfolk, Virginia, June 1996*. Wooden Artifacts Group, American Institute for Conservation, [1997]. 61 pp.; bw illus. (See especially Leroy Graves and Joanna Ruth Harris, "Southern Sofas"; Mark Minor, "Laser Reproduction of Brass/Wood Inlay in Furniture by Charles Honoré Lannuier"; and Mark Kutney, Chris Swan, and F. Cary Howlett, "Conservator, Curator, Craftsman: Collaborations at Colonial Williamsburg.")

[Wooden Artifacts Group, American Institute for Conservation]. *Postprints of the Wooden Artifacts Group: Presented at the 25th Annual Meeting of the American Institute for Conservation, San Diego, California, June 1997*. Wooden Artifacts Group, American Institute for Conservation, [1998]. 62 pp.; bw illus.

Wright, Virginia. *Modern Furniture in Canada, 1920 to 1970*. Toronto, Buffalo, and London: University of Toronto Press, 1997. 209 pp.; 8 color and 206 bw illus., bibliography, index.

Yelavich, Susan. *Design for Life: Our Daily Lives, the Spaces We Shape, and the Ways We Communicate, as Seen through the Collections of the Cooper-Hewitt, National Design Museum*. Edited by Stephen Doyle. New York: Cooper-Hewitt, National Design Museum, Smithsonian Institution, and Rizzoli, 1997. 192 pp.; numerous color illus., checklist.

Zea, Philip. *A Deerfield Sampler*. Deerfield, Mass.: Historic Deerfield, Inc., 1998. 38 pp.; color and bw illus.

Zea, Philip. Review of Nancy Goyne Evans, *American Windsor Chairs*. In *Pennsylvania Magazine of History and Biography* 121, no. 4 (October 1997): 383–86.

Zimmerman, Philip D. Review of Nancy Goyne Evans, *American Windsor Chairs*. In *Journal of Early Southern Decorative Arts* 28, no. 1 (summer 1997): 105–8.

Zimmerman, Philip D. "The Stratford, Connecticut, Bureau Table: A Reexamination." *Antiques* 153, no. 5 (May 1998): 740–45. 5 color and 1 bw illus.

Index

Academie or Store House of Armory & Blazon (Holme), 198
Ackermann, Rudolph, 129, 130, 132, 134, 135, 136, 138, 140
Adam, Robert and James, 134
Adams, Samuel, 209
Advertisements, 73(fig.), 164(fig.); by Christian M. Nestell, 101(& fig.), 102(& fig. 4); by ornamental painters, 104
Advice books, immigrant, 43–44, 45, 47, 48, 76(n9)
Affleck, Thomas, 81, 93
Aldrich, Mimi, 235(n10)
Alexander, John D., Jr., 237(n12)
Allen, Abner, 169
Allen, Ezra, 169, 171, 173, 183, 190–91
Alling, David, 149, 154
Alte und Neue Welt, Die (The Old and New World), 45, 46, 74, 77(n16)
American Chairs: Queen Anne and Chippendale (Kirk), 81, 96–98
American eagle. *See* Patriotic motifs
American Furniture, Queen Anne and Chippendale Periods (Downs), 89–90, 248, 265
American Furniture, The Federal Period in the Henry Francis du Pont Winterthur Museum (Montgomery), 165, 249
American Interpreter/Der Amerikanische Dolmetscher, The, 48
American Seating Furniture, 1630–1730 (Forman), 249
Ames, Ezra, 144, 145, 155
Andrews, Edward Deming, 252, 254, 256, 257, 259
Andrews, Faith, 252, 259
Angier, Harlan, 167
Animal motifs, 114–18, 114(figs.), 115(fig.), 116(figs.), 117(figs.), 144–45
Anthony, Daniel, 102(fig. 3)
Antiquities of Ireland, The, 113
Appleton, George S., 73
Apthorp, Charles, 20, 22, 27
Arabesques, 138
Armchairs: Boston baroque, 7(fig. 9), 11(& fig.), 12(fig. 16), 13–16, 13(fig. 18), 14(fig. 20), 37(n9); Hunzinger, 241(fig.); New York painted, 147(fig.), 151(fig.); rococo, 86(fig.), 87(figs.), 89–90, 89(fig.); from the South, 270–71
Art and Architecture of Free Masonry, The (Curl), 255
Art history, 253

Art in the House (von Falke), 241
Art of Drawing and Painting in Water-Colours, The, 114
Art of Painting in Water Colours, The, 124
Ash, 207–8, 212(n6), 213(n12), 234(n10)
Assimilation, 59
Attributions: Boston baroque and mistaken, 33–34, 40(n35); and Nathan Lombard, 165, 167–68; and Randolph labeled chairs, 81–94, 96–98; and Waldo chair, 197, 209, 211
Averill, William, 213(n18)

Backstools: Boston baroque, 6(fig.), 7–9, 18–20, 20(fig. 33), 37(n9), 38(n20); London, 20(fig. 32)
Bacon, Roger, 10
Ballard, Daniel, 1
Baltimore: and German trade, 76(n10); ornamental painting in, 143, 145–46, 150–51, 152–53, 152(fig.), 153(fig. 95), 154(& fig.), 155
Banding, 171, 194(n10)
Bangs, Jeremy, 234(n9)
Banister, John, 35(& fig.), 36
Barbour, Frederick, 167
Bard Graduate Center for Studies in the Decorative Arts, 260
Barnes, Alice (Bradford), 235(n10)
Barnes, John (first generation), 235(n10)
Barnes, John (third generation), 235(n10)
Barnes, Jonathan, 233(n7), 235(n10)
Barnes, Mary (Bartlett), 235(n10)
Barnes, Mary (Plummer), 235(n10)
Barnes, Phoebe (Finney), 233(n7)
Barnes, William, 235(n10)
Baroque: and Boston seating furniture, 2–33; as design term, 249; introduction of, 232(n1); and Williamsburg furniture, 37(n12)
Barrett, Charles, Sr., 34
Barrett, John, 28, 29(fig. 47)
Barrett, Samuel, 156
Barrow, John S., 105
Barry, Joseph B., 65, 66
Bartlett, Anna (Clark), 233(n7)
Bartlett, Benjamin, 233(n7)
Bartlett, Elizabeth (Bartlett), 233(n7)
Bartlett, Hannah (Pope), 233(n7)
Bartlett, Isaac, 222(fig. 12), 233(n7)
Bartlett, Joseph (second generation), 233(n7)
Bartlett, Joseph (third generation), 233(n7), 235(n10)

Bartlett, Joseph (fourth generation), 233(n7)
Bartlett, Joseph (sixth generation), 233(n7)
Bartlett, Lydia (Griswold), 233(n7)
Bartlett, Margaret (Barnes), 233(n7)
Bartlett, Robert, 233(n7)
Bartlett, Samuel, 233(n7)
Bartlett, Zacheus (captain), 233(n7)
Bartlett family, 222, 223, 233(n7)
Bartolozzi, Francesco, 108
Bauduy, Peter, 140
Baxter, Thomas, 1
Bayard, William, 246
Beach, Miss, 108
Bealing, Richard, 261
Beane, Nellie Fairbanks, 235(n10)
Beard, Geoffrey, 260–63
Beckerdite, Luke, 264
Beech, 212(n6)
Beehive motif, 118, 145
Belknap, Zedekiah, 169(fig. 9)
Belter, Johann Heinrich, 73
Benedict, William, 170
Bentley, William (reverend), 108
Bermuda Group, The, 18, 19(fig. 31)
Biedermeier design, 54–59, 62, 65–67, 76(n1), 78(nn 32, 41)
Binny and Ronaldson, 136, 141
Bird motifs, 115(fig.), 116–17(& figs.), 145; and Lombard furniture, 185, 195(n20)
Bivins, John, 249, 264, 265, 266
Bolemius and Company, A. W., 51
Booke Containing Such Beasts As Are Most Usefull For Such As Practice Drawing, Graveing, Armes Painting, [and] Chaseing, 115
Border patterns: feather motifs, 117(fig. 28), 126(fig. 47); floral/foliage, 119(fig. 33), 121, 124(& fig. 42), 125(figs. 43, 44), 126–27, 126(figs.), 127(figs. 48, 49); fruit motifs, 129–30, 130(figs.), 131(fig. 60); Greek key, 133(& fig. 66), 150, 163(n111); guilloche, 134(& figs.), 150–52; Roman fasces, 138(& fig.), 154; shell motif, 133(& fig. 65); textile derived, 135(figs. 69, 70)
Bosley, James, 247
Boston: armchairs, 7(fig. 9), 11(& fig.), 12(fig. 16), 13–16, 13(fig. 18), 14(fig. 20); backstools, 6(fig.), 7–9, 18–20, 20(fig. 33); baroque seating furniture, 1–36; desk-and-bookcases, 16(figs.); easy chairs, 8(fig. 11), 9–11, 9(fig.), 10(fig.), 16, 18(fig.), 19–20, 21(fig. 34), 23(fig.), 28–33, 30(fig.), 31(fig.), 32(fig.), 33(fig. 53); Plymouth County and influences from, 224–25; side chairs, 2(figs.), 3–6, 3(fig.), 4(figs.), 5(fig.), 7–9, 7(fig. 8), 8(fig. 12), 12(fig. 17), 14(fig. 21), 15–18, 17(fig.), 19(fig. 29), 22(fig. 36), 24–28(& figs.), 29(fig. 48), 33(fig. 52); turned great chairs, 220–22, 220(fig.), 233(n5)
Botanical Magazine, 124
Bouvier, Michel, 67
Bower, Samuel J., 104
Bowers, Samuel, 105
Bowfront furniture, 175–76
Bow-knot motif, 119(fig. 34), 125–26, 125(fig. 45)
Bowles, Carington, 121, 123
Boynton, Thomas, 148, 150, 155
Bradford, Rebecca (Bartlett), 235(n10)
Bradford, William, 231, 235(n10)
Branson, Benjamin, 143
Breck, Samuel, 102
Bretter, Frances F., 243–48
Brewster chairs, 215, 233(n2)
Bright, George, 29
Brinkerhoff, James, 246
British Architect; or, The Builder's Treasure of Staircases, The (Swan), 268
British influences: and Boston baroque seating furniture, 12–13, 20–21, 36(n4); and German craftsmen, 55–56, 59, 66, 68; and southern furniture, 268
Bromfield family, 27–28
Bromme, Traugott, 45, 47
Brooklyn Museum of Art, 239(& fig.), 240(fig.), 241–42
Brown, Abraham, 192, 196(n25)
Brown, Daniel Putnam, Jr., 10
Brown, Dona, 259
Brown, George, 49
Brown, Moses, 25, 34
Buck, Charles N., 77(n27)
Buck, Susan L., 257, 258
Buckland, William, 264(fig.), 268
Bulloch, A. S., 247
Burdon, Aaron, 196(n25)
Burgess, John Cart, 118, 120, 121
Burks, Jean, 253, 258–59
Burroughs, Paul H., 264
Burton, E. Milby, 264, 266
Busby, C. A., 134
Butterfly motif, 118(& fig. 29)

Cabinet-Maker and Upholsterer's Drawing Book (Sheraton), 55, 122(fig. 39), 123, 124, 127(fig. 50), 137
Cabinet-Maker and Upholsterer's Guide, The (Hepplewhite), 170, 191
Cabot, William, 34
Cadwalader, Elizabeth (Lloyd), 81
Cadwalader, John, 81, 93
Campbell, Duncan, 246
Campbell, Maria (Bayard), 246
Candee, Richard M., 105
Candle stands, 186–90, 188(fig. 46), 189(figs.), 190(figs.), 191(figs.), 195(n22)
Cane chairs, 3, 36(n4)
Card tables: German influences and, 59, 61(figs.); by Nathan Lombard, 186, 187(fig. 44), 188(fig. 45); Randolph labeled, 93
Carnation motif, 123(& fig.), 124(fig. 41)
Carpenter, Ralph, 40(n35)
Carpenters, 209, 213(n18)
Carrington, Edward, 104
Carter family, 37(n12)
Carver, John, 226, 234(n9), 235(n10)
Carver, Mary (Barnes), 235(n10)
Carver chairs, 215
Carving: and attribution of Randolph chairs, 89, 92(& figs.), 93(figs.), 95(n7), 96, 97; Boston baroque, 15(& figs. 23, 24), 16(figs.), 21, 34; and German craftsmen, 59, 73; joined chairs and, 197; and Lombard furniture, 193
Caulkins, Frances Manwaring, 211
Chairs: Boston baroque, 1–36; four-footed turned, joined, 199, 200, 201(fig.), 202(figs.), 207(& fig.); neoclassical, 194(n4); plain, 201–2, 203(fig.), 204(fig.); three-post, joined, 197–201, 198(figs.), 199(figs.), 200(fig.), 202–9, 205(figs.), 212(nn 5, 6); turned great, 215, 216(fig.), 218(fig. 2), 220(fig.), 221(fig.), 222(fig. 11), 223(fig. 13), 224(fig. 16), 225(fig.), 226(fig.), 227(fig.), 228(fig.), 229(fig.), 230(figs.), 233(nn 5, 7), 234(n9), 235(n10), 237(nn 11, 12). *See also* Armchairs; Chairs, side; Easy chairs
Chairs, side: Baltimore painted, 152(fig.); Boston, 2–3, 2(figs.), 3–6, 3(fig.), 4(figs.), 5(fig.), 7(fig. 8), 8(fig. 12), 12(fig. 17), 14(fig. 21), 15–18, 17(fig.), 19(fig. 29), 22(fig. 36), 24(figs.), 25(figs.), 26(fig.), 27(figs.), 28(fig.), 29(fig. 48), 33(fig. 52); Boston baroque, 24–28, 39(n21); London, 15(fig. 22), 22(fig. 37); Massachusetts painted, 148(fig. 88); New York painted, 144(&

fig.), 148(& fig. 89), 149, 150(fig.); Philadelphia rococo, 81–94, 82(figs.), 85(figs.), 86(fig.), 87(figs.); Windsor painted, 103(figs. 5, 7)
Chandler, Adeline F. (Harlow), 235(n10)
Chandler, Albert H. Churchill, 235(n10)
Chandler, Eliza (Churchill), 235(n10)
Chandler, John, 234(n9)
Chandler, Joseph, 235(n10)
Chandler, Joseph Everett, 235(n10)
Chandler, Lydia (Ward), 234(n9)
Chapin, Eliphalet, 165
Chapin, L. D., 132
Charles, Mary, 191
Chaudron, Simon, 57
Cheney, Silas, 146
Cherry, 207, 208, 212(n6), 213(n12)
Cherub motif, 141(& figs.), 155
Chests of drawers: by Nathan Lombard, 167, 168(& figs. 5, 6), 171–77, 172(figs.), 173(fig.), 174(figs.), 175(figs.), 176(fig.), 177(figs.), 179(fig. 28), 194(n11); from Philadelphia, 69(& fig. 25)
Childs, Charles O., 195(n20)
Chinese influence, 38(n16)
Chinnery, Victor, 200, 213(nn 12, 14)
Chippendale, Thomas, 261; and ornamental painting designs, 120, 124, 129–30, 134, 135, 136
Chippendale style, 249
Christian M. Nestell, 101(fig.), 102(fig. 4)
Churchill, Eleazor, 235(n10)
Churchill, Experience (Ellis), 235(n10)
Churchill, Hannah (Barnes), 235(n10)
Churchill, Hannah (Hosea), 235(n10)
Churchill, John, 235(n10)
Churchill, Lucy (Burbank), 235(n10)
Churchill, Peleg, 235(n10)
Churchill, Stephen (third generation), 235(n10)
Churchill, Stephen (fourth generation), 235(n10)
Churchill, Stephen (fifth generation), 235(n10)
Churchill family, 228
Clark, James, 233(n7)
Clark, Simeon and Susanna, 195(n12)
Classical design: German influences and late, 41, 54, 58, 67, 68–72 (*see also* Biedermeier design); ornamental painting and, 161(n76)
Clocks: cases by Nathan Lombard, 182, 185–86, 187(figs. 42, 43); cases from Virginia, 265(fig.), 269; German imported, 51

Coffers, 46(fig.), 58–59
Collection of Designs for Household Furniture and Interior Decoration, A (Smith), 129
Colonial Williamsburg Foundation, 249, 263(fig.), 264, 265
Columbian Academy of Painting and Drawing, 101, 108–9
Commons, John R., 24
Complete Address Book for Merchants, Manufacturers, Apothecaries, Smelters, Glass Houses, and Hotels, 50
Complete Book of Shaker Furniture, The (Rieman and Burks), 253
Complete Mercantile Guide to the Continent of Europe (Rördansz), 50
Comstock, Helen, 235(n10)
Connecticut: chairs from, 233(n5), 234(n9), 237(n11); Elderkin in, 210–11; joined chairs from, 198(figs.), 200, 202(figs.), 227; ornamental painting in, 146(fig.), 153(fig. 94)
Conservation, 248
Construction: and attribution of Randolph chairs, 83–91, 88(fig.), 96–97; Boston baroque seating furniture, 20, 25–26; and Hunzinger furniture, 242; Lombard furniture, 171–73, 172(figs.), 175(& figs. 20, 21), 176–77, 179–80, 180(fig. 31), 182, 183(fig. 36), 184, 195(n17); Philadelphia German-influenced furniture, 65, 66; plain chairs, 202; three-posted joined chairs, 197, 201–2, 203–4, 205(fig. 12), 208–9, 208(figs.), 212(n6), 213(nn 14, 15, 16); turned great chairs, 219(fig. 8), 231(figs.), 232(& fig.)
Continental European influence, 267. *See also* French influences; German influences
Convolvulus. *See* Morning glory motif
Copley, John Singleton, 28, 29(fig. 47)
Corbit, Daniel, 91
Corbit, William, 91
Cornelius, Charles Over, 243
Craftsmen: in Boston and Newport, 35, 40(n36); carpenters and furniture making, 209; German immigrant, 42–44, 45–49, 77(n21); in Sutton, Massachusetts, 192–93
Crest rails, 92(figs.)
Crout, J. and A., 69–71
Crunden, John, 134
Cupboards, 204, 206(fig.)
Curl, James Stevens, 255

Dalhoff, Nicholas, 49
Darling, William, Jr., 196(n25)
Dating, 215–17, 224, 231–32, 232(n1), 249–50; and Lannuier's furniture, 246
Davidson, George, 105, 145, 146, 149, 151–52, 155
Davies, Robert, 144
de Bouverie, Jacob, 26
de Chaumont, James Leray, 247
Decoration: and attribution of Randolph chairs, 83–92, 92(figs.), 93(& figs.), 96–98; color and Shaker furniture, 254, 257–58; German influences and, 54, 69; Hunzinger and, 241; joined, turned chairs and, 197, 202; and Lombard furniture, 171, 173–75, 174(figs. 17, 18), 175(fig. 19), 176, 177(fig. 25), 179(& figs.), 180–90, 180(fig. 30), 181(fig. 33), 182(figs.), 184(fig. 39), 187(fig. 43), 189(figs. 48, 49), 192(fig. 55), 193. *See also* Carving; Inlay; Ornamental painting; Turnings
De Coster, Charles, 196(n25)
Delaware chairs, 89(fig.), 90(fig.)
Derby, Elias Hasket, 150
Design: and attribution of Randolph chairs, 83–92, 85(fig. 6), 93, 96–98; Boston seating furniture and baroque, 2–33; as a commodity, 1; dating schemes and, 232(n1); German influences, 41, 52–59, 52(fig.), 55(fig.), 62–76, 64(fig. 16), 67(fig. 22), 70(fig. 27), 71(fig. 30), 74(fig.), 75(fig.); Hunzinger's furniture and, 241; influences on turned chairs, 217–32; and Lannuier, 246; neat and plain style, 268; Shaker, 252–55; southern furniture and, 269; terms, 249–50; three-posted, joined chairs and, 199–207
Design books: and German craftsmen, 55, 73–75; Nathan Lombard and, 191; and southern furniture, 268
Desk-and-bookcases: Boston baroque, 16(figs.); Nathan Lombard, 164(fig.), 165–68, 166(figs.), 168(fig. 7), 178(figs.), 179(figs.), 180–82(& figs.), 183(fig. 36); by Randolph, 93. *See also* Secretaries
deutsche Auswanderer nach den Vereinigten Staaten von Nordamerika, Der, 43–44
DeWitt Wallace Gallery, 270
Dillaway, Thomas, 1
Directions for House and Ship Painting (Reynolds), 156
Dobson, J., 73
Doggett, John, 149, 153

Dolbear, Benjamin, 19
Dominique, Charles, 47
Doolittle, Amos, 140
Dorr, Sullivan, 104
Downe, William, 35
Downs, Joseph, 90, 243, 248, 263–64, 265
Dressing table, 69, 71(fig. 29)
Dryen, Edward, 37(n7)
Ducoff-Barone, Deborah, 66
Duden, Gottfried, 43
Dudley, Jonathan, 170
du Pont, Henry Francis, 165
Dwight, Timothy, 100

East, John, 12, 32
Easy chairs, Boston baroque, 8(fig. 11), 9–11, 9(fig.), 10(fig.), 16, 18(fig.), 19–20, 21(fig. 34), 23(fig.), 28–33, 30(fig.), 31(fig.), 32(fig.), 33(fig. 53), 38(n18)
Economic development model, 267–68
Eddy, Jeremiah, 34, 35, 40(n34)
Eddy family, 33–34
Edsall, Thomas, 220
Education/training: and Nathan Lombard, 191; and ornamental painting, 99, 100–101, 108
Eighteenth-Century American Arts: The M. and M. Karolik Collection (Hipkiss), 82
Elderkin, John, 197, 198(figs.), 210–11, 214(n20)
Elementary View of the Fine Arts (Enfield), 109(fig. 12), 110
Elfe, Thomas, 269
Eliot, John, 233(n5)
Ellery, Elizabeth (Almy), 25
Ellery, William, 25
Ellery, William, Jr., 25, 39(n27)
Ellis, Benjamin, 235(n10)
Ellis family, 227
Elm, 212(n6)
Employment, 45–46
Enfield, William, 109(fig. 12)
England: backstool from, 20(fig. 32); chairs from, 22(fig. 37), 199(figs.), 200–202, 200(fig.), 203(fig.); upholstery in, 260–63. *See also* British influences
Evans, Nancy Goyne, 14, 248–51

Faden, William, 112(fig. 16)
Fairbanks, Columbus, 235(n10)
Fairbanks, Jonathan, 235(n10)
Fairbanks, Joseph, 235(n10)
Fairbanks, Keturah (Luce), 235(n10)
Fairbanks, Nathaniel, 235(n10)
Fairbanks family, 229
Fancy goods, imported, 50–51, 51(fig.)
Faneuil, Benjamin, 1
Fasces (Roman), 138(& fig.), 154
Fayerweather, Jonathan, 24
Feather motif, 125(& fig. 45), 126(fig. 47), 145, 147–48
Feet. *See* Legs/feet
Feke, Robert, 35(fig.)
Fiedler, Joseph, 67, 67(fig. 22), 79(n47)
Fine Points of Furniture: Early American (Sack), 82
Finials, 218(Fig. 3), 222, 228–29
Finish, 92, 104, 257
Finlay, Hugh and John, 143, 145–46, 149–52, 152(fig.), 154(& fig.), 155
Finney, Josiah, 233(n7)
Firescreens, by Nathan Lombard, 167, 190–91, 192(figs.)
Fitch, Mary, 39(n27)
Fitch, Thomas, 2–3, 12, 17, 31–32, 35, 37(n7), 38(n19); style and, 1, 6
Flayderman (Philip) sale in 1930, 33–34, 40(n33)
Fledman, Joseph G., 78(n39)
Flint, Richard W., 239
Flora of North America, 125
Florist, 121
Flower motifs, 118–25, 118(fig. 30), 119(figs.), 120(figs.), 121(fig.), 122(figs.), 123(fig.), 124(figs.), 125(figs.), 145–47, 146(fig.), 147(fig.), 148(figs.)
Foliage motifs, 122(fig. 39), 123, 126–27(& figs.), 128–29, 128(fig. 53), 129(figs. 55, 56)
Folwell, Samuel, 111
Forman, Benno M., 3, 6, 10, 249–50
Freemasonry, 107, 118; and Shaker furniture, 255–56, 257, 258
French influences: and English upholstery, 261; and German craftsmen, 55, 59, 62, 66–67, 67(fig. 21), 68; and Lannuier, 244, 246
French Restoration style, 69
Freudenvoll, Charles, 74
Freudenvoll, D., 71(fig. 30), 74–75, 75(fig.)
Freudenvoll, John, 74–75
Frichot, Denis-Michel, 247
Fruit motif, 127–28, 128(figs. 51, 52), 129, 130(figs.), 148–49, 150(fig.)

Fuller, Frank, 40(n35)
Furniture of George Hunzinger; Invention and Innovation in Nineteenth-Century America, The (Harwood), 239–42
Furniture of the American South, 263(fig.), 266(fig.)
Furniture of the Pilgrim Century (Nutting), 197, 198(fig. 2)

Gaillardia, 124–25
Gall, Ludwig, 43
Gardner, Caleb, 32
Garvan, Francis P., 84, 195(n22)
Gentleman and Cabinet-Maker's Director, The (Chippendale), 120, 124
Geometrical forms, 133–34, 133(fig. 66), 134(figs.)
Georgian style, 250
German aid societies, 45–46
German influences: and 1820–1850 design, 41, 52–59, 52(fig.), 62–76, 64(fig. 16), 67(fig. 22), 70(fig. 27); on Philadelphia design, 71(fig. 30), 74(fig.), 75(fig.)
Germany: economy and emigration from, 42–43; furniture from, 53(fig.), 56(fig.), 60(fig. 11), 61(fig. 13). *See also* German influences
Gilbert, Christopher, 260
Gilding, 104
Gilmor, Robert, Jr., 154
Gilpin, Thomas, 79(n42)
Gilpin family, 62
Girard, Stephen, 57–58, 62, 78(n38)
Gladding, Kinsley C., 105
Goddard, John, 34
Goehmann, Charles H. L., 73(& fig.)
Golda, Clement, 214(n20)
Gonzales, Roger, 10
Gothic style, 90
Gragg, Samuel, 145(& fig.)
Grandeur on the Appoquinimink (Sweeney), 91
Grant, Samuel, 4–5, 11, 17–19, 22–25, 28–30, 32, 34, 35, 37(n9), 249; trade network, 1–2
Grape motif, 129–30, 130(figs.)
Gratz family, 62, 65
Gray, William, 156
Grear, Malcolm, 248
Greek key, 133–34, 133(fig. 66), 150, 163(n111)
Green, Calvin, 258
Green, Nathaniel, 4, 30

288   INDEX

Greene, Richard Ward, 104
Greenleaf, Stephen, 13
Grendy, Giles, 26–27
Griffin motif, 137–38, 137(fig.), 154(& fig.)
Guild system, German, 47, 76(n6)
Guilloche border, 134(& figs.), 150–52
Gusler, Wallace, 264, 265,
Gutekunst, Frederick, Jr., 47
Gutekunst, Frederick, Sr., 47, 52(fig.)

Hadley, Rick, 270
Hagen, Ernest, 243
Hanke, J. W., 74(& fig.)
Hardware, 137
Harlow, Adeline, 235(n10)
Harlow, Jedidah (Churchill), 235(n10)
Harlow, Thomas, 235(n10)
Harwood, Barry R., 239–42
Haslett, William, 106
Hass and Götz, 51
Hatheway, Rufus, 145
Hay, Anthony, 269
Hayden, Dolores, 259
Hayward, Charles Cotton, 140
Hayward, Joanna (Winslow), 235(n10)
Hayward, Nathan, 235(n10)
Hayward, Thomas and James, 36
Head, Elizabeth White (Frazier), 234(n9)
Head, Jane (MacKenzie), 234(n9)
Head, John, 234(n9)
Head, Joseph, 234(n9)
Head, Lydia (Chandler), 234(n9)
Helenium, 124–25
Hepplewhite, George, 135, 141–42, 170, 191
Hepplewhite style, 249
Hermann Unterstützungs Brüdershaft (Hermann Benevolent Brotherhood), 45
Hewson, John, 131
Hill, Peter, 78(n39)
Hipkiss, Edwin J., 82
History and Status of the Germans in America (Löher), 45
History of Four-Footed Beasts and Serpents (Topsel), 115
History of New London, Connecticut, The (Caulkins), 211
History of the Town of Sutton, Massachusetts, 170
Hoare, Richard, 26
Hoehling, Adolph, 47
Holland, John, 15

Holland, Sarah (May), 15, 38(n17)
Holme, Randle, 198
Holst, Charles, 49
"Holy City," 254–55, 258
Honeysuckle motif, 125(& fig. 44)
Honoré Lannuier, Cabinetmaker from Paris: The Life and Work of a French Ébéniste in Federal New York (Kenny, Bretter, and Leben), 242–48
Hooglant, Anna, 31
Hope, Thomas, 117, 126, 129, 131–32, 134, 135, 136
Horton, Frank L., 263, 264, 271
Household Furniture and Interior Decoration (Hope), 117, 131–32
How, Thomas, 261
Howard, Jonathan, 196(n25)
Howland, John, 234(n9)
Howland, Thomas, 235(n10)
Howland family, 234(n9)
Hubard, Master, 112
Hulme, F. Edward, 133
Humphrey, John, 196(n25)
Hunt motif, 136(& figs.), 153(& fig. 95)
Hunzinger, George Jakob, 239–42, 239(fig.), 240(fig.), 241(fig.)
Hurst, Ronald L., 264–71
Huse family, 27

Imitations, painted, 142(& figs.), 155–56
Immigrants: Dutch and Rhenish, 217; German, 41–46; Irish, 45; and southern furniture, 267, 269
Impecunious Collector's Guide to American Antiques, The (Kirk), 251
Inlay: and Lannuier, 247; and Lombard furniture, 171, 174, 175(& fig. 19), 179(figs.), 180, 182(& figs.), 183, 184(fig. 39), 185–86, 187(fig. 43), 188, 189(figs. 48, 49), 190, 192(fig. 55), 193; and Providence furniture, 196(n24)
Inscriptions, 167(& fig.), 168, 169(fig. 8), 194(n5). *See also* Labels
Invenzioni Diverse di Mobili ed Utensilj Sacri e Profani (Roccheggiani), 129(fig. 54)
Irish immigrants, 45
Irish-stitch needlework, 32, 39(n32)

Jackson, Allen D., 235(n10)
Jackson, John, 4
Jackson, John (eighth generation), 235(n10)

Jackson, John (ninth generation), 235(n10)
Jacob, Richard, 199
Jameson, John, 69
Jobe, Brock, 248, 250, 266
Johnson, James, 1
Joints, mortise-and-tenon, 208, 209(fig.), 213(n15)
Journal for Cabinetmakers and Upholsterers (Kimbel), 69
Journal of Early Southern Decorative Arts, 264–65
Judd, Donald, 259

Kamil, Neil, 1
Kammen, Michael, 259
Kane, Patricia E., 82–83
Kauffmann, Angelica, 108
Kaufmann, Johann Gottfried, 53(fig.)
Kenny, Peter M., 243–48
Kimbel, Wilhelm, 69, 70(fig. 27)
Kindig, Joe, Jr., 82–83, 84
King, Samuel, 13(fig. 19)
King, William, 269
Kirk, John T., 81, 82, 83, 88, 92–93, 96–98, 251–60
Küchler, Carl, 72, 74
Kuhn family, 62, 65

Labels: and Lannuier, 247; Nestell, 103(& fig. 6); and Randolph chairs, 82(fig.), 85(fig. 5), 92–93, 97–98. *See also* Inscriptions
Labor relations, 49
Labrobe, Benjamin, 255
Laisdell, Betsey (Lelley), 183
Laisdell, Daniel, 183
Landscape themes, 108(fig.), 109–14, 109(figs.), 110(fig.), 111(figs.), 112(figs.), 113(figs.), 143–45, 144(fig.)
Language, 48, 49
Lannuier, Honoré, 243–48
Lannuier, Nicolas, 244, 245–46
Lannuier, Therese (Baptiste), 245
Lapiere, Francis, 261
Latrobe, Benjamin Henry, 151, 153–54, 163(n111)
Leach, John, 1
Leather chairs, Boston, 2–3, 2(figs.), 7(fig. 9), 9, 11(& fig.), 12(figs.)
Leben, Ulrich, 243–48
Lee, Thomas, 269
Lee family, 233(n5)
Legs/feet: and attribution of Randolph

chairs, 89; baroque style and, 4–6, 7, 11, 16, 19, 21, 37(n7); and furniture by Nathan Lombard, 168(figs. 6, 7), 171, 173, 175, 179, 188, 190
Lehman, Arnold L., 239
Leuchs, J. C., 74
Lewis, Reginald, 84
Light-wood furniture, 69–72
Ligon, Richard, 130
Lincoln, John, 4
Lion's mask motif, 136–37, 136(fig. 73)
Lipp, G. J., 55(fig.)
"Little Known Masterpieces," 185
Lock, Mathias, 123
Löher, Franz, 45
Lombard, Alanson A., 170, 193, 194(n6)
Lombard, Ariel, 169
Lombard, Delight (Allen), 169, 194(n6)
Lombard, Joseph, 168–69
Lombard, Mary, 168
Lombard, Nathan, 165, 168–70, 169(fig. 9), 194(nn 6, 9); furniture by, 166(figs.), 168(figs.), 170–93, 173(fig.), 174(figs.), 176(fig.), 177(figs.), 178(figs.), 181(figs.), 183(figs.), 184(figs.), 185(fig.), 186(fig.), 187(figs.), 188(figs.), 189(figs.), 190(figs.), 191(figs.), 192(figs.)
London: furniture from, 20(fig. 32), 22(fig. 37)
London Court of Aldermen, 209
London Turner's Company, 201–2
Lothrop, Samuel, 210
Lotter, Tobias Conrad, 169(fig. 10)
Loud & Brothers, 51–52, 58(fig. 9), 59, 69
Luce, Deborah (Woolen), 235(n10)
Luce, Joseph, 235(n10)
Luckie, Benjamin, 1
Lyon, Charles Woolsley, 165, 167

Mahogany, 190
Manigault, Peter, 268
Mannerist style, 232(n1)
Maple, 212(n6), 213(n12)
Map of the Inhabited Part of Canada, A (Faden), 112(fig. 16)
Maps, 112(fig. 16), 169(fig. 10)
Maryland. *See* Baltimore
Mason, Ralph, 220
Mason, Sanford, 105
Massachusetts: cupboard from, 204, 206(fig.); joined chairs from, 200, 201(fig.), 204(fig.), 207(fig.); Nathan Lombard's furniture, 165, 166(figs.), 168(figs.), 170–93, 173(fig.), 174(figs.), 176(fig.), 177(figs.), 178(figs.), 181(figs.), 183(figs.), 184(figs.), 185(fig.), 186(fig.), 187(figs.), 188(figs.), 189(figs.), 190(figs.), 191(figs.), 192(figs.); ornamental painting in, 148(fig. 88), 149(fig.). *See also* Boston; Plymouth County, Massachusetts; Sutton, Massachusetts
Material culture studies approach, 266
Mather family, 233(n5)
Matthaey, Carl, 74
Mattocks, Samuel, Sr. and Jr., 1, 4
May, Samuel, 38(n17)
Mayhew, Thomas, 210, 261
McElroy's Philadelphia Directory, 48
Mentz, George W., 73
Mésangère, Pierre de la, 62, 67(& fig. 21), 79(n46)
Messinger, Henry, 220
"Methodological Study in the Identification of Some Important Philadelphia Chippendale Furniture, A," 81
Metropolitan Museum of Art, 243, 249
Meubles-Zeichnungen für Tischler (Lipp), 55(fig.)
Miller, Alan, 2
Miller, Henry Wilder, 105
Mitchell, David H., 235(n10)
Modernism, Hunzinger and, 241
Moheagan (Norwich), Connecticut, 210–11
Molitor, Bernard, 244
Montgomery, Charles F., 165, 249
Moore, J. W., 73
Morland, George, 108
Morning glory motif, 122(& fig. 38), 147, 148(fig. 88)
Morse, Adams, 196(n25)
Morse, Sylvester, 196(n25)
Museum of Early Southern Decorative Arts (MESDA), 263, 249, 264
Musical instruments, 51–52, 59
Music trophy, 135(fig. 71), 136, 152–53, 153(fig. 94)
Myers, Louis Guerineau, 243
My Immigration to the United States of North America (Gall), 43
Mythological themes, 137–40, 137(fig.), 139(figs.), 154–55, 154(fig.)

National Aegis, 170
Neat and plain style, 268
Needham, Mary, 191

Neoclassical style: Lombard furniture and, 170, 185, 186; ornament and, 137; and Shaker design, 252, 253, 255, 257; and southern furniture, 269
Nestell, Betsey Horton (Bosworth), 106
Nestell, Christian I., 99
Nestell, Christian Michael, 99–107, 107(fig.); drawing book, 99(fig.), 107–43, 108(fig.), 109(figs. 10, 11), 110(fig.), 111(figs.), 112(fig. 17), 113(figs.), 114(figs.), 115(fig.), 116(figs.), 117(figs.), 118(figs.), 119(figs.), 120(figs.), 121(fig.), 122(fig. 38), 123(fig.), 124(figs.), 125(figs.), 126(figs.), 127(figs. 48, 49), 128(figs.), 129(figs. 55, 56), 130(figs.), 131(figs.), 132(figs.), 133(figs.), 134(figs.), 135(figs.), 136(figs.), 137(fig.), 138(fig.), 139(figs.), 140(figs.), 141(figs.), 142(figs.)
Nestell, John J., 99
Nestell, Mary (Swan), 99
Nestell, Michael, 99
Netherlands, turned chairs and the, 217–19, 218(fig. 2), 225, 233(n3)
Neues Journal für Möbelschreiner (New Journal for Cabinetmakers) (Hanke), 74(& fig.)
Neuestes Mainzer Moebel-Journal (New Mainz Furniture Journal) (Freudenvoll), 71(fig. 30), 74–75, 75(fig.)
New England Furniture at Winterthur: Queen Anne and Chippendale Periods (Richards and Evans), 248–51
New Lebanon Meetinghouse, 254–55
New London, Connecticut, 210, 211
Newport, Rhode Island, 33–36
Newspapers, German-language, 46, 48
New York City: craft community in, 100; and German immigration, 44, 45; Lannuier and cabinet trade in, 245; ornamental painting in, 143–44, 144(fig.), 146–47, 147(fig.), 148(fig. 89), 149, 150(& fig.), 151(fig.), 155; sofa, 72(fig.), 73
New York Daily Tribune, 46
Nolen and Gridley, 147, 149, 150, 155
Norwich, Connecticut, 227
Nutting, Wallace, 197, 198(fig. 2), 209, 215, 232(n1), 233(n2)

Oak, 207, 212(n6), 213(n12)
Oak Furniture: The British Tradition (Chinnery), 200
Oeben, Jean-François, 62

Oldmixon, John, 11
Oliver, Andrew, 17
Oliver, Andrew, Jr., 17, 19(fig. 30), 39(n27)
Oliver, Mary (Fitch), 17, 19(fig. 30)
Oppenheimer family, 57, 78(n37)
Ormsbee, Thomas Hamilton, 243
Ornamental painting, 103–6. See also Nestell, Christian Michael
Ornamentation. See Decoration
Oxidation patterns, 92–93, 97–98

Paintings/portraits, 13(fig. 19), 19(figs. 30, 31), 29(fig. 47), 35(fig.); and Hunzinger, 242; Isaac Bartlett tintype, 222(fig. 12); Lombard portrait, 169(fig. 9)
Patriotic motifs, 140–41(& figs.), 145, 155; and Nathan Lombard furniture, 180, 182(fig. 34), 183, 184, 185, 195(n22)
Patrons: and English upholstery, 260, 261; Lannuier's, 246–47
Patternbooks. See Design books
Patterson, John, 155
Pavey, Jess, 38(n17)
Peacock motif, 117(& figs.), 145(& fig.)
Peck, Amelia, 33
Pendants, architectural, 204–5
Pennery, Walter, 69, 71(fig. 29), 72
Penniman, John Ritto, 106, 150
Pennsylvania. See Philadelphia
Pergolesi, Michelangelo, 126, 127, 131, 134, 135, 136, 140
Perkins, Ann (Foster), 4
Perkins, Daniel (reverend), 4
Perkins, Edmund, 1, 4, 23
Perkins, Henry and William, 1
Perkins, John, 23
Perry, Francis, 209
Philadelphia: chests from, 69(& fig. 25); dressing table from, 69, 71(fig. 29); fall-front secretaries from, 57–58, 57(fig.), 59, 62–67, 63(fig.), 64(fig. 15), 65(figs.), 66(fig.), 68(fig. 23), 69, 70(fig. 28); German immigrants in, 44–50, 69–76, 77(nn 21, 27); pianofortes from, 58(figs.), 59; pier and card tables from, 59, 60(fig. 10), 61(fig. 12), 69(& fig. 26); rococo chairs from, 81–94, 82(figs.), 85(figs.), 86(fig.), 87(figs.); work table from, 68(fig. 24), 69
Philadelphia Cabinet and Chair Makers' Union Book of Prices for Manufacturing Cabinet Ware, The, 62

Phill, Thomas, 4, 37(n7), 261
Phyfe, Duncan, 245, 246
Pianos, 51–52, 58(figs.), 59
Pickering, Theophilus (reverend), 37(n9)
Pilgrim Hall, 215, 219
Pilgrim Society, 234(n9)
Pineapple motif, 130–31, 131(fig. 60), 149
Pitman, William M., 104, 105
Plimoth Plantation, 213(n11)
Plymouth County, Massachusetts, chairs from, 215–32, 216(fig.), 221(fig.), 222(fig. 11), 223(fig. 13), 224(fig. 16), 225(fig.), 226(fig.), 227(fig.), 228(fig.), 229(fig.), 230(figs.), 233(n5)
Poictevin, Jean, 261
Pommels, 219(fig. 6), 226–27
Pommer, Charles, 47
Poplar, 212(n6)
Porter, Rufus, 106, 144
Pottie, George, 117
Potvin, Ronald, 40(n36)
Pouget fils, 125
Practical Essay on the Art of Flower Painting (Burgess), 118
Presbury, Deborah (Skiff), 235(n10)
Presbury, Stephen, 235(n10)
Preston, Titus, 146
Price, William, 12
Prices: and Boston baroque seating furniture, 24–25, 31; and English furniture, 261; Philadelphia secretaries and, 62, 78(n38); and Randolph desk-and-bookcase, 93
Priddy, Sumpter, 264
Prior, Jane Otis, 150
Production, standardized, 22–23, 24–33, 39(n25)
Proud brothers, 101
Providence, Rhode Island: map of, 102(fig. 3); neoclassical inlays and furniture from, 196(n24); Nestell in, 101, 102–3; ornamental painting in, 103–6; Windsor painted chairs from, 103(& figs. 5, 7)
Prown, Jonathan, 264–71
Pugin, Augustus Welby Northmore, 213(n11), 241
Puig, Francis J., 83
Putnam, Joseph, 23
Pyncheon, John, Jr., 211

Queen Anne style, 249, 250
Quervelle, Anthony, 60(fig. 10), 61(fig. 12), 79(n44)

Radde, William, 73
Rademacher, C., 73
Ragan, Richard, 151
Rails, front/side/rear, and attribution of Randolph chairs, 84, 85–86, 87(fig. 9), 88(& fig.), 91(fig.), 95(n9), 96, 97
Randolph, Benjamin, 81, 82(figs.), 85(figs.), 93, 98
Rauschenberg, Bradford, 265
Ray, Mary Lynn, 259
Rea, Daniel, Jr., 145, 146, 155–56
Redwood, Abraham, 32
Redwood, Abraham, II, 13(& fig. 19), 14
Regency style, 69
Remey, George, 9, 38(n20)
Report on a Journey to the Western States of North America (Duden), 43
Repository, The, 132, 138
Restoration: and attribution of Randolph chairs, 84(& fig.), 87–88, 91–92, 92(figs.), 96–97; and turned great chairs, 235(n10)
Revival style, 261
Reynolds, Hezekiah, 156
Rhode Island. See Newport, Rhode Island; Providence, Rhode Island
Richards, Nancy, 248–51
Ridgeway, R., 231
Ridgway, Samuel, 1
Rieman, Tim, 253, 259
Rife, Peter, 265(fig.), 269
Ritter, J. G., 73
Robbins family, 233(n5)
Roberts, Richard, 4
Roberts, Thomas, 4, 19, 20(fig. 32)
Robertson, Alexander, 108
Robertson, Archibald, 101, 108–9
Robertson, Hannah, 111
Robinson, George, 15
Roccheggiani, Lorenzo, 129(fig. 54)
Rococo: as design term, 249; and ornamental painting, 126; Randolph chairs and, 81
Rococo revival, 73–75; German influences and, 41, 54
Roman motifs, 136, 137, 138
Rördansz, C. W., 50
Rose motif, 118–21, 118(fig. 30), 119(figs.), 120(figs.), 146–47, 146(fig.)
Round Barn, at Hancock, Massachusetts, 254–55
Royall, Anne Newport, 102
Russell, Allen D., 235(n10)
Russell, Mary Winslow (Hayward), 235(n10)

Russell, Nathaniel, II, 235(n10)
Russell, William S., 235(n10)
Ruthven, James, 245

Sack, Albert, 82, 89
Saunders, Mrs., 108
Savage, Thomas, 264, 266, 267
Sayward, Jonathan, 28–29
Schermerhorn, Arnout, 5
Scherr, Emilius N., 58(fig. 8), 59
Scholarship, material culture, 240–42, 243–47, 251–60, 260–63, 264–71; reviewing and correcting, 81, 94
Schwartz, Marvin D., 239
Scollay, John, 28–29, 32
Scott, Charles, 165–67, 166(fig. 2)
Scott, Peter, 37(n12), 269
Sears, William Bernard, 264(fig.), 268
Secretaries: German fall-front, 53(fig.), 56(fig.), 78(n37); German-influenced Philadelphia, 79(n44); Philadelphia fall-front, 57–58, 57(fig.), 59, 62–67, 63(fig.), 64(fig. 15), 65(figs.), 66(fig.), 68(fig. 23), 69, 70(fig. 28). *See also* Desk-and-bookcases
Seymour, Thomas, 150
Shaker Experience in America: A History of the United Society of Believers, The (Stein), 251
Shaker furniture, 251–60
Shaker World: Art, Life, Belief, The (Kirk), 251–60
Shaw, John, 269
Shearer, John, 269
Sheeler, Charles, 259
Shell motif, 132–33, 132(figs.), 133(figs. 64, 65), 149–50, 151(fig.)
Sheraton, Thomas, 108, 122(fig. 39), 123, 124, 127(& fig. 50), 137, 138–39, 141, 143
Sheraton style, 249
Short, William, 167–68, 190
Sibley, Jonathan, 196(n25)
Sideboards, 182–85, 183(fig. 37), 184(figs.), 185(fig.), 186(fig.), 195(nn 19, 20), 264(fig.)
Sievers, Jacob, 49
Signs, 104–5
Skiff, Lydia (Snow), 235(n10)
Skiff, Stephen, 235(n10)
Skillin, John, 155
Sloane, Jeanne, 35
Smibert, John, 17, 18, 19(figs. 30, 31), 38(n19)

Smith, George, 49, 120, 124, 129, 134, 135, 136
Smith, Robert C., 79(n44), 81
Smith, Samuel, 210
Society of Journeymen Cabinetmakers, 49
Sofa, 72(fig.), 73
South Carolina, furniture from, 233(n5), 266(fig.)
Southern Antiques (Burroughs), 264
Southern Furniture, 1680–1830: The Colonial Williamsburg Collection (Hurst and Prown), 264–71
Southern furniture studies, 263–71
Speyer, Philipp, 50
Spitler, Johannes, 266(fig.), 269
Splat design, 90–92, 92(figs.), 93(figs.)
Spruance, Sarah C. (Corbit), 91
St. George, Robert Blair, 215–16, 217, 231, 233(n6), 235(n10)
Stampa, P., 110–11
Standish, Mary (Carver), 235(n10)
Standish, Thomas, 235(n10)
Star motif, 151–52
Stedman, George, 176, 192
Stein, Stephen J., 251
Stockel, Theobald, 47
Stretcher design, 10–11, 16, 19–20, 21, 38(n15)
Stringing, 171, 173, 174, 175, 176, 179, 182, 185, 186, 190
Strong Museum, 239
Strycker family, 233(n5)
Style. *See* Design
Sutton, Massachusetts, 169, 192–93
Swan, Abraham, 268
Sweeney, John, 91
Swiss immigrants, 41
Symbolism: and ornamental painting, 111, 118, 120, 137; Shaker furniture and, 255, 258
Syz, J. G., 51

Tables: dining, 37(n12); Philadelphia dressing, 69, 71(fig. 29); pier, 59, 60(figs.), 69(& fig. 26), 153(fig. 95); work, 68(fig. 24), 69. *See also* Card tables; Sideboards
Tan-and-ebony color scheme, 230
Tayloe family, 268
Tenney, Daniel, 192–93, 196(n25)
Textile arts, 135, 138, 139, 145
Thomlinson, John, 35
Thonet, Michael, 241
Thornton, Peter, 232(n3)

Tinkham, Ephraim, II, 215, 216–17
Tinkham shop tradition, 215
Topsel, Edward, 115
Townsend, Job, 33–34, 40(n33)
Tracy, Berry B., 243
Tracy, Hiram, 170
Trade: Boston chairmakers and, 1–2; Dutch chairs and, 233(n3); German-American, 50–52, 72, 73, 76(n10), 77(nn 26, 27); levels of production and, 39(n25); Newport-Boston seating furniture, 33–36; and New York City, 100; and Providence, 102–3
Trade manuals/catalogues, 50–51, 73, 135, 142
Trent, Robert F., 197, 235(n10)
Trophy motif, 135–37, 135(fig. 71), 136(figs.), 152–54, 153(figs.)
Tufts family, 233(n5)
Tulip motif, 121(fig.), 122, 147
Turnings, 218–32, 218(fig. 3), 219(figs.), 223(figs. 14, 15)
Typography, 134, 140–41

University of Delaware, Winterthur Program in Early American Culture, 250
Upholsterers and Interior Furnishing in England, 1530–1840 (Beard), 260–63
Upholstery: and Boston baroque seating furniture, 30–33; English, 260–63
Urns, 141–42, 141(fig. 80), 155; and Nathan Lombard furniture, 180, 184(& fig. 39), 190, 192(fig. 55); and turned great chairs, 222, 223

Van Rensselaer, Harriet (Bayard), 246
Van Rensselaer, Stephen, IV, 246
Van Renssalaer family, 144
Vaughan, George, 93
Vermont: ornamental painting in, 148, 150, 155; Stedman and Lombard connection, 176, 191–92
"Very Pink of the Mode: Boston Georgian Chairs, Their Export and Their Influence," 2
Vincent, Clement, 1, 29
Violets motif, 124(& fig. 42)
Virginia, furniture from, 37(n12), 233(n5), 264(fig.), 265(fig.), 266(fig.)
von Falke, Jacob, 241

Wainwright, John, 18, 38(n20)
Wainwright, Nicholas, 81
Waldo, Abigail Elderkin, 210
Waldo, Cornelius, 209
Waldo, Daniel, 144, 209
Waldo, John, 209
Waldo, Nathan, 209
Waldo, Rebecca (Adams), 209
Waldo, Susanna (Adams), 209
Waldo chair, 197, 198(figs.), 202–9, 205(figs.), 208(fig. 16), 209(fig.), 213(n16)
Walker, Mack, 41, 42, 47
Walpole, Robert (sir), 18–19
Warren, Mary (Winslow), 235(n10)
Waxman, Lorraine, 243
Webb, Adrian, 165–67, 166(fig. 2)
Wedgwood, Josiah, 131
Weis, Chrisostomus, 43
Welch, John, 1, 15, 21, 35
Wells, William, 210
Wendel, Jacob and John, 17
Wesselhoeft, J. G., 46, 50, 51, 74
West, Elizabeth (Derby), 150, 153
Wheaton, Stephen, 144
Whipple, Peter, 265(fig.), 269
Whipple and Low, 105
White, Bruce, 248
White, Cornelius, 235(n10)
White, Gideon, 235(n10)
White, Joanna (Howland), 235(n10)
Whiting, Elizabeth (Adams), 231
Whiting, Samuel (reverend), 231
Whittenburg, James P., 267
Whittock, Nathaniel, 142
Williamsburg, Virginia, 37(n12)
Willig, George, 51
Winslow, Edward, 235(n10)
Winslow, Isaac, 228, 235(n10)
Winslow, Joanna (White), 235(n10)
Winslow, John, 235(n10)
Winslow, Josiah, 235(n10)
Winslow, Pelham, 235(n10)
Winslow, Sarah (Wensley), 235(n10)
Winter, William, 257
Winterthur Museum, 90, 165, 243, 248–51
Winterthur Program in Early American Culture. *See* University of Delaware, Winterthur Program in Early American Culture
Winthrop, John, Jr., 210, 211
Wölfer, Marius, 64(fig. 16), 74
Woodbury, Zadock, 196(n25)
Woods: and New England joiners, 213(n12); turned great chairs and, 234(n9), 235(n10); and the Waldo chair, 207–8
Woodward, Abijah, 171, 186, 188
Woodward, Julia Ann (Lombard), 171, 188
Woollenweber, L. A., 73
Wreath motif, 131–32, 131(fig. 61), 134–35, 136, 149, 152, 153–54
Wygal, Sebastian, 269

Zeitz and Company, 73
Ziegler, Alexander, 43–44
Zogry, Kenneth, 266